Where to wa
Herefordshire
Staffordshire, Warwickshire,
Worcestershire & the former
West Midlands County

THE *WHERE TO WATCH BIRDS* SERIES

Where to watch birds in

Herefordshire, Shropshire, Staffordshire, Warwickshire, Worcestershire & the former West Midlands County

Second edition

Graham Harrison and Jack Sankey

Graham Harrison

Christopher Helm

A & C Black · London

Second edition 1997
First edition 1987

© 1997 Graham Harrison and Jack Sankey
Line drawings by Jack Sankey and Brett Westwood

Christopher Helm (Publishers) Ltd, a subsidiary of
A & C Black, 35 Bedford Row, London WC1R 4JH

0-7136-4478-8

A CIP catalogue record for this book
is available from the British Library

Typeset and designed by D & N Publishing
Membury Business Park, Lambourn Woodlands, Hungerford, Berkshire

Printed and bound by Redwood Books, Trowbridge, Wiltshire, UK

CONTENTS

Contents

ACKNOWLEDGEMENTS

We have received considerable help from many people and wish to express our gratitude to all of them.

We would especially thank Leo Smith for much help with the original Shropshire sites and the following for their expert advice and constructive comments: Mrs Lilian Allender and the Whitfield Valley Wildlife Volunteers, Michael Boote for Doxey, Jonathan Bowley for Coombe Abbey and Sowe Valley, Dr Joan Daniels for Fenns and Whixall Mosses, Peter Dedicoat for Belvide, Ivor Evans and his team of Gerry Bilbao and Chris Wells for Herefordshire, Frank Gribble and Bill Low for many Staffordshire sites, Richard Harbird for some Worcestershire sites, Tim Hextell for the Black Country and Paul Hodges for Coombe Abbey. Maurice Arnold, Charles Brown, Eric Clare, Bert Coleman, Edwin Hopkins, Peter Rollin, Jim Winsper and many others gave us the benefit of their local knowledge. We are also grateful to the staff of the County Wildlife Trusts, RSPB wardens and Country Park rangers for their help and assistance. Above all, we freely acknowledge the debt we owe to the editors of various Bird Reports and to those whose records we culled from them to compile the species sections.

Many of Brett Westwood's original drawings have been reused, for which we once again express our sincere thanks. Additional illustrations have been provided by Jack Sankey and Graham wishes to express a special debt of gratitude to him for these. Both of us are also indebted to Robert Kirk and the staff at A & C Black for their guidance and encouragement in the preparation of this book.

Finally, Jack would like to thank his mother for once again suffering neglect during a busy period. Graham would like to thank his wife, Janet, for her constructive comments, meticulous checking of drafts and help with drawing so many of the maps; and his daughters, Sue and Jenny, for their encouragement and tolerance of the disruption to their lives.

Graham R. Harrison

Jack Sankey

ACKNOWLEDGMENTS

INTRODUCTION

Herefordshire, Shropshire, Staffordshire, Warwickshire, Worcestershire and the former West Midlands County are collectively known as the West Midlands. This is a region of contrasts from the bleak moors of the Peak District to the mellow hills of the Cotswolds; or from the wooded hillsides and streams of the Welsh border country to the lush valleys of the Avon, Severn and Trent.

Within its rich mosaic of habitats can be found northerly species such as Twite and Black Grouse; southerly ones such as Rufous Nightingale and Hobby; westerly ones like Pied Flycatcher and Common Buzzard; and easterly ones including Red-legged Partridge and Corn Bunting. The hub of the region is Birmingham, where Black Redstarts maintain a tenuous presence, while with the Marsh Warbler in Worcestershire the region clings on to a national rarity.

Since writing the first edition we have been surprised how much the birdlife has changed in the space of a decade. Declines in once common farmland birds, such as Turtle Dove, Tree Sparrow and Corn Bunting, have been well publicised. But many typical upland birds like Tree Pipit, Whinchat and Wood Warbler have become scarce too. Conversely, Pied Flycatchers and many of the raptors are now more numerous and widespread. Changes in behaviour are also apparent, with waders appearing earlier in spring and Barn Swallows no longer roosting in reedbeds. The reasons for these are probably complex, but one significant factor has been the gradual drying out of wetlands through increasing drainage and below average rainfall. Breeding waders, such as Northern Lapwing, Common Snipe, Eurasian Curlew and Common Redshank have all declined as a result, as have Yellow Wagtails. A decline in passage Common Greenshank is also apparent, while Grey Plover have seemingly increased.

In this book we tell you not only where to look for these and other birds, but when to look and what to expect. We have written it for beginners and experts; residents and visitors alike. The sites chosen are representative of the places with most birds, the best examples of each habitat, or those close to Birmingham, the Black Country, Coventry and the Potteries where most people live. Only sites with some form of legitimate access have been included. Some sites may alter, perhaps for the worse, but we have omitted those where this is most likely. Our selection is by no means exhaustive and many a good days' birding could be enjoyed by exploring elsewhere.

Despite anticipated criticism, we have chosen to use the new bird names published in *British Birds* in January 1993. We make no apologies for this, as we believe they will only gain widespread acceptance through general use.

Between us we have personally visited every site to check details of habitat and access, but these can quickly become out of date. We therefore apologise for any inaccuracies. With growing concern about the effects of traffic on our environment, we have this time included brief notes about public transport. Surely those of us with an interest in the natural environment should set an example by adapting our travel habits. So why not give it a try – you'll be surprised where you can get to by train and bus! We have also included notes on access for disabled people.

With beginners and overseas visitors in mind, we have tried to indicate the months, seasons and weather conditions under which certain birds might occur. In so doing, we have listed those birds that might reasonably be seen. It would be unrealistic to expect them all in a single visit, particularly those such as waders, terns and passage migrants whose appearances in an area such as this depend so much on a combination of factors. Equally others not listed might turn up, but that is the joy of birdwatching! We chose generally to omit any reference to common birds, such as Robin and Blue Tit, since even those unfamiliar with British birds are likely to encounter these somewhere during their visits.

Finally, we trust everyone will understand the need to withhold certain information. Some sites are too sensitive to mention and some birds too susceptible to disturbance. We have put the welfare of the birds first, but at the same time, have tried to suggest where every typical species might be seen. We ask you please to repay this faith by visiting, watching and leaving sites and birds undisturbed for others to enjoy.

Note: Since publication of the new bird names in 1993, Nuthatch has been changed again, from Wood Nuthatch to European Nuthatch, but this further change has not been incorporated in this edition.

HOW TO USE THIS BOOK

Over 100 sites are covered by this book, some of them grouped into areas. They are arranged systematically in a clockwise direction, beginning with the Peak District in north Staffordshire and concluding with the Northern Mosses of Shropshire. These areas were used in preference to counties, firstly, because they make it easy to identify neighbouring sites that can be visited on the same day and, secondly, because a number of the region's important sites overlap county boundaries. Each site is treated consistently, with sections on habitat, species, timing, access and a calendar, except where it is more meaningful to deal with these for the area as a whole.

Habitat

The description begins with the broad location of each site and, where relevant, details of its area and who administers it. It then aims to provide the reader with a mental picture by describing the natural and man-made features and the range of vegetation to be found, particularly that most relevant to its birds. We make no excuse for describing some sites in detail, as a thorough knowledge and understanding of the habitats makes it that much easier to find the birds. Some habitats are continually changing, especially gravel pits and young forestry plantations, and as they do so they may become less attractive to some birds and more attractive to others.

Species

This section begins with a statement of the main ornithological interest of each site. Following this is an account of the birds to be found. It was not our intention to provide a complete list of every species ever seen at each site. Rather we have given an idea of the more interesting ones that are typically to be found. Thus the commoner species have normally been omitted, while a selection of rare or unusual species are mentioned only as examples of what might occur.

Most species' accounts are arranged to give an idea of how the birdlife changes through the year. They also indicate why the birds are using the site. For example, whether they are breeding, feeding or roosting; or whether they are passing through or arriving during periods of flood or extreme cold. Where possible an indication is given of how often each species occurs and in what numbers, so that visitors know whether to expect a single bird, small party or large flock. Numbers and frequency have generally been based on the period 1990–95, which for convenience is referred to as 'recent'.

Timing

The best times of year are given in the species accounts and calendars. This section therefore concentrates on the best times of day. In a densely populated area such as the West Midlands, disturbance is a constant consideration, particularly from recreational activities and especially water-based sports. We have tried to assess the effects as accurately as possible, but recreational activities are always liable to change at short notice. Invariably they intensify rather than reduce.

As a general rule, early morning visits are best, when disturbance is least and birds are most active. Where evening visits are better, these are specified. Weather is the other important factor. In winter, periods of flooding or severe frost attract some species, but drive away others, and the site accounts mention these. Shallow waters, in particular, freeze before deeper ones. In spring and autumn wind directions and weather systems affect bird migration across the region as a whole, but are less critical at individual sites. For an overview of the general effects of weather see the section on 'A Portrait of the Six Counties'.

Access

Directions are given to every site from the nearest main road. Often there are alternative approaches, but to save space only one has been described. Other routes can be followed using the relevant site map and/or Ordnance Survey Landranger Map identified in the main area headings. (This section should always be read in conjunction with the site maps.) Parking arrangements are described and details of footpath access are given where this is relevant. Information is also included on facilities such as hides, visitor centres, toilets and access for the disabled.

This time we have also included notes on the nearest public transport services. We regret being unable to give more details, but services change so frequently that the information would be out of date before it was published. However, Centro and the County Councils are extremely helpful should you need more information. Contacts are included in the section on 'Useful Addresses'.

Where access to a site is restricted to members of an organisation, or is strictly by permit only, this is clearly stated and visitors are asked to respect this. However, visitors should note that the Wildlife Trusts may issue permits for members of other trusts to visit their reserves.

Although we believe the details given to be correct at the time of writing, access, facilities and ownership can change and the information given cannot guarantee right of entry.

Calendar

This provides a quick checklist of the birds likely to be seen, given sufficient time and the right weather conditions, except that common species have not usually been individually named. Species are normally listed in the order of the Voous classification, which is that followed by most contemporary field guides.

The first list includes birds which might be seen at any time of year. Others cover the main passage or wintering times: spring is defined as March or April until June, which is when most waders, terns and migrants pass through and summer visitors arrive; autumn is defined as July to September, which is when most summer visitors depart and waders, terns and migrants again pass through; winter is classed as October to February or March, which is when wildfowl are most numerous and winter visitors arrive at the beginning of the period and leave at the end. Where the birds of spring and autumn are very similar, then the periods have been combined.

Some species will inevitably fail to conform to these, or any other, arbitrary divisions, being either restricted within the periods or spreading outside them. However, if there is no qualifying comment, the bird concerned might be expected at any time during the period for which it is mentioned. The terms 'scarce' and 'rare' refer to frequency of occurrence rather than total numbers. To find when peak numbers are most likely, refer to the species section for each site.

We have tried to ensure that your visit will be both enjoyable and rewarding. But birds undertake complex movements in response to a whole range of unpredictable circumstances, such as disturbance and weather, and it is impossible to guarantee the presence of any of those mentioned. Inevitably there will be times when a site fails to live up to its expectations and we would ask for your forbearance in this. Hopefully such occasions will be few and offset by those when a site exceeds its expectations.

Key to the Maps

◀◖▤◗▶	Motorways and junctions	▨	Built-up areas
▬▬▬	Class A and B roads	※※	Deciduous and mixed woodland
▬▬	Other roads	♦♦♦♦♦	Coniferous woodland
▬ ▬ ▬	Unmetalled tracks		Water
🅿	Car parks	～ ～	Marsh
-------	Footpaths		Sand or mud
+++○+++	Railways and stations	ⅠⅠⅠⅠⅠⅠⅠⅠⅠ	Steep slopes
⌒⌒⌒⌒	Canals	:........:	Site boundaries (where appropriate)
≈≈≈	Main rivers	■	Hides
∼∼∼	Other rivers and streams	△	Triangulation point

13

A PORTRAIT OF THE SIX COUNTIES

To most people this is the region of motor cars, Spaghetti Junction and Birmingham. Yet there is much more to this area than that. Its six constituent counties cover 5000 square miles (13,000 km^2) and are home to five million people. The countryside is extremely varied, ranging in altitude from 40 to 2306 ft (12 to 703 m). The climate is varied too, with the Gulf Stream bringing relatively mild winters and early springs to the Avon and Severn Valleys, while the Peak District experiences heavy snowfalls. The mean January temperature is above freezing everywhere, but this disguises the propensity for extremely cold nights and prolonged frosts. East of the Severn the climate is dry, with less than 30 in (750 mm) of rain each year, while to the west and north rainfall increases steadily until it exceeds 40 in (1000 mm) in the Black Mountains and the Peak District.

Weather and topography strongly influence bird migration. Although movements are never as spectacular as around the coasts, some, like the overland migrations of Common Shelduck and Common Scoter, occur regularly. Others are very unpredictable. With favourable weather most long-distance migrants probably overfly the region undetected. But adverse conditions, for example cool, damp days in spring, force species such as Common Swifts and hirundines to lower levels. Equally, vigorous weather systems at critical times in spring can disrupt the movements of waders and terns, grounding many birds. At such times many species follow the river valleys. In autumn prolonged easterly winds usually bring more waders, while on misty mornings migrant passerines pass across hills such as Bredon and the Malverns. Storms and cold also have their effect, with strong westerly winds during September or October often resulting in a few 'wrecked' seabirds and cold weather on the Continent, especially around the Baltic, bringing an increase in winter wildfowl.

To journey across the region from southeast to northwest is to step backwards in time. Beneath your feet the rocks get progressively older, whilst around you man's influence on the landscape gives way to nature's. The newest rocks are the Jurassic beds of the Cotswolds. They are followed by the Trias of the great Midlands Plain and then by the Carboniferous deposits, which include both the coal measures that kindled the Industrial Revolution and the grits and limestones of the Peak District. Further west, Old Red Sandstones underlie most of Herefordshire, and finally the oldest rocks are the Silurian, Ordovician, Cambrian and pre-Cambrian formations that are the backbones of the Shropshire Hills. Within this structure are localised intrusions of igneous and metamorphic rocks, most notably the Malvern Hills.

The geology has shaped the scenery. More importantly, it has governed man's activities. The south and east is so intensively farmed that little semi-natural habitat survives and the best birdwatching sites are man-made ones as at Draycote Water. By contrast, in the north and west natural areas such as the meres, mosses and moors are more important than individual sites.

Standing on the Cotswolds – at Edge Hill, Broadway Hill or Bredon Hill – you are surrounded by warm, honey-coloured stone walls and picturesque villages. On misty autumn mornings migrant birds follow this line of hills, but on a clear day the great, flat Midlands Plain stretches before you. In the foreground the heavy clays of southeast Warwickshire and Worcestershire are the arable and horticultural centre of the region, with fields of corn and vivid oilseed rape standing alongside remnants of old ridge-and-furrow. Flocks of Northern Lapwings and European Golden Plover visit the unimproved pastures in the winter and Hobbies and Rufous Nightingales breed in the summer. But farming has left precious little land for nature, especially around Evesham, where greenhouses, polythene cloches and the other paraphernalia of market gardening and horticulture proliferate.

Shakespeare's Avon is the first of the region's four great rivers to be encountered. Dotted throughout its valley are charming half-timbered villages, grand country houses and parklands whose subtle blend of grasslands, lakes and woods supports many commoner birds. In winter the flood meadows above Tewkesbury hold many wildfowl and waders, including Tundra Swans, and just upstream the Marsh Warbler still hangs on in what was once its national stronghold. Around Coventry were several sand and gravel quarries, of which Brandon Marsh has become an outstanding wetland. North of the river is mixed farming country, with small fields and well timbered hedgerows. Small woods are liberally scattered throughout, many reputedly remnants of the once extensive hunting forests of Feckenham and Arden. One site of special importance is Upton Warren, where brine seepage into shallow subsidence pools creates an excellent wader habitat.

The raw materials yielded by the coal measures spawned the great industrial empires of Birmingham, the Black Country, Coventry, and the Potteries. Today these areas house nearly three million people and surviving semi-natural habitats are few amidst a mass of concrete, bricks and mortar. But industrial decline has created a niche for the Black Redstart in Birmingham. The city was once the hub of a thriving canal network and several feeder reservoirs were built to replenish this, of which Chasewater is good for wildfowl and excellent for gulls.

Coventry is a much newer city, substantially rebuilt since the Second World War blitz, but along the River Sowe many birds visit the mining subsidence pools and marshes. Whilst Birmingham and Coventry grew progressively outwards from single centres, engulfing small villages as they went, the Black Country towns of Dudley, Stourbridge, Walsall, West Bromwich and Wolverhampton spread simultaneously, trapping isolated pockets of countryside between them. Today these pockets bring precious countryside to a vast population, introducing them through places like the RSPB's Sandwell Valley reserve to a variety of birdlife from warblers and woodpeckers to waders and wildfowl.

Some 40 miles (60 km) to the north, the 'five towns' of the Potteries grew in similar fashion to the Black Country. Today, with the bottle kilns, collieries and foundries gone, reclaimed slag heaps are producing good birdwatching sites, with wildfowl visiting Westport Lake and marsh species the Whitfield Valley.

Urban influence has spread well beyond our towns and cities. In the Tame Valley east of Birmingham, old gravel pits, subsidence pools, a reservoir, river purification scheme and water park form an ornithologically outstanding chain of wetlands, with a wide range of birds that even includes coastal species such as Common Tern nesting right in the heart

Principal Birdwatching Sites

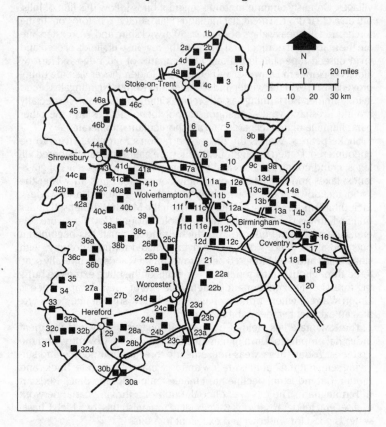

1 The Peak District
  a The Dales
  b The North Staffordshire Moors
2 Rudyard and Tittesworth
  a Rudyard Reservoir
  b Tittesworth Reservoir
3 The Churnet Valley
4 The Potteries
  a Westport Lake
  b Whitfield Valley and Ford Green
    Marsh
  c Park Hall Country Park
  d Greenway Bank and Knypersley
5 Blithfield Reservoir
6 Doxey Marshes
7 Belvide Reservoir, Gailey Reservoir
  and Chillington Lower Avenue
  a Belvide Reservoir and

    Chillington Lower Avenue
  b Gailey Reservoirs
8 Cannock Chase
9 Lower Tame and Trent Valleys
  a Elford Gravel Pits
  b Branston Water Park
  c Whitemoor Haye
10 Chasewater
11 The Black Country
  a Walsall Area
  b Sandwell Valley
  c Sheepwash Urban Park
  d Buckpool and Fens Pool
  e Blackbrook Valley
  f Himley and Baggeridge
12 Birmingham District
  a Edgbaston Reservoir
  b Bartley Reservoir

of the country. Winter concentrations of diving duck are also impressive.

Tracts of heathland are a feature of the landscape north of Birmingham. The best is Cannock Chase, with its superb mosaic of dry and wet heath intermingled with broad-leaved and coniferous woodland. Outstanding amongst its heath and woodland birds is a good population of European Nightjars. Similar heaths occur at Sutton Park, around Kidderminster and south of the Potteries, but their birdlife has been diminished by afforestation, fragmentation and recreation pressure.

The River Trent skirts Cannock Chase and beyond that lies the Vale of Trent. Gravel pits and flood meadows around the confluence with the Tame hold wintering wildfowl and interesting breeding birds. Doxey Marshes are another superb wetland, especially good for Water Rail and Common Snipe. But the prime sites are Belvide and Blithfield reservoirs, both of which are excellent for wildfowl, waders and gulls. Another arable belt, with fields of barley, wheat, potatoes and sugar beet, stretches from here to north Shropshire. In summer this is a good area for Corn Buntings and occasionally even Common Quail are heard. In Shropshire interest centres more on natural sites, particularly the glacial meres around Ellesmere, which are good for wildfowl, and mosses such as Fenns and Whixall.

Across in Staffordshire the picturesque Churnet Valley is clothed with mixed woodlands, such as those at the RSPB's Coombes Valley reserve. All the birds typical of upland woods and fast-flowing streams can be found here. At the head of the Churnet Valley, the twin reservoirs of Rudyard and Tittesworth hold wintering wildfowl and passage waders, especially Eurasian Curlew. This is also one of the few areas in the region where Common Sandpipers nest.

Above the Churnet the land rises up to the plateaux and craggy summits of the Peak District. To the east, white drystone walls mark the limestone country, dissected by the majestic dales with their crystal streams, ashwoods and sheer rock faces. Again, the woodland and riparian birds are similar to the Churnet Valley, but with the addition of Goosanders along the Dove. To the west are tracts of windswept grass and heather moor, interspersed with upland pastures, rocky crags and deep, wooded cloughs. This is an outstanding area for upland breeding birds, especially waders, Red and Black Grouse, Ring Ouzel and Twite.

Westwards from Birmingham is the Severn. Through much of Shropshire it meanders across flood meadows which upstream of the spectacular Ironbridge Gorge hold wintering wildfowl, including wild swans. Above the gorge, the region's fourth outcrop of coal measures became the birthplace of the Industrial Revolution. Ironbridge is now both a world heritage site and part of Telford New Town. Once through the Gorge, the Severn follows a direct course down to the Bristol Channel. On its west banks are Chelmarsh Reservoir, one of the foremost sites in Shropshire for wildfowl and waders, and the Wyre Forest, which is one of Britain's finest and most extensive forests. As well as Common Redstart, Wood Warbler and Pied Flycatcher, which are the typical birds of western oakwoods, Common Crossbill and Hawfinch can also be found.

Rising abruptly out of the Severn plain is the distinctive outline of the Malverns. The hills are the haunt of Northern Wheatears and Tree Pipits in summer and a variety of passage migrants, particularly in autumn. From the summits of the Malverns the views are spectacular. To the east is the Midlands Plain with the hazy outline of the Cotswolds receding into the distance. To the west lie the rolling hills of Herefordshire.

Noted for its rich, red soils and famous red-and-white cattle, Herefordshire must surely be one of England's loveliest and least spoilt counties. Lying in a bowl ringed by the Malverns, the Black Mountains and the Shropshire Hills, this is a landscape of arable fields, lush pastures, hop-yards and cider orchards. Woodlands abound, particularly on the steep hillsides, with oak the native tree, but beech on the limestones. This is mistletoe country, while Pied Flycatcher is *the* bird of Herefordshire.

Through the bowl flows the Wye – the last of the region's four great rivers. This must be one of the most beautiful rivers in England, particularly where it flows through the magnificent, wooded gorge at Symonds Yat. Here the spectacular beauty of the scenery is matched only by the breath-taking agility of the resident Peregrine Falcons. With few enclosed waters, the Wye is a major habitat for wildfowl and waders in Herefordshire. Mute Swans, Goosanders, wintering ducks and passage waders can be found all along its course, with particular concentrations around the Lugg confluence and downstream of Hay-on-Wye especially after winter flooding. Then the numbers of dabbling duck increase and wild swans may arrive.

In the extreme southwest the plateau of the Brecon Beacons rises to over 2300 ft (700 m) – the highest point of the region. Its rocky crags and scree slopes are the summer haunt of Northern Wheatear and Ring Ouzel, while on the plateau the windswept heather moor holds a few Red Grouse. Down below, the secluded Olchon Valley holds the typical species of upland streams and woods.

The south Shropshire Hills are heavily dissected by numerous streams and rivers, breaking down in the east into parallel ridges of which Wenlock Edge is the longest. Here rough hill grazing and rich valley pastures combine to produce an unspoilt landscape where sheep outnumber people. This is the countryside of wooded hillsides and sheepwalks that belongs to Common Buzzard and Common Raven. Many woods have been replanted with conifers, creating a niche for Siskin and Common Crossbill. At the same time sufficient broadleaved woodland remains for other arboreal species to be widespread and for Hawfinches to occur here and there. The streams are home to Dippers and Grey Wagtails. Finally, amongst the acid heath, heather moor and rocky outcrops of the Clee Hills, Long Mynd and Stiperstones, Red Grouse are resident and summer brings Whinchat, Northern Wheatear and Ring Ouzel.

In this portrait we have attempted to give a flavour of the region and its birdlife. The following chapters describe the better sites in detail. Even now, though, it should be apparent that the six counties have much to offer the birdwatcher. Where else are upland and lowland, northerly and southerly, or easterly and westerly species brought into such close proximity? Add to this a good range of passage birds and the chance of a rarity here and there and the prospects for a successful day's birdwatching are good.

The southernmost part of the Peak District National Park protrudes into Staffordshire, where it embraces two quite distinct habitats. To the east, where the Carboniferous limestone outcrops, are the famous dales, of which majestic Dovedale is the best known. To the west, on the Millstone Grit, are the bleak and sombre North Staffordshire Moors.

THE DALES

Habitat

The eastern side of the National Park in Staffordshire is part of a great limestone dome that forms a plateau of short, nutritious swards grazed by cattle and sheep. Fields are enclosed by drystone walls of white limestone and trees are few, although some farmsteads nestle behind a belt of sycamores.

The glory of this area is the dales – spectacular ravines with crystal-clear rivers, a mantle of ash woodland or thorn scrub, and towering limestone cliffs. Much of the area belongs to the National Trust (NT). Dovedale, which marks the Derbyshire border, is the narrowest and most spectacular. It is also the most popular and thronged with summer visitors. Interesting birds can be seen here, but most birdwatchers prefer the Hamps or Manifold Valleys.

The Manifold below Wetton Mill is typical dales country and is easily explored from the footpath along the old railway track. Just below the mill the river disappears down a sink-hole in summer, leaving a dry bed for several miles. In winter, though, it flows throughout its course. In spring and summer, the small riverside meadows are dotted with the delicate flowers so typical of limestone country. Rising abruptly from the valley floor are steep slopes of grassland or ash woodland. On the upper slopes these give way to gorse or thorn scrub, whilst the summits are marked by sheer cliffs or crags of bare limestone, with here and there natural caves. In places, vast quarries disfigure the landscape. Most of the woodland birds can be seen at the Staffordshire Wildlife Trust's (SWT) reserve at Castern Wood in the Manifold Valley.

Species

Breeding woodland and waterside birds in superb scenery are the main interest.

In early spring the plateau tops come alive with tumbling Northern Lapwings, the bubbling calls of Eurasian Curlews and the outpourings of Sky Larks. Less obtrusively, Meadow Pipits perch on drystone walls, joined later by a few Northern Wheatears and perhaps a Whinchat.

The rivers are home to both Dippers and Common Kingfishers. The latter prefer the deeper, slower reaches with overhanging banks for nesting. During a dry season, they often catch the fish trapped in the small pools that are left behind when the river disappears underground. Dippers frequently feed among the boulder-strewn shallows or shingle banks and nest beneath a nearby bridge or overhanging bank. Pied and Grey Wagtails also inhabit the riverside, especially in the vicinity of mills and water-falls. Goosander have begun to colonise the quieter stretches in summer, with here and there a pair nesting. Occasionally a pair of Grey Herons nests as well.

Amongst the ashwoods Chaffinch and Willow Warbler are the com-monest species, while Blackcap, Garden Warbler, Spotted Flycatcher and the occasional Green Woodpecker, Marsh Tit or Wood Nuthatch occur along with other regular woodland birds. Of the specialities, Wood War-blers and Pied Flycatchers can be found in one or two woods with closed canopies, while Tree Pipits and Common Redstarts occur where there are scattered trees and scrub. Goldfinch, Linnet, Common Whitethroat and an occasional Whinchat inhabit the scrub on the upper slopes, with Lin-net and Common Whitethroat especially fond of gorse. Most of the wood-land birds, including all three woodpeckers, Tree Pipits, warblers and Pied Flycatchers can be seen at Castern Wood.

Overhead, Rooks are common, Wood Pigeons and Stock Doves fly to and fro across the valley and noisy flocks of Eurasian Jackdaws spiral around the crags, caves and quarries. Common Swifts are regularly over-head in summer and sometimes nest behind fissures in the limestone. Likewise some House Martin colonies may be found on the exposed crags. Common Kestrels are the most frequently seen raptor.

Most summer visitors leave during August and it is quiet until late Sep-tember or October. Then flocks of Fieldfare and Redwing relish the berries on the thorn scrub. Once these are eaten, they turn to the fields or move elsewhere, leaving the resident birds alone once more. Sometimes a Common Stonechat is seen in autumn or a flock of Siskin in winter.

Timing

Early morning, when songbirds are most vocal, is the best time to visit the woods. The dales get very crowded on warm, sunny days, particularly at weekends and bank holidays, forcing many species of birds into remote inaccessible spots. Even Dippers and riparian birds such as Pied and Grey Wagtail are elusive when crowds of people are about.

Access

Dovedale Approach from the A515 Ashbourne to Buxton road. From the south, 1 mile (1.6 km) after Ashbourne, turn left onto a minor road and follow signs to Thorpe. Turn left into the village and, following signs to Ilam, bear right in the centre, continue down the hill and across the river bridge. Then turn immediately right, pass the entrance to the Isaac Wal-ton Hotel and park in the car park on the right. From here follow the main footpath along the river to Milldale, a distance of 3 miles (4.8 km). There is a limited bus service between Ashbourne and Ilam which passes the end of Dovedale, about 0.25 miles (0.4 km) short of the car park.

From the north, turn right off the A515 about 4 miles (6.4 km) south of the junction with the A5012 and take the narrow lane signposted Alstone-field. At the bottom of the steep hill, cross the river and turn left into Mill-dale, through the village and up the hill to the car park. Return to the village on foot, cross the river and follow the footpath southwards. Again, there is a limited bus service between Ashbourne and Alstonefield. Alight at the junction for Milldale, which is about 0.5 miles (0.8 km) from the vil-lage.

Manifold Valley Continue from Milldale (or through Alstonefield) to

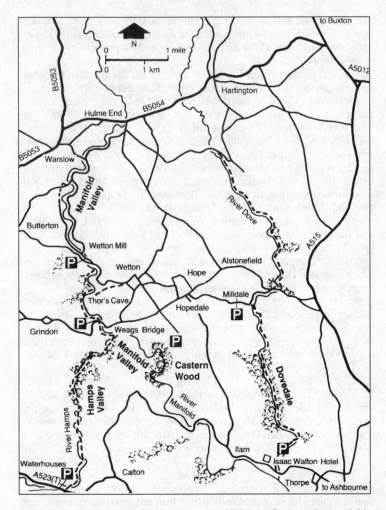

Hopedale, then take a right turn signposted Wetton. Park on the roadside by the Y junction at the western end of the village, follow the farm track for a short distance, then take the footpath on the right to reach Thor's Cave and spectacular views along the valley. Check the thorn scrub here-abouts for chats and warblers. Return to the road, drive down steep hill to the river and car park at Wetton Mill. Follow the Manifold Way southwards along the disused railway for woodland, scrub and water-side species.

The Manifold Way may be followed as far as Weags Bridge, 2 miles (3 km), then onwards up the Hamps Valley to the A523 at Waterhouses, a total distance of 6 miles (9.5 km). Alternatively, park in the car park off the A523 at Waterhouses to walk the route in reverse, or explore from the riverside car park at Weags Bridge (to reach this carry straight on from Alstonefield towards Grindon instead of turning right into Wetton). There are various bus services to Waterhouses, including that from Derby to Manchester, and a limited service from Leek to Grindon, from where it is a 1.5-mile (2.4 km) walk to Weags Bridge.

Castern Wood Access is restricted to SWT members only. Continue straight on from Hopedale towards Weags Bridge and take the first lane on the left, which is a cul-de-sac. At the end of the lane, turn right by a tall public footpath sign, through a gate and into a field. Follow a track to a small parking area at the end. Please close all gates and keep dogs on a lead.

Calendar

All Year: Common Kestrel, Stock Dove, Common Kingfisher, all three woodpeckers, Pied Wagtail, Dipper, Marsh Tit, Wood Nuthatch, corvids and common woodland birds.

March–September: Grey Heron and Goosander (scarce), Northern Lapwing, Eurasian Curlew, Sky Lark, Meadow Pipit, Goldfinch and Linnet (a few of the last four may be resident). Summer visitors from mid-April: Common Swift (May to August), House Martin, Tree Pipit, Grey Wagtail, Common Redstart, Whinchat (scarce), Northern Wheatear, Common Whitethroat, common woodland warblers including Wood Warbler, Spotted Flycatcher (not before May) and Pied Flycatcher.

October–February: Common Stonechat (October and November), winter thrushes and Siskin.

THE NORTH STAFFORDSHIRE MOORS

Habitat

The main areas of moorland lie between Leek and Buxton, reaching a height of 1684 ft (513 m) on Oliver Hill. Although this is no great altitude, the climate is most inhospitable; rainfall is heavy and snow frequently lies in winter. By moorland standards the area is well populated, with numerous scattered farmsteads and villages. It is also surprisingly accessible, being crossed by the A53 and numerous minor roads. Beware in winter though, as roads are frequently blocked by drifting snow.

The land north and west of the A53 is generally highest, with heather moor and areas of cotton-grass to the north, and rocky outcrops, steep-sided valleys and fast-flowing streams in the extreme west. The Roaches and Ramshaw Rocks stand up as exposed sandstone crags, smoothed and contoured by rain and frost. Below them is a bleak, rolling landscape of heather, cotton grass, bracken, rushy pastures and peat bogs, relieved only where drystone walls enclose sheep pastures and rough grazing. East of the A53 are large expanses of heather moor, with heavily grazed, improved pastures on the lower slopes. There are also two areas of rushy grassland used by the Ministry of Defence.

There are isolated patches of scrub woodland, usually birch, willow or pine, or a small conifer plantation. Sessile oakwoods occur in the valleys. Small dairy farms once contributed to the intricate mosaic of habitats that was so ideal for breeding birds. Unfortunately, most have now been converted into heavily stocked sheep farms and their pastures drained, improved and used for silage. This, together with mounting recreational pressures, including birdwatching, has contributed to the decline of many species. Fortunately, the SWT has recently received a grant from the National Heritage Memorial Lottery Fund, which will enable it to acquire 240 acres (97 ha) of moorland and woodland. This will link together the Peak Park's Roaches and Warslow Moors estates and, with sympathetic management, it is hoped that some of these declines can be reversed. As yet, there are no access arrangements for this area.

Species

There is an outstanding range of moorland species, especially in summer.

Seasonal contrasts are most marked. Severe winters force all but the hardiest species to forsake the moors and only the grouse and a few Meadow Pipits, corvids and Reed Buntings can be regarded as truly resident.

Much of the remaining heather is managed as grouse moor, with a widespread, if declining, population of Red Grouse. A covey often bursts unexpectedly from cover, but beware of game birds 'whirring' low across the moor and disappearing into heather again – there are Grey Partridge here too!

Black Grouse still survive on the moors

Black Grouse have declined still further and, with no more than ten males at a single lek, their future is in serious jeopardy. However, a new hide now overlooks the lek site, so they can be watched without disturbance, but please keep visits to a minimum and enter and leave the hide quietly. Males often return to the lek in February, but most activity is in spring, quickly subsiding after May. Most birds gather in the early morning or late evening. Sometimes lekking occurs in autumn too, but only in the early morning. Just occasionally a Black Grouse is encountered in the middle of the day, perched on a drystone wall or in a tree. Since bilberry is a favourite food, look where it invades the edges of scrub woodland. In winter, birds also feed in birch scrub and sallow thickets.

Meadow Pipits reappear in March and soon become the commonest, most widespread breeding species, but often are involuntary hosts to Common Cuckoos. Eurasian Curlews also begin to return in March, and by April they too are widespread. Huge flocks of Redwing and Fieldfare also pause on their journeys northwards, roosting at times in the heather at Swallow Moss, as do Pied Wagtails.

Snow may still be lying when the first Ring Ouzels and Northern Wheatears return to their territories in late March or early April. Ring Ouzels, now below 20 pairs, prefer the broken terrain west of the A53, especially where upland pastures give way to boulder-strewn open moorland with nearby streams. Their sharp decline is thought to be due to increased rock climbing, walking and hang-gliding in their favoured area. Conversely, Northern Wheatears, which favour drystone walls, derelict barns and scree slopes, have spread eastwards across the A53 and doubled their numbers. This may be because the increased intensity of grazing has produced the short turf they require for feeding.

Late spring or early summer is best for breeding birds. Whinchats will have returned to their territories, with most around Goldsitch and Swallow Mosses along with Reed Buntings. Despite their being up to 100 pairs, Twite can be difficult to find, but their favoured area is to the north around Knotbury. They return late, sometimes not until June, and can be very unobtrusive when feeding with Linnets in hayfields off the moor. Occasionally in late summer small flocks are seen perched on telegraph wires or feeding on roadside thistles or ragwort.

As with most moorland, the area is important for breeding waders. In addition to Eurasian Curlew, the mosses and damp rushy pastures hold Northern Lapwing and Common Snipe. All three species have declined as a result of improved drainage and conversion to drier silage fields. Even so, Northern Lapwing and Common Snipe remain widespread and numerous, though Common Redshank has sadly disappeared. On the higher, more remote moors three or four pairs of European Golden Plover nest each year, though they too are in decline. Passage may bring parties of Whimbrel flying over in May and August, occasionally pausing to rest awhile. In recent years small 'trips' of Dotterel have also rested at Gun Hill or the airfield at Morridge in early May.

Raptors are another moorland speciality. Common Kestrels are always around, and Merlin and Hobby also breed, though not necessarily annually. Hen Harriers have bred too, but now seem to be very scarce, but regular winter visitors. Often they come into roost at Swallow Moss. A pair or two of Merlins nest most years and their arrival and departure usually coincides with that of the Meadow Pipits on which they prey. Occasionally one stays through the winter, giving a tantalising glimpse as it dashes low and twisting across the heather. Likewise little is seen of a Hobby in fast aerial pursuit of prey, but on warm summer days one might leisurely hunt insects across the moor. Peregrine Falcons occur sporadically, with sightings increasing as their population spreads. Exceptionally a Common Buzzard or a rarer Rough-legged Buzzard, Red Kite or Marsh Harrier passes through. Two other moorland predators are the Short-eared and Long-eared Owls. Short-eared breed sporadically, but regularly quarter rough grassland or young forestry plantations in their quest for voles. Long-eared are more nocturnal and best located by the hunger calls of their young coming from a patch of scrub late on a summer's evening. Common Ravens now inhabit the Swallow Moss and Knotbury areas too.

Other breeding species include a few Common Stonechats amongst gorse and scrub; Common Redpolls in small birches and sallow thickets; and one or two Common Teal in wet ground such as that at Goldsitch Moss. Swarms of hatching insects also attract feeding Common Swifts and hirundines.

The scrub, woodland and streams should not be neglected, especially the Blackbrook Valley. In the open scrub, Willow Warblers are abundant and Tree Pipits quite numerous. Within the woods, Chaffinch is the commonest bird, but several pairs of Common Redstarts breed in the older oak and rowan woods and Pied Flycatchers nest sparingly. Other species present in reasonable numbers are Eurasian Sparrowhawk, Common Pheasant, Woodcock, Tawny Owl, Green Woodpecker, Blackcap, Wood Warbler, Eurasian Jay and Goldfinch. On the fast, tumbling streams both Dipper and Grey Wagtail are frequently seen, while some 30 pairs of Eurasian Jackdaws nest on a cliff overlooking the River Dane and Stock Doves breed in deserted farm buildings.

After breeding, most small birds leave their moorland homes and move to lower ground. Those remaining tend to flock around a good food source. From late September onwards Redwings and Fieldfares move in to feast on berries, with perhaps a late Ring Ouzel seeking out the rowans. Small flocks of finches at this time often include Bramblings, Goldfinches and Common Redpoll. From time to time late autumn also brings a Common Stonechat or rarely a Snow Bunting, while Great Grey Shrike has been seen then and in spring.

Timing

As usual, early morning is the best time as songsters re-establish their territories in spring or resume the endless routine of feeding their young in summer. Raptors are more active from mid-morning onwards, once the ground has warmed up and insects are on the wing. Overflying migrants are often brought down by heavy rain or thunderstorms, and in winter they may pass through in large numbers in advance of hard weather. Black Grouse are most active very early in the morning and, in spring, again in the late evening. The moors are becoming increasingly popular for recreation. Rock-climbers regularly use Ramshaw Rocks and the Roaches, hang-gliders use Hen Cloud and to the east of the A53 the military has a large firing range. (Watch out for red flags which give warning of firing.) The army also uses the area around Swallow Moss for exercises.

Access

The moors are best approached from the A53 Leek to Buxton road. For the Roaches turn westwards off the A53 at Upper Hulme, 3 miles (4.8 km) to the north of Leek. After 1 mile (1.6 km) park by the roadside and explore on foot. One suggestion is to take the path that skirts the southern side of Hen Cloud, follow this round to the summit and then head towards the Roaches. From here there is a good expanse of heather moor to the right and superb views beyond the old pinewood on the left. Continue along the Roaches for 2 miles (3.2 km) into Roach End. From Roach End take the rough track that descends into the Blackbrook Valley. For woodland species follow the path on the left just before the renovated farmhouse and continue into Back Forest. Wander along the tracks in the wood and down to the stream and the River Dane. Return via the top edge of the wood to check for birds feeding on bilberries or heather.

For moorland species stay on the main track from Roach End, past the renovated farmhouse and down into Blackbrook Valley. Look out for Ring Ouzels across the valley. Cross the stream by the footbridge and climb up the hillside opposite to the top of Gradbach Hill, then turn right along the path to regain the road at Goldsitch Moss, where a check should be made for waders. This walk could be made in reverse, beginning at Goldsitch Moss, where cars can be parked by the roadside, or alternatively shortened by beginning at Roach End. However, parking is very limited at Roach End and difficult in the Roaches generally, so try to avoid busy times. Alternatively, there is plenty of parking at nearby Tittesworth Reservoir, for which a small charge is made, and a park-and-ride bus

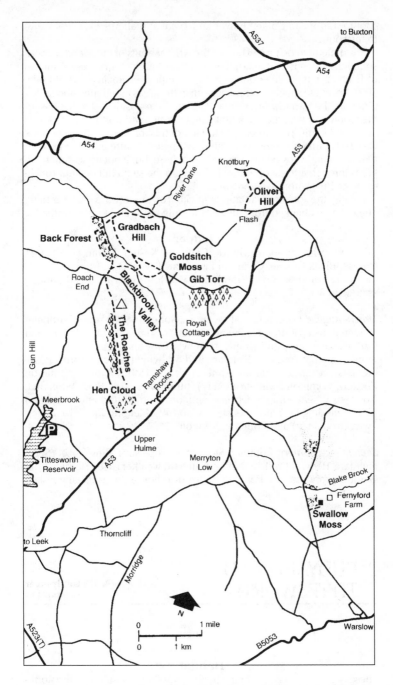

service in summer from here to the Roaches. Additionally the Hanley–Sheffield bus service operates along the A53.

Another good area for typical moorland birds is Oliver Hill, which is conveniently crossed by a footpath from Flash to Knotbury. This is a good

27

spot for European Golden Plover and Twite and affords excellent views to the south.

It is difficult to be precise about the whereabouts of moorland birds as so much depends on the condition of their habitat. This is especially so of heather, which deteriorates both through over-grazing and old age. Most moorland species should be seen in the areas mentioned above, but if not, try the Swallow Moss area. Park on the roadside just to the east of the wood and take the track that leads off the road northwards towards Fernyford Farm. The old barn to the left of this track overlooks the Black Grouse lek and has been converted by English Nature into a hide. With patience good views should be had from here, but if not try scanning the fields through a telescope from halfway up the steep hill that approaches Blake Brook from the northwest.

Finally, the forestry plantations at Gib Torr are always worth a look. They can be checked from the surrounding roads and public footpaths.

Calendar

All Year: Eurasian Sparrowhawk, Common Kestrel, Merlin (rare), Red Grouse, Black Grouse, Common Pheasant, Tawny Owl, Dipper, corvids including Common Raven (rare), and Meadow Pipits and Reed Bunting (scarce in winter).

March–August: Common Teal (scarce), Dotterel (May; rare), European Golden Plover, Northern Lapwing, Common Snipe, Woodcock, Eurasian Curlew, Long-eared and Short-eared Owls, Grey and Pied Wagtails, Common Stonechat (scarce), Fieldfare and Redwing (leave in April). Possible passage waders. From April onwards: Hobby (rare), Common Cuckoo, Common Swift (from May), hirundines, Tree Pipit, Whinchat, Northern Wheatear, Ring Ouzel, common open ground and woodland birds including Common Redstart, Wood Warbler and Pied Flycatcher, Twite (from May) and Common Redpoll.

September–February: Common Stonechat (Sep–Nov), Ring Ouzel (Sep), Fieldfare, Redwing and finches (rare in hard weather). Hen Harrier (from October: very scarce). Possible raptor or other rarity, especially in late autumn.

2 RUDYARD AND TITTESWORTH

OS Landranger
Map 118

Habitat

These two reservoirs lie near the head of the Churnet Valley, to the north-west and north of Leek, respectively.

The British Waterways (BW) canal-feeder reservoir at Rudyard covers 175 acres (71 ha). Situated in a deep, natural valley, the lake is narrow but almost 2 miles (3.2 km) long. Viewed from the A523, high to the east, its setting is magnificent, with steep, wooded slopes and open hillsides above. The lake is quite deep and the banks shelve steeply, so there is little marginal vegetation except at the northern end where the banks are more gradual. Here water horsetail, yellow flag and reed-grass grades into alder and willow scrub, providing cover for nesting birds. Low water levels expose mud which attracts a few migrant waders. Sailing and fishing are both popular and many people visit the lake in summer. The valley is well wooded, with two small copses on the eastern side, Rea Cliffe Wood covering much of the western shore and lower down the valley the Staffordshire Wildlife Trust's (SWT) woodland and wetland reserve at Longsdon Wood. Between them these contain oak, beech and other broadleaved trees plus some larch and other conifers. Alders thrive down at the water's edge, particularly along the feeder stream below the dam, and there are flood meadows between the river and canal.

Tittesworth Reservoir is larger, with 189 acres (76 ha) of water and an additional 1275 acres (515 ha) of surrounding land owned by Severn Trent Water (STW). Principally a water-supply reservoir, it is also used for game fishing and has a very popular picnic area. Like Rudyard, it was formed by damming a natural valley, but here the shoreline shelves gradually and is more irregular. The surrounding countryside is more open too, with plenty of grazing for winter wildfowl and hedges of hawthorn and blackthorn to provide winter food for birds. The River Churnet feeds the reservoir from the northeast. The indented eastern shore is partly covered by young broadleaved woodland backed by plantations of pine and larch, while much of the western shore is bordered by Hindclough Wood – an ancient oak woodland, which is a haven for red deer. Common spotted orchids flourish in the conservation area beneath the dam. North of the causeway is another conservation area primarily for birds. A screened path gives access to a hide on the east bank. Water levels are controlled through a weir to provide suitable conditions for breeding and passage waders and an island provides safe nest sites. The area is also good for dabbling duck in winter. Of the two reservoirs, Tittesworth is likely to prove the most productive.

Given time, Longsdon Mill Pool might also be worth a look. Formerly a favoured haunt of Whooper Swans, this tiny depression in a rough, upland meadow, is also fished and more often than not is devoid of birds. However, its marginal vegetation provides some cover and wildfowl do visit from time to time, while Eurasian Curlew may roost in good numbers in March.

Species

Winter wildfowl and passage waders and terns are the main interest, though both sites can be erratic.

A few pairs of common waterbirds usually breed, with Great Crested Grebe, Canada Goose, Mallard and Tufted Duck at both reservoirs, Little Grebe at Tittesworth and Mute Swan at Rudyard. By autumn, 200 Canada Geese may have assembled at Rudyard (exceptionally 400) and around 100 at Tittesworth, while at Rudyard some 20 Grey Herons come from the nearby heronry to fish. Eurasian Wigeon start arriving in September and by the turn of the year 200 or more graze the grassy surrounds of Tittesworth. The species is less regular at Rudyard, but 150 may be present, while even Longsdon might hold 100. Up to 150 Mallard frequent both reservoirs, though numbers are lower some years. At Tittesworth, much depends on the water level in the marshy areas favoured by dabbling duck. Common Teal are very unpredictable, with numbers fluctuating from a few to 200 or so. Highest counts are usually in the autumn at Rudyard, but small numbers might also be seen at Longsdon. Small numbers of Common Shelduck, Gadwall, Northern Pintail and Northern Shoveler appear irregularly too, and Garganey has been noted in spring.

Diving birds are equally variable, but Common Pochard and Tufted Duck are usually present in winter. Rudyard seldom has more than a couple of dozen of each, but occasionally 100, while Tittesworth holds around 25 Tufted Duck and sometimes over 100 Common Pochard. A few Common Goldeneye and Goosander also regularly visit both waters. Up to 100 Common Coot frequent Tittesworth, Great Cormorants and Ruddy Duck are noted on occasions, Common Scoter are sometimes seen on passage and other sea-duck or scarce wildfowl have been recorded.

From 1976–87 Whooper Swans frequented the area, but with few recent records it must now be regarded as a scarce and irregular winter visitor. This also applies to Tundra Swans, which occasionally appear at Tittesworth between October and March, the largest herd being one of 50. Geese are equally enigmatic. The resident Canada Geese are joined from time to time by other species. Small numbers are assumed to be feral birds, but skeins of 100 or more Pink-footed Geese have been seen flying over Tittesworth and down the Churnet Valley. Similar flocks over-fly other parts of north Staffordshire and almost certainly indicate movements of wild birds from the Lancashire mosses.

Wader passage begins in March, when 100 or more Eurasian Curlew may visit Tittesworth *en route* to their moorland breeding haunts. In the evening most leave to roost at Longsdon. Little Ringed Plover and Common Sandpiper return in April, with two or three pairs of each usually breeding at Tittesworth and a pair of Little Ringed Plovers at Rudyard. With high water levels, spring wader passage is often poor, though the commoner species are regularly noted and Oystercatcher, Great Ringed Plover, Sanderling and Common Greenshank are occasionally seen. Rarer spring visitors have included Little and Temminck's Stints, Whimbrel and Wood Sandpiper. Tittesworth is generally the better reservoir at this season and has held a Kentish Plover.

Following a good breeding season, there may be several hundred Northern Lapwings and up to ten Little Ringed Plovers and Common Sandpipers by July. Soon they are joined by one or two Green Sandpipers and perhaps a Wood Sandpiper. August then brings a few of the commoner species, including Common Greenshank. Less regularly, Little Stint, Curlew Sandpiper, Black-tailed Godwit, Spotted Redshank or Turnstone might appear. Eurasian Curlew and Common Snipe move down from the moors to flock at the reservoirs. Eurasian Curlew are seldom so numerous as in spring, but up to 50 Common Snipe may probe for food at either Rudyard or Tittesworth from August to October. Some may stay well into a frost-free winter, being joined perhaps by a Jack Snipe.

Passage gulls and terns are scarce, but one or two Common or Arctic Terns move through in spring or autumn, while a Black Tern, couple of Little Gulls or a storm-driven Kittiwake are occasionally seen. In winter, the reservoirs, particularly Tittesworth, hold a few gulls and a Water Rail might secrete itself among the marginal vegetation – the habitat at Longsdon being particularly suitable. Common Kingfishers are resident, often breeding in the vicinity; Grey and Pied Wagtails frequent the shorelines and streams below the dams; one or two pairs of Yellow Wagtail and

Sedge Warbler breed and Dippers occur on the Churnet above Tittes-worth. A few White Wagtails pass through in spring as do flocks of hirundines, Meadow Pipits and Mistle Thrushes in autumn.

There is also a good range of common woodland birds, especially around Rudyard. The heronry in Longsdon Wood contains about 20 nests and other residents include Little and Tawny Owls, all three species of woodpecker, Marsh and Willow Tits, and Wood Nuthatch. Summer brings Common Redstart, Spotted Flycatcher, passage Pied Flycatcher and many warblers, including Grasshopper and Wood Warbler, into the valley. Woodcock also breed in the conifer plantations, but more occur in winter. This is also the season when Fieldfare and Redwing visit and Siskin and Common Redpoll congregate, especially in the alders below the dam at Rudyard. Bramblings visit most winters too, with sometimes several hundred at Rudyard. Although Eurasian Sparrowhawk and Com-mon Kestrel are the commonest raptors, passage might bring a Hen Har-rier, Osprey, Hobby or Peregrine Falcon to enliven the day. Unusual sightings have included Great Northern Diver, Slavonian Grebe, Little Egret, Green-winged Teal and a Fulmar flying over.

Timing
Both reservoirs are fished, the picnic areas are extremely popular in sum-mer and there is sailing on Rudyard too. Early visits are therefore advis-able, particularly in spring and summer. In winter, weather is more important than disturbance. Freezing conditions or heavy snowfalls fur-ther north may well bring fresh wildfowl, possibly including geese.

Access
Rudyard Approach from the A523 Leek to Macclesfield road. About 1.5 miles (2.4 km) north of Leek turn westwards onto the B5331 and follow this towards Rudyard. Just before entering the village, there is a car park on the left (south) side of the road by the railway bridge. Park here and either follow the Staffordshire Way northwards to the perimeter path around the reservoir, or southwards for 1.5 miles (2.4 km) to Longsdon Wood (where access is restricted to public rights-of-way).

Alternatively continue along the A523 for a further 3 miles (4.8 km), then turn westwards at Ryecroft Gate. In a few yards, immediately over the old railway bridge, turn left and follow a track alongside the old rail-way line. At the fork, either park to explore the western shore on foot, or bear to the left, drive under the bridge and park along the eastern shore. A bus service from Leek (Derby to Manchester) passes along the A523. Alight at Ryecroft Gate and follow above directions to the reservoir.

Tittesworth Approach from the A53 Leek to Buxton road. Some 2.5 miles (4 km) north of Leek turn westwards at the Three Horseshoes Inn in Blackshaw Moor towards Meerbrook. Access to the car park, visitor centre, cafe and toilets is on the left about 1 mile (1.6 km) further on. A small charge is made for parking. Bus services run from Leek to Black-shaw Moor, including a Hanley to Sheffield service. Alight at the Three Horseshoes and walk to the reservoir. For those also visiting the moors, there is a park-and-ride service in summer from the reservoir to the Roach-es. The visitor centre and the hide have facilities for the disabled.

Longsdon Mill Pool Turn northwards off the A53 Stoke to Leek road at the cross-roads 0.25 miles (0.4 km) to the east of Longsdon Church. After

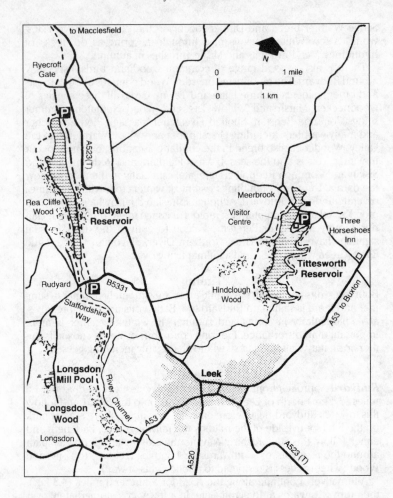

0.5 miles (0.8 km) turn right and the pool is on the left of the lane about 0.5 miles (0.8 km) further on. View from the road.

Calendar

All Year: Little Grebe, Great Crested Grebe, Grey Heron, Mute Swan, Canada Geese, Mallard, Tufted Duck, Ruddy Duck (scarce), Eurasian Sparrowhawk, Common Kestrel, Common Coot, Woodcock, Northern Lapwing, Little and Tawny Owls, Common Kingfisher, all three woodpeckers, Grey and Pied Wagtails, Dipper, Marsh and Willow Tits, Wood Nuthatch and common passerines.

April–June: Common waders such as Little Ringed Plover, Dunlin, Eurasian Curlew and Common Sandpiper; perhaps scarcer waders such as Oystercatcher, Great Ringed Plover, Sanderling and Common Greenshank; possible Kittiwake, Little Gull or Common, Arctic or Black Tern; Yellow Wagtail, White Wagtail (April; scarce), Common Redstart, Spotted Flycatcher (from May), Pied Flycatcher and warblers including Grasshopper, Sedge and Wood. Maybe Garganey or a passing raptor.

July–September: Common waders including Little and Great Ringed Plovers, Dunlin, Common Snipe, Eurasian Curlew, Common Redshank, Common Greenshank and Green and Common Sandpipers; perhaps scarcer waders such as Oystercatcher, Little Stint, Curlew Sandpiper (rare), Black-tailed Godwit, Spotted Redshank, Wood Sandpiper or Turnstone; possible Little Gull or terns as above. Departing summer visitors; maybe a passing raptor.

October–March: Great Cormorant (scarce), Tundra Swan (rare), Whooper Swan (rare), Pink-footed Goose (scarce), Common Shelduck (early and late), Eurasian Wigeon, Gadwall (scarce), Common Teal, Northern Pintail (rare), Northern Shoveler (scarce), Common Pochard, Common Goldeneye, Goosander, Water Rail, Jack Snipe (scarce), Common Snipe, Eurasian Curlew (March), gulls including perhaps Kittiwake, Meadow Pipits (March and October) and flocks of thrushes and finches including Brambling. Perhaps scarce waterfowl, sea-duck or raptor.

3 THE CHURNET VALLEY

OS Landranger
Maps 118 & 119

Habitat

The Churnet rises on the moors of north Staffordshire and flows 25 miles (40 km) to join the Dove near Uttoxeter. Gouged out by glacial meltwaters, its valley is 330 ft (100 m) deep and gorge-like in places. The main river is sluggish, with broad meanders in the lower reaches, but the tributaries are faster flowing, with shallows, shingle spits and boulder-strewn reaches.

Small, lush, grazing meadows line the narrow valley, which is followed by the Caldon Canal and a railway. The land between these and the river is often marshy and liable to flood. Meadows are enclosed by hawthorn hedges, alders flourish along the canal and riverbanks, and there is a profusion of tall herbage. Reed-grass provides cover for nesting birds in many places. Mixed woodland clothes the steep hillsides, forming an almost continuous canopy from Longsdon down to Alton. In parts the ancient woodland has been replaced by coniferous plantations, often with an amenity fringe of oak, ash or sycamore and an understorey of rhododendron that provides winter roost sites.

Hardwoods survive in good variety too. The National Trust (NT) has a nature reserve at Hawksmoor, with stunted oaks and birches scattered over a hillside of bracken, heather and bilberry, while Staffordshire County Council (SCC) has a nature park at Consall. Here both river and canal flow through a remote and very beautiful bowl of semi-natural ash woodland. In addition, there are pools, streams, botanically interesting wet flushes, unimproved grassland and bilberry-rich heath. With such diversity, the fauna is also good, with 15 mammal and 16 butterfly species recorded. Part of the park is an SSSI. Equally beautiful is the area around Oakamoor where private and Forest Enterprise (FE) woodlands blend into an exquisite mixture of hard and softwoods.

For birds, the sessile oakwoods are most important and many are now protected by the RSPB and other conservation bodies. Coombes Valley is typical of most and the easiest to visit. Here, in addition to the oaks, are ash, birch, holly, rowan and wych elm above a shrub layer of bird cherry, blackthorn, hazel, guelder rose and other food plants. There are also hillsides of bracken and heather, meadows by the stream and a small pool overlooked by a hide. A second hide in the oaks that overhang the stream gives excellent views of many woodland species.

Species

Woodland and waterside birds are the main attraction of this picturesque valley, particularly in spring and summer.

Early spring is good for resident woodland birds. Even on chilly mornings, the three woodpeckers, Wood Nuthatch, Eurasian Treecreeper, thrushes, tits and finches are active and easily observed in the bare trees. Look in the pine and spruce plantations for Goldcrests, Coal Tits and Common Redpoll, or perhaps Siskin.

For migrant songbirds, many of which do not return to these upland valley woods until late spring, mid-May is better. Then the woods resound to a chorus of warblers. Willow Warblers are commonest, but Garden Warblers and Blackcaps are both numerous and there are smaller numbers of Lesser Whitethroat and Chiffchaff. A few pairs of Spotted Flycatchers hawk insects; Tree Pipits display on bracken slopes with scattered trees; and Common Whitethroats, Yellowhammers and a few Linnets nest in gorse and thorn scrub. In the background, Sky Larks sing and Common Cuckoos call. A few pairs of Northern Lapwing, and one or two Common Snipe and Yellow Wagtails, breed in some of the damper meadows.

Three migrant songsters are especially characteristic of the Churnet Valley. Wherever there is a closed canopy and sparse shrub layer, such as under beeches or in hanging oakwoods, Wood Warblers can be heard. In contrast, Common Redstarts prefer an open canopy and well developed shrub layer and such conditions at Coombes Valley support around 30 pairs. Similar numbers of Pied Flycatchers occur here too. They like steeply sloping oakwoods overhanging a stream, and commonly breed in the nest boxes outside the tree-hide.

Common Redstarts are particularly numerous in the Churnet woodlands

Eurasian Sparrowhawks can be seen soaring on thermals and Common Kestrels hovering in search of prey, while occasionally a larger raptor, such as Northern Goshawk or Common Buzzard, strays into the area. Rooks, Carrion Crows and Eurasian Jackdaws are all numerous, while the Magpie and Eurasian Jay populations are far healthier than is good for the smaller songbirds. In the evening, Woodcocks rode over the tree-tops, Tawny Owls call and one or two pairs of Long-eared Owls are regularly present, though locating them is difficult unless they call.

In high summer the woods are quiet as parent birds busily feed their young and shortly afterwards migrant birds depart and resident adults go into moult. In irruption years, though, this is when the 'chip, chip' calls of Common Crossbills might be heard.

Activity revives again from early October onwards, when hordes of Redwings and Fieldfares strip the woods and hedgerows of berries. A good year brings several thousand of each and large roosts gather, especially in woods with an understorey of rhododendron. With them come migrant Blackbirds, Song Thrushes, Mistle Thrushes and perhaps a late Ring Ouzel. If there is a good crop of beechmast, a few Brambling may join the usual flocks of foraging Chaffinches and tits. Chaffinches also feed in the meadows and ploughed fields, where they are often joined by other finches and buntings. Small parties of Bullfinches are also noted at this time, while flocks of Goldfinches, Common Redpoll and Siskin regularly come to feed among the alders. Most birds arriving in these autumn influxes remain until either their food supply is exhausted or severe weather forces them to seek a milder clime.

Waterside birds can be seen throughout the year. The streams that twist and fall down the steep slopes into the Churnet are a favoured haunt of Dippers and Grey Wagtails, but Common Kingfishers prefer the stiller reaches of the main river. All three species can be seen from the pool hide at Coombes Valley. Mallard and Moorhen raise broods along the canal, where hirundines regularly feed and Grey Herons come from the nearby Longsdon heronry to fish.

Timing

Early morning is invariably best for songbirds, especially in spring and early summer. By high summer all woodland species are more secretive. A late evening visit is necessary for roding Woodcock and owls. Timing matters less in winter, when disturbance is reduced and most birds are active throughout the day. The numbers of small birds such as Goldcrest, however, can be decimated by a hard winter, when all but the hardiest species will forsake the area altogether. Remember, too, that little will be seen in wet or windy weather. Waterbirds can be seen at most times.

Access

Coombes Valley All the characteristic birds can be seen at this RSPB reserve. Leave the A520 Leek to Stone road eastwards on one of the minor roads leading to Basford Bridge (Cheddleton Railway Centre). Continue past the old station for 0.75 miles (1.2 km) to Basford Green and then turn left into a narrow lane that climbs steeply. The reserve is on the right-hand side in just over 1.5 miles (2.5 km). Park in the car park and contact the warden in the Information Centre for further details. Alternatively, approach from the A523 Ashbourne to Leek road. About 2.75 miles (4.4 km) from Leek turn southwards onto a minor road and follow this to the reserve, which is on the left in about a mile (1.6 km). Various bus services pass along the A523 from Leek.

The best points to explore the Churnet Valley are as follows.

Consall Nature Park Turn eastwards off the A522 onto a narrow lane, just south of Wetley Rocks. Follow this into Consall, turn left in the village

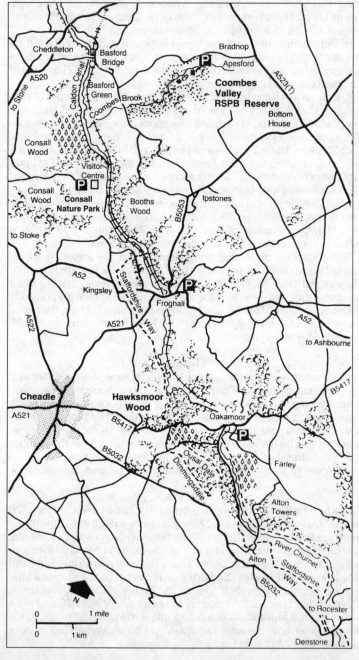

and continue to the end of the lane, where there is a car park, toilets and visitor centre (summer only), with facilities for the disabled. From here there are two waymarked trails around the park and signposted walks across the valley to the RSPB's Booths Wood opposite. Alternatively, follow the Staffordshire Way southwards to Froghall, where both woodland and waterside species can be seen along this scenic valley. The walk can be done in reverse, commencing at Froghall, on the A52 Stoke to Ashbourne road, where cars can be parked in the SCC picnic area. The Leek–Cheadle bus service passes through Froghall.

Alton to Oakamoor For car access take the narrow lane which runs along the south side of the river. Alton Village is reached from the B5032 Rocester to Cheadle road. (Do not follow the signs to Alton Towers.) Turn left just before the bridge in the village into the little lane that follows the river. In about 1 mile (1.6 km) park by the roadside and follow the Staffordshire Way into Dimmingsdale – a small valley to the left of the road. After 0.3 miles (0.5 km) one path follows Dimmingsdale to the left, while the Staffordshire Way continues straight ahead into Ousal Dale. Follow either path to a little lane, then return by the other route to complete a good circular walk.

Continue by car to Oakamoor and turn left onto the B5417 towards Cheadle. In a little over 1 mile (2 km) park on the right-hand side and explore the open hillsides and woods of the NT nature reserve at Hawksmoor Wood. (A guide book to the nature trails on the reserve is available in Oakamoor.) SCC has another picnic area on the B5417 at Oakamoor. From here there is a pleasant, easy walk of 2 miles (3.2 km) to Alton and 4.5 miles (7.2 km) to Denstone along the old railway line. There is a bus service from Uttoxeter to Alton.

Finally, the really energetic can follow the Staffordshire Way for nearly 20 miles (32 km) from Rudyard in the north to Rocester in the south.

Calendar

All Year: Grey Heron, Mallard, Eurasian Sparrowhawk, Common Kestrel, Moorhen, Northern Lapwing, Common Snipe (scarce), Woodcock, Tawny Owl, Long-eared Owl, Common Kingfisher, all three woodpeckers, Sky Lark, Grey Wagtail, Dipper, Wood Nuthatch, Eurasian Treecreeper, corvids, Common Redpoll and other common scrub and woodland birds.

April–September: Common Cuckoo, hirundines, Tree Pipit, Yellow Wagtail (scarce), Common Redstart; woodland and scrub warblers including Wood Warbler; Spotted and Pied Flycatchers; and Common Crossbill (July onwards, in irruption years).

October–March: Thrushes including Fieldfare and Redwing, flocks of finches and buntings including Brambling and Siskin. Perhaps Ring Ouzel (October) or passage raptor.

Stoke-on-Trent has undergone an urban renaissance, exemplified by the 1986 National Garden Festival. No longer a place of grimy collieries, belching chimneys and innumerable bottle kilns, it is now a greener, more pleasant city following a massive programme of derelict land reclamation. Stoke developed through the gradual coalescence of its 'five towns'. This left pockets of undeveloped land, to which subsidence and dereliction contributed further. Such areas soon became 'wastelands' of willowherb, nettle, thistle and rank grass, with marshy hollows of rush, sedge, reedmace and reed-grass where subsidence caused flooding.

Elsewhere, old spoil mounds, devoid of top soil and prone to gully erosion because of their steepness, were slowly recolonised by coarse grassland and scrub. All too often such areas became much abused wastes, serving as playgrounds, exercise areas for dogs and rubbish tips. The derelict land reclamation programme has managed and accelerated natural regeneration so as to create more useful and attractive open spaces.

In some respects industrial dereliction will be missed. Northern Wheatear, Yellow Wagtail, and Meadow and Tree Pipits, for example, are all recorded as having nested on the slag heaps of Etruria and Longton and perhaps some of these might still be found on one of the few remaining tips. Common Kestrels and occasionally owls still nest in derelict buildings and Meadow Pipits breed in fair numbers among the rank grasslands. Such areas also support a few pairs of Grey Partridge – now a scarce bird in its more familiar farmland habitat. In late summer and autumn, thistleheads and weed seeds draw parties of Goldfinches and other finches.

The marshy ground of subsidence areas provides a safe winter refuge for Mallard, Common Teal and even Common Snipe. Where subsidence has been severe enough to create standing water, Great Crested and Little Grebes and Mute Swan may breed and Common Kingfishers can be seen. In addition to the reclamation sites, there are one or two other interesting areas, such as Trentham Park which, despite intensive leisure and recreational use, still supports a thriving heronry with some 16 nests.

WESTPORT LAKE

Habitat
Opened in 1971, Westport Lake Park covers 100 acres (40 ha) and is administered by the City of Stoke-on-Trent. Its principal feature is a shallow 25-acre (10 ha) lake formed by the subsidence of marl workings. To the south is another, smaller pool backed by scrub, while to the east is formal grassland, with scattered trees. The northern shore is flanked by birch woodland and thorn scrub, with willows along the shoreline. Behind the western shore is a designated nature reserve, with a small stream, three small, reed-fringed pools and marshy areas of reed-grass and water horsetail overhung by willows and set within an area of alder woodland.

Species
Westport Lake is the best site in the Potteries for wintering wildfowl and gulls, and for passage terns and waders.

Numbers are not spectacular, but the variety is good. Great Crested Grebes, Mute Swans, Canada Geese, Mallard, Tufted Duck (sporadically) and Common Coot breed, though many have declined since terrapins arrived. Typically some 50 Mute Swans are present throughout the year, being joined in winter by 100–200 Tufted Duck, 30–40 Common Pochard, a dozen Great Crested Grebes, 20 Common Goldeneye, 200 Common Coot and an occasional Goosander. The lake is less favoured by dabbling duck, but up to 100 Mallard and a few Eurasian Wigeon, Gadwall and Northern Shoveler can usually be seen, while Northern Pintail and, less often, Common Teal and Ruddy Duck make irregular visits. One or two Great Cormorants and Common Shelduck are noted most years, the latter usually at passage times, while recent appearances of scarcer species such as Black-throated Diver, Red-necked Grebe, Whooper Swan, Brent Geese, Garganey and Common Scoter have repaid regular watching.

Most of the gulls from the Potteries roost on meres and lakes in Cheshire, so numbers at Westport are seldom large. Normal maxima are around 4,000 Black-headed Gulls, up to 1,000 Lesser Black-backed, 500 Herring, a few Common and one or two Great Black-backed. Despite these small numbers, one or two of the rarer Yellow-legged, Mediterranean, Iceland or Glaucous Gulls are seen most winters, though the latter is scarce in mild winters. Kittiwakes are almost annual visitors, often in spring. Even the rare Bonaparte's and Ring-billed Gulls have appeared.

Spring, and more especially autumn, bring a few passage waders and terns. Among the waders, Common Sandpiper, Little Ringed Plover and Dunlin are most regular, with other species occurring from time to time. Of these, Red Knot, Little Stint, Curlew Sandpiper, Whimbrel and Spotted Redshank are perhaps most noteworthy. Little Gulls pass through most years, usually in autumn, but terns have been very scarce in recent years. Nonetheless, there is a chance of Common, Arctic or even a Sandwich or Little Tern, either in spring or autumn. Black Terns are equally scarce, but more likely in autumn. Unexpected visitors have included Arctic Skua and Little Auk.

A passage of Meadow Pipits, perhaps enlivened by a White Wagtail, often heralds the onset of spring. Soon flocks of Common Swifts and hirundines congregate over the lake to feed and warblers, including a few Sedge and Reed Warblers, add their songs to the lengthening summer days. With luck, something like a Turtle Dove, or Pied Flycatcher might pass through. Among the breeding birds, Willow Tit and two or three pairs of Reed Bunting are noteworthy.

Return passage sees a good variety of summering chats and warblers moving through in August and September, followed by Barn Swallows and then Sky Larks, Meadow Pipits, Song Thrushes and Blackbirds. Late autumn might also bring a Rock or Water Pipit, or raptor such as Common Buzzard or Merlin. Finally, as winter sets in, the alders are visited by feeding flocks of Common Redpoll, Siskin and Goldfinches, while over 100 Magpies come to roost. Recent highlights have included Yellow-browed Warbler and Arctic Redpoll.

Timing

As a main venue for sailing, fishing, swimming and casual recreation, Westport is popular at all times and very crowded on summer weekends. Sailing is prohibited from November to March, so this enables duck numbers to build up. Early morning is likely to be the quietest time, but late afternoon can be good for gulls. Cold winters bring most birds.

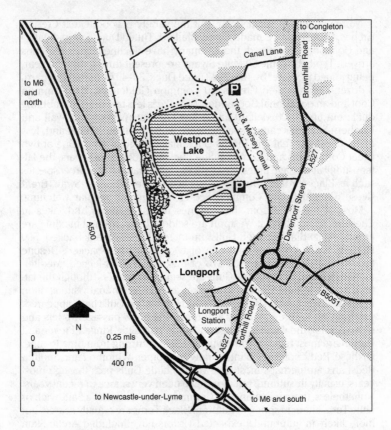

Access

Westport is just under 1 mile (1.5 km) west of Burslem town centre, off the A527 Newcastle to Congleton road. From the A500 Potteries spine road turn eastwards onto Porthill Road (A527), cross the railway and canal bridges and at the roundabout continue into Davenport Street. Take the first turn left onto a track which passes beneath a height control barrier, crosses back over the canal and leads into Westport Lake Park, where car parking overlooks the lake and there are toilet facilities. Follow the established paths to explore the park. There are facilities here for the disabled.

Alternatively, continue along the A527 for a further 0.3 miles (0.5 km) and turn left into Canal Lane. Follow the lane round to the left and there is a car park on the left at the end. Cross over the canal bridge and follow the paths around the lake. Several bus services pass along Davenport Street.

Calendar

All Year: Great Crested Grebe, Mute Swan, Canada Goose, Mallard, Common Coot and common passerines including Willow Tit and Reed Bunting.

April–June: Common Shelduck (scarce); Little Ringed Plover, Dunlin, Common Sandpiper and perhaps other scarcer waders; Kittiwake or occasional tern (scarce); Common Swift, White Wagtail (scarce), hirundines and warblers including Sedge and Reed Warbler. Possible scarcer passage migrant or rarity.

July–September: Little Ringed Plover, Dunlin, Common Sandpiper and perhaps other scarcer waders; maybe Little Gull or terns, including perhaps Black; Barn Swallow and passage chats and warblers.

October–March: Great Cormorant (scarce), Common Shelduck (scarce), Eurasian Wigeon, Gadwall, Common Teal (scarce), Northern Pintail (scarce), Northern Shoveler, Common Pochard, Tufted Duck, Common Goldeneye, Goosander (scarce) and Ruddy Duck (scarce); gulls including occasional rarity or Kittiwake (March); Sky Lark (October), Meadow Pipit (October and March), Rock or Water Pipit (rare), thrushes, Magpie (roost) and flocks of passerines including Goldfinch, Siskin and Common Redpoll. Perhaps a passage raptor, scarce wildfowl or vagrant seabird.

WHITFIELD VALLEY AND FORD GREEN MARSH

Habitat
Whitfield Valley lies northeast of Burslem and is Stoke-on-Trent's first designated Local Nature Reserve. It contains extensive areas of open ground that extend for 2 miles (3.2 km) from Ford Green to the former Chatterley-Whitfield Colliery, now a mining museum, with open countryside beyond. Within it is a mixture of dry, acidic grassland; damp, boggy grassland; old hawthorn hedges; willow, birch and hawthorn scrub; small pools with stands of emergent vegetation; and a stream with sandy banks. Near Chell Heath a larger pool, with a stand of reedmace, nestles beneath the reclaimed colliery spoil mound with its sparse covering of scrub.

The focal point is Ford Green Marsh, at the southern end. This is a small area of open water, large enough to hold a few wildfowl, and marshy ground with stands of reedmace and reed-grass that are relatively safe from disturbance. The marsh has been designated an SSSI – the first in Stoke-on-Trent – for its ornithological interest. Adjacent to it is an old pumping station, which the Whitfield Valley Wildlife Volunteers have converted into a nature centre with hide.

Species
Once an important roost for thousands of Barn Swallows, which have now virtually disappeared, this site is nevertheless still good for other species.

The emergent vegetation provides cover for several broods of Common Coot and one or two of Tufted Duck, Little and perhaps Great Crested Grebes. It also provides nest sites for a few pairs of Sedge and Reed Warblers, while Common Kingfishers are seen and may nest along the stream. On the grassy heaths, Sky Larks, Meadow Pipits and, more sparingly, Whinchats breed, and a Grasshopper Warbler 'reels' from rank vegetation. Grey Partridge are also present and Common Quail has been heard, while the scrub holds Reed Bunting and a few warblers. Common Swifts and House Martins feed on the multitude of insects, while small mammals attract feeding Common Kestrels or sometimes a Barn Owl in winter. Eurasian Sparrowhawks are regular visitors too.

Autumn might still see a small hirundine or wagtail roost, or a solitary Water Rail skulking amongst the reedmace. It also brings Common Snipe, which increase to 50–100 during winter, and one or two Jack Snipe. Winter wildfowl include a few Mallard and Common Teal, and sometimes one or two Gadwall, Northern Shoveler or Common Pochard. Away from the pools, Redwings and Fieldfares occur in small numbers.

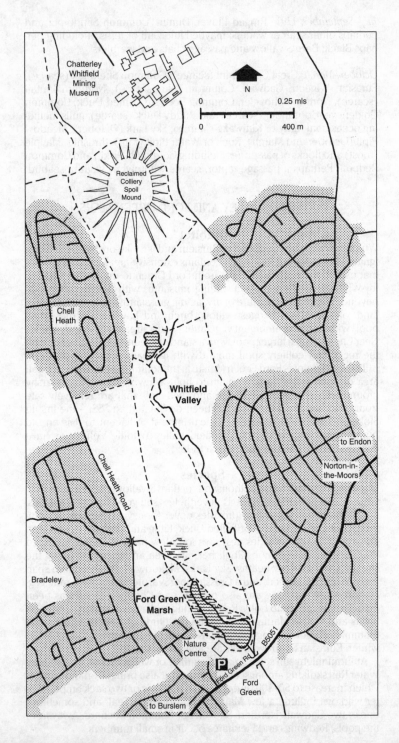

Spring sees a return passage of any of the wagtails, with a chance of a White amongst the Pied Wagtails.

Timing
The area is well used by local inhabitants at all times. Best times are early mornings, before there has been any disturbance, or dusk for owls and roosting birds.

Access
Ford Green lies 1.5 miles (2.4 km) northeast of Burslem town centre, immediately north of the B5051. Leave Burslem along Moorland Road (B5051) and at the double mini-roundabouts continue into Ford Green Road. Park in the car park adjacent to Ford Green Museum, which is on the left, near the bottom of the hill. The old pumping station is next to the car park and paths lead from here around the marsh and up both sides of the valley, making a good circular walk. The nature centre (open 11.00 am–4.00 pm daily except Fridays) has access for the disabled. Buses from Hanley and Newcastle pass along Ford Green Road.

Calendar
All Year: Little and Great Crested Grebes, Tufted Duck, Eurasian Sparrowhawk, Common Kestrel, Grey Partridge, Common Coot, Common Kingfisher and common passerines including Reed Bunting.

March–June: Common Swift (from May), hirundines, wagtails including perhaps White, Whinchat (rare); warblers including Grasshopper, Sedge and Reed; and common passerines.

August–September: Barn Swallows (few) and wagtails including Grey and perhaps Yellow.

October–March: Gadwall (scarce), Common Teal, Mallard, Northern Shoveler (scarce), Common Pochard (scarce), Water Rail (scarce), Jack Snipe (scarce), Common Snipe, Barn Owl (rare), Pied Wagtail, Redwing and Fieldfare.

PARK HALL COUNTRY PARK

Habitat
Between the housing estates of Bentilee and Weston Coyney, the hilly 333-acre (135 ha) Park Hall site is an ambitious reclamation scheme by Staffordshire County Council and the City of Stoke-on Trent to create a Country Park. The area was despoiled firstly by coal mining, then by sand and gravel extraction and finally by waste disposal. The result was a desolate and dangerous wasteland of pit shafts, sludge tips, settling lagoons and unfenced canyons, but is now a mosaic of heathland, woodland, secluded valleys and pools.

The park sits astride a sandstone ridge and parts still support the indigenous heathland flora, with small patches of heather, gorse and scrub. There is also an old pinewood. Extensive grasslands were sewn with wildflower seed and nearly 100,000 trees were planted. In the southwestern corner, the Lady's Corner Pools provide a home for a few wildfowl.

Species

In summer Sky Larks, Meadow Pipits and a few Grey Partridge breed on the grassy heath, with Linnets and Yellowhammers in the gorse and scrub. More sparingly, one or two pairs of Whinchat occur and a Grasshopper Warbler might be heard 'reeling'.

Spring and autumn bring passage Northern Wheatears and just occasionally a migrant such as Common Stonechat, Lesser Whitethroat or even Ring Ouzel.

The heath is good for raptors too, with Common Kestrel and Eurasian Sparrowhawk regularly seen throughout the year and records of Rough-legged Buzzard, Northern Goshawk, Hobby and Red Kite. Little Owls are often in the vicinity and Tawny Owls may sometimes breed. In winter 200–300 European Golden Plover frequent the fields at the top.

In the pinewoods the high-pitched calls of Goldcrests mingle with the trills from a few pairs of Common Redpoll, or in winter with the contact calls of foraging tits and finches. The pinewoods are also a traditional winter roost for up to five Long-eared Owls.

The reedy pools near Lady's Corner provide just sufficient cover for Little Grebe, Mallard and Tufted Duck to breed. More interestingly in winter they harbour a few Common Snipe and very occasionally a couple of Jack Snipe or Water Rail.

Park Hall is a traditional roosting site for Long-eared Owls

Overall this is a developing site with considerable potential. Not a great deal is known about its birdlife at present, but among the unexpected so far has been European Nightjar.

Timing
An early morning visit, when birds are singing and not too many people have arrived, is recommended in summer. Otherwise not really critical, though parts are very exposed so little may be seen in windy weather.

Access
The main entrance to the country park is north of the B5040. About 0.75 miles (1.2 km) west of the traffic lights in Weston Coyney turn right into Hulme Road and follow the signs to the Visitor Centre on the right-hand side, where there are toilets and plenty of parking. The whole park can be explored from here. For Lady's Corner pools and marsh use the car park on the right-hand side of Hulme Road before the Visitor Centre.

For the pinewood, follow the A520 Stone to Leek road for 0.5 miles (0.8 km) north of the traffic lights in Weston Coyney. Turn left at the end of the houses into the country park's car park.

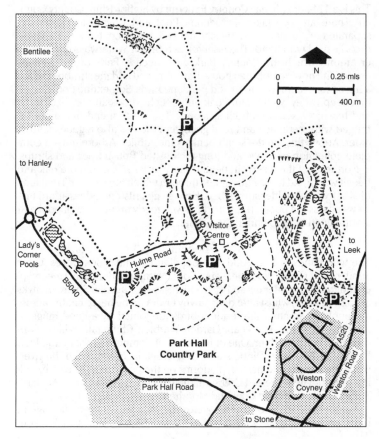

A network of footpaths provides circular walks from any of the car parks. The Visitor Centre is open Sunday afternoons in the summer. Buses from Hanley and Newcastle pass the entrances to the park.

Calendar

All Year: Little Grebe, Mallard, Tufted Duck, Eurasian Sparrowhawk, Common Kestrel, Grey Partridge, Little and Tawny Owls, Sky Lark, Meadow Pipit, Goldcrest, Linnet, Common Redpoll, Yellowhammer and other common passerines.

April–September: Whinchat (scarce), Northern Wheatear and Grasshopper Warbler (scarce). Perhaps Common Stonechat, Ring Ouzel, Lesser Whitethroat or a passage raptor.

October–March: Water Rail (rare), European Golden Plover, Jack Snipe (rare), Common Snipe, Long-eared Owl and foraging flocks of tits and finches. Perhaps a passing raptor.

GREENWAY BANK AND KNYPERSLEY

Habitat

This is a 114-acre (46 ha) Country Park run by Staffordshire County Council. There are two lakes, Serpentine Pool and Knypersley Reservoir, separated by a dam and mostly flanked by steep banks of mature broadleaved woodland. The reservoir is a British Waterways canal feeder around which the Country Park gives access. Parts of the gardens around the now demolished house have survived and the shrubberies are a haven for common garden and parkland birds. Serpentine Pool nestles in a deep valley, with mature oak and beech woods and areas of birch and hawthorn scrub on both its slopes. The western end of the pool is fringed with reedmace and reed-grass, and there is also a good stand of alder. Above this, on the south bank, is the Jubilee Arboretum – a complete collection of native and long-established British trees and shrubs.

Northeast of the reservoir, behind the Warder's Tower, more oak and beech woodland leads into a gorge through which the Head of Trent tumbles across its boulder-strewn bed. Here steep gritstone ridges afford fine views across the pools. There are also wet, reedy areas, a small pool and several dead trees to enrich the habitat.

Species

The woodlands hold a good bird population, with Stock Doves, Great Spotted and Green Woodpeckers, Wood Nuthatch, Eurasian Treecreeper and the commoner tits and crows all resident. Eurasian Sparrowhawks are also present, whilst after dark Tawny Owls can be heard calling across the pools. In summer the resident birds are joined by a good range of migrants including Blackcap, Garden Warbler, Chiffchaff, Willow Warbler and Wood Warbler. One or two pairs of Common Redstart and Pied Flycatcher also nest. Dippers and Grey Wagtails breed along the river, while the islands and nesting platforms on the pools provide safe breeding sites for Great Crested Grebes, Little Grebes, Canada Geese, Mallard, Tufted Duck, Common Coot and Moorhen.

Numbers of some of these species increase in winter as immigrant birds arrive, bringing with them small numbers of Eurasian Wigeon,

Common Teal and Common Pochard. Common Goldeneye are also occasionally present and other, more interesting species, such as Whooper Swan, occur from time to time. Among the passerines, flocks of tits and finches feeding on beech mast may include 50 or so Brambling.

Passage may also bring an occasional wader or tern, while a recent report of a European Serin raises speculation as to what regular watching might reveal.

Timing

To get the full benefit of birdsong in spring, visit as early in the morning as possible. Otherwise timing is not too critical, though fine afternoons can be busy and less will be seen when it is wet or windy.

Access

Leave the A527 Newcastle to Congleton road 1.75 miles (2.8 km) south of Biddulph (just north of Brindley Ford), turning eastwards onto minor roads and following the brown signs to Greenway Bank Country Park. There are two car parks on the left, one in the former kitchen garden at the top of the hill, where there are also toilets, and another at the foot, overlooking Knypersley Reservoir. Well marked paths lead from these around the pools and into woodlands. There are bus services from Hanley and Newcastle along the A527. Alight at Brindley Ford and follow

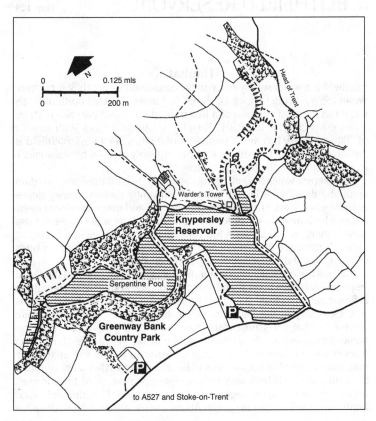

above directions. It is about 1 mile (1.6 km) to Greenway Bank. The park is open from 10.00 am–9.00 pm April to September and 10.00 am to dusk between October and March. Outside these hours the toilets and gates are locked, preventing cars from entering or leaving.

Calendar

All Year: Little and Great Crested Grebes, Canada Goose, Mallard, Tufted Duck, Eurasian Sparrowhawk, Common Coot, Moorhen, Stock Dove, Tawny Owl, Green and Great Spotted Woodpeckers, Grey Wagtail, Dipper, Wood Nuthatch, Eurasian Treecreeper and common garden, parkland and woodland birds.

April–September: Common Redstart, woodland warblers including Wood, Pied Flycatcher and perhaps passage wader or tern.

October–March: Eurasian Wigeon, Common Teal, Common Pochard, Common Goldeneye (occasional) and perhaps scarcer wildfowl. Finch flocks may include Brambling.

5 BLITHFIELD RESERVOIR
OS Landranger
Map 128

Habitat

Blithfield is a water-supply reservoir administered by South Staffordshire Water (SSW). Lying in open countryside 4 miles (6.4 km) north of Rugeley, it has the configuration of a letter Y and is divided into two parts by a causeway carrying the B5013 Rugeley to Uttoxeter road. With an area of 790 acres (320 ha) and a perimeter of 9 miles (14.4 km), Blithfield is the largest water in the region. It is also arguably the best ornithologically, and is certainly the best for waders.

The deepest water is south of the causeway, behind the dam. This dam apart, the shoreline is largely natural, with gently shelving, grassy slopes grazed by wildfowl. The shoreline is indented and many bays have rushy edges which provide cover for dabbling duck. Low water levels expose muddy margins that attract a few migrant waders. Sailing and fly-fishing cause disturbance on this deeper, southern section. Nevertheless birds still make good use of it, especially Eurasian Wigeon.

North of the causeway the water divides into the two arms of the Y, fed respectively by the River Blithe (west) and Tad Brook (east). Here there is fly-fishing, both from bank and boat, but no sailing, so disturbance is less, especially in the Tad arm, which has been set aside as a nature reserve. The habitat is more varied too, so it usually holds more birds. The banks shelve very gently, so even a moderate fall in water level uncovers a good area of mud and a recently constructed scrape will enable the optimum depth of water for birds to be maintained. After a dry summer, the mud exposed in both arms can be quite extensive, providing the most important habitat in the region for autumn waders. Unfortunately such conditions rarely occur in spring. Above the expanses of mud, the arms are flanked by marshy areas of rush and reed-grass. The Blithe is also lined by alders. Dense willow scrub encroaches onto the mudflats. Whilst this provides cover and nest sites for Great Crested Grebes, it threatens to engulf the wader habitat and is therefore controlled.

Stansley Wood, on the point between the two arms, is a remnant of mature deciduous woodland. Despite much felling and replanting with conifers, it still holds a good mix of typical woodland birds. On the eastern shore of Tad Bay, the plantations of spruce and larch are ornithologically less interesting.

Species

There is usually something interesting to be seen throughout the year. Apart from waders, Blithfield is nationally important for its number and variety of wintering wildfowl.

All the commoner species occur in good numbers at some time of the year. Canada Geese, Mallard, Tufted Duck, Common Coot and occasionally Gadwall breed, but attempts by Little and Great Crested Grebes often fail. Birds from a wide area form post-breeding flocks in late summer which may reach 100 Mute Swans, 250 Tufted Duck and 150 Great Crested Grebe. Common Shelduck also pass through at this time, with others in late autumn and again in spring. August to October is consistently good for Northern Pintail and Garganey, with the former frequently reaching double figures at this time then peaking again in winter. September and October are best for Northern Shoveler, with 250 or more present. Other species begin to arrive at this time too, and from then until February over 2,000 wildfowl are usually present, with almost 3,000 in November and December. This is when many species peak, with 500–1,000 Canada Geese, 1,000+ Common Teal and around 1,000 Mallard. A few Gadwall also winter. Blithfield is especially important for Eurasian Wigeon, with January and February counts of this Russian visitor frequently exceeding 700 and even topping 1,000.

Wintering diving duck are more puzzling. Common Pochard flocks barely total 100, though they may reach 200 on occasions, and there are even fewer Tufted Duck. Common Coot are also scarce, with no more than 100 or so. These meagre counts contrast sharply with those for some other diving birds. By January up to 50 Common Goldeneye have normally assembled and they may be joined by others in March or April, when the drakes are displaying. Goosander also reach their peak after the New Year, with gatherings up to 100 in late winter, when rafts of Ruddy Duck assemble and one or two Smew normally appear. Numbers of Great Crested Grebes and Great Cormorants are variable, with many of the latter quickly dispersing after their early morning fishing expeditions.

Among the scarcer wildfowl, Tundra Swans and a few sea-duck pass through every year. Indeed, a few Tundra Swans, on occasions as many as 30, may drop in at any time between late autumn and March. Though much rarer, Whooper Swans also visit. The most regular sea-duck is Common Scoter, with small parties pausing briefly in spring, late summer and autumn during their overland migrations, though a few Greater Scaup are also seen most winters. Other sea-duck, divers and the rarer grebes are more erratic visitors, whose arrival often coincides with storms in the North Sea or extreme cold in the Baltic. Small parties of geese also visit. Usually these are suspected of being feral birds, but occasional skeins of overflying Pink-footed Geese in midwinter almost certainly come from the Lancashire mosses, while parties of White-fronted Geese, particularly between December and March, may also be wild. Autumn often produces intriguing parties of other geese, such as around a dozen Barnacle Geese or smaller flocks of Brent or Bean Geese.

Winter is also the time for gulls. Blithfield has a large gull roost that regularly holds one or two rarities. Black-headed Gulls predominate with 20,000–25,000, but Lesser Black-backed Gulls may approach 2,000, Herring Gulls 1,000 and Common Gulls 100, with slightly more Great Black-backed Gulls. It is always worth searching through the flocks for Mediterranean and Yellow-legged Gulls, one or two of which are now regular. From December onwards Glaucous and Iceland Gulls may also appear. Most records are of single birds, but two or three may be seen together, especially Iceland Gulls. Winter also brings mixed finch and bunting flocks, with maybe several Tree Sparrows and a few Brambling or Twite, while the alders are often visited by Siskin and Common Redpoll.

Spring passage begins in March, when winter visitors such as Redwing and Fieldfare depart for northern climes and Meadow Pipits return. The end of the month often sees the first Sand Martins and Northern Wheatears arrive, although most summer visitors do not show until April. Then many Pied and a few White Wagtails pass through, followed in May by an occasional Garganey and parties of up to 40 Yellow Wagtails, a pair of which may breed. With the latter might be a Blue-headed Wagtail. There is also a heavy passage of Common Swifts, a steady stream of other common migrants and a good chance of a passing raptor such as Osprey, Hobby or Marsh Harrier.

Waders in spring are few, but very varied. Commonest are Oystercatcher, Great Ringed Plover, Dunlin, Eurasian Curlew, Common Redshank and Common Sandpiper, though even these seldom reach double figures. Two or three Sanderlings, Common Greenshanks and Turnstones appear in most springs and some years a pair or two of Little Ringed Plovers attempt to breed. Less often Grey Plover, Red Knot, Little Stint, Ruff, Black-tailed or Bar-tailed Godwit, Whimbrel or Wood Sandpiper pass through. Although the first waders may come in February or March, late April and early May is when most pass through. Kittiwakes are sometimes seen in March, while Little Gulls and terns regularly move through in late April and May. Arctic is the first tern to arrive, followed by Common. Neither is especially numerous, but if over-flying Arctic Terns are brought down by adverse weather, then dozens might occur, perhaps accompanied by an Arctic Skua. Black Terns also make erratic appearances, as do solitary Sandwich and Little Terns in April and June respectively.

Common Kingfishers nest nearby and in the surrounding areas Eurasian Sparrowhawk, Little Owl, Tawny Owl, all three woodpeckers, Marsh Tit and a good range of woodland songsters breed, including both Common Redstart and Pied Flycatcher.

From July onwards waders become the prime interest. Although numbers are insignificant nationally, they are excellent for an inland location and outstanding for the West Midlands. July and August normally bring good numbers of Little Ringed Plovers, half-a-dozen Common Redshank, 20 Common Sandpipers and the first Green Sandpipers and Eurasian Curlew. They are followed by some 30 Great Ringed Plover and Dunlin. A few Oystercatchers, Red Knot, Black-tailed Godwits, Whimbrel and Spotted Redshank usually pass through about this time too, along with slightly more Common Greenshank. Blithfield is very good for Ruff, with around a dozen present at some time between July and September. It is also the most reliable place in the region for Little Stint and Curlew Sandpiper. Most years bring just two or three of each, but occasionally a dozen

Blithfield is outstanding for passage waders such as Curlew Sandpiper (foreground), Dunlin and Ruff (background)

or more appear. Among other visitors might be a Sanderling, Wood Sandpiper, Turnstone or rarely a Temminck's Stint.

From August onwards there is a good chance of Grey Plover or a few Bar-tailed Godwits. By September, Common Snipe are congregating, to be joined in October perhaps by a few Jack Snipe or a Water Rail. Several hundred Northern Lapwing may also have gathered and Dunlin, too, can be numerous in late autumn, with sometimes 100 in a tight, wheeling flock. If the weather stays mild a few might remain through the winter, accompanied perhaps by a Ruff or Common Redshank.

August and September bring flocks of departing hirundines and wagtails, plus steady movements of warblers and chats. Little Gulls and terns return in small numbers, with again the chance of a party of Black Terns or a single Sandwich or Little Tern. Little Egret, Eurasian Spoonbill and White-winged Black Tern have been seen at this time too. Shortly afterwards the first autumn gales are awaited with high hopes. Seldom do they disappoint. A few Kittiwakes or other seabirds are quite likely. Shags and Arctic Skuas are commonest, while the highlights of recent years have included Long-tailed Skua and Sabine's Gull. From October onwards Sky Larks and Meadow Pipits pass through, winter thrushes return, and a few Rock Pipits feed around the water's edge, while from November a late Common Stonechat or even a Snow Bunting is possible.

With so much potential prey, one or two Peregrine Falcons are now regularly present outside the breeding season, Merlins are noted on rare occasions in autumn, and July and August usually bring a Hobby or Osprey. Above all, star birds in recent years have included Black-winged Stilt, two Pectoral Sandpipers, two Bonaparte's Gulls, White-throated Needletail Swift, Horned Lark and Arctic Warbler.

Timing

Early morning is best, as some species tend to move away as human disturbance increases. The causeway gets very busy on fine afternoons, but access to the rest of the reservoir is restricted, so disturbance should be minimal, although trespass is increasing. Sailing is confined to south of the causeway and October to March is the close season for fishing.

In spring, southerly winds and overcast conditions may bring passerines, or deep depressions waders and Arctic Terns. Black Terns and Little Gulls tend to arrive on light easterly winds in settled weather, as do autumn passage migrants. Vagrant seabirds are most likely after autumn gales, while wildfowl numbers increase in cold weather, when divers or the rarer grebes sometimes appear.

Access
The reservoir is crossed on a causeway by the B5013 Rugeley to Uttoxeter road. There is limited parking at either end of this causeway which is ideal for a quick visit, as many wildfowl and gulls can be seen from here. Parts of the reservoir can also be viewed from a minor road off the B5013 that skirts the eastern shore for a short distance. Entry to the confines of the reservoir is strictly by permit only, obtainable from the West Midland Bird Club. This allows access right round the reservoir, giving serious bird-watchers much better views and use of the hides provided by SSW, who have also provided an excellent education centre for schools. There is a limited bus service from Uttoxeter to Abbots Bromley. Alight at the B5013 junction about 0.75 miles (1.2 km) outside Abbots Bromley, from where it is a 1-mile (1.6 km) walk to the causeway.

Calendar
All Year: Little Grebe, Great Crested Grebe, Great Cormorant (scarce in spring), Grey Heron, Mute Swan, Canada Goose, Gadwall, Mallard, Tufted Duck, Eurasian Sparrowhawk, Common Kestrel, Common Coot, Northern Lapwing, Little Owl, Tawny Owl, Common Kingfisher, all three woodpeckers and common woodland passerines.

April–June: Common Shelduck, Garganey (scarce), Common Scoter (scarce), Hobby, Oystercatcher, Little Ringed Plover, Great Ringed Plover, Sanderling, Dunlin, Eurasian Curlew, Common Redshank, Common Greenshank, Common Sandpiper and Turnstone; maybe scarcer wader such as Grey Plover, Red Knot, Little Stint, Ruff, Black- or Bar-tailed Godwits, Whimbrel or Wood Sandpiper; Little Gull (scarce); terns including a few Black and perhaps Sandwich or Little; Common Swift (from May), hirundines, wagtails including White (scarce) and Blue-headed (rare), Common Redstart, Northern Wheatear, Pied Flycatcher and common woodland warblers. Possible passage raptor or rarity.

July–September: Common Shelduck, Eurasian Wigeon, Common Teal, Northern Pintail, Garganey, Northern Shoveler, Common Pochard, Common Scoter (scarce), Ruddy Duck, Osprey (scarce), Hobby, Peregrine Falcon, Oystercatcher, Little Ringed Plover, Great Ringed Plover, Grey Plover, Red Knot, Sanderling (scarce), Little Stint, Curlew Sandpiper, Dunlin, Ruff, Common Snipe, Black- and Bar-tailed Godwits, Whimbrel, Eurasian Curlew, Spotted Redshank, Common Redshank, Common Greenshank, Green Sandpiper, Wood Sandpiper (scarce), Common Sandpiper, Turnstone (scarce), Little Gull (scarce) and terns including a few Black and perhaps Sandwich or Little. Hirundines, wagtails, chats, warblers and other common passage migrants. Possible passage raptor or rarity.

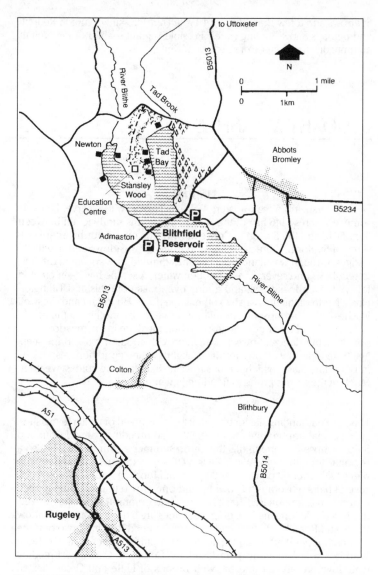

October–March: Tundra Swan (scarce), Whooper Swan (rare), grey geese (rare), Common Shelduck (late autumn), Eurasian Wigeon, Common Teal, Northern Pintail, Northern Shoveler, Common Pochard, Greater Scaup (scarce), Common Scoter (scarce), Common Goldeneye, Smew (scarce), Goosander, Ruddy Duck, Merlin (rare), Peregrine Falcon, Water Rail (scarce), European Golden Plover, Grey Plover (autumn), Dunlin (autumn), Jack Snipe (scarce), Common Snipe, Eurasian Curlew (autumn); perhaps wintering Ruff, Common Redshank or Green Sandpiper; gulls including one or two Mediterranean, Yellow-legged and from December Iceland and Glaucous; Kittiwake (autumn and March; scarce), Sky Lark (autumn), Meadow Pipit (October and March), Rock Pipit (October), Grey Wagtail, Common Stonechat, winter thrushes; mixed finch and bunting flocks including Tree

Sparrows and a few Brambling and Twite (rare); Siskin, Common Redpoll and perhaps Snow Bunting (rare). Possible vagrant seabird or rare gull in autumn; diver, rare grebe or sea-duck in winter.

6 DOXEY MARSHES

OS Landranger
Map 127

Habitat

Doxey Marshes is a Staffordshire Wildlife Trust (SWT) reserve. It covers some 360 acres (146 ha) of the Sow Valley and is sandwiched between the A5013 and the Euston to Crewe railway line on the northwestern out-skirts of Stafford. There is a transition from dry meadows and hawthorn hedges, through washlands and marshes drained by a system of ditches, to reedbeds and several areas of open water. A scrape has been created for waders and wildfowl, and a hide overlooks both this and Tillington Flash. North of the river are two other large pools, Boundary and Creswell Flashes, while an observation platform overlooks another to the south.

The purity of the water and the rich botanical life in the meadows sup-ports an abundance of insects, which provide food for birds. Brine seep-age from old salt workings results in slightly saline conditions, especially in Boundary Flash, which inhibits freezing in all but the coldest weather. Much of the area is prone to flooding in winter.

Species

This is an outstanding site for birds that typically breed or winter in marshes.

Of special importance are the eight or so breeding pairs of Common Snipe, whose drumming fills the air on summer evenings. This is also a regional stronghold for Water Rails, with some 15 pairs, and Sedge War-blers, with over 60 pairs. Over 20 pairs of Moorhen and Common Coot, several pairs of Northern Lapwing, and one or two pairs of Little Ringed Plover and Common Redshank breed, while Common Kingfisher are reg-ularly seen. Among the breeding passerines are a dozen pairs of Meadow Pipits and Reed Warblers, nearly 60 pairs of Reed Buntings, two or three of Grasshopper Warbler and up to ten of Common Whitethroat. The Reed Warblers are frequently parasitised by Common Cuckoos. Breeding waterfowl are also of interest, with broods of Little and Great Crested Grebes, Mute Swan, Canada Geese, Common Teal, Gadwall, Mallard, Northern Shoveler and Tufted and Ruddy Ducks to be seen.

Small numbers of Green and Common Sandpipers pass through in July and August, as does the occasional Great Ringed Plover, Black-tailed Godwit, Common Greenshank or Wood Sandpiper. One or two of these may hang around into autumn. Exceptionally a Spotted Crake might be glimpsed in late summer. August and September see Common Swifts and hirundines departing, Goldfinches flocking and summer migrants, such as Northern Wheatears and Whinchats, resting or feeding on their way south. Late in the evening a few hirundines and Yellow Wagtails come to roost, perhaps pursued by a swooping Hobby. Soon these species will have left, to be replaced in winter by up to 500 roosting Pied Wagtails.

October brings an influx of Common Snipe from the Continent and by late autumn around 500 probe the mud for food. With them come about a dozen Jack Snipe: they are generally more skulking, but sometimes venture out at dusk. Between 30–40 Water Rails are around at this time as well. Many Common Snipe, Jack Snipe and Water Rails use the marsh only to feed and rest before passing onwards, but some will remain through a mild winter, when floods sometimes force them into the open to feed. Indeed, Jack Snipe counts are often highest in February, although more birds are almost certainly present, but concealed, at passage times. A few Dunlin or a solitary Green Sandpiper might also overwinter and 1,000 or so Northern Lapwings feed across the marsh, sometimes in company with European Golden Plover.

*In autumn Doxey attracts good numbers of Common Snipe
and a few Jack Snipe (foreground)*

Autumn also sees wildfowl beginning to arrive. Common Teal and Mallard are most numerous, each peaking at around 250 during the winter. Up to 25 Northern Shoveler are often present too, along with smaller numbers of Mute Swan and Eurasian Wigeon, but Gadwall and Northern Pintail are only occasional visitors. A flock of some 300 Canada Geese also makes periodic visits, joined sometimes by feral geese. However, the larger skeins seen on occasions may have involved wild birds. A few Common Shelduck are noted on passage in spring and, less often, in autumn. Garganey has been recorded at these times too. Diving wildfowl are fewer in number, with perhaps 40–50 each of Tufted Duck, Common Pochard and Common Coot. Common Goldeneye are very rarely seen, but Goosander is now an established visitor, with a few mostly between December and March. Flood-water might encourage a small herd of Tundra Swans to join the resident Mute Swans for a while.

A few Common Stonechats and Grey Wagtails arrive in autumn and one or two often stay for the winter. From October onwards, parties of Redwing and Fieldfare are very evident in the meadows and hedgerows. Even a Short-eared Owl or Hen Harrier might stay for a few days. Common Kestrels regularly hover over the marsh, while Eurasian Sparrowhawks and the occasional Merlin create periodic panics among wintering flocks of Meadow Pipits, Linnets, Chaffinches and maybe Brambling. Small parties of Siskin and Common Redpoll feed in the alders.

By April, summer visitors return and one or two waders such as Great Ringed Plover, Common Greenshank or even a Grey Plover or Turnstone pause briefly on their way north. A few Northern Wheatears and Whinchats move through too, Common Swifts and hirundines swoop across the pools and there is always a chance of Common or Black Terns, though both are very scarce.

Vagrant divers, grebes and sea-duck have occurred, but rarities more appropriate to the site have included White Stork, Eurasian Spoonbill and both Marsh and River Warblers.

Timing
Not particularly critical, but early morning or just before dusk are usually less disturbed and birds are more active.

Access
Leave the M6 at Junction 14 and turn south southwards along Eccleshall Road (A5013) towards the town centre. Take the first right into Creswell Farm Drive and follow this round to the right to a car park at the end. From here a footpath runs behind the houses and into the reserve. There are bus services from Stafford along Eccleshall Road to the end of Creswell Farm Drive, from where it is only a short walk into the reserve.

Alternatively, follow the Stafford ring road clockwise, pass the railway station and at the next roundabout, bear left into Doxey Road, cross the river and turn right at the mini-roundabout into the pay-and-display car park opposite Sainsbury's. From here take the footpath along the south side of the River Sow, cross over the old railway bridge to the north side, and follow the waymarked posts to the hide and pools. There are Inter-City trains to Stafford station, from where it is only a short walk to Doxey Road and the footpath along the riverbank to the reserve.

Calendar
All Year: Little Grebe, Great Crested Grebe, Mute Swan, Canada Goose, Common Teal, Gadwall, Mallard, Northern Shoveler, Tufted Duck, Ruddy Duck, Eurasian Sparrowhawk, Common Kestrel, Water Rail, Moorhen, Common Coot, Northern Lapwing, Common Snipe, Common Kingfisher, Meadow Pipit, Reed Bunting and common passerines.

April–June: Common Shelduck (scarce), Garganey (rare), Hobby, Little Ringed Plover, Common Redshank; maybe common passage waders such as Great Ringed Plover, Common Sandpiper or scarcer species such as Grey Plover, Common Greenshank or Turnstone; perhaps passage tern; Common Cuckoo, Common Swift (After April); Grasshopper, Sedge and Reed Warblers; Common Whitethroat and regular passage migrants such as Northern Wheatear and Whinchat.

July–September: Garganey (rare), Hobby; common waders such as Little Ringed Plover, Common Redshank, Green and Common Sandpipers, or scarcer species such as Great Ringed Plover, Common Greenshank, or Wood Sandpiper; hirundines, Yellow Wagtail (scarce) and other regular passage migrants such as Northern Wheatear and Whinchat. Exceptionally Spotted Crake.

October–March: Tundra Swan (rare), Common Shelduck (scarce), Eurasian Wigeon, Northern Pintail (rare), Common Pochard, Common Goldeneye (rare), Goosander, Hen Harrier (rare), Merlin (scarce), Water Rail, Jack Snipe, European Golden Plover, Dunlin (scarce), Green Sandpiper

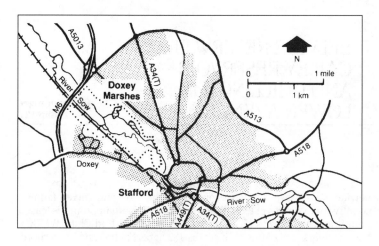

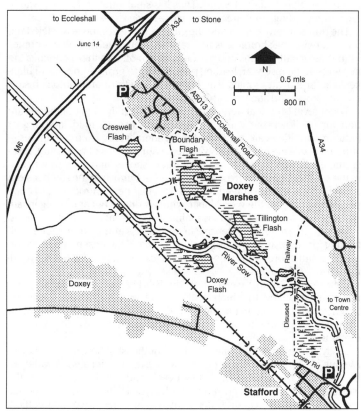

(scarce), Short-eared Owl (rare), Grey and Pied Wagtails, Common Stonechat, Fieldfare, Redwing and flocks of finches, including Brambling (scarce), Siskin and Common Redpoll.

7 BELVIDE RESERVOIR, GAILEY RESERVOIR AND CHILLINGTON LOWER AVENUE

OS Landranger Map 127

Habitat

Belvide is a canal-feeder reservoir situated in low-lying, mixed farming country some 7 miles (11.2 km) northwest of Wolverhampton. It is leased from British Waterways (BW) by the West Midland Bird Club (WMBC). Immediately south of the A5, it covers 182 acres (74 ha) and has a shore-line of less than 3 miles (4.8 km). Thus it is small enough for easy watching and recording, and offers good, close-range views.

The northeasterly corner and the eastern shore comprise a brick dam, but otherwise the shoreline is natural and gently shelving. Water comes from three small streams and agricultural run-off into these enriches the nutrients in the reservoir, leading periodically to profuse growths of blanketweed and algal blooms. The luxuriant growth of amphibious bistort provides food and shelter for birds.

Water level is critical here. When it is consistently high conditions are best for wildfowl, but when it fluctuates to expose mud in spring or autumn conditions are better for birds generally. For such a small reservoir, the shoreline is remarkably varied, with patches of oozy mud, rushes and grasses on the western and northern shores, and great water-grass in the southern bays. There is a large stand of bulrush in the southeastern corner, where common reed has also recently been introduced to compensate, in part, for the West Marsh, which is drying out and being invaded by scrub. A feeding station is maintained in front of one of the hides.

Behind the shoreline extensive areas of grass and rush provide rough grazing for cattle and cover for nesting birds and the Reservoir Plantation on the south shore holds woodland species. Other small areas of woodland also border the site.

Four miles (6.4 km) east of Belvide, BW has two more canal-feeder reservoirs at Gailey, to which WMBC members have access. These are much smaller and generally less productive than Belvide, their main attraction being the heronry on the island and the roost of Great Cormorants.

Lastly, a little under 1.5 miles (2.4 km) southeast of Belvide is the Lower Avenue at Chillington. It comprises a wide avenue with a good variety of broadleaved trees, including a few beech and hornbeam towards the western end, and a rich and varied shrub layer. Halfway along is a bridge over the Shropshire Union Canal, which is in a deep, wooded cutting.

Species

Belvide's prime interest is as a breeding, moulting and wintering site for wildfowl. Indeed, it has held as many as 5,000 birds in winter, giving a higher density than anywhere else in the region. Add to this a winter gull roost, passage waders and terns, and the promise of a rarity, and there is clearly plenty of interest at all times.

Breeding waterfowl include Gadwall in increasing numbers, Little and Great Crested Grebes, Canada Geese, Mallard, Northern Shoveler, Tufted Duck, Ruddy Duck and Common Coot, though their success depends on suitable water levels. Several pairs of Northern Lapwing and one or two pairs of Little Ringed Plover and Common Redshank also breed, while a pair of Common Terns may nest on the tern raft.

Eurasian Curlew, nesting on nearby farmland, are regularly seen or heard. The new reedbed and the West Marsh together hold about a dozen pairs of Reed Warbler, while Sedge Warblers and Reed Buntings are slightly more plentiful. The reservoir surrounds hold several pairs of Common and Lesser Whitethroats, Blackcap, and Willow Warbler, plus small numbers of Garden Warbler, Chiffchaff and Spotted Flycatcher, and usually a pair of Yellow Wagtails and Grasshopper Warblers. Great and Lesser Spotted Woodpeckers, Wood Nuthatch and, sometimes, Pied Flycatcher occur in Reservoir Plantation. As many as half-a-dozen Common Buzzards can be seen at times throughout the year, Peregrine Falcons are regular outside the breeding season, Hobbies are frequent from spring to autumn and Merlin is increasing as a passage or wintering bird.

Despite its small size and disturbance from anglers, Belvide still holds flocks of moulting wildfowl, though recent low water levels have greatly reduced numbers. In late summer up to 500 Mallard, 1,000 Common Coot and 50 Mute Swans may be present, but similar influxes of drake Common Pochard and Tufted Duck have not materialised lately. Several thousand Common Swifts and hirundines can descend on the reservoir to feed during the summer, especially in poor weather.

Return wader passage begins in late June, peaks in August and then slowly subsides, petering out in November. Often first to show are Green Sandpiper and Little Ringed Plover, with up to 20 of the latter as migrants join local birds. Small numbers of Ruff, Dunlin, Common Greenshank and Common Sandpiper are usually present in August and September too, while any combination of Oystercatcher, Red Knot, Sanderling, Black- and Bar-tailed Godwits, Whimbrel, Spotted Redshank, Wood Sandpiper and Turnstone might appear. Little Stints and Curlew Sandpipers, sometimes in small flocks, are seen most years, often juveniles in September. Finally, Grey Plover and a few more Dunlin pass through between September and November.

Autumn also holds promise of a small passage of Arctic, Common and Black Terns, plus perhaps a Little or Sandwich Tern. Black Terns can be numerous in suitable weather conditions. Usually one or two Little Gulls come as well. Departing summer visitors frequently include Northern Wheatears, Whinchat (especially at the western end) and perhaps something like a Common Redstart, while later on a few Common Stonechats or a Rock Pipit might be seen. Finally, flocks of Redwings and Fieldfares arrive for the winter. Autumn raptors could include Marsh Harrier or Osprey; and other, rarer sightings have included Eurasian Spoonbill, Little Egret, Pectoral Sandpiper, Grey Phalarope, White-winged Black Tern and Wryneck.

From September onwards wildfowl steadily increase. Typical winter maxima are 100 Northern Shoveler, 600 Mallard, 500 or more Common

Teal and 200 Eurasian Wigeon. Good numbers of Gadwall are now regular and small numbers of Common Shelduck are sometimes seen, mostly in spring and autumn.

Ruddy Duck used to be Belvide's speciality, but the large autumn flocks of earlier years have now dwindled to fewer than 50. Great Cormorants reach a similar number in late autumn, but Common Goldeneye do not reach their peak of 50–70 until March. The winter peaks for Common Pochard and Tufted Duck are around 200 and 100 respectively, though the latter reach 300 on occasions. Of the three sawbills, Smew and Red-breasted Merganser occur only occasionally in ones and twos, whereas Goosander have topped 100 several times and recently set a new regional record of 190. Other wintering waterfowl include some 200–300 Common Coot, and a few Little and Great Crested Grebes, with the latter peaking at 50 between November and January. Such large numbers of waterfowl inevitably bring some scarce species. Northern Pintail are now annual visitors in winter, as are Garganey in spring and autumn; while Black-necked Grebe, Tundra Swans, Barnacle Geese and Common Scoter are noted most years, along with a diver, rarer grebe or other sea-duck.

Goosander (foreground) and Common Goldeneye are among the wildfowl that winter at Belvide

Winter also brings a reasonable gull roost, with up to 6,000 Black-headed, 400 Lesser Black-backed and 50 Herring Gulls. Common and Great Black-backed Gulls also occur in fluctuating numbers. Amongst them may be a rarer gull, such as Yellow-legged and Mediterranean Gulls in autumn, or Iceland and Glaucous Gulls in mid-winter, while a few Kittiwakes could pass through at any time between October and April. In addition to the wildfowl and gulls, flocks of Northern Lapwing and 100 or more European Golden Plover frequent the surrounding area, while up to 100 Common

Snipe, half-a-dozen Jack Snipe and Water Rail stay hidden in the marginal vegetation. Good flocks of larks, pipits, finches and buntings feed on open ground. Meadow Pipits and Linnets are often most numerous and with them may be the occasional Twite or Water Pipit. In hard weather especially, many small birds can be watched at the feeding station, while dusk may see over 100 Reed Buntings roosting in one of the reedbeds.

By March wildfowl are departing, though one or two Eurasian Wigeon and Common Goldeneye can stay well into May or even later, and the return of Common Redshanks and Little Ringed Plovers heralds the onset of spring. Flocks of Meadow Pipits frequently follow and the first Northern Wheatears often appear along the dam. With them may be a Rock Pipit, or Common Stonechat. Early April brings hirundines and wagtails, including good numbers of Sand Martins, Pied and Yellow Wagtails. With them usually come one or two White Wagtails and maybe a Blue-headed. A few Bramblings are also regular in the Reservoir Plantation at this time. There is normally some mud in spring, so wader passage is better than at many reservoirs. Occasional birds are seen even in winter, but the main passage is in April and May. Generally it brings Great and Little Ringed Plovers, Sanderling, Dunlin, Ruff, Black-tailed Godwit, Whimbrel, Common Greenshank, Common Sandpiper, and less often Grey Plover, Red Knot, Bar-tailed Godwit, Spotted Redshank or Turnstone. Variety in spring is usually less than in autumn and visits more fleeting, but there is still the chance of a semi-rarity such as Avocet, Temminck's Stint or Curlew Sandpiper.

Little Gulls and terns pass through in spring as well. Numbers are generally small, but deep depressions in late April or early May might bring several Arctic Terns. Common and Black Terns usually come later, but the latter are very unpredictable, while Sandwich and Little Terns are scarce. Spring is also good for predators, with Marsh Harrier or Osprey in most years, while Short-eared Owl has also occurred. Amongst recent spring and summer rarities have been Little Egret, American Wigeon, Common Crane, Icterine Warbler, Firecrest and Little Bunting.

Gailey holds similar birds to Belvide, with regular movement between the two occasioned by disturbance. However, numbers are less and it is more attractive to diving species than surface-feeders, with a good share of unusual birds such as divers, rarer grebes and sea-duck. The main interest, though, is the excellent views of the heronry, with up to 50 nests on the island despite recent tree-felling. During winter up to 50 Great Cormorants come in to roost.

Chillington Lower Avenue used to be good for Hawfinches, but recently sightings have been very scarce. Nonetheless a glimpse of this elusive bird foraging beneath its favourite hornbeams and beeches might just be had at first light on a winter's morning. Lower Avenue is also good for resident woodland species like Great and Lesser Spotted Woodpecker, Wood Nuthatch, Eurasian Treecreeper and tits. Summer brings warblers, Turtle Dove and Common Cuckoo, while winter sees flocks of Fieldfare, Redwing and finches arrive, with maybe a few Brambling.

Timing

Belvide is little disturbed, except by anglers in late winter particularly. Water level and weather are more important. The former depends on BW activities, but in spring it is usually lower than most water-supply reservoirs, making this a good place for waders. In spring, southerly winds with overcast conditions bring passerines, but deep depressions can be good for waders and terns. In autumn, westerly gales or light easterly winds are most productive. Because it is small, shallow and sheltered from the wind, the reservoir virtually freezes over in very cold weather and few birds remain.

Gailey is best visited at the height of the Grey Heron's breeding season from March to June. Great Cormorants come to roost at dusk on winter evenings, but are not always present. Sailing and fishing create some disturbance.

Lower Avenue can get quite busy, so an early morning or weekday visit is recommended.

Access

Access to Belvide and Gailey is strictly by permit only, available from the WMBC.

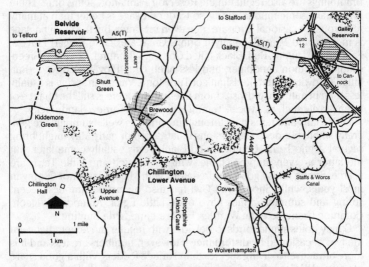

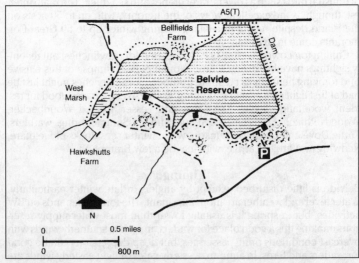

Gailey Leave M6 at Junction 12, take the A5 eastwards and then the first left turn into a narrow lane. Continue round the left-hand bend and park on the verge, making sure there is room for agricultural machinery to pass. Access is by the fishing club, but do not use their car park.

Belvide Leave the M6 at Junction 12 and take the A5 westwards. Stay on the A5 at the Gailey Roundabout (junction with A449), then take the third turning left into Horsebrook Lane, leading towards Brewood. Continue down this lane for 0.6 miles (1 km) and then turn right into Shutt Green Lane. Cross over the canal, go through the tiny hamlet of Shutt Green and there is a car park on your right in a field adjoining a small wood. The gate is locked, but keys are issued to permit holders. Park here and walk through the wood to the reservoir and hides. A hide with facilities for the disabled is under construction. To avoid disturbing ground-nesting birds visitors are asked to keep off the northern shore during the breeding season.

Chillington Lower Avenue Continue along Horsebrook Lane into Brewood. Follow signs out of the village for Coven. After 0.5 miles (0.8 km) turn right at the crossroads into Codsall Road. In 0.5 miles (0.8 km) turn left into another lane and park on the verge where the Lower Avenue footpath strikes off to the left. Remember to try the less used footpath to the right of this road as well.

There is no bus service to Belvide along the A5, but there is a service from Wolverhampton to Brewood, from where it is 1.5 miles (2.4 km) to the reservoir along Horsebrook Lane and Shutt Green Lane.

Calendar

All Year: Little Grebe, Great Crested Grebe, Great Cormorant (scarce in spring: roost at Gailey), Grey Heron (particularly Gailey), Canada Goose, Gadwall, Mallard, Northern Shoveler, Tufted Duck, Ruddy Duck, Common Buzzard, Common Coot, Northern Lapwing, Great and Lesser Spotted Woodpeckers, Eurasian Treecreeper, Wood Nuthatch, Hawfinch (Lower Avenue; rare), Reed Bunting and common passerines.

March–June: Common Shelduck, Garganey (scarce), Merlin (scarce), Little Ringed Plover, Great Ringed Plover, Dunlin, Ruff, Black-tailed Godwit, Eurasian Curlew and Common Redshank; maybe scarcer wader such as Red Knot, Spotted Redshank or Common Greenshank; Meadow Pipit, Common Stonechat and Brambling (scarce). From mid-April: Hobby, Sanderling, Whimbrel, Common Sandpiper or scarcer wader such as Grey Plover, Bar-tailed Godwit or Turnstone; Little Gull (scarce), terns including possible Sandwich, Little and Black; Turtle Dove (scarce), Common Cuckoo, Common Swift (from May), hirundines, Rock Pipit (rare), Yellow Wagtail, Blue-headed Wagtail (rare), Pied Wagtail, White Wagtail (scarce), Northern Wheatear; warblers including Grasshopper, Sedge and Reed; Spotted and Pied Flycatchers and other common summer visitors. Passing raptors including Marsh Harrier and Osprey. Maybe rarity.

July–September: Garganey (scarce), Northern Pintail (scarce), Hobby, Peregrine Falcon; common waders including Little Ringed Plover, Ruff, Eurasian Curlew, Common Redshank, Common Greenshank or scarcer wader such as Oystercatcher, Grey Plover, Red Knot, Sanderling, Little Stint, Curlew Sandpiper, Black- and Bar-tailed Godwits, Whimbrel, Spotted Redshank, Wood Sandpiper and Turnstone; Little Gull (scarce), terns including possible Sandwich, Little and Black; and departing summer visitors. Passing raptors. Maybe rarity.

October–February: Tundra Swans (scarce), Common Shelduck, Eurasian Wigeon, Common Teal, Northern Pintail (scarce), Common Pochard, Common Goldeneye, Smew (scarce), Red-breasted Merganser (scarce), Goosander, Merlin (scarce), Peregrine Falcon, Water Rail, Grey Plover (October or November; scarce), European Golden Plover, Jack Snipe (scarce), Common Snipe; gulls including possible Mediterranean, Yellow-legged, or (after December) Iceland and Glaucous; Kittiwake (scarce), Rock Pipit (scarce), Common Stonechat, winter thrushes and flocks of larks, pipits, finches and buntings with occasional Water Pipit (rare), Brambling (scarce) or Twite (rare). Maybe a diver, rarer grebe or sea-duck.

8 CANNOCK CHASE
OS Landranger
Maps 127 & 128

Habitat
The 16,500 acres (6700 ha) of Cannock Chase form the smallest Area of Outstanding Natural Beauty (AONB) in Britain. A magnificent expanse of semi-natural oak and birch woodland, lowland heath (here at its most northerly limit) and conifer plantations, the Chase is owned largely by Forest Enterprise (FE) and Staffordshire County Council (SCC). On fine summer weekends it attracts literally thousands of visitors and cars are now excluded from parts in order to prevent erosion.

An upland plateau dissected by narrow valleys, the Chase reaches a height of 800 ft (243 m) at its northern end, from where wooded slopes descend into the Trent Valley. Capped by Bunter sands and gravels, the soils are acidic and poor. Browsing by five species of deer, and formerly grazing by sheep, have inhibited natural regeneration and encouraged an open, heath flora, with extensive sweeps of bracken and heather. Tiny streams meander along the valleys and mires have developed where drainage is impeded. Some valleys are quite distinctive, with the Oldacre Valley lined with willows and the Sherbrook Valley with old, coppiced alders.

Precious broadleaved woodland still survives. There are pedunculate oakwoods at Seven Springs and Sycamore Hill, and a superb sessile oakwood at Brocton Coppice, where a feeding station is maintained. The Brocton oaks are mostly 200 to 300 years old, but their invertebrate fauna suggest a woodland with much more ancient origins. With reduced grazing, birch, sycamore and Scots pine are freely regenerating and hawthorn, crab apple, holly, rowan, willow and elder are all becoming steadily established. Over the last 70 years, some 6700 acres (2700 ha) of the southern and eastern sides of the Chase have been planted with serried ranks of larch, spruce, Corsican and Scots pines, bordered by birch, beech and oak. Now the oldest are being clear-felled and replanted, creating a wider age structure to the benefit of birds.

Standing water is scarce, but there are a few small pools within the plantations where birds sometimes drink and bathe. Waterfowl are few, however, except in the flooded Brocton Quarry with its towering exposure of Bunter pebble beds.

Species

Scrub, woodland and even wetland birds are all interesting, but most bird-watchers are seeking heathland species, particularly European Nightjar.

Meadow Pipit and Linnet breed commonly on the heath and over 50 pairs of Tree Pipit are spread widely across areas with scattered trees. Willow Warblers, Chaffinches and Yellowhammers are plentiful and the calls of Green Woodpeckers and Common Cuckoos carry across the heather. Two or three pairs of Common Stonechats usually breed, favouring areas with gorse. More occur on passage along with a few Whinchats, though the latter is now rare. Reed Buntings also nest along valleys such as Sherbrook.

The heath is best savoured on a balmy, summer's evening. As the sun sinks, Hobbies, which are present throughout the summer, come to hunt, Grasshopper Warblers 'reel' and Woodcock rode. The latter can be seen at some 25 widely scattered, heathland localities. Finally, when only silhouettes show against a darkening sky, European Nightjars begin to churr. With some 30 or more 'churring' males the Chase is unquestionably the Midland's stronghold for this species. Open heath with scattered trees, such as that bordering the Sherbrook Valley, or conifer plantations less than five years old are most favoured.

*At dusk on the Chase, European Nightjars hawk insects and
Woodcock rode above the trees*

In late summer, passage Northern Wheatears visit the heath, followed in early autumn by occasional Ring Ouzels. The latter favour the rich harvest of rowan and elder berries in the Oldacre Valley. With the first autumn frosts, flocks of Fieldfare and Redwing descend on the same food source. Sometimes a passing raptor, most probably a ring-tailed Hen Harrier, may pause for a few days, or even stay the winter. A favoured spot is by the glacial boulder on Chase Road.

The birdlife of the broadleaved woodlands is extremely good. Among the commoner species, Tawny Owl, Great and Lesser Spotted Woodpeckers, Wood Nuthatch, Eurasian Treecreeper, Eurasian Jay and a good range of tits and finches are resident, while summer visitors include Chiffchaff, Willow Warbler, Blackcap, Garden Warbler and Spotted Flycatcher. Most can be seen at Brocton Coppice or Seven Springs, which are also the best places for Common Redstart, Wood Warbler and Pied Flycatcher. Some 25 pairs of Common Redstarts nest across the Chase, but Wood Warbler, with just 10 pairs, and Pied Flycatcher, with only three or four pairs, are more localised. Small numbers of Willow Tits and Lesser Spotted Woodpeckers also occur among the valley willows and alders, especially along the Sherbrook Valley. The same areas are visited in winter by flocks of Goldfinch, Common Redpoll and Siskin, plus mixed parties of foraging tits, Goldcrests and a few Eurasian Treecreepers. At this time the heaths hold small numbers of Sky Larks and Meadow Pipits, Grey Wagtails visit the streams and one or two Common Snipe and Woodcock feed in the valley mires.

Goldcrests and Coal Tits are widespread and plentiful in the conifer plantations throughout the year and Common Redpolls can usually be found. Always check parties of Goldcrests carefully as Firecrests have been seen both in spring and autumn. The heart of the plantations are too dark and lifeless to harbour many birds. However, Great Spotted Woodpeckers feed on old decaying tree stumps, and Chaffinches, Blue and Great Tits, Robins and Hedge Accentors frequent the woodland fringe. A real surprise was the recent discovery of Wood Larks – a species long since lost to the region. Their precise location is not being disclosed in the hope that recolonisation will ensue, but it is always worth looking round any suitable forest clearing.

Common Crossbills are recorded virtually every year and breeding has occurred. A few may be resident, their numbers replenished by fresh immigrants from June onwards during irruption years. Although larch, pine and spruce cones are their main food, birds sometimes use young oaks as perches and song posts. In springtime large flocks of Siskin, sometimes up to 100 strong, also feed among spruce and pines. Most soon leave, but increasingly a few linger later each year, though breeding is as yet sporadic. A third finch to look for is Brambling. Seldom numerous in the Midlands, small numbers sometimes feed and roost with Chaffinches, particularly in March and April, with the feeding station at Brocton Coppice a likely place.

The forest holds predators too. Eurasian Sparrowhawks are the commonest and on bright days several might spiral together on a rising thermal. Northern Goshawks, though less evident, might also be seen, especially in April. From time to time a larger raptor, such as a Common Buzzard, passes over, usually being mobbed by the local crows. Within the plantations, a few pairs of the nocturnal Long-eared Owl nest. The best chance of finding them is to listen on a still summer night for the 'squeaky-gate' calls of hungry youngsters.

Moorhen and Mallard inhabit the small pools, but most waterfowl are at Brocton Pool. Little and Great Crested Grebes and Tufted Duck all breed here, a small flock of Canada Geese is regularly present and Common Kingfishers are seen from time to time.

Among the more exciting sightings recently have been Red Kite, Rough-legged Buzzard, Common Raven and Arctic Redpoll.

Timing

On fine summer days the Chase is thronged with visitors, though few venture far from the car parks. Nevertheless, afternoons are best avoided. For woodland birds, try first thing in the morning when they are most active. Visit in the evening for Grasshopper Warbler, Woodcock, Long-eared Owl and European Nightjar, the latter seldom being seen or heard until it is virtually dark. Warm, still evenings with plenty of flying insects are best. In winter, weather is most important. Avoid wet or windy conditions. Cold, clear mornings with a light sprinkling of snow can be good, as birds are actively feeding to regain the body-weight lost overnight. The stands of conifers are fairly quiet and undisturbed at most times.

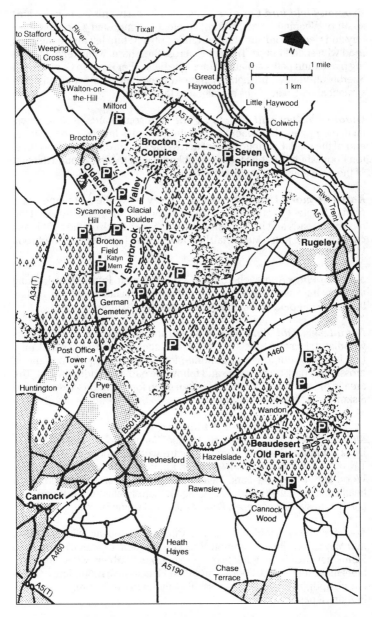

Access

Cannock Chase lies between the A34 Cannock–Stafford and the A513 Stafford–Rugeley roads, and either side of the A460 Cannock–Rugeley road. The heathland has a well defined pattern of peripheral car parks and footpaths into the area. The FE plantations can be explored on foot using the many forest roads. Buses use the A34 between Stafford and Cannock and the A513 between Stafford and Lichfield.
The best access points are:

Brocton Field and Coppice Leave the A34 eastwards 2.5 miles (4 km) south of Weeping Cross, Stafford, where it is signposted 'German Cemetery and Hednesford'. In a further 1 mile (1.6 km) turn left onto a metalled road with speed ramps. This leads across the Chase, with plenty of parking places and paths radiating across the heath. For Brocton Coppice and Sherbrook Valley turn right by the old gravel pit. The coppice is then straight ahead, with paths off right into the valley.

Oldacre Valley and Brocton Pool Turn southwards in Brocton village, then right into Oldacre Lane, where there is limited parking at the end of the road. Continue on foot across the old gravel workings to Brocton Pool, where a public hide overlooks the water. A track round the east of the pool goes out into Oldacre Valley.

Katyn Memorial and Sherbrook Valley Leave the A34 at the crossroads 2.5 miles (4 km) north of Cannock towards Rugeley. Turn left at the next crossroads and in 0.75 miles (1.2 km) take a track on the right into a car park by the Katyn Memorial. Follow the main footpath into Sherbrook Valley.

Seven Springs Approach from the A513 Stafford to Rugeley road, taking a narrow track westwards opposite the turning to Little Haywood. Follow this to the car park among birch trees and then explore on foot.

Beaudesert Old Park This is one of the better areas of coniferous woodland. Leave the A460 Cannock to Rugeley road to the east 1 mile (1.6 km) south of Rugeley. Continue for 1·25 miles (2 km) to Wandon crossroads, park on the verge and follow the paths and rides on foot. The area to the south and southeast is often good for Common Crossbills and Siskin.

Calendar

All Year: Little Grebe, Great Crested Grebe, Canada Goose, Mallard, Tufted Duck, Northern Goshawk, Eurasian Sparrowhawk, Moorhen, Woodcock, Tawny Owl, Long-eared Owl, Common Kingfisher, all three woodpeckers, Wood Lark (rare), Sky Lark, Meadow Pipit, Reed Bunting and common heath and woodland birds including Goldcrest, Willow Tit, Wood Nuthatch, Eurasian Treecreeper, Eurasian Jay and Common Redpoll.

April–September: Hobby, Common Cuckoo, European Nightjar (after mid-May), Tree Pipit, Common Redstart, Whinchat (scarce), Common Stonechat, Northern Wheatear, Grasshopper Warbler; woodland warblers including Wood; Spotted and Pied Flycatchers; Brambling and Siskin in April; and Common Crossbill (July onwards: in irruption years). Perhaps a passing raptor.

October–March: Common Snipe, Grey Wagtail, Ring Ouzel (October; rare), Fieldfare, Redwing, Common Crossbill (after irruptions) and flocks of tits and finches including Brambling (scarce) and Siskin. Possible Hen Harrier (rare) or passing raptor.

9 LOWER TAME AND TRENT VALLEYS

OS Landranger
Map 128

Habitat

Flat, featureless agricultural land is characteristic of the Tame and Trent valleys from Tamworth downstream to Burton-on-Trent. However, there are some good washlands and numerous sand and gravel pits have gradually spread down the valley as areas closer to Birmingham became exhausted. Most pits are private and many are still operational, so there is no access and viewing is restricted to roads and public rights-of-way. Nonetheless, two or three sites provide interesting birdwatching.

At Elford there are half-a-dozen or so worked-out pits which can be viewed from a public footpath. Willow and birch scrub have regenerated vigorously, substantially reducing the amount of open water, but there is still one flooded pit with innumerable tiny islands. In addition two areas of woodland – an oak-pine wood to the east with a magnificent display of bluebells in May, and an ash-sycamore wood to the west add diversity. To the north a wet ditch separates the gravel pits from a large set-aside field that stretches down to the River Tame.

On the outskirts of Burton-on-Trent, East Staffordshire District Council has created Branston Water Park out of more disused gravel workings. The central feature is a lake with stands of common reed in the southwest corner. Along the eastern shore poplar, birch and hawthorn provide a mature, but narrow, woodland fringe, whilst to the west thick hawthorn hedges border the Trent and Mersey Canal. On the other side of the canal are three more old, flooded pits flanked by willow scrub, bramble and patches of gorse.

Outside the scope of this book, but less than a mile (1.6 km) across the Trent in Derbyshire, is Drakelow Wildfowl Reserve. This comprises 50 acres (20 ha) of old gravel pits and flyash lagoons skilfully converted into a year-round habitat for wildfowl. It especially attracts passage waders and, in winter, diving duck and roosting gulls.

Between Elford and Branston other gravel pits can be glimpsed from the road, while the washlands around the confluence of the Mease, Tame and Trent are good for wintering wildfowl, with Whitemoor Haye a favoured spot.

Species

Wildfowl and waders are the main interest throughout the year.

At the gravel pits and on the rivers and canals, breeding waterfowl include Great Crested Grebe, Mute Swan, Canada Goose, Mallard, Tufted Duck and perhaps Common Teal (at Branston) or Ruddy Duck. Common

Shelduck are a special feature of Branston, with a pair or so breeding and a post-breeding flock of around 50. Up to 40 Little Grebes might gather at Elford in late summer too, while Common Kingfishers are resident and could appear anywhere along the valleys. Among other breeding species, Black-headed Gulls and Common Terns nest sporadically at Elford and Branston respectively, though their nests are sometimes washed out. The terns often fish the canal. Turtle Doves breed sparingly and warblers are widespread in summer, with plenty of Sedge Warblers and Common Whitethroats, a few Reed Warblers and perhaps a Grasshopper Warbler. Raptors include breeding Eurasian Sparrowhawks and occasional Hobbies in summer.

During winter, birds are spread more evenly at sites throughout the valleys, especially when floodwaters are receding. Likely maxima at any one locality are up to 200–300 Canada Geese, 250 Mallard, 100 Common Teal, 75 Mute Swans, 50 Eurasian Wigeon and 25 Gadwall. The latter two species generally favour Elford, though 70 Gadwall have been seen at Branston. A few Northern Shoveler also visit the gravel pits most years, but Northern Pintail are irregular, occurring mostly after flooding.

Several Great Cormorants frequent the valley, while normal maxima for other diving species are 200 Common Coot, 100 Tufted Duck and 50 Common Pochard. A few Common Goldeneye visit Branston and this is the best water for sawbills, though all three species are very occasional. Various geese are also reported from here, though most are probably feral birds. Scarcer species to occur have been Slavonian and Black-necked Grebes, Shag, Garganey and Greater Scaup. If the weather stays mild, several Common Snipe and here and there a Jack Snipe or Water Rail may remain through the winter, with the latter sometimes staying on to breed.

The meadows at Whitemoor Haye are a traditional winter haunt of Tundra Swans, with a herd of 30 or more in most years. Sometimes they are joined by a small flock of White-fronted Geese. Northern Lapwings tend to be widely scattered, but flocks can coalesce to bring as many as 1,000 together, with perhaps 200 European Golden Plover, a few Eurasian Curlew or a Ruff amongst them. Large flocks of Black-headed Gulls, Wood Pigeons, Stock Doves, Meadow Pipits, Eurasian Jackdaws and other open ground species, including a few Tree Sparrows, also feed across the washlands. Sometimes these attract the attention of a Merlin or Peregrine Falcon, while a Short-eared Owl might hunt for voles. Small coveys of Red-legged and Grey Partridges are occasionally seen too, Common Quail has been heard calling in summer, and Corn Buntings breed in the valleys, with Whitemoor Haye again a good area.

In spring a few pairs of Oystercatcher, Little Ringed Plover, Northern Lapwing and perhaps Great Ringed Plover or Common Redshank return to nest, while passage brings a good variety of the commoner waders, with Common Sandpiper regular and Great Ringed Plover most numerous. Other passage birds include an occasional tern, Kittiwake or Little Gull, fair numbers of Yellow Wagtails, a scatter of Northern Wheatears and one or two Whinchats and Common Stonechats.

Autumn sees a similar passage, but with up to a dozen Green and half as many Common Sandpipers along with smaller numbers of other waders. Among the scarcer species to have occurred recently have been Little Stint, both Black- and Bar-tailed Godwits, Spotted Redshank and Wood Sandpiper.

Though not noted for rarities, a Purple Heron was seen at Branston and a European Serin at Elford, though tantalisingly both were over-flying birds.

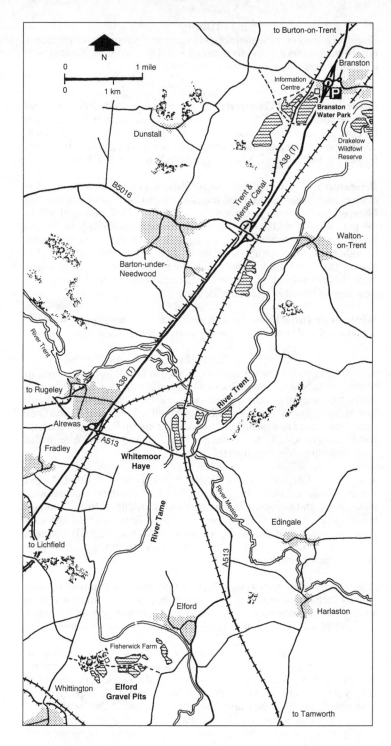

Timing

Branston is busy on nice afternoons in summer. Otherwise disturbance is not a great problem, but early morning is still the best time. Visits as winter floodwaters subside can be productive.

Access

Elford Leave the A513 Tamworth–Rugeley road westwards at the south end of Elford village. Park on the verge near the entrance to the gravel pit, which is about 0.5 miles (0.8 km) down the lane. Then, where the road turns left, take the public footpath straight ahead between the old pits and on towards Fisherwick Farm. There is a bus service from Tamworth to Elford.

Branston The entrance to the Water Park, which has a car park, information centre and toilets, is off the northbound carriageway of the A38 between Barton-under-Needwood and Branston. Park here and follow the path round the lake. Also follow the towpath southwards to the first bridge, cross the canal and follow the public footpath to view the pits on the other side. For a circular walk, turn right after a short distance and follow the path that skirts the pits back to the road and into Branston. Buses from Burton-on-Trent, including the Birmingham–Lichfield–Burton service, stop at Branston and Alrewas.

Whitemoor Haye Leave the A38 eastwards onto the A513 at Alrewas, take the first right and view from the roads or public footpaths.

Calendar

All Year: Little and Great Crested Grebes, Great Cormorant (scarce in spring), Mute Swan, Canada Goose, Common Shelduck, Gadwall (scarce in breeding season), Common Teal (scarce in breeding season), Mallard, Tufted Duck, Ruddy Duck, Eurasian Sparrowhawk, Red-legged and Grey Partridges, Water Rail (scarce in summer), Common Coot, Northern Lapwing, Black-headed Gull, Common Kingfisher and common farmland birds including Corn Bunting (scarce).

March–June: Garganey (rare), Oystercatcher, Little and Great Ringed Plovers, Common Redshank and maybe other common waders, Kittiwake (rare) and Common Stonechat. From mid-April: Hobby, Common Quail (rare), Common Sandpiper, Common Tern, maybe Little Gull (rare) or other tern, Turtle Dove (scarce), Yellow Wagtail, Northern Wheatear, Whinchat (scarce) and warblers including Grasshopper (scarce), Sedge and Reed.

July–September: Garganey (rare), Hobby, Common Quail (rare); common waders including Green and Common Sandpipers and maybe scarcer species such as Little Stint, Black- or Bar-tailed Godwit, Spotted Redshank or Wood Sandpiper; Common Tern and departing summer visitors.

October–March: Tundra Swan, White-fronted Goose (scarce), Eurasian Wigeon, Northern Pintail (irregular), Northern Shoveler, Common Pochard, Common Goldeneye, sawbills (rare), Merlin (rare), Peregrine Falcon (scarce), European Golden Plover, Ruff (rare), Jack Snipe (scarce), Common Snipe, Eurasian Curlew (scarce), Short-eared Owl (scarce) and flocks of pigeons, pipits, corvids and other open ground species including Tree Sparrows (scarce). Perhaps rarer grebe, sea-duck or vagrant seabird.

Habitat

Chasewater is a British Waterways (BW) canal-feeder reservoir of almost 250 acres (100 ha) set amidst former heath, marsh and bog. Over the years the landscape was steadily eroded by mining and encroached upon by the factories and houses of Brownhills, Chasetown and Norton East. Then, with the development of the amusement park, it became a focus for leisure activity. Now the southern end is threatened by the proposed Birmingham Northern Relief Road and the northern end by a reclamation and coal recovery scheme.

The central feature is the reservoir, which is divided into two by a causeway carrying the Chasewater Light Railway. South of this causeway, the main body of water (217 acres or 88 ha) is used for fishing, sailing, windsurfing, water-skiing and powerboat racing. This disturbance makes the much smaller body of water to the north, known as Jeffrey's Swag, especially important as a quiet refuge for wildfowl.

Approaching from the A5, you are confronted by a derelict stadium and trotting track on your right and an amusement park along the southern shore to your left. Do not be deterred. Despite the deafening go-karts and general hurly-burly, this is often the shoreline that waders, pipits and wagtails prefer! Around the western shore, the reclaimed grassland is of little value, but below the embankment the small pools, scrub and fields of Willow Vale are of interest.

On the opposite (eastern) side of the reservoir is the dam. Beneath this, Anglesey Basin and the canal-feeder are bordered to the south by dry heath and to the north by a richly varied marsh noted for its passage migrants and winter roosts. The heathland continues north of the reservoir, where it is interspersed with scrub, marsh, woodland, a small pool and open ground with alder plantations beyond. Together these make an excellent habitat for passerines. The shoreline between the dam and Target Point is good for waders, but beyond the Point it becomes peaty and less attractive.

North of the railway line are old pit mounds and slurry beds, a pool and marsh suitable for breeding duck and waders, and patches of dense willow scrub. Similar dense patches of willow along Big Crane Brook and around Jeffrey's Swag shelter breeding and passage warblers, while the patches of gorse and broom on the adjacent heath are the most likely places for chats.

Species

Winter wildfowl and gulls, and passage waders and terns are the main interest, but above all Chasewater is known for its rarities.

Wildfowl numbers increase from August onwards and most species peak in December. After this there is a steady decline, until by April few birds are left. Diving duck and Common Coot predominate, with typical maxima of 800 for Tufted Duck and Common Coot, and 100 to 150 for Common Goldeneye. The water is much less attractive to Common Pochard, but following the main arrival in October 100 or so remain through the winter. Of the other diving duck, one or two Ruddy Duck, or perhaps Goosander or Red-breasted Merganser, can also be expected during the winter, while Greater Scaup and Common Scoter occur most years, the latter usually in spring, late summer or autumn. Smew are unpredictable, but a couple may arrive during very hard weather.

Great Crested Grebes are present through from autumn to spring, usually in small numbers. Little Grebes are scarce and tend to frequent the smaller pools in preference to the main reservoir. At some time during the winter a diver or rarer grebe is likely, with recent records of all except Black-throated Diver.

Dabbling duck are less numerous, with typically only 150 or so Mallard, 40–50 Common Teal, a dozen or so Eurasian Wigeon and Gadwall, and a few Northern Pintail and Northern Shoveler. Common Shelduck and Garganey pass through at their migration times. There is a small herd of resident Mute Swans, which increases to a peak of 50 to 70 between September and January, while between October and March a small party of Tundra Swans may fly through or pause briefly to rest and feed. Canada Geese are usually present outside the breeding season, but in very variable numbers. Other geese, such as a party of Brents, might drop in during the winter, when up to 50 Great Cormorants could also be present.

As winter progresses and wildfowl numbers begin to decline during February and March, attention turns to gulls. Having spent the day gorging on farmland or landfill sites, thousands flock into the reservoir every evening to bathe and roost. They are there from autumn through to spring, though the rarer gulls are more likely in late winter. Sometimes powerboats and water-skiers disturb roosts, causing many birds to leave, most probably for Blithfield Reservoir. When undisturbed, however, this is the best place in the region to study gulls.

Numbers vary with the weather, being greater on cold nights, when Black-headed Gulls usually peak at around 10,000 in December and January. The proportion of larger gulls is above average, though, with 2,000 or more Lesser Black-backs, perhaps 1,000 Herring Gulls, a few hundred Great Black-backs and up to 25 Common Gulls likely. Amongst these one or two Yellow-legged and Mediterranean Gulls, or from December Iceland or Glaucous Gulls, are regularly present. Indeed, Chasewater has always been a good, consistent site for these rarer gulls and even a Pomarine Skua was once discovered amongst them.

Spring wader passage begins in March with the return of breeding Little Ringed Plovers and migrant Oystercatchers and Great Ringed Plovers. It continues with Common Sandpipers in April and culminates in a few frenetic days in May when small parties of Great Ringed Plover and Dunlin, one or two Grey Plover, Sanderling or Turnstone, and perhaps a party of Bar-tailed Godwits pass swiftly through. Sanderling in particular favour the shoreline near the sailing club. Common Swifts, hirundines and both Pied and Yellow Wagtails are also regular spring migrants, with usually a few White Wagtails too.

Return passage is more protracted and sedate. The water level is kept as high as possible for water sports, but if it does fall the exposed muddy margins attract a good variety of waders, mostly along the southern shore or east of Target Point. Again the commoner species are the more likely, particularly Great Ringed Plover, Dunlin and Common Sandpiper. They are usually joined in August by Common Greenshank, Whimbrel and Ruff; then by Grey Plover; and in October by one or two Common Redshank or Red Knot. Less often, Little Stint, Curlew Sandpiper Black-tailed Godwit or Wood Sandpiper appear. A further passage of Dunlin sometimes leads to a few staying into the winter.

Adult Iceland Gull (left) and immature Glaucous Gull are typical of the unusual gulls for which Chasewater is renowned

Unlike waders, terns and gulls are unaffected by water level. Spring passage sometimes begins with a few Kittiwakes in March, but most terns and Little Gulls pass quickly through in late April or early May. Numbers are usually small, but large flocks of Black Terns appear spasmodically, usually on light easterly winds, while vigorous depressions can bring impressive numbers of Arctic Terns and Little Gulls. Common Terns are regular both in spring and autumn, when either Sandwich or Little might also occur. Autumn sometimes brings a few Little Gulls as well and passage often concludes with one or two Kittiwakes in November, though both species may reappear again around the turn of the year.

The surrounds of Chasewater are almost as interesting as the reservoir itself. In summer the heath supports many Sky Larks, Meadow Pipits and Willow Warblers and, with luck, even a Grasshopper Warbler might be heard. Eurasian Jays and Common Redpolls frequent the scrub, and passage Northern Wheatears and the occasional Whinchat flit across the heather or perch upright on convenient gorse bushes. In winter the damp hollows and marshy areas, such as behind the dam and at Willow Vale, hold good numbers of Common Snipe and Jack Snipe and one or two Water Rails, while a Short-eared Owl might be seen searching for voles on the heath. Indeed, the heath is a good spot for raptors, with regular sightings of Eurasian Sparrowhawks and Common Kestrels and always a chance of Peregrine Falcon. Apart from Meadow Pipits and passage Northern Wheatears, few species frequent the reclaimed grasslands, but the alder plantations are visited by wintering flocks of Siskin and Common Redpoll.

Do not overlook the marsh behind the dam. Apart from the species already mentioned, Willow Tit, Bullfinch, Reed Bunting and several warblers nest amidst the dense willow scrub and rank vegetation. Then, in late summer, there is a steady stream of migrant warblers, especially Willow Warblers, followed in autumn by flocks of Linnets and Goldfinches. Several species also use the willows as a winter roost.

Along the railway line the tall thorn scrub holds breeding Lesser Whitethroats and is used by Eurasian Jays moving to or from the nearby

Brownhills Common. In winter the surrounding pastures are visited by flocks of Fieldfare and Redwing, or Sky Larks, Meadow Pipits and finches. These often include Common Redpoll and sometimes a few Brambling or Twite, though large flocks of the latter are a thing of the past. Try the old pit mounds, where there might also be Grey or Red-legged Partridge, or watch from the edge of Southacres Farm for finches going in and out of the weeds. Remember, though, there is no access to this private farmland. Finally, in winter a Rock Pipit or Water Pipit may be feeding around the shoreline.

Chasewater has long held a reputation for rarities and, indeed, with Lesser Scaup can even lay claim to a first for Britain. In more recent times Fulmar, Great Bittern, Horned Lark and Arctic Redpoll have maintained its reputation.

Timing

Early in the day is the best time to visit, as water sports and general activity intensify in the afternoons. If there is disturbance on the main reservoir in winter, check Jeffrey's Swag for wildfowl. Wildfowl increase in cold weather, when shallower waters are frozen. In spring, passerines tend to arrive with southerly winds and overcast conditions, but storms or deep depressions may bring waders and Arctic Terns. Black Terns and Little Gulls tend to arrive on light easterly winds in settled weather. Vagrant seabirds are most likely after autumn gales, while divers or the rarer grebes usually come with very cold weather. The colder nights also seem to be the better ones for Glaucous and Iceland Gulls. Disturbance is greatest in high summer, when orchids, sundews, dragonflies and butterflies compensate for the lack of birds.

Access

Approach from the A5, which at this point is a dual carriageway. The only access is from the eastbound carriageway, so when travelling westwards proceed past the entrance, right around the roundabout at the junction with the A452 and back along the eastbound carriageway. Take the second left into Pool Road and left again into the amusement park. Some of the car parks here overlook the southern shore, so are ideal for the elderly or disabled and also enable the winter gull roost to be studied from the comfort of your car! There are well defined and obvious footpaths around the reservoir and its surrounds.

Jeffrey's Swag and the northern area can be reached from Norton East, where cars can be parked along the road. There is also a car park at the end of Church Street, Chasetown, giving access to the northern side (see map). Various bus services from Brownhills to Cannock, and one from Birmingham to Cannock, pass Brownhills West (A5/A452 junction), from where it is a 0.75-mile (1.2 km) walk to the reservoir.

Calendar

All Year: Little Grebe, Mute Swan, Mallard, Tufted Duck (rare in summer), Eurasian Sparrowhawk, Common Kestrel, Red-legged Partridge, Grey Partridge, Water Rail (scarce in summer), Common Coot, Common Snipe (scarce in summer), Sky Lark, Meadow Pipit and common heathland, scrub and woodland birds, including Willow Tit, Eurasian Jay, Common Redpoll, Bullfinch and Reed Bunting.

April–June: Common Shelduck, Garganey (rare); common waders including Oystercatcher, Little and Great Ringed Plovers, Dunlin, Common

Sandpiper and scarcer species such as Grey Plover, Sanderling, Bar-tailed Godwit or Turnstone; Little Gull (scarce); terns including occasional Sandwich (rare), Little (rare) and Black; Common Swift, hirundines; Yellow, Pied and White (scarce) Wagtails; Whinchat, Northern Wheatear; warblers including Grasshopper (scarce), Sedge and Reed Warblers, and Lesser Whitethroat. Possible passage raptor or rarity.

July–September: Great Crested Grebe, Canada Goose, Garganey (rare), Peregrine Falcon (scarce); common waders including Little and Great Ringed Plovers, Dunlin, Ruff, Common Redshank, Common Greenshank, Common Sandpiper and scarcer species such as Grey Plover, Red Knot, Little Stint, Curlew Sandpiper, Black-tailed Godwit and Wood Sandpiper; Little Gull (scarce); terns including occasional Sandwich (rare), Little (rare) and Black; hirundines, Whinchat, Northern Wheatear and other departing summer visitors. Possible passage raptor or rarity.

October–March: Great Crested Grebe, Great Cormorant, Tundra Swan (scarce), Canada Goose, Common Shelduck, Eurasian Wigeon, Gadwall, Common Teal, Northern Pintail (scarce), Common Pochard, Greater

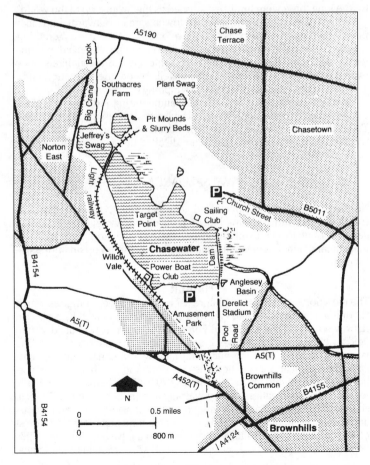

Scaup (scarce), Common Scoter (scarce), Common Goldeneye, Smew (rare), Red-breasted Merganser (rare), Goosander (scarce), Ruddy Duck, Peregrine Falcon (scarce), Dunlin, Jack Snipe; gulls regularly including Mediterranean, Yellow-legged, or after December Iceland or Glaucous; Kittiwake (mainly autumn and March), Short-eared Owl (scarce), Rock Pipit (October), Water Pipit (rare), Fieldfare, Redwing; and winter passerine flocks including Brambling (scarce), Siskin and Twite (rare). Maybe a vagrant seabird, diver, rare grebe or sea-duck. Possible rarity.

11 THE BLACK COUNTRY

OS Landranger
Map 139

The Black Country lies between Wolverhampton, Walsall, West Bromwich and Dudley. During the Industrial Revolution countless settlements sprang up around a multitude of mines, mills, factories and quarries. Before long these were firmly established as the 'workshop of the world'.

Villages grew into towns, and the towns spread outwards until they met. Somehow a few pockets of undeveloped land survived, increasingly isolated from the countryside beyond. Some of these, prized and protected as urban lungs, now provide some fascinating habitats. Two examples are Sandwell Valley and Saltwells Wood, the latter, ironically, adjacent to the enormous Merry Hill shopping centre.

Heavily dependent on traditional manufacturing industry, the Black Country has suffered badly from the industrial recession of the 1980s. Today there are countless acres of derelict land, much of it too toxic for wildlife. The more interesting sites are detailed below.

WALSALL AREA

Northeast of Walsall are three small areas, all close to the A461 Walsall–Lichfield road and the Daw End branch of the Wyrley and Essington canal. Though insignificant in themselves, in combination they make an ideal local patch. Regular watching has already turned up an impressive list of birds.

Habitat

The most northerly site is the 91-acre (37 ha) Clayhanger Common, which is bounded to the north and east by a canal and to the west by a disused railway. Once part of the Royal Forest of Cannock, it was divided into fields enclosed by thorn hedges before becoming a colliery waste tip. The land was low-lying and the enclosing railway and canal embankments caused frequent and severe flooding. The Common next became a household waste site, which raised its level by 20 ft (7 m) before being finally reclaimed as a recreation area by Walsall Metropolitan Borough Council. North of Clayhanger Road is grassland sown with wildflowers and plantations of willow, poplar, alder and birch, which form part of the new Forest of Mercia. Aquatic plants have been added to the two small pools in this area. South of the road is a subsidence pool, with a margin of reedmace, reed-grass and willow scrub, and an island with alders and willows that affords sanctuary to wildfowl. Within the surrounding rough grassland a few birches, pines and patches of gorse provide reminders of the former heath. They are reinforced by willow scrub and newly planted oaks. Further west, alongside the old railway track, is another subsidence pool, this time with substantial margins of rush and sedge as well as reedmace. The surrounding rough grazing land also contains some gorse.

Yet two more subsidence pools are at Stubbers Green, 1.75 miles (2.8 km) further south. That north of the road is fringed with reedmace, backed by willows and alders and encroached upon by landfill operations. The pool south of the road is larger and more open, with some reedmace and reed-grass and an area of exposed mud on the western shore. Otherwise the shoreline comprises mature willow scrub, bramble and gorse. Sailing causes some disturbance. Further east is a wet, marshy field with muddy areas, rushes and sedges. The whole area is surrounded by rough pastures grazed by ponies.

Thirdly, a further 1.5 miles (2.4 km) southwest, is Park Lime Pits Local Nature Reserve. This comprises two deep, flooded pits surrounded by 57 acres (23 ha) of arable farmland managed under the Government's Stewardship scheme to be both productive and rich in wildlife. Both pools have some marginal vegetation, including reedmace, and the larger of the two incorporates an island surmounted by beech trees. A belt of mature woodland, including alder, sycamore, oak and many fine beeches, encloses the pools. Reinforcing this is perimeter planting of similar species, especially alder and willow. Thorn scrub is well developed along the stream courses and the understorey along the south side is diverse. Farmland management provides hay meadows for ground-nesting birds and winter stubbles for finches and buntings. The reserve forms part of the Beacon Regional Park and is crossed by the Beacon Way, from which the surrounding countryside can be explored.

Species

Spring is perhaps most rewarding with resident birds nesting and migrants arriving.

A few pairs of Little Grebe, Mute Swan, Canada Geese, Mallard, Tufted Duck, Ruddy Duck, Common Coot and Moorhen breed, while Great Crested Grebes may attempt to nest. Common Kingfishers can be seen throughout the year. The management regime makes the farmland around Park Lime Pits especially good, with nesting Grey Partridges, Northern Lapwings, Sky Larks, Yellowhammers, Reed Buntings and, sparingly, even Tree Sparrows and Yellow Wagtails. It also attracts predators, with Eurasian Sparrowhawk, Common Kestrel and Little Owl nesting in the area. The mature woodland holds Stock Dove, Great Spotted and Green Woodpeckers, Mistle Thrush, Willow Tit and Bullfinch. Wood Nuthatch and Eurasian Treecreepers are also seen, but less regularly.

Spring passage normally brings a few Meadow Pipits and Sand Martins, or an occasional Eurasian Curlew or Woodcock. Most years Northern Wheatears, or perhaps a Common Redstart, will pause briefly, while scarcer migrants could include Turtle Dove, Common Stonechat, Whinchat and Spotted or Pied Flycatcher. Warblers are well represented, with a few of the regular species staying to breed, including Sedge Warbler and Lesser Whitethroat. Grasshopper and Reed Warblers occur irregularly. Keeping a watchful eye on their potential hosts are a scattering of Common Cuckoos and Clayhanger might hold a 'drumming' Common Snipe.

Tree Sparrows nest sparingly around Park Lime Pits

Stubbers Green is best for wader passage, with Little Ringed Plover annual and one or two of the commoner species such as Great Ringed Plover and Common Redshank passing through. Even the more enclosed pools at Park Lime Pits might attract a Common or Green Sandpiper. A Hobby could be seen anywhere, while migrant Ospreys and Firecrest have been recorded at Park Lime Pits and a Short-eared Owl seen at Stubbers Green.

Autumn brings similar species, but with the addition of a few more hirundines, Sky Larks and Pied Wagtails. Indeed, a small roost of Barn Swallows might form at Clayhanger or Stubbers Green, but nothing like the size the latter used to attract. Waders are fewer, but Green Sandpipers are regular at Stubbers Green and there is always a chance of something like Oystercatcher, Ruff or even Wood Sandpiper. One or two terns could also be seen, while a party of late-staying Dunlin might join the wintering Common Snipe. Away from the pools, Siskin, Redwing and Fieldfare arrive for the winter, with often a roost of up to 200 of the latter two species at Park Lime Pits.

The farmland here and at Stubbers Green is equally productive in winter, with flocks of 500 Black-headed Gulls, 250 Northern Lapwings and Lesser Black-backed Gulls and sometimes 50 or so European Golden Plover. Eurasian Jackdaws, Carrion Crows, Rooks and Common Starlings also gather, as do flocks of finches and buntings which may include a few Brambling at either end of the winter. Magpies are numerous and the passerine flocks might attract a passing Merlin.

Grey Herons visit all the pools and the resident wildfowl are joined for the winter by a few Common Teal, Northern Shoveler and Common Pochard. Sometimes a Northern Pintail or Greater Scaup appears and Mandarin Duck, Ruddy Shelduck and Red-crested Pochard have all been noted. Stubbers Green is best for waterfowl, with around 100 Mallard and up to 50 Common Teal, Common Pochard, Tufted Duck and Common

Coot. It also attracts a few gulls, including Common Gulls and perhaps a rarity such as Yellow-legged Gull.

Although few rarities can be expected, Night Heron has occurred at Park Lime Pits and both Twite and Wryneck at Clayhanger.

Timing

Early morning visits are best, especially at migration times, before birds are disturbed. In spring, song is also best early in the morning. Weather

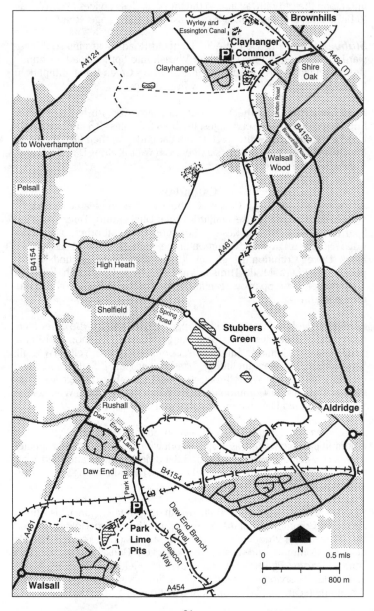

matters less, although overnight rain or fog may ground migrants.

Access

Clayhanger Common Leave the Lichfield Road (A461) northwestwards by turning into Brownhills Road (B4152). Continue across into Lindon Road and after 0.25 miles (0.4 km) turn left into Clayhanger Road. There is a car park on the right in 0.25 miles (0.4 km), opposite the junction with High Street. Follow the paths onto the common on both sides of the road. From the south side, also follow the track behind the houses and along the old railway line to the far pool. Bus services from Walsall to Brownhills and Brownhills West pass along Clayhanger Road.

Stubbers Green Leave the A461 Lichfield Road by turning southeastwards 2.75 miles (4.4 km) north of Walsall into Spring Road. Continue straight ahead at the roundabout into Stubbers Green Road and park in the lay-by alongside the pools. View from the road.

Park Lime Pits Leave the A461 southeastwards from Rushall along Daw End Lane, following reserve signs. In about 0.5 miles (0.8 km), turn right into Park Road, follow the track to the car park and then take the paths into the reserve. There are bus services from Walsall along Daw End Lane, from which the reserve is a short walk.

Calendar

All Year: Little and Great Crested Grebe, Grey Heron (scarce in spring), Mute Swan, Canada Goose, Mallard, Tufted Duck, Ruddy Duck, Eurasian Sparrowhawk, Common Kestrel, Common Coot, Moorhen, Grey Partridge, Northern Lapwing, Common Snipe (rare in summer), Little Owl, Stock Dove, Common Kingfisher, Green and Great Spotted Woodpeckers, Sky Lark, Mistle Thrush, Willow Tit, Wood Nuthatch, Eurasian Treecreeper, Tree Sparrow, Bullfinch, Yellowhammer and other common passerines.

April–June: Hobby (scarce); Little Ringed Plover and maybe other common passage waders such as Great Ringed Plover, Common Redshank, and Green and Common Sandpipers; Common Cuckoo, Yellow Wagtail, Sand Martin; warblers including Grasshopper (rare), Sedge and Reed (scarce) and Lesser Whitethroat; and perhaps other passage migrants such as Turtle Dove, Common Redstart, Whinchat, Northern Wheatear or Spotted and Pied Flycatchers. Possible rarity.

July–September: Hobby (scarce); Green Sandpiper and maybe other common passage waders as in spring, but with chance of scarcer species such as Oystercatcher, Ruff or Wood Sandpiper; Yellow and Pied Wagtails, hirundines (perhaps Barn Swallow roost) and departing summer visitors. Possible rarity.

October–March: Common Teal, Northern Pintail (rare), Northern Shoveler, Common Pochard, Merlin (rare), European Golden Plover, Dunlin (scarce), Woodcock (scarce), Eurasian Curlew (scarce); Black-headed, Common and Lesser Black-backed Gulls; Short-eared Owl (rare), Meadow Pipit (October and March), Fieldfare, Redwing, Siskin and flocks of corvids, Common Starlings, finches and buntings including Brambling (scarce). Maybe unusual waterfowl or gull.

SANDWELL VALLEY

Habitat

Between Birmingham and West Bromwich is a large lung of open land that might be many miles from either. For here the pleasant countryside is dotted with woods and lakes, marred only by the M5/M6 motorway interchange at its very centre. The heavily polluted River Tame also flows through the valley. Across much of the area, gappy hedges enclose rough pastures grazed by the skewbald and piebald ponies so characteristic of the Black Country. This untended countryside is a haven for Carrion Crows and Magpies, their depravations doing much to limit the populations of small birds. Four golf courses also attract passage Northern Wheatears.

Two areas are specially important. Firstly, in a meander of the River Tame, the Environment Agency's (EA) Forge Mill Lake acts as a balancing reservoir. There are two small islands and the RSPB leases 25 acres (10 ha) at the eastern end for a nature reserve. This includes a marsh, fields and hedgerows – all overlooked by a Nature Centre. Hides give closer views across the lake and marsh and there is a feeding station.

Secondly, there is Sandwell Borough Council's 1000-acre (400 ha) expanse of Sandwell Valley Country Park. This lies on the opposite side of Forge Lane to the balancing lake and is bisected by the M5. The area west of the motorway is used for formal recreation and holds few birds, except in the marshy woodland of Sots Hole. To the east the landscape is surprisingly varied, with woodland, scrub and rough grassland set amidst marginal farmland with neglected hedges. Interest centres on the small Swan Pool, which despite board and dinghy sailing and fishing, still attracts birds.

Species

Sandwell Valley is excellent for birds at any time of the year, but especially at migration times.

Most of the commoner passerines and a good range of woodland species are resident, including Stock Dove, Little and Tawny Owls, all three woodpeckers, Willow Tit, Wood Nuthatch and Eurasian Treecreeper. Cool, damp days in spring and summer bring hundreds of Common Swifts from their breeding sites in the conurbation to feed low over Forge Mill Lake along with a few passage martins and Barn Swallows from nearby farms. Late in summer they might fall prey to a dashing, migrant Hobby. A dozen or more Reed Buntings, Yellowhammers and Common Whitethroats sing from hedgerows and scrub, with two or three pairs of Lesser Whitethroat where growth is tallest and thickest, and Grasshopper Warblers sometimes breed. Willow Warblers are widespread, and areas such as Priory Wood hold several Blackcaps and a few Garden Warblers as well as the woodland species already mentioned. Around the lakes and pools several pairs of Canada Geese and a few pairs of Little Grebe, Great Crested Grebe, Mute Swan, Mallard, Tufted Duck, Ruddy Duck, Common Coot and Sedge and Reed Warblers attempt to breed. Northern Lapwing also nest in good numbers, while low water levels sometimes entice Little Ringed Plovers and Common Redshank to attempt breeding. Common Kingfishers are resident in the area.

Late summer and autumn bring a variety of waders with one or two Oystercatchers, Little and Great Ringed Plovers, Dunlin, Ruff, Common Redshank, Common Greenshank and both Common and Green Sandpipers all liable to occur. With luck, something like a Little Stint, Curlew

Sandpiper or even a Grey Phalarope might appear. Usually there are one or two terns as well, including perhaps Sandwich or Black. Small numbers of hirundines and various other passerines also move through. Tree Pipit, Northern Wheatear and Whinchat all visit grassy areas or scrub, while a Common Redstart or maybe a Pied Flycatcher might work its way along a hedgerow. Later on, Meadow Pipits pass through and a Common Stonechat could settle in for the winter.

Arriving winter visitors soon become the centre of attention. Hidden in the marsh may be 50 Common Snipe, half-a-dozen Jack Snipe, one or two Water Rails and a Woodcock. On the lake a dozen Great Cormorants gather to fish, while Grey Herons stalk along the shore. Among the mixed finch and bunting flocks searching for seeds could be Tree Sparrows, a few pairs of which breed locally. They particularly favour the paddocks around Park Farm and Swan Pool, as do Little Owls. Small flocks of Siskin and Common Redpoll also occur. Common Kestrels regularly hover over the motorway verges, Merlins make rare appearances, a Short-eared Owl might search rough grassland for voles and roosting Long-eared Owls are sometimes found.

Winter waterfowl congregate on Forge Mill Lake. Most common species occur, including Great Crested Grebes and Mute Swans. Up to 400 Canada Geese assemble from late summer into autumn. Other species reach their maxima in midwinter, with 50–100 Common Pochard, a few more Tufted Duck, 50 Common Teal and 150 Common Coot. Small numbers of Eurasian Wigeon, Northern Shoveler and a few Gadwall, Common Goldeneye, Goosander and Ruddy Duck are often present as well. Common Shelduck and Northern Pintail sometimes occur early in the year, or in autumn. Expectations are always high, and recent years have brought all three rarer grebes and various unusual duck including Common Eider, Long-tailed Duck and Velvet Scoter. Sea-duck often settle first on Swan Pool, transferring to Forge Mill Lake only when disturbed. By comparison, gulls are few and the scarcer species infrequent.

March sees Fieldfare and Redwing moving north for the summer and the resident Eurasian Sparrowhawks displaying. A Common Buzzard might pass through or a Merlin chase the first Meadow Pipits. Little Ringed Plovers return to their territories followed by a steady trickle of waders. Species are similar to autumn, but with the probable addition of Sanderling and Black-tailed Godwit and a chance of a diminutive Temminck's Stint. One or two Common Terns and less often Kittiwake, Arctic or Sandwich Terns might also pass through in April or early May, while Black Terns characteristically appear some years but not others. Spring brings good, if variable, numbers of Yellow Wagtails, while Ring Ouzel is regular and Turtle Dove is noted most years as are Common Cuckoo, Spotted Flycatcher and similar species to those in autumn. With them might be a Rock or Water Pipit, White Wagtail or raptor such as Osprey or Peregrine Falcon. Firecrests have been seen several times and both Fulmar and Northern Gannet have appeared just 4 miles (6.4 km) from the centre of Birmingham!

Timing

Human disturbance is the main factor. Weekends and bank holidays are very busy, and this is also when most water sports occur. The RSPB visitor centre is used by school parties during term time. Bright spring mornings are best for birdsong. Autumn wader passage is best after a dry summer, when water levels are low. Wildfowl on Forge Mill Lake tend to be more numerous in very cold weather and most vagrants usually arrive after a stormy spell.

Access

Sandwell Valley Country Park Leave the M5 at Junction 1 onto the A41 Birmingham to West Bromwich road and turn eastwards towards Birmingham. Pass the West Bromwich Albion football ground and take the next turn left into Park Lane. Continue for about 1.5 miles (2.4 km) to the car park on the left by Swan Pool. Explore from here. Birmingham–West Bromwich buses pass the football ground.

Sandwell Valley RSPB Reserve Continue along Park Lane (which becomes Forge Lane). At the end turn right into Newton Road, continue over the railway bridge and take the second right into Hampstead Road. After 0.6 miles (1 km), turn right into Tanhouse Avenue (immediately before Hampstead School) and then left to the Nature Centre (following signs) where there are toilets and car parking.

Alternatively approach from M6 (Junction 7) by turning southwards onto the A34 towards Birmingham. At the traffic lights, turn right onto the A4041 towards West Bromwich, left after 1 mile (1.6 km) into Hampstead Road and then follow the above directions. There are bus services along Tanhouse Lane from Birmingham and West Bromwich.

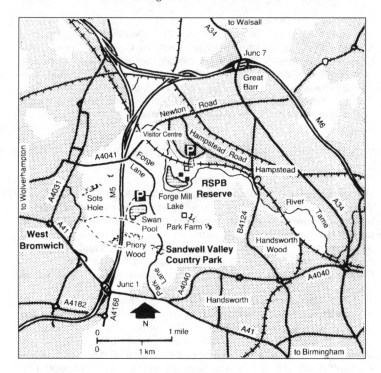

Calendar

All Year: Little and Great Crested Grebes, Mute Swan, Canada Goose, Mallard, Tufted Duck, Ruddy Duck, Eurasian Sparrowhawk, Common Kestrel, Common Coot, Northern Lapwing, Common Snipe (scarce in summer),

Woodcock, Little and Tawny Owls, Stock Dove, Common Kingfisher, all three woodpeckers, Willow Tit, Wood Nuthatch, Eurasian Treecreeper, Tree Sparrow, Reed Bunting, Yellowhammer and other common passerines.

April–June: Common waders such as Oystercatcher, Little Ringed Plover, Great Ringed Plover, Dunlin, Common Redshank, Green and Common Sandpipers, or scarcer waders such as Sanderling or Black-tailed Godwit; Kittiwake (rare); passage terns including Sandwich (rare) and Black (scarce); Turtle Dove (scarce), Common Cuckoo, Common Swift (after April), hirundines; Yellow, Pied and White (scarce) Wagtails; Whinchat (rare), Northern Wheatear; warblers including Grasshopper (scarce), Sedge and Reed; Ring Ouzel (scarce) and Spotted Flycatcher. Maybe passing raptor or rarity.

July–September: Grey Heron, Hobby (scarce); common waders such as Oystercatcher, Little and Great Ringed Plovers, Dunlin, Ruff, Common Redshank, Common Greenshank, Green and Common Sandpipers or scarcer waders such as Little Stint or Curlew Sandpiper; terns including perhaps Sandwich (rare) and Black; Common Swift (scarce in September), hirundines, Whinchat (rare), Northern Wheatear and other departing summer visitors including perhaps Tree Pipit, Common Redstart or Pied Flycatcher. Maybe passing raptor or rarity.

October–March: Great Cormorant, Grey Heron, Common Shelduck, Eurasian Wigeon, Gadwall, Common Teal, Northern Pintail (rare), Northern Shoveler, Common Pochard, Common Goldeneye, Goosander (scarce), Merlin (rare), Water Rail (scarce), Jack Snipe (scarce), Dunlin (scarce), Long- and Short-eared Owls, Meadow Pipit (October and March), Common Stonechat, Fieldfare, Redwing, Siskin, Common Redpoll and mixed flocks of Tree Sparrows, finches and buntings. Maybe rarer grebe, sea-duck, unusual waterfowl or passing raptor.

SHEEPWASH URBAN PARK

Habitat

Sheepwash is a joint venture between Sandwell Metropolitan Borough Council and the Black Country Development Corporation to create an urban park from derelict land in the very heart of the Black Country. At present large areas of rough grassland are broken up by new plantations of young native hardwoods, including oak, alder, birch and willow that have yet to mature. Gorse adds variety and gives a heathy feel in parts. Even within the park's short life, regular watching has produced an impressive list of birds.

The park is bisected by a canalised and rather sterile River Tame. At the centre a large lake has margins of common reed and reedmace and half-a-dozen islands designed specifically to attract wildfowl and waders. One island has been sliced in half to expose a sand face into which pipes have been inserted as artificial nest holes for Sand Martins. Another has a shallow scrape for waders. A smaller, higher pool also has a good margin of common reed.

The habitats between the river and the railway are established and mature. They include some old pastures with thick thorn hedges, two or three pools fringed with reedmace and a backdrop of alders and willows.

Species

This is an excellent oasis in an urban desert, with many over-flying birds dropping in briefly to rest or feed.

For its location, the breeding community is extremely varied. Nesting waterfowl include Little Grebe, Mute Swan, Canada Goose, Mallard and occasionally Great Crested Grebe and Tufted Duck; waders are represented by three or four pairs of Little Ringed Plover and Northern Lapwing; while passerines include Meadow Pipit, Pied and Grey Wagtails, Willow Tit, Goldfinch, Linnet, Bullfinch, Reed Bunting and several common warblers including Common Whitethroat, Sedge and Reed Warblers. To these can be added Common Kestrel and Red-legged Partridge in the area.

Grey Wagtails breed at Sheepwash Urban Park and can be seen at many Black Country sites in winter

Late summer and autumn bring a post-breeding flock of around 100 Canada Geese, up to 200 Common Swifts, a small passage of waders and maybe one or two Arctic, Common or Black Terns. Great Ringed Plover, Dunlin and both Green and Common Sandpipers are the most regular waders to occur, while Sanderling, Ruff, Black-tailed Godwit, Common Greenshank and Turnstone are among the less usual. Small flocks of hirundines, especially House Martins and Barn Swallows, gather over the lake to feed and are sometimes harassed by a Hobby. A family party of Spotted Flycatchers might also be seen making forays after passing insects and one or two Yellow Wagtails and Whinchats are virtually annual. Lesser Whitethroats are fairly regular too, while Northern Wheatear, Common Redstart or exceptionally Pied Flycatcher might be seen. As the days shorten, so several hundred Pied Wagtails come in to roost and a Common Stonechat or Rock Pipit might show.

Winter brings a variety of wildfowl, with around 100 Mallard, 50 Common Teal, 30 Tufted Duck and 25 Common Pochard. Eurasian Wigeon and Northern Shoveler are less frequent and both Gadwall and Common Goldeneye scarce. One or two Common Shelduck are noted most years at passage times, while Ruddy Shelduck, Common Scoter, Long-tailed Duck and Goosander have all been recorded. Some 20 Common Snipe may winter too, though their numbers are declining. With them are usually one or two Jack Snipe and perhaps a Woodcock or

Water Rail. The latter often favours the entrance to the culvert carrying the Tame underneath the railway. Up to 300 European Golden Plover and a similar number of Northern Lapwings are occasional visitors too. A few gulls are usually present, with Black-headed most numerous, but several larger gulls too. Yellow-legged and Mediterranean Gulls have been found amongst them most years. The riverside alders attract a few Siskin and Common Redpoll and the rough grassland small flocks of pipits, finches and buntings, including perhaps Brambling.

Spring passage often begins with a Common Stonechat or even a Black Redstart. Yellow Wagtails, Northern Wheatears and Whinchats are annual visitors; Common Cuckoos, White Wagtails and Common Redstarts are occasionally seen or heard; and Water Pipit, Lesser Whitethroat and Ring Ouzel have been recorded. Although hirundines are regular, Sand Martins have so far resolutely shunned the artificial nest holes. One or two of the commoner waders also pass through again and there is a chance of Kittiwake or terns as well. Waders are generally similar to those in autumn, but perhaps with Oystercatcher, Eurasian Curlew and Common Redshank as well. Two unusual records have been Red Knot and Wood Sandpiper. Great Cormorants, Shags, Grey Herons and Common Kingfishers have all fished the waters on occasions. Common Buzzard and Peregrine Falcon are occasionally seen, while unusual visitors have included Black-necked Grebe, Little Gull, Cetti's Warbler and Bearded Tit.

Timing

Early morning is best before there is any disturbance. Over-flying migrants may be grounded by heavy rain or mist and stay only a short while to feed or rest before moving on.

Access

Leave the M5 at Junction 1 and turn westwards onto the A41 West Bromwich Expressway. At the second roundabout turn left, then right at the next roundabout onto the A4035 (Dudley Street). Continue along this road, which becomes Great Bridge Street, for 1 mile (1.6 km), then turn left into Whitehall Road (B4166) and first right into Sheepwash Lane. The entrance to the park is on the left in just under 0.25 miles (0.4 km). The Birmingham–West Bromwich–Dudley bus service passes along Great Bridge Street.

Calendar

All Year: Little and Great Crested Grebes, Great Cormorant (scarce in summer), Grey Heron (scarce in spring), Mute Swan, Canada Goose, Mallard, Tufted Duck, Common Kestrel, Red-legged Partridge, Northern Lapwing, Common Kingfisher (scarce), Willow Tit, Goldfinch, Linnet, Bullfinch, Reed Bunting

April–June: Little Ringed Plover and other common waders such as Oystercatcher, Great Ringed Plover, Dunlin, Eurasian Curlew, Common Redshank, Green and Common Sandpipers or scarcer species such as Red Knot or Wood Sandpiper; terns (rare), hirundines, Meadow Pipit; Yellow, Grey, Pied and White (scarce) Wagtails; Black Redstart (rare); summer visitors such as Common Cuckoo, Common Redstart, Whinchat, Northern Wheatear or scarcer species such as Water Pipit, Lesser Whitethroat or Ring Ouzel; warblers including Sedge and Reed Warbler and Common Whitethroat. Maybe passing raptor or rarity.

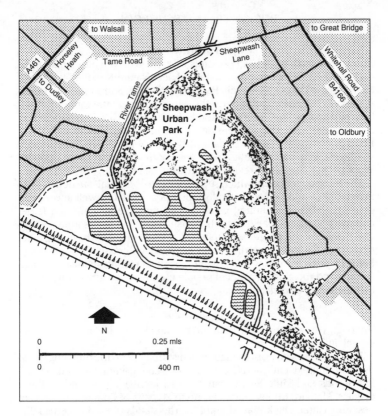

July–September: Hobby (rare); perhaps common passage waders such as Great Ringed Plover, Dunlin or Green and Common Sandpipers or scarcer wader such as Sanderling, Ruff, Black-tailed Godwit, Common Greenshank or Turnstone; maybe a tern including perhaps Black (scarce); Common Swift (scarce in September), hirundines, Meadow Pipit, Yellow, Grey and Pied Wagtail; warblers including Sedge and Reed Warbler and Common Whitethroat; and maybe other passage migrants such as Common Redstart, Whinchat or Spotted and Pied Flycatchers. Maybe passing raptor or rarity.

October–March: Common Shelduck (scarce), Eurasian Wigeon, Gadwall (scarce), Common Teal, Northern Shoveler, Common Pochard, Common Goldeneye (scarce), Water Rail (scarce), European Golden Plover, Jack Snipe (scarce), Common Snipe, Woodcock (scarce); gulls including Mediterranean (rare) and Yellow-legged (rare); Kittiwake (autumn and March; rare), Rock Pipit (October; rare), Pied Wagtail (roost), Common Stonechat (scarce), Siskin, Common Redpoll and flocks of pipits, finches and buntings including Brambling (scarce). Maybe sea-duck, rare or unusual wildfowl.

BUCKPOOL AND FENS POOL

Habitat

Known also as Brierley Hill Pools, this wilderness of wetlands, grasslands and scrub has now been designated a Local Nature Reserve by Dudley Metropolitan Borough Council. Part is also an SSSI. Surrounded by housing estates, and new factories on the enormous tip of the former Round Oak steelworks, the reserve extends for 2 miles (3.2 km) along the Stourbridge Canal. The northeastern end around Fens, Middle and Grove Pools is generally best for birds, but Buckpool Dingle, in the extreme southwest, is a natural valley with oakwoods that hold Great Spotted Woodpecker, Eurasian Treecreeper and Eurasian Jay.

The three larger pools, which supply water to the canal, are rich in fish, invertebrates and plants. Several smaller pools are also well known for their amphibians, including great crested newts, and there is a large colony of southern marsh orchids. Marsh vegetation varies from sedges and rushes on the poorer soils to a lush growth of tall herbs in nutrient-rich areas. On the former industrial areas, rough grassland is gradually being invaded by willow and hawthorn scrub, creating an ideal nesting, feeding and roosting area. Local people use the valley for various activities, including fishing.

Species

Although very disturbed, this site still manages to hold some good birds, especially in winter.

Few nests are safe from predation or disturbance, so the breeding community is limited. Little and Great Crested Grebes usually succeed in rearing broods and Mute Swans can be seen incubating or tending their cygnets. Mallard, Ruddy Duck and up to 20 pairs of Common Coot also nest and Tufted Duck may attempt to. The stands of reedmace usually host two or three pairs of Reed Warblers, their rhythmic songs contrasting with those of Sedge Warblers in the nearby scrub. A few pairs of Common and Lesser Whitethroats, and one or two Blackcaps, Willow Tits and perhaps Garden Warblers, Reed Buntings and Yellowhammers also breed along with many commoner species. Common Kingfishers nest in Buckpool Dingle and Grey Wagtails have bred.

Most winters a few Common Snipe, plus one or two Jack Snipe and Water Rail, conceal themselves among the marginal vegetation. Joining them at dusk might be a Woodcock. Waterfowl typically number up to 200 Common Coot, 75 Canada Geese, 50 Mallard, 50–100 Tufted Duck and 20 Common Pochard. Other species are more erratic, but any of Common Shelduck, Eurasian Wigeon, Gadwall, Northern Shoveler, Common Teal, Common Goldeneye, Goosander and Ruddy Duck could be seen. Outstanding in a long list of scarcer waterfowl are Red-necked Grebe, Ferruginous Duck, Greater Scaup, Smew and four Long-tailed Ducks, while among the few winter gulls both Mediterranean and Ring-billed Gulls have been seen.

A surprising variety of birds pass through in spring and autumn. One or two of the commoner waders appear most years, with Common Sandpipers regular at both seasons. Less expected was a recent Black-tailed Godwit. A few terns are also likely, with Black Tern most frequent. Common and Arctic Tern passage is very slight and Sandwich Tern has been seen. Among the passerines, spring brings a few Meadow Pipits, hirundines and Common Swifts, but most common summer visitors have occurred at sometime with Northern Wheatear, Whinchat or Common Redstart perhaps most likely.

There is even a chance of a White Wagtail or Rock Pipit in spring, with the latter perhaps again in autumn. Goldfinches feed on thistle heads early in autumn and later Redwings and Fieldfares strip the hawthorn scrub of berries. One or two Bramblings might also pass through.

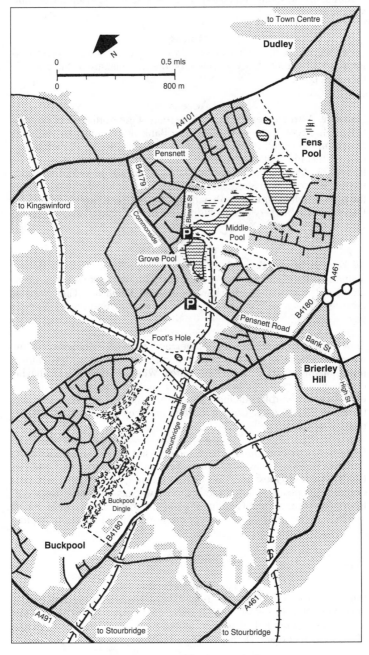

For an urban site, raptors are good, with Common Buzzard and Peregrine Falcon increasingly appearing, the latter mainly in winter and spring. Summer sightings of Hobby are also increasing, while Eurasian Sparrowhawk has bred and even Marsh Harrier and Merlin have been recorded.

Rarities are few, but Great Bittern and a splendid Night Heron were outstanding.

Timing

Local people use the area at all times for many purposes, especially during school holidays. Early morning, before there is any disturbance, is therefore best.

Access

Leave the A461 Dudley to Stourbridge road at the north end of Brierley Hill High Street. Turn westwards into Bank Street and carry straight ahead into Pensnett Road, where there is a car park on the left at the foot of the hill. Paths from here lead up to Fens Pool or down to Buckpool. Alternatively, continue straight ahead into Commonside, turn right into Blewitt Street and there is a track between the houses on the right which leads to a small parking area between Grove and Middle Pools. Several bus services, including one from Birmingham, pass along Commonside.

Calendar

All Year: Little and Great Crested Grebes, Mute Swan, Canada Goose, Mallard, Tufted Duck (scarce in summer), Ruddy Duck (scarce), Common Coot, Eurasian Sparrowhawk, Common Kingfisher, Grey Wagtail (scarce), Willow Tit, Yellowhammer, Reed Bunting and other common passerines.

April–September: Common Sandpiper and perhaps another common wader; maybe terns including Black; Common Swift (after April), hirundines, Meadow Pipits, Rock Pipit (rare), White Wagtail (rare); maybe common passage migrants such as Common Redstart, Whinchat, Northern Wheatear; warblers including Sedge and Reed Warblers, Lesser and Common Whitethroats, Garden Warbler (scarce) and Blackcap. Maybe passing raptor.

October–March: Common Pochard and occasionally Common Shelduck, Eurasian Wigeon, Gadwall, Common Teal, Northern Shoveler, Common Goldeneye and Goosander; Water Rail (scarce), Jack Snipe (scarce), Common Snipe, Woodcock (scarce), a few gulls, Fieldfare, Redwing, Brambling (scarce) and Goldfinch (early autumn). Perhaps rarer grebe, sea-duck, other unusual waterfowl or rare gull. Maybe a passing raptor.

BLACKBROOK VALLEY

Habitat

Dudley Metropolitan Borough Council has designated some 2 miles (3.2 km) of the Blackbrook Valley a Local Nature Reserve. At the heart of the reserve are Netherton Hill, Netherton Reservoir and the 62 acres (25 ha) of Saltwells Wood and Doulton's Claypit SSSI.

Saltwells is primarily a pedunculate oak and birch wood, with a closed canopy, sparse shrub layer containing some holly, and a field layer of bracken. Some trees are 200 years old and believed to be relics of the old Pensnett Chase. The valleys of the two small, fast-flowing streams are more varied, with beech, ash, lime, grey poplar and sycamore above a rich shrub layer. Alders occupy the southeast corner.

Doulton's Claypit, quarried last century for fireclay, now exhibits various stages in the natural succession to oak woodland. Damp patches and wet flushes line the quarry floor, with birch scrub and developing oak wood-land to the south and east. Open grassland, gorse and hawthorn scrub, and some grazing meadows complete the range of habitats in the area.

Netherton, or Lodge Farm, Reservoir is a small canal-feeder with a fringe of willow and thorn scrub, while to the north Netherton Hill pro-vides an expanse of rough grass with extensive areas of gorse, hawthorn and willow scrub. The reservoir is fished and used for water-skiing, while local residents use the whole area for recreation.

Species

For an urban location, this is a good place for wetland and woodland birds.

The sparse shrub layer at Saltwells Wood limits the range of breeding species, but there are good numbers of hole-nesters, with two or three pairs of Wood Nuthatch, Great Spotted and Green Woodpeckers, Stock Dove and Tawny Owl. Other arboreal species such as Eurasian Sparrow-hawk, Mistle Thrush, Spotted Flycatcher and Eurasian Treecreeper also nest and there are good numbers of most common woodland passer-ines, including a few pairs of Bullfinches, Chiffchaffs, Blackcaps and perhaps a Garden Warbler. Surprisingly for an urban site, Wood Warblers bred until recently, but lately only passage birds have been reported. Around the claypit, Common Whitethroats and Linnets inhab-it the gorse, while Eurasian Jays are especially numerous in the birches and young oaks.

In autumn and winter, parties of Common Redpoll hang from birch twigs, Fieldfares and Redwings feed on holly and other berries and for-aging flocks of tits and Goldcrests wander about the valley. Sometimes Siskin visit the alder plantation, a few Bramblings join Chaffinches to search for beechmast, or a Lesser Spotted Woodpecker scours the canopy. Thrushes and Common Starlings feed across the meadows, Common Kestrels prey on small mammals, Green Woodpeckers seek out anthills and small flocks of finches feed on a variety of seeds. At dusk, just as thousands of Wood Pigeons come to roost in Saltwells Wood, one or two Woodcock leave to feed in the damper areas. Even a Grey Wagtail or Jack Snipe could be seen along the streams or in a wet flush.

Netherton Reservoir holds a few waterfowl, with Great Crested Grebe, Mallard and Common Coot breeding here or on the canal. Winter brings 50 or so Mallard and Tufted Duck; a handful of Little Grebes, Eurasian Wigeon, Common Teal, Gadwall and Common Pochard; and occasion-ally a Northern Shoveler or Common Goldeneye. Greater Cormorants are also seen from time to time and Shags have appeared more than once. Very rarely Common Scoter pause on passage, while Ferruginous Duck, Greater Scaup and Common Eider have all been noted. Several hundred gulls, mostly Black-headed, may also be present. Passage brings a few Kittiwakes and terns, the former usually in spring and the latter more like-ly in autumn. One or two waders also pass through, usually Common

Sandpipers, though occasionally a Common Greenshank or Green Sandpiper shows in autumn. Common Kingfishers also frequent the area.

Red-legged Partridge are resident on Netherton Hill, while summer brings both Common and Lesser Whitethroats to nest. Common Cuckoos are sometimes heard in spring and constant watching has also shown the hill to be a regular stop-over for migrants, with Tree and Meadow Pipits, Yellow Wagtail, Whinchat, Northern Wheatear and Ring Ouzel most regular amongst a wide range of species.

Passing raptors also visit the valley, with records of Common Buzzard, Osprey, Hobby, Merlin and Peregrine Falcon.

Timing

There is considerable disturbance from recreational activity at all times, but especially during school holidays. Early morning, before disturbance,

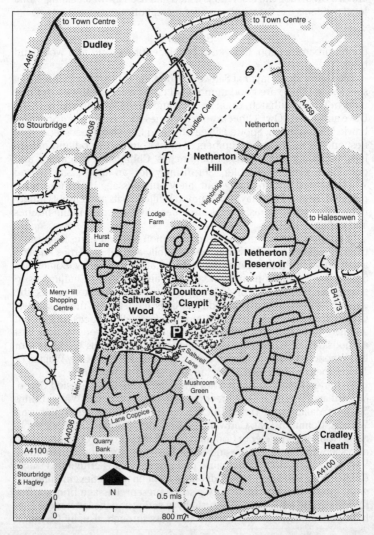

is the best time, with the woods better in spring and the hill on calm, misty autumn mornings. Family birders could always combine a visit with one to Merry Hill shopping centre.

Access

Approach via the A4036 from Dudley or Stourbridge. At the roundabout leading to the Merry Hill Shopping Centre turn eastwards into Coppice Lane and follow the brown signs to Saltwells Nature Reserve. In just over 0.5 miles (0.8 km) turn left into Saltwell Lane and park in the reserve car park. The whole area can be explored from here. There are numerous other access points, but parking may prove difficult. Various bus services from Dudley pass along Merry Hill, Hurst Lane and Highbridge Road.

Calendar

All Year: Great Crested Grebe, Mallard, Eurasian Sparrowhawk, Common Kestrel, Red-legged Partridge, Common Coot, Stock Dove, Wood Pigeon, Tawny Owl, Common Kingfisher, Green and Great Spotted Woodpeckers, Mistle Thrush, Goldcrest, Wood Nuthatch, Eurasian Treecreeper, Eurasian Jay, Common Starling, Linnet, Common Redpoll, Bullfinch, Yellowhammer and other common woodland birds.

April–September: Green Sandpiper (July–August; scarce), Common Sandpiper (scarce; not May and June), Common Cuckoo, Meadow Pipit, Lesser and Common Whitethroat, Garden Warbler, Blackcap, Wood Warbler (scarce), Chiffchaff, Willow Warbler and Spotted Flycatcher. Passing migrants might include Tree Pipit, Yellow Wagtail, Whinchat, Northern Wheatear or Ring Ouzel. Maybe a tern or passing raptor.

October–March: Great Cormorant (scarce); Tufted Duck and maybe Eurasian Wigeon, Common Teal, Gadwall, Common Pochard or occasional Northern Shoveler or Common Goldeneye; Jack Snipe (rare), Woodcock (scarce); a few gulls including perhaps Kittiwake (autumn or March), Lesser Spotted Woodpecker, Grey Wagtail (scarce), thrushes including Fieldfare and Redwing, small finch flocks perhaps including Brambling (scarce) and Siskin. Maybe scarce wildfowl or vagrant seabird.

HIMLEY AND BAGGERIDGE

Habitat

The parkland of Himley Hall and the adjoining Baggeridge Wood, though on the outskirts of the Black Country, are never far from urban influence. The central feature of the parkland is the Great Pool. Beyond this is Himley Hall, now an educational centre, and behind that a backcloth of majestic beeches. In the valley above the Great Pool, the feeder stream has been dammed to create four smaller, reed-fringed pools. Higher up is Baggeridge Country Park, with its oak-birch woodland and stands of beech and alder. The whole area is administered as country parks by Dudley Borough Council and Staffordshire County Council respectively.

Species

Although not outstanding for birds, this is a good place for beginners to familiarise themselves with some of the commoner species. Regular watching could well be rewarded with something more interesting.

The wealth of tall, mature trees well suits Rooks, Eurasian Jackdaws and Stock Doves and noisy activity around the rookery is an early sign of spring. This is a good area for Green Woodpeckers, particularly the birch-woods, and Eurasian Jays favour this habitat too, while Great Spotted Woodpeckers and Wood Nuthatch prefer the oaks and beeches. Lesser Spotted Woodpeckers are present, but more elusive. Small birds such as tits and finches are plentiful, despite some falling prey to Eurasian Spar-rowhawks. In summer they are joined by warblers, including one or two Wood Warblers, or perhaps a pair of Common Redstarts. The last migrant to arrive is usually the unobtrusive Spotted Flycatcher, which is seldom seen before early May. On the pools, broods of Mallard, Moorhen, Common Coot and Great Crested and Little Grebes can be seen, while in the reeds a few pairs of Reed Warbler busily tend their young. As night falls a roding Woodcock might show against the darkening sky.

Once the leaves start to fall, parties of tits and Chaffinches begin search-ing for beechmast. With them may be a handful of Brambling, their dis-tinctive white rumps identifying them as they take flight. In autumn the pools usually hold one or two Water Rails.

From September onwards small flocks of wildfowl build up on the Great Pool. Most numerous are Mallard, Tufted Duck and Common Pochard, with the latter sometimes exceeding 100. Some 20 or so Mute Swans may also be seen late in the year. A few Little Grebes are regularly present too, while Common Teal, Eurasian Wigeon, Northern Shoveler, Ruddy Duck and even a Goosander might appear. Grey Herons also fish here frequently. Midwinter could bring something even more unusual, such as a diver or rarer grebe.

The alders, especially along the feeder stream, are always worth check-ing in winter for parties of Goldfinch, Siskin and Common Redpoll, whilst the weirs are often frequented by Pied and Grey Wagtails.

Recent interesting records have included Common Buzzard, Little Gull and Pied Flycatcher.

Timing

Himley Park is extremely popular at weekends and evenings during the summer, so an early visit is recommended. During the winter, weekend sailing may disturb wildfowl and in very cold weather the pools ice over completely. On the whole the woods are quieter.

Access

From the A449 Wolverhampton to Kidderminster road turn eastwards at the traffic lights by Himley Church and take the B4176 towards Dudley. The entrance to Himley Hall is on the left in about 0.5 miles (0.8 km). Alternatively, leave the A449 at the roundabout junction with the A463 (Wodehouse Lane) and follow this road for 1 mile (1.6 km) when the entrance to Baggeridge Country Park is on the right. There is plenty of car parking at both entrances (Baggeridge is cheaper!) and obvious paths lead to the lake, millpools and woods. Toilets are available and Baggeridge has a small visitor centre (opening limited). Several buses serve the area.

Calendar

All Year: Little Grebe, Great Crested Grebe, Mallard, Eurasian Sparrow-hawk, Moorhen, Common Coot, Woodcock, Stock Dove, all three wood-peckers, Wood Nuthatch, Eurasian Jay, Eurasian Jackdaw, Rook and other common woodland birds.

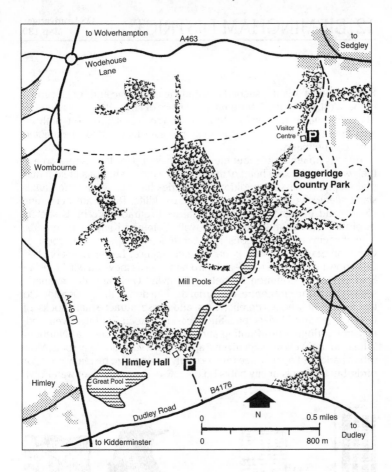

April–September: Common migrants including Common Redstart, Reed and Wood Warblers and Spotted Flycatcher.

September–March: Grey Heron, Mute Swan; Common Pochard and perhaps Eurasian Wigeon, Common Teal, Northern Shoveler, Ruddy Duck or Goosander; Water Rail (scarce); Grey and Pied Wagtails; and parties of tits and finches including Goldfinch, Siskin, Common Redpoll and maybe Brambling (scarce). Possible diver, rare grebe or unusual waterfowl.

Birmingham is Britain's second city and the economic and social capital of the West Midlands. A bustling, busy mass of concrete, bricks and tarmac, it is unlikely to be visited by anyone in search of birds. Yet for those with time to spare, some surprisingly pleasant places and unexpected birds can be found.

There is no great river, but the canals make up for this as they weave their way into the very heart of the city. Once the arteries of a great industrial empire, today the traditional industries have gone and the canals stand silent save for pleasure boats and wildlife. Rivers are becoming cleaner and, though the Rea is too canalised to attract many birds, stretches of the Cole are much improved, with Common Kingfishers in parts.

In the city centre pigeons rule supreme, the spectacular roost of Common Starlings having gone. In recompense, Lesser Black-backed Gulls now nest on roof tops – as far from the sea as they can get! Eurasian Sparrowhawks, Common Kestrels and Tawny Owls are also regularly seen close to the city centre. Industrial decline during the 1980s added to the legacy of weedy, derelict sites and these attract small flocks of Goldfinches and Linnets, plus the occasional Reed Bunting. Even Red-legged Partridge, Corn Bunting and passing migrants such as Northern Wheatear and Yellow Wagtail have appeared in such unlikely spots. Most urban parks and open spaces are too tidily managed to be really good for birds, but the pools in city parks hold a few of the commoner waterfowl.

Black Redstarts breed in parts of Birmingham

Birmingham's real speciality is the Black Redstart, which arrives in late April or May and stays until August or September. Locations are hard to identify as the large derelict buildings and structures that it favours are constantly being redeveloped. Old power stations, gas works, railway stations and factories are always worth a look, especially those close to water. Try exploring the canal towpaths in the early morning, particularly on Sundays when there is less traffic noise, and listen for the males singing from the highest roofs and chimneys.

In the leafy suburbs, small woodland birds are often more numerous than in the surrounding countryside despite the deprivations inflicted by Eurasian Jays, Magpies and Carrion Crows. Woodpeckers, thrushes, warblers, tits and finches all occur. Even this far inland, gulls are numerous and parties, mostly of Black-headed Gulls, can be seen standing around on school playing fields and recreation grounds.

Some of the better sites are described below.

EDGBASTON RESERVOIR

Habitat

Just 1.5 miles (2.4 km) from the centre of Birmingham is Edgbaston Reservoir – a 64-acre (26 ha) canal-feeder reservoir with gently shelving, gravelly shores and a few marshy creeks. Hemmed in on three sides by housing and on the fourth by old factories, its setting is truly urban, but a little mixed broadleaved woodland and a variety of mature trees and herbaceous plants create a richer habitat than is found in the more formally managed parks. Of interest to botanists are amphibious bistort and flowering rush. Despite disturbance from fishing, boating, sailing and general public access, regular watching has produced a good bird list. The area is administered by Birmingham City Council. Almost adjoining is Harborne Walkway, a linear strip of developing woodland along a disused railway line that leads to a small West Midland Bird Club (WMBC) reserve of scrub and woodland.

Species

It would be unwise to have great expectations of this site, which is mentioned principally because it is so close to the city centre and the many hotels and conference facilities along the Hagley Road.

A few pairs of Great Crested Grebe, Mallard and Common Coot breed and these along with Canada Geese, Tufted Duck and Common Pochard are winter regulars. Occasionally they are joined by one or two Eurasian Wigeon, Common Teal, Gadwall, Northern Shoveler or Common Goldeneye. On a good night up to 6,000 gulls roost as well. Most are Black-headed, with a scattering of Common, Lesser Black-backed and Herring Gulls with them. Two or three Great Black-backed Gulls or a Kittiwake might add to the variety, while Yellow-legged and Glaucous Gulls have been recorded. Surprisingly the region's first ever Laughing Gull was also seen here. The list of vagrant wildfowl is also impressive, though recent sightings have been confined to Black-throated Diver, Shag, Common Scoter and Red-breasted Merganser.

Small numbers of terns are noted on passage, mainly in spring, with Commons most regular, Arctics occasional and Black Terns unpredictable. Waders are rare, but one or two of the commoner species may stop briefly to feed or rest, especially if the water level is low in autumn.

Parkland and garden birds include Tawny Owl, Great Spotted Woodpecker, Wood Nuthatch and Eurasian Treecreeper along with many commoner species. Pied Wagtails are quite numerous, Grey Wagtails sometimes breed and small numbers of the commoner migrants such as Meadow Pipit and Willow Warbler regularly pass through. Common

Swifts frequently come to feed and less often migrants such as Sand Martins, Northern Wheatear or even a Black Redstart are seen. In autumn, Linnets gather to pick up seeds from any exposed mud, and a Rock Pipit could work steadily around the shoreline. Occasionally a Chaffinch flock is joined by one or two Brambling and a Peregrine Falcon recently made an appearance. Although casual visits are unlikely to produce anything rare, regular watching has demonstrated the wide range of migrating birds that pass over a major city.

Timing

The reservoir is a popular and well-used recreational facility at all times. Nevertheless it repays regular visits, particularly during the winter. It is quietest on weekdays outside the school holidays, when it is the ideal place to while away a lunch-hour or take an early morning or evening stroll whilst staying on business in a nearby hotel. Often it is most productive after a dry spell, when the water level is down.

Access

The best approach is from the Hagley Road (A456 Birmingham to Kidderminster). At the Ivy Bush public house, about 0.5 miles (0.8 km) west of the Five Ways underpass, turn northwards into Monument Road. Then

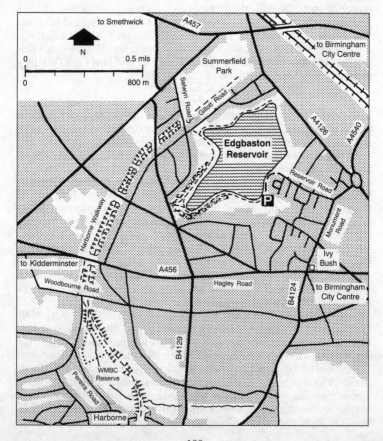

take the fourth turn left into Reservoir Road and the entrance faces you at the end. Park overlooking the reservoir (good for the disabled) and follow the paths around. There are several bus services from Birmingham city centre to the Ivy Bush and a circular route passes along Monument Road.

Harborne Walkway is reached by leaving the reservoir on the north side, turning left into Gillott Road and then immediately right into Selwyn Road. Cross the bridge, turn right into Summerfield Park and double back beneath the same bridge onto the walkway. At the end of the cutting in 1 mile (1.6 km), take a right fork down to the WMBC reserve. The gate is kept locked, so contact WMBC for access details.

Calendar

All Year: Great Crested Grebe, Canada Goose, Mallard, Common Coot, Tawny Owl, Great Spotted Woodpecker, Grey and Pied Wagtails, Wood Nuthatch, Eurasian Treecreeper and other common garden and parkland birds.

April–September: Maybe commoner wader or tern, including Black Tern; Common Swift (after April), White Wagtail (spring; rare), warblers, Linnets (from August) and maybe other passage migrants.

October–March: Common Pochard, Tufted Duck and maybe Eurasian Wigeon, Gadwall, Common Teal, Northern Shoveler or Common Goldeneye; roosting gulls including perhaps Yellow-legged, Iceland and Glaucous (after December), or Kittiwake; Meadow Pipit (March); and finches possibly including Brambling (rare). Maybe a diver, rarer grebe, sea-duck, passing raptor or Rock Pipit (autumn).

BARTLEY RESERVOIR

Habitat

Bartley lies just over 5 miles (8 km) southwest of the city centre. Once this 114-acre (46 ha) water-supply reservoir was 'Mecca' for Birmingham's birdwatchers. Then Bill Oddie immortalised it in *Gone Birding* as a place totally devoid of birds! All too often this is true, but regular watching still produces a good list.

Once deep in open country, Bartley is now overshadowed by the tower blocks of Birmingham. With solid concrete banks and short grass swards fortified by a chain-link perimeter fence, it is bleak and uninviting. As the water has already been partially treated, Severn Trent Water (STW) is very sensitive about possible pollution and uses bird-scarers to dissuade gulls from roosting, with questionable success. For the same reason recreational activity was originally resisted, but sailing and windsurfing now occur.

West of the reservoir is Birmingham City Council's Bromwich Wood, a small oakwood carpeted with bluebells in spring. There are also ash, sweet chestnut, wild cherry, alder and rowan above an understorey that abounds with autumn berries on hawthorn, elder, holly, rose, honeysuckle and bramble.

Species

Winter wildfowl and gulls are the main interest, but Bartley can be agonisingly erratic. Often a couple of Common Goldeneye are all that are present during the day. Even the gull roost is unpredictable, with several thousand birds one night and none the next.

In a mild winter, a few Great Crested Grebes, Mallard, Common Pochard, Tufted Duck and Common Coot are all that can be expected, with Great Cormorants making occasional visits. Eurasian Wigeon are less regular, but small numbers are often present, and most of the other common wildfowl also appear at some time or another, albeit infrequently in ones and twos. Some species like Common Shelduck and Common Scoter are fairly regular passage migrants. Indeed, Common Scoter is almost annual in spring, late summer, or more especially autumn when ducks and immatures move overland. Hard weather can also be productive, as Bartley is deep and therefore freezes over later than most waters. As a result it acts as a refuge for wildfowl from miles around. During a prolonged freeze, a diver, Shag, one of the rarer grebes or a sea-duck is quite likely to appear and perhaps stay for several days or even weeks.

The coldest nights also attract the most roosting gulls, with up to 3,000 Black-headed, 1,000 Lesser Black-backed, 100 or so Herring and a scatter of Common and Great Black-backed Gulls. Exceptionally a Kittiwake, Mediterranean, Yellow-legged or Iceland Gull is found amongst them.

Once the wintering wildfowl and gulls have left, the reservoir is largely deserted, although Mallard breed. A few waders and terns are noted each spring and autumn, staying only for a short time if at all. This is hardly surprising, since even with a low water level the shoreline is suited only to such birds as Common Sandpiper or Rock Pipit. Nevertheless, very small numbers of the commoner waders such as Oystercatcher, Little and Great Ringed Plovers, Dunlin and Common Sandpiper do pause briefly, perhaps more often in spring than autumn, while other species occur from time to time. A few terns also pass through in April and May and again in August and September, with sometimes as many as 20. Common and Black Terns are most regular, but Arctic and even Sandwich Terns have been recorded. Small numbers of hirundines, wagtails, chats and warblers are also noted on both passages, with one or two White Wagtails a regular feature of spring. By October, as wildfowl are gathering again, parties of Meadow Pipits and Sky Larks move westwards, particularly on misty mornings. This is the most likely time to find a Rock Pipit, while wandering raptors, such as Common Buzzard and Peregrine Falcon, could appear at any time.

Bromwich Wood holds a few woodland residents including Stock Dove, Great Spotted Woodpecker, Wood Nuthatch, Eurasian Treecreeper and Eurasian Jay. In spring they are joined by warblers, including Blackcap and Garden Warbler, and by Spotted Flycatcher. The general area holds Common Kestrel, Little Owl, Common Cuckoo and breeding Yellowhammer and Reed Bunting. Green Woodpeckers are occasional visitors, while from late autumn onwards small flocks of Fieldfares, Redwings, finches and buntings can be found among the adjoining fields and hedgerows.

Bartley has a long tradition of turning up unusual birds and recent sightings of Fulmar, Stone-curlew and Richard's Pipit have helped maintain its reputation.

Timing

Water sports mostly take place at weekends, while bird-scaring in the winter seems to be erratic. Southerly winds are usually best for bringing migrants in spring, while misty mornings with an east wind are best in autumn. In winter, the reservoir holds most birds in very cold weather. Periods during or immediately after storms could bring vagrant wildfowl.

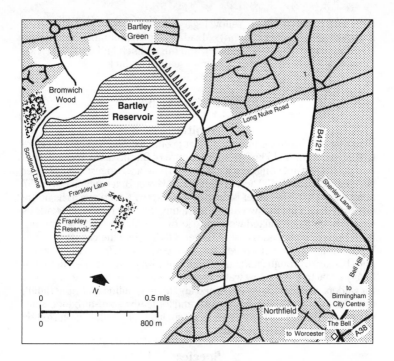

Access

Approach from the A38 Birmingham to Worcester road. Turn northwards at the traffic lights by the Bell Inn at Northfield, carry on down Bell Hill and into Shenley Lane. Continue over the next hill and turn left at the foot into Long Nuke Road. Go to the end and then either turn right to view the reservoir from the dam, or better still turn left, second right to follow Frankley Lane around the south side of the water and then right again into Scotland Lane. View the reservoir from anywhere along this lane, where parking is easy. Access points into Bromwich Wood, on the opposite side of the road, are obvious. There are bus services from Birmingham city centre to the reservoir.

Calendar

All Year: Mallard, Common Kestrel, Stock Dove, Little Owl, Green Woodpecker (scarce), Great Spotted Woodpecker, Wood Nuthatch, Eurasian Treecreeper, Eurasian Jay, Yellowhammer Reed Bunting and other common passerines.

April–September: Maybe a common wader such as Oystercatcher, Little or Great Ringed Plover, Dunlin or Common Sandpiper; perhaps terns including maybe Black; Common Cuckoo, passage hirundines, wagtails including White (spring; rare) and chats; common woodland warblers and Spotted Flycatcher. Maybe Common Scoter, passage raptor or rarity.

October–March: Great Crested Grebe, Great Cormorant (scarce), Common Shelduck (scarce), Eurasian Wigeon and maybe other common dabbling duck, Common Pochard, Tufted Duck, Common Scoter (scarce), Common Goldeneye, Common Coot; roosting gulls perhaps including Mediterranean, Yellow-legged, Iceland (from December) or Kittiwake; Sky Larks (autumn), Meadow Pipits (autumn), Rock Pipit (October; rare), Fieldfare, Redwing and mixed finch and bunting flocks. Perhaps a diver, rarer grebe or vagrant seabird or duck.

BITTELL RESERVOIRS

Habitat

Bittell Reservoirs nestle into the folds of some extremely pleasant countryside just 8 miles (13 km) from the centre of Birmingham and still within sight of the giant Longbridge car plant. There are two reservoirs, Upper Bittell which covers 100 acres (40 ha) and Lower Bittell which covers 57 acres (23 ha), but the latter is divided into two by a road across its northern corner. Linking the two reservoirs, a tiny fast-flowing stream winds its way through damp, mixed woodland known as Mill Shrub. A feeder arm from Upper Bittell passes east of Lower Bittell to join the canal.

Excluding dams, both reservoirs have gently shelving, natural shorelines backed by rough grassland where wildfowl graze. After a summer of heavy canal traffic, the low water level also exposes muddy feeding areas for waders. Both reservoirs are fished and there is sailing on Upper Bittell, but no public access except on roads and footpaths, so disturbance is not too great. Lower Bittell is quieter, more sheltered, and often preferred by wildfowl despite its smaller size.

Species

At times there is a considerable movement of birds between Bittell and Bartley, but Bittell usually carries the greater number and variety. Again winter wildfowl and gulls are the main attraction.

The commoner wildfowl often peak in late summer or early autumn, when there are typically 500 or so Canada Geese and 150–200 Mallard. Tufted Duck and Common Coot are less numerous, both peaking at 25–30 in midwinter, while Great Crested Grebes reach 20 at times. From late autumn to early spring up to 50 Common Teal and Common Pochard can be seen. Small numbers of Eurasian Wigeon, Northern Pintail, Northern Shoveler and Ruddy Duck are also present, while up to a dozen Common Goldeneye usually arrive in November and stay until the following March. Less regular are Common Shelduck, Gadwall and Goosander, though one or two appear most years as does a Garganey in spring. Sea-duck are rare, but a few Common Scoter are sometimes seen on their overland migrations, or a Greater Scaup makes a brief winter visit.

Parties of Tundra Swans are occasionally noted, usually flying over, and a few geese appear from time to time. These are usually considered to be feral birds, though some such as a party of Brent Geese or the four White-fronted and four Barnacle Geese that arrived together on one occasion could be wild. Other recent site rarities have included Red-throated and Great Northern Divers, Shag, Ring-necked Duck, Greater Scaup, Smew and Red-breasted Merganser.

Up to 3,000 gulls roost, predominantly Black-headed, but with 50 or so Lesser Black-backed and a few Herring and Common Gulls. Amongst them may be the odd Great Black-backed Gull or, with luck, a rarer Yellow-legged or Mediterranean Gull. There is also a chance of an Iceland or Glaucous Gull, though neither is as frequent as in the past.

At times Great Cormorants dive for fish, up to a dozen Grey Herons stand poised to pounce, and Common Snipe feed amongst clumps of rush and sedge. Skulking with them may be one or two Water Rails and Jack Snipe, then at dusk Woodcock come down to feed.

As the wildfowl and gulls depart at the onset of spring, thoughts turn to waders, terns and summer migrants. Early passage may bring a Kittiwake or Oystercatcher, but it is April and May before movement really peaks. Waders in spring are few and their stay brief, but Little Ringed Plover, Dunlin and Common Sandpiper are seen most years, with perhaps Great Ringed Plover, Sanderling, Eurasian Curlew and Common Redshank. Grey Plover, Bar-tailed Godwit, Whimbrel, Common Greenshank and Wood Sandpiper have also occurred at this time, while an excellent recent site record was two Avocets. Little Gulls and terns are equally sparse, but there is always the chance of a Sandwich or Little Tern as well as the more usual 'Commic' and Black Terns.

Most commoner summer migrants pass through or stay to nest. Pied Wagtails show early, sometimes with an accompanying White Wagtail, and a few Northern Wheatears and Whinchats are seen most years. Later hundreds of Common Swifts and hirundines feed over the water on cool days and a pair of Yellow Wagtails or perhaps Grasshopper Warblers may nest. The woodland along Mill Shrub holds migrant Willow Warblers, Chiffchaffs, Blackcaps and Garden Warblers plus the three resident woodpeckers, Marsh Tits, Wood Nuthatches, Eurasian Treecreepers and, in the damper parts, Willow Tits. The thick hedgerows shelter broods of Lesser Whitethroats and Bullfinches. The latter also occur in willow scrub along with Sedge Warblers and Reed Buntings, while Reed Warblers nest in the reedbeds. Tree Sparrows also nest in the area and Common Kingfishers usually raise a brood or two somewhere nearby. Breeding attempts by Spotted Flycatchers, though, are often unsuccessful. Breeding waterfowl are not outstanding, but a few Little and Great Crested Grebes, Mallard, Tufted Duck and Common Coot usually nest.

Lower water levels in autumn usually attract more waders. Passage begins in July, when Green and Common Sandpipers may reach their peak, and continues through August and September. Most of the species that pass through in spring return again, but with others such as Little Stint, Curlew Sandpiper, Ruff and Spotted Redshank which favour autumn. Again tern numbers are generally small, but Arctic and Common are regular, with sometimes a larger party of either the latter or the more erratic Black Tern. A Little or Sandwich Tern, or a Little Gull, might also appear. Passerine passage is also similar to that in spring, but with more Meadow Pipits and a better chance of Rock Pipit. Hopefully something scarcer will turn up, such as the recent three Little Egrets. Of the raptors, Peregrine Falcons are seen most years, mainly in autumn, and Red Kite, Osprey, Common Buzzard, Hobby and Merlin have all been recorded.

Although the wildfowl and gulls inevitably command attention, the variety of common passerines is good in winter too. Chaffinches, Greenfinches and a few Yellowhammers feed in nearby fields, with one or two Bramblings sometimes joining them in late autumn or early spring. In hard weather birds frequently gather around cattle and sheep troughs. The large alders along Mill Shrub are a regular haunt for flocks of Siskin and Common Redpoll, the former up to 100 strong. Parties of Bullfinches and Long-tailed Tits also frequent this sheltered valley as do Redwings and Fieldfares in late autumn and winter. One or two Grey Wagtails usually winter along the stream and sometimes stay to breed.

Timing

There are usually birds to be seen at any time of day or year. Weekends are busiest and that is when most sailing and fishing occurs. Otherwise weather is a key factor. In spring the best birds usually arrive in southerly airstreams with overcast skies, while a dry summer is often followed by a good wader passage. Autumn gales may bring something unusual, but winter wildfowl may be driven out by an extremely cold spell, when both reservoirs can freeze.

Access

Approach from the B4120 Alvechurch to Lickey Road, which skirts the southern shore of Lower Bittell. Views from this narrow road are restricted and parking is difficult, with double yellow lines around the bends, so turn northwards into the lane towards Hopwood, park on the verge and walk back to view from the main road. Alternatively continue towards Hopwood, park on the verge where the lane bends sharp right and view from the causeway. A telescope is advisable and you will be looking southwards, so beware of the position of the sun, especially in winter.

For Upper Bittell return to the bend and proceed on foot up the rough track through Mill Shrub. Do not take cars along as it is a private track. Follow the track round to the right by a small pond, cross the style ahead and view the reservoir from the top of the dam. Return to the main track, turn right past the sailing club and right again at the end to follow the North Worcestershire Path past Cofton Richards Farm to the northern shore. Again a telescope is advisable as views are distant. For permission to enter the reservoirs contact British Waterways. Continuing along this path leads to the A441 at Hopwood. Buses from Birmingham to Redditch run along this road.

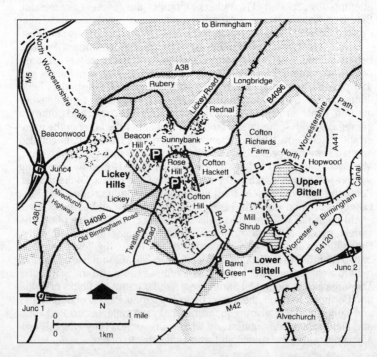

Calendar

All Year: Little and Great Crested Grebes, Mute Swan, Canada Goose, Mallard, Tufted Duck, Eurasian Sparrowhawk, Common Coot, Common Kingfisher, all three woodpeckers, Marsh and Willow Tit, Wood Nuthatch, Eurasian Treecreeper, Tree Sparrow (scarce), Bullfinch, Reed Bunting and other common passerines.

April–June: Common Shelduck (scarce), Garganey (scarce); common passage waders such as Little Ringed Plover, Dunlin and Common Sandpiper; scarcer waders such as Oystercatcher, Great Ringed Plover, Sanderling, Eurasian Curlew and Common Redshank, and rarely Grey Plover, Bar-tailed Godwit, Whimbrel, Common Greenshank and Wood Sandpiper; Little Gull (rare); terns including perhaps Sandwich, Little or Black; Common Swift (after April), hirundines; Yellow, Pied and White (scarce) Wagtail; passage chats; common scrub and woodland warblers including Grasshopper (rare), Sedge and Reed. Perhaps a passing raptor or a rarity.

July–September: Grey Heron, Common Shelduck (scarce), Garganey (scarce); Green Sandpiper and other common passage waders as in spring, scarcer waders such as Little Stint, Curlew Sandpiper, Ruff and Spotted Redshank; Little Gull (rare); and terns and common passage migrants as in spring. Perhaps a passing raptor or a rarity.

October–March: Great Cormorant (scarce), Grey Heron, Tundra Swan (rare), Common Shelduck (scarce), Eurasian Wigeon, Gadwall (scarce), Common Teal, Northern Pintail (scarce), Northern Shoveler, Common Pochard, Tufted Duck, Common Goldeneye, Goosander (scarce), Ruddy Duck, Water Rail (scarce), Jack Snipe (scarce), Common Snipe, Woodcock (scarce); roosting gulls perhaps including Mediterranean, Yellow-legged, or from December Iceland or Glaucous; Kittiwake (March), Meadow Pipit (October), Rock Pipit (October; scarce), Grey Wagtail, Fieldfare, Redwing; mixed finch and bunting flocks including Brambling (scarce); Siskin and Common Redpoll. Maybe a diver, rarer grebe, seabird, sea-duck or other unusual wildfowl.

LICKEY HILLS (see map p. 106)

Habitat

Barely 1 mile (1.6 km) to the west of Bittell Reservoirs and right on the city boundary, the Lickey Hills rise like a knife edge to a height of 956 ft (291 m). Birmingham City Council manages the hills as a Country Park. From the summits there are panoramic views across attractive, undulating countryside to the south and west, and across Birmingham to the north and east.

Some summits and hillsides, such as Beacon Hill, are open grasslands, but the majority are clothed with plantations of pine and larch interspersed with broadleaves among which oak, beech, birch and sycamore are all locally dominant. On the steeper, more open hillsides are patches of bilberry, gorse and heather. Along the valleys the more open oak canopy has a rich understorey of hazel, holly, rowan and bramble, but beneath the pines and beeches are nothing but fallen needles and leaves. There is plenty of birch scrub too, especially among the wetter areas.

The older pinewoods are mostly along the main ridge from Cofton Hill, with the larch plantations on the lower, western slopes. The best broad-leaved woods are in the valley running down from Twatling Road, at Sunnybank on the opposite side of Rose Hill and at the Worcestershire Wildlife Trust's (WWT) Beaconwood reserve.

The hills are popular for walking, horse riding and many other recreational pursuits. When snow is lying, Beacon Hill is used for skiing and sledging. Despite all this, the birdlife remains good.

Species

Few rare or unusual birds are likely, but a good range of typical woodland species makes this an ideal place for beginners. In winter it is one of the most reliable places for Brambling.

Resident songbirds like Wren, Hedge Accentor, Robin, Song Thrush, Blackbird, Blue and Great Tits, and Chaffinch are widespread and easily located once they start to sing in spring. This is also the best time to seek out the less common residents. Eurasian Treecreepers are quite numerous and well distributed both in conifers and broadleaved trees. Though less widespread, Wood Nuthatches are more obvious as they call shrilly from the canopy of mature oaks and beeches.

Woodpeckers are commoner than sometimes thought. Green Woodpeckers often seek anthills amongst the short hillside turf; but Great Spotted Woodpeckers are more arboreal, favouring the mature stands of

The raucous calls of Eurasian Jays echo through Lickey Woods

oak and beech, but often nesting in a rotting birch stump. Hardest to spot are Lesser Spotted Woodpeckers as they flutter between the topmost branches of oaks and beeches. All three are readily located by their calls. Among the other residents, the noisy Eurasian Jays, Magpies and Carrion Crows also make their presence only too apparent. Summer visitors are plentiful on the hills. Chiffchaffs and Willow Warblers return early to their territories, the former using the highest branches as song posts. Blackcaps and Garden Warblers, on the other hand, keep more to the shrub layer. Among the scarcer migrants, a few pairs of Wood Warbler are spread thinly in beech and oakwoods with little undergrowth, Tree Pipits and Common Redstarts nest here and there in small numbers, and Pied Flycatchers are recent colonists to nest boxes at Beaconwood.

The conifer woods are good for Goldcrests, Coal Tits and Common Redpolls. In irruption years, small flocks of Common Crossbills may arrive in the larch and pinewoods at any time from June onwards, sometimes passing quickly on but at other times staying for the winter.

The beechwoods, particularly those adjoining Twatling Road are good in winter, especially when there is plenty of mast for Chaffinches and Bramblings. The former regularly number up to 200, but Brambling are much more erratic. Often a handful of Great Tits and one or two Marsh Tits feed with them or join other tits such as Long-tailed in the birchwoods. Eurasian Treecreepers, Willow Tits and Lesser Spotted Woodpeckers may also be around. Streamside alders and willows attract small flocks of Common Redpoll and up to 100 Siskin.

In springtime, the resident Eurasian Sparrowhawks begin to display above the trees, and a Common Buzzard or Peregrine Falcon could sail lazily past. In autumn a migrant Ring Ouzel might visit the hills, probably where there are plenty of elder or rowan berries. Rarities are few, but a Dartford Warbler late in 1995 was one of the least expected finds for the region.

Timing

Early morning in spring is the best time to visit. For resident birds, go before the trees are in leaf, but for summer visitors wait until May. Weekdays or early Sunday mornings are generally the quietest. Avoid the hills on sunny weekend afternoons, especially in summer when they are very busy and birds become secretive. In winter, timing is less critical, though it is surprising how many people are still around.

Access

Approach from the A38 Birmingham to Worcester road. At the roundabout outside the Longbridge car plant, take Lickey Road (B4096) to the south, continue beyond the end of the dual carriageway and turn right at the roundabout into Rose Hill. Part way up the hill, on the right-hand side, is a car park from where the hills can be explored to north and south on a variety of tracks. Alternatively, continue up Rose Hill and turn left at the crossroads into Twatling Road. You can then turn left along Warren Lane to another parking area and a Visitor Centre, or follow the road to the right and park on the left-hand verge. Paths from both points lead southwards through the beech and oakwoods.

For Beaconwood, continue along Rose Hill, which becomes Old Birmingham Road, take the first right into Alvechurch Highway and then second right into Birmingham Road. The entrance to the reserve is at the end of this cul-de-sac. Access is by permit only from WWT. There are bus services from Birmingham city centre to the roundabout at the bottom of Rose Hill.

Calendar

All Year: Eurasian Sparrowhawk, Common Kestrel, Stock Dove, Tawny Owl, all three woodpeckers, Goldcrest, Marsh and Willow Tits, Wood Nuthatch, Eurasian Treecreeper, Eurasian Jay, Common Redpoll and other common woodland birds.

April–September: Common Cuckoo, Tree Pipit (scarce), Common Redstart (scarce); woodland warblers including Wood; Spotted and Pied Flycatchers; Common Crossbills (from July; irruption years). Possible passing raptor or scarce migrant such as Ring Ouzel (autumn).

October–March: Flocks of tits and finches including Brambling, Siskin and Common Crossbills (after irruptions). Maybe passing raptor.

SUTTON PARK

Habitat

Entirely surrounded by urban development, this incomparable 2500 acres (1000 ha) of heath and wood is one of the largest and finest urban parks in Europe. It has survived as it was a gift, firstly from Henry Vlll to the Bishop of Exeter, and then to the inhabitants of Sutton Coldfield. It is now run by Birmingham City Council.

The natural vegetation is a mosaic of heath, bog, marsh and wood. Across much of the park the poor, acidic soils support only heather, western gorse or heath grasses such as wavy hair-grass and mat-grass. In the wetter hollows and valleys such as Longmoor, cross-leaved heath, purple moor-grass and cotton-grass take over, with sphagnum mosses in the boggier spots. These wet places form a very important habitat for all forms of wildlife.

Oak is dominant in the older woods, but there is a lot of birch and rowan, and holly is a feature of the understorey. The older oaks harbour myriad insects, rotting birches provide a wealth of nest sites, and rowan and holly a rich harvest of autumn berries. Parts of the higher, drier ground are covered by bracken or grass heath, with scattered clumps of birch which are becoming invasive and forming open woodland. Along the streams and around the pools, particularly Bracebridge, Blackroot and Wyndley Pools, the woodland is wetter and dominated by tall alders.

Species

The main interest is passage and breeding passerines.

Movements begin with parties of Meadow Pipits and perhaps a Common Stonechat in March. Northern Wheatears and occasionally a Whinchat follow in April, while in May a migrant Hobby may glide across the heath in pursuit of insects. Sky Larks and Meadow Pipits both breed on the grassy heaths and just occasionally a non-breeding Eurasian Curlew is seen in summer. Yellowhammers, Linnets and Common Whitethroats nest amongst the gorse, with the latter also in scattered hawthorns, and Common Cuckoos call from suitable vantage points.

After the breeding season, Sky Larks, pipits and chats pass through on their return journey south. The heath can be good for Common Stonechats, with up to 10 on passage and one or two sometimes staying well into autumn. Often they are attracted to areas burnt by summer fires, as are passage Northern Wheatears and Whinchats. Once the summer visitors have gone, the open heath is largely empty save for the small resident populations of Common Pheasant and Grey and Red-legged Partridge. However, Common Kestrels and Eurasian Sparrowhawks are frequently seen at all times and seasons, with both breeding.

Half-a-dozen pairs of Reed Buntings nest in the wetter parts and on still, summer evenings three or four Common Snipe display over marshy, boggy valleys such as Longmoor. Overhead, one or two Woodcock rode, while from deep within the lush valley vegetation a Grasshopper Warbler 'reels'. Winter brings more Common Snipe, possibly a Jack Snipe (with others again in spring) and Water Rails to the marshy valleys and pool margins, while in the twilight a party of Corn Buntings might come in to roost or Woodcock drop down to the water's edge to feed.

The range of woodland species is good. Commonest and most wide-spread are Willow Warblers and Chaffinches. Mistle Thrushes, Magpies, Eurasian Jays and Carrion Crows are also numerous and widespread, with roosts of the latter reaching 500 in winter. Chiffchaffs, Blackcaps and Garden Warblers are spread throughout the older deciduous woodland, all three woodpeckers are probably present, though Lesser Spotted is elusive, and there are several pairs of Eurasian Treecreepers and Wood Nuthatches. Conversely, Spotted Flycatchers are scarce, while Wood Warblers often sing, but seldom breed. Common Redstarts formerly bred, but now only appear on passage, mainly in autumn, but Pied Flycatchers have recently held territories for the first time. Where the open heath merges into light birch woodland, the musical song of a Tree Pipit may be heard, but this is a declining species with just one or two pairs at best. In the wetter ground, Willow Tits nest in rotting tree stumps, while Marsh Tits are rarely far from mature trees. Three or four pairs of each nest most years. Flocks of Common Redpoll and Siskin join with tits to feed on birches in early autumn, but soon move to the mature alders for the rest of the winter. Neither is numerous, with 50–100 about average. A few Common Redpolls also breed, mainly in the conifers along with Coal Tits and Goldcrests. In winter, the commoner pigeons, thrushes and finches, including a few Bramblings, roost in the same plantations, while Common Crossbills are always a possibility in irruption years.

Around the many pools in summer Reed and Sedge Warblers nest regularly in the reeds and sallows, Grey Wagtails have bred on occasions, and Common Kingfishers are sometimes glimpsed darting across the water. Waterfowl are of secondary interest, but a few pairs of Great Crested Grebe, Mute Swan, Canada Goose, Mallard, Tufted Duck, Moorhen and Common Coot all nest, while Little Grebes sometimes attempt to do so. Small numbers of these species also occur in winter, augmented from time to time by the occasional Eurasian Wigeon, Common Teal, Northern Shoveler, Common Pochard, Common Goldeneye or Ruddy Duck. Less often Gadwall, Goosander or a passing Common Shelduck may drop in for a short stay. Waders are rare, but a few gulls and terns are fairly regular. Common Terns mostly occur in spring and have attempted to breed, while Black Terns sometimes appear on light easterly winds in spring or autumn.

Recent sightings of Smew in winter and both Osprey and Ring Ouzel on spring passage should stimulate more interest in this area.

Timing

Sutton Park is very popular for all kinds of casual and organised recreation from walking, exercising dogs and picnicking to road and cross-country racing. Boating and fishing are also popular. With so much activity, it pays to arrive early in the morning before everyone else, especially in spring and summer. Fortunately birds are most active then as well. In summer, a late evening visit to Longmoor or one of the other valleys can also prove worthwhile. Timing matters less in autumn and winter, but avoid major events.

Access

Sutton Park lies 0.5 miles (0.8 km) to the west of Sutton Coldfield town centre (which is on the A453 Birmingham to Tamworth road) and is surrounded by roads. There are several gates, any one of which will give reasonable access, and cars can be driven into certain parts of the park. For Longmoor Valley enter from Chester Road North (A452 Stonebridge to Brownhills road) at Banners Gate, which is at the junction with Monmouth Drive. Indeed this is as good as anywhere to begin any exploration of the wilder, more remote parts of the park. There are train and bus services to Sutton Coldfield from Birmingham, from which the park is just a short walk. A bus service also runs from Birmingham to Banners Gate.

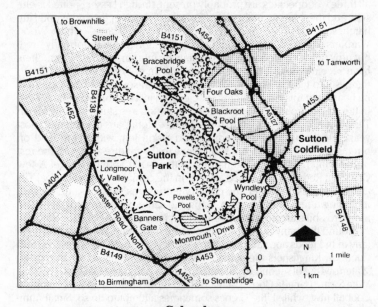

Calendar

All Year: Little Grebe (scarce), Great Crested Grebe, Mute Swan, Canada Goose, Mallard, Tufted Duck, Eurasian Sparrowhawk, Common Kestrel, Red-legged and Grey Partridges, Common Pheasant, Moorhen, Common Coot, Common Snipe, Woodcock, Common Kingfisher, all three woodpeckers (Lesser Spotted rare), Sky Lark, Grey Wagtail, Mistle Thrush, Goldcrest, Marsh and Willow Tits, Wood Nuthatch, Eurasian Treecreeper, Eurasian Jay, Linnet, Common Redpoll, Yellowhammer, Reed Bunting, Corn Bunting (occasional roost) and other common heath and woodland passerines.

March–June: Winter visitors leave by April. Meadow Pipits and Common Stonechat (scarce). From April: Hobby (scarce), Eurasian Curlew (rare), Common Tern (scarce), Black Tern (rare), Common Cuckoo, Tree Pipit (scarce), Common Redstart (scarce), Whinchat (scarce), Northern Wheatear; warblers including Grasshopper (scarce), Sedge and Reed,

Common Whitethroat and Wood Warbler (scarce); Spotted and Pied Fly-catchers (scarce). Maybe common wader, passing raptor or scarce passage migrant.

July–September. Generally quiet as summer visitors depart. Terns including perhaps Black; Whinchat, Common Stonechat, Northern Wheatear and other common passage migrants; and Common Crossbill (irruption years). Maybe common wader, passing raptor or scarce passage migrant.

October–February: Common Teal, Common Pochard; maybe Eurasian Wigeon, Northern Shoveler, Common Goldeneye or Ruddy Duck or scarcer wildfowl such as Common Sheiduck, Gadwall or Goosander; Water Rail, Jack Snipe (scarce); larks, pipits and Common Stonechat (October and November); roosting pigeons, thrushes, corvids and finches including Brambling (scarce); Siskin and Common Crossbill (after irruptions). Maybe unusual wildfowl or passing raptor.

13 THE MIDDLE TAME VALLEY

OS Landranger Maps 139 & 140

Habitat

The Middle Tame Valley lies due south of Tamworth and 9 miles (14.4 km) to the northeast of Birmingham. It contains a complex chain of pools, marshes, scrub and rough grassland some 10 miles (16 km) long. Although some of the habitats are transient, the ability of birds to move from place to place makes this one of the most important ornithological areas in the whole of the Midlands and arguably one of the most important inland areas in the country. The valley is an incongruous blend of man-made industrial areas set in pleasant countryside, yet never far from urban influence. Working from south to north the principal sites are listed below.

SHUSTOKE RESERVOIR

This is a Severn Trent Water (STW) reservoir of 100 acres (40 ha) with a steeply shelving, concrete-lined shoreline surrounded by grassy banks. Along the northern shore the River Bourne is lined with alders and conifers. There is some disturbance from sailing and game fishing, and now access to the general public. At times the reservoir acts as an important refuge for wildfowl, especially diving duck.

LADYWALK RESERVE

This 125-acre (50 ha) reserve is run jointly by PowerGen and the West Midland Bird Club (WMBC). Situated in a broad meander of the River

Tame, it consists principally of several flooded gravel pits and some old lagoons which were filled with pulverised flyash from the former power station. These now support a profuse growth of southern marsh orchids

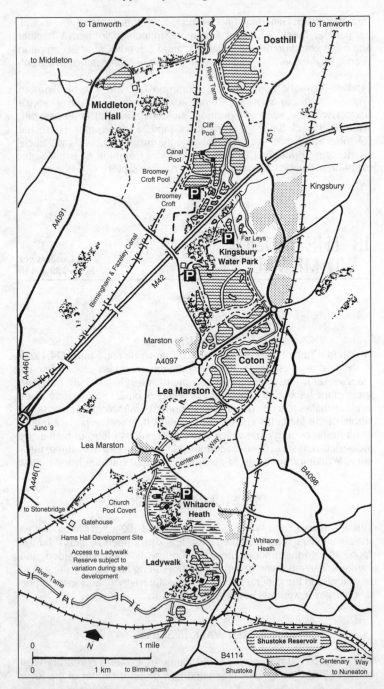

each spring. There is also a large reedbed, plenty of willow scrub, developing birch and alder woodland and well vegetated islands to provide cover for nesting and roosting birds. Four hides overlook the reserve and there are feeding stations and a scrape. There is also an educational reserve at Church Pool Covert.

WHITACRE HEATH

This small 70-acre (26 ha) Warwickshire Wildlife Trust (WWT) reserve is on the opposite bank of the river a short distance downstream of Ladywalk. It too originates from disused gravel pits. There are five pools, a scrape, dense stands of emergent and marginal vegetation, notably common reed and reedmace, willow carr, rough grassland, scrub and developing birch and alder woodland. There are four hides and a feeding station.

LEA MARSTON AND COTON

Sand and gravel extraction was used to create several large lakes along the River Tame. Originally these were to be part of a river purification scheme, but the main river presently flows only through the most westerly one, known as Lea Marston. This requires constant dredging by the Environment Agency (EA), so is unsuitable for recreational use. Being relatively undisturbed and having a long central island as a safe sanctuary, the lake is one of the main foci for wildfowl in the valley, especially diving duck. Tree planting and landscaping have still to mature and the site is presently rather bleak and open.

The future use of the eastern lakes on both sides of the river, and known as Coton, is uncertain. Meanwhile they remain as typical flooded gravel pits surrounded by rough ground that provides an abundance of weed seeds for birds in winter.

KINGSBURY WATER PARK

This is the focal point of the Tame Valley wetlands – a fascinating complex of old sand and gravel quarries reclaimed by Warwickshire County Council as a Country Park. The Water Park covers over 600 acres (250 ha) and contains more than 20 lakes and pools of various sizes. Recreational pursuits include hydroplane racing, water-skiing, sailing, windsurfing, fishing, camping, caravanning and various casual activities. Yet this is still an outstanding place for birds. The park is dissected by the M42 motorway, with most public activities and noisy pursuits kept to the south of it, leaving the north for more specialised, quieter pursuits. This includes a good nature reserve overlooked by two public hides.

The reserve area comprises one main gravel pit, known as Cliff Pool, which has several shingle islands and a small scrape. Water levels can be regulated to some extent for birds, but flooding from the main river cannot be prevented. Adjoining this pool is a restored gravel pit which provides important grazing for wildfowl. Immediately south of the nature reserve, both Broomey Croft and Canal Pools hold wildfowl, and two large islands were created in the latter specifically to encourage breeding ducks, waders and terns. In the centre of the park old silt beds and ash lagoons support a vigorous regeneration of willow and alder scrub, with some reedmace and common reed. There are also extensive areas of rough grassland, bramble and hawthorn. Further south are two large and several smaller pools which, though primarily used for active recreation, often hold good numbers of wildfowl.

MIDDLETON HALL AND DOSTHILL

At Middleton a small, reed-fringed pool and adjoining wood are administered by the Middleton Hall Trust.

East of this are extensive sand and gravel pits, some still operational. Of these, the flooded pit across the river at Dosthill is one of the largest areas of water in the valley. It is also one of the least disturbed and, with a large island for nesting and roosting, is a key site for wildfowl, waders and terns. However, planning permission is being sought to use it for water-skiing.

ALVECOTE POOLS

The WWT reserve of Alvecote Pools covers 664 acres (264 ha) situated on the Anker, a tributary of the Tame, but is included here because birds often move between it and the above sites. Colliery subsidence has created several shallow pools, with the river flowing through the three largest ones. The range of habitats includes extensive reedbeds, fen, marsh, alder and willow carr, scrub and colliery spoil heaps as well as the river and pools. The surrounding pastures flood in winter. The pools contain several old tree stumps which are much appreciated by passage terns. Generally, this is an open landscape, with treeless, prairie farming to the north, but there are a few scattered oaks, birches, alders and willows. The main Euston to Crewe railway line passes through the site and the M42 motorway skirts it to the east.

Species

The Middle Tame Valley wetlands will captivate birdwatchers at any time. For variety of breeding birds, they are unsurpassed in the Midlands, and both wintering wildfowl and passage waders are outstanding.

To strangers, perhaps the biggest surprise is to find that typical seaside quartet – Common Shelduck, Oystercatcher, Great Ringed Plover and Common Tern – all nesting just about as far from the sea as they could possibly get. Four or five broods of Common Shelduck appear most years at either Alvecote, Dosthill, Ladywalk or Kingsbury. All too often they hatch then disappear, victims of pike or other predators. The two waders fair little better. If not washed out by spring floods, two or three broods of Great Ringed Plover normally fledge, while Oystercatchers seem to be established at last after several abortive breeding attempts. In contrast, Common Terns are well established, with around 30 pairs each year producing 60 to 70 young. They can be fickle, but usually favour Dosthill or the Canal Pool at Kingsbury, with the same sites also having small colonies of Black-headed Gulls.

At least six pairs of Little Ringed Plover are spread throughout the valley. An opportunist species, it nests wherever conditions are suitable, but Coton, Dosthill, Ladywalk and Kingsbury are all regular haunts. Some half-a-dozen pairs of Common Redshank also nest at Alvecote, Dosthill, Lady-

Common Tern, Great Ringed Plover and Oystercatcher (from left to right) are among the unexpected birds breeding in the Middle Tame Valley

walk and Kingsbury, either on small islands or in damp pastures. Several pairs of Northern Lapwing complete the breeding waders of the valley.

Breeding waterfowl are just as outstanding. Little and Great Crested Grebes, Mute Swan, Greylag and Canada Geese, Mallard, Tufted Duck and Common Coot nest in varying numbers at several places each year. With them, the odd pair of Common Pochard breed at Alvecote, a few pairs of Gadwall and Northern Shoveler may be seen and several broods of Ruddy Duck emerge from the shelter of the reeds, particularly at Alvecote, Dosthill and Middleton. Common Teal nest erratically and sparingly, with Ladywalk and Whitacre Heath likely areas. These, together with Dosthill and Kingsbury, are also the most likely places to find a Garganey. A drake, or sometimes a pair, of this scarce, elusive duck appears somewhere in the valley every year and breeding has occurred.

The valley is also rich in warblers, with nine breeding species. Early in spring every thorn bush and reedbed seems to reverberate to their songs. Many of these early songsters are merely passing migrants, but there are healthy breeding populations too. Sedge and Willow Warblers are the commonest and most widespread, with other species having more exacting habitat requirements. Despite the almost total lack of woodland, Chiffchaffs, Blackcaps and the scarcer Garden Warbler still sing wherever there are a few mature trees with a dense shrub growth beneath them. Scattered thorn thickets make the ideal home for several pairs of Common Whitethroats, while Lesser Whitethroats 'rattle' from deep within the taller, thicker hawthorn hedges. Most Reed Warblers nest in the reedbeds at Alvecote and Ladywalk, but a few sing from reedmace elsewhere. Despite its general decline, half-a-dozen Grasshopper Warblers can still be heard in the valley, though their numbers vary from year to year. It is always worth listening for them in patches of bramble or damp areas of rank grass. A new arrival in the valley is Cetti's Warbler, seen at Kingsbury and Ladywalk, and raising the prospect of a tenth breeding species. The best sites for warblers are Alvecote, Ladywalk, Whitacre Heath and above all Kingsbury, where all nine species can be seen.

Some other breeding species also warrant mention. Here and there among the reedbeds Water Rails occasionally raise a brood, as do Common Kingfishers along the smaller, unpolluted streams, their numbers fluctuating with the severity of the preceding winter. A few Sand Martins also nest in the river banks and a pair of Grey Wagtails might breed as well, with more seen in winter. Two, sometimes three, species of owl nest, with Little Owls in the older hedgerow trees, Tawny Owls in the small copses and developing woodland and very sparingly a pair of Long-eared Owls too. At Kingsbury, Ladywalk (especially Church Pool Covert) and Whitacre Heath, the woodland, copses and regenerating scrub on the old silt beds hold a variety of woodland birds including Eurasian Sparrowhawk, the declining Turtle Dove, all three woodpeckers, Spotted Flycatcher, Marsh and Willow Tits, Wood Nuthatch, Eurasian Treecreeper, Eurasian Jay and Bullfinch. Finally, Common Kestrels and Common Cuckoos are widespread; Meadow Pipits, Reed Buntings and a few Yellow Wagtails nest amongst rank grass in damp meadows; and the wastelands and valley farms hold both partridges, Tree Sparrows and Yellowhammers. Even the jangling song of the once common Corn Bunting can still be heard across some open arable fields. In cool, overcast conditions, countless Common Swifts and hirundines skim across the water or hug the sheltered slopes of grassy banks in their search for flying insects.

Once the breeding season is over, return wader passage is eagerly awaited, although it is seldom so good as in spring. Alvecote, Coton, Dosthill, Ladywalk and Kingsbury can usually be relied upon for small numbers of the commoner species such as Oystercatcher, Great Ringed Plover, Dunlin, Common Redshank and Common Sandpiper. For Little Ringed Plovers and Green Sandpipers try Kingsbury or Ladywalk, where up to a dozen often gather in July or August. With them might be a more elegant, speckled Wood Sandpiper. Little Stint, Ruff, Black-tailed Godwit, Common Greenshank and Spotted Redshank are also annual visitors to the valley, though not necessarily to every site, while Grey Plover, Red Knot, Curlew Sandpiper, Bar-tailed Godwit, Whimbrel and Turnstone occur somewhere most years. Eurasian Curlew are uncommon, but a small flock around 25 roosts in the Ladywalk area from July to October and then again in February and March. Among the scarcer autumn visitors of recent years, Avocet, Temminck's Stint and Grey Phalarope are noteworthy. One or two Dunlin, Common Redshank or, less often a Common Sandpiper, may linger until December, but overwintering is rare. Green Sandpipers, however, are regular winter visitors.

By late summer there are approaching 100 Common Terns at Kingsbury and smaller numbers elsewhere in the valley, with occasionally an Arctic, Sandwich or Little Tern, or a Little Gull, as well. Exceptionally they attract the attention of a passing Arctic Skua. Black Terns tend to be spasmodic visitors, either coming in small parties or not at all. Although seldom reaching double figures, large flocks have been known. Autumn brings good numbers of hirundines, Meadow Pipits and wagtails, especially Yellow Wagtails, along with a few Northern Wheatears, Whinchats and perhaps a Common Redstart.

The Middle Tame Valley is also regionally important for Mute Swans. Birds begin to gather for their annual moult in June, often at Alvecote or Kingsbury, and by July or August a herd in excess of 100 may be in the valley. Wild swans pass along the valley too, usually parties of Tundra Swans in late autumn, winter or early spring. Alvecote, Dosthill and Kingsbury are regularly visited, but birds could easily drop into a meadow well away from the main localities. Whooper Swans have been recorded, but are extremely rare.

A huge flock of Canada Geese gathers at Kingsbury in the autumn, often accompanied by around 50 feral Greylag Geese. The vast majority of both species remain together until February or March, during which time they may attract other geese. Mostly these are single birds of dubious origin, but the occasional small party, especially of White-fronted Geese, sometimes suggests genuinely wild birds.

Winter wildfowl are impressive both in variety and number. Flocks of Mallard begin to form in late summer, followed by Common Teal and then Eurasian Wigeon. Typical peaks are 200–250 Mallard in autumn and 150–200 Common Teal in midwinter, with such numbers occurring at Alvecote, Kingsbury and Ladywalk. Eurasian Wigeon reach their peak in late winter, when up to 200 are in the Dosthill, Kingsbury–Coton and Ladywalk–Shustoke areas. The valley is very attractive to Northern Shoveler, especially in autumn when Kingsbury often holds over 100; Coton and Ladywalk are also favoured sites. One or two Northern Pintail can be seen at various times too, while Gadwall approach 30–50 at Kingsbury and Coton during late autumn. Up to 30 can also be seen at Ladywalk, with smaller numbers at Middleton and elsewhere.

Numbers of diving duck are huge, with Common Pochard often well in excess of 1,000 and both Tufted Duck and Common Coot consistently approaching that figure. Generally these enormous flocks settle in the Coton–Lea Marston area, but several hundred Common Coot occur at Kingsbury and much smaller numbers of all three species can usually be found elsewhere as well. Common Goldeneye are most numerous at Dosthill or Kingsbury, with between 50 and 100 during the winter months, but Coton and Ladywalk also hold smaller numbers. In freezing weather they often take to the river. Goosanders are scarce, with just one or two in the valley that might be seen anywhere, though they show a tendency to visit Dosthill or Shustoke to feed and Ladywalk to rest. Smew, too, are seen most winters, usually just a single bird but sometimes as many as four, with Kingsbury, Coton and Dosthill the best areas. Small numbers of Ruddy Duck also appear at most sites, with Coton having held 200. Apart from ducks, over 100 Great Crested Grebes gather, mostly at Kingsbury, 100 or more Great Cormorants assemble here or at Ladywalk, and around 30 Grey Herons come into Ladywalk of an evening to roost.

Amongst such huge concentrations, keen eyes naturally spot a few rarities. Up to five Greater Scaup are seen most years, but beware of Common Pochard hybrids looking very like pure Greater Scaup. Coton is the best site, but one or two occasionally visit Kingsbury or Ladywalk. A Ferruginous Duck has regularly visited Lea Marston in recent winters, but for how much longer remains to be seen. Other recent vagrants have included Red-throated and Great Northern Divers, the three rarer grebes, Shag, Ring-necked Duck, Common Eider and Long-tailed Duck.

Up to 10,000 Black-headed Gulls and over 1,000 Lesser Black-backed Gulls roost in the valley, often at Coton and Dosthill respectively, though site fidelity is variable. With them are a few hundred Herring and Great Black-backed Gulls. Also pre-roost flocks gather at Kingsbury and Ladywalk. Many of the gulls spend the day feeding at Packington Landfill site, some 3 miles (4.8 km) to the south. Most winters one or two Mediterranean, Yellow-legged, Iceland or Glaucous Gulls are identified.

Several Water Rails winter among reedbeds, reedmace and other marginal vegetation, notably at Alvecote, Kingsbury and Ladywalk, and very cold weather might bring them out into the open. The feeding station at Ladywalk is always a good place to try. Common Snipe also congregate, mostly at Dosthill and Alvecote, though in declining numbers with maximum counts of around 50. Jack Snipe are scarce or overlooked, but an overwintering bird is sometimes forced into the open by heavy snow or extreme cold. One or two Woodcock also occur in winter and even a Great Bittern might be seen, especially if harsh conditions persist for any length of time.

The valley is very attractive to plovers and passerines. Flocks of Northern Lapwings up to 2,000 strong are a familiar sight and a well-established flock of 500–1,000 European Golden Plover gathers on the arable fields in the Kingsbury area. Similar numbers, along with large flocks of Wood Pigeons, also occur at Alvecote. One or two Rock Pipits sometimes feed along the shorelines in October and November, particularly at Shustoke, while a few Water Pipits have become a regular autumn feature, perhaps staying throughout the winter to be joined by others in March and April. Other passerines congregate around the wealth of disturbed ground, where they feast on weed seeds. Larks, pipits, finches and Reed Buntings are the commoner species, with perhaps a sprinkle of Tree Sparrows, Yellowhammers or Corn Buntings for good measure. Spring flocks sometimes contain a handful of Bramblings. Excellent views of the resident and wintering birds can be had from the hides overlooking the feeding stations, especially at Ladywalk where good numbers of Reed Buntings and a few Tree Sparrows visit in winter and even Lesser Whitethroats in late summer. In autumn, large flocks of Redwing and Fieldfare feed along the hedgerows before moving to pastures later in winter. They frequently favour the hedges and fields alongside the canals. Parties of Common Redpoll and Siskin work their way through the alders and birches, particularly at Alvecote, Kingsbury and Ladywalk, while loose groups of Bullfinches are seen especially in autumn. Autumn also brings a few Common Stonechats, one or two of which may overwinter. Others then pass through again in February and March.

The wealth of prey attracts predators. Common Kestrels and Eurasian Sparrowhawks breed and are seen most frequently, but one or two Merlins regularly winter in the valley and might appear anywhere. Peregrine Falcons were also seen daily before Hams Hall power station was demolished, but now they are only occasional visitors outside the breeding season. At dusk a Barn Owl, still a rarity in the Midlands, might hunt a patch of rough grassland, while Short-eared Owls search for voles amongst areas of rank, tussocky grass, especially around Coton and Dosthill. In a really good year several systematically quarter the area, though just one or two are more usual. There are also four Long-eared Owl roosts, holding as many as 16 birds. Of the remaining raptors, Common Buzzards are increasing, while Hobbies and migrant Marsh Harriers and Ospreys are annual visitors. Rarer sightings have included Red Kite and Honey-buzzard.

Even in the teeth of a biting cold March wind, small parties of thrushes and Meadow Pipits moving through the valley are a sure sign that spring is on the way. Late in the month the first Oystercatchers, Little Ringed Plovers, Great Ringed Plovers, Northern Wheatears and Sand Martins may appear. They are followed in April by good numbers of Yellow Wagtails and several Pied Wagtails, with usually a couple of Whites or perhaps a Blue-headed Wagtail among them. One or two passage Whinchats, Common Redstarts, or even a Black Redstart or Ring Ouzel, could be seen too.

This is a time of great anticipation, for spring invariably brings the best birds. Among the passage waders, Dunlin and Common Sandpiper are most regular and numerous, but Grey Plover, Black-tailed Godwit, Whimbrel, Eurasian Curlew, Common Greenshank and both Green and, sparingly, Wood Sandpipers appear annually. A few Sanderlings and Turnstones also occur most years, but Ruff are more erratic with none some years, but a good flock in others. Of the scarcer waders, Red Knot, Little and Temminck's Stints, Curlew Sandpiper, Bar-tailed Godwit, Spotted Redshank and even Avocet have all been seen. With the waders may come a passage of gulls and terns. A few Kittiwakes, Little Gulls and Arctic, Common and Black Terns are seen most years. Tern numbers vary greatly, depending on the weather, with scarcely any one year, but then perhaps 50 or more the next. Just occasionally a Sandwich or Little Tern is seen and both the rarer Roseate and Caspian Terns have been recorded. Early May is usually best for waders and terns.

Among a host of highlights have been Eurasian Spoonbill, Night Heron, Little Egret and the region's first Red-breasted Flycatcher.

Timing

The beauty of this chain of wetlands is that birds disturbed from one site simply move elsewhere. Timing is not therefore especially critical. For those who like peace and quiet though, early mornings are best. Sailing on Shustoke often empties the reservoir of birds and Kingsbury gets extremely busy, even in the winter. Traffic noise from the M42 and from hydroplane racing can also be a nuisance to those trying to listen to birds. Fine weekends and Bank Holidays are the busiest times, particularly in summer.

In spring, cold or stormy weather often grounds overflying waders, terns and passerines, while a warm, southerly airstream may bring an overshooting 'southern' heron or other rarity. Common Swifts and hirundines are most numerous on cool, overcast days. Winter wildfowl are more plentiful in very cold weather, when they are also forced to concentrate into a few unfrozen spots. These conditions also bring shy species such as Water Rail and Jack Snipe into the open. At any time of year after heavy rain the whole valley complex is prone to flash flooding, which can prevent access to some parts.

Access

Leave the M42 at Junction 10 (the A5) for Alvecote, or Junction 9 (the A446) for all other sites as detailed below. The Birmingham–Tamworth bus service passes Junction 9 (for Ladywalk) and along the A4097 (for Whitacre Heath via Lea Marston village (1 mile (1.6 km); Coton and Lea Marston) and the A51 through Kingsbury (for Water Park) and Dosthill (short walk along public footpath). The Centenary Way links Shustoke, Whitacre Heath, Lea Marston, Coton and Kingsbury Water Park.

Shustoke Reservoir Take the A446 southwards and then turn eastwards at the first roundabout onto the B4114 Birmingham to Nuneaton road. Continue through Coleshill and on to Shustoke, about 2 miles (3.2 km). Turn left in the village to the reservoir, where there is a car park and footpath access to the reservoir.

Ladywalk Take the A446 southwards and then turn left in about 0.5 miles (0.8 km) towards Lea Marston. Where the road turns sharp left, continue straight ahead, over the railway line and report to the gatehouse at the entrance of the new Hams Hall development. Admittance is strictly by permit, available only to WMBC members.

Whitacre Heath Take the same route to Hams Hall, but follow the road round to the left at the entrance to Hams Hall and continue into Lea Marston village. Turn right in the village, cross over the river, pass the entrance to Lea Marston purification lake on your left (stopping to make a quick check) and over the railway line. The reserve is then on the right-hand side. Access is restricted to WWT members only and is through a locked gate.

Lea Marston and Coton Take the A4097 towards Kingsbury. Turn right at the first roundabout and continue for about 0.5 miles (0.8 km). Park on the verge, but take care as this road is busier than it looks. Lea Marston purification lake is then on the right-hand side and can be viewed from the road. Mornings are best, as later in the day you will be looking into the light. The lake itself is an operational area to which there is strictly no access. Coton, on the opposite side of the road, is also strictly private, but the pools west of the river can be viewed quite adequately from the road. Those to the east are best viewed from the public footpath which leaves the road on the left immediately before the railway bridge. Because of the distances involved, a telescope is desirable at both sites.

Kingsbury Water Park Take the A4097 towards Kingsbury, but turn left at the first roundabout. Follow the lane round to the left, pass the main entrance to the Water Park on the right, go over the motorway and then turn immediately right into a tiny lane. Take the entrance on the left signed to Broomey Croft, follow the road round to the right, leaving the caravan site on your left, pass through the lifting barriers (parking charge on exit) and continue to the car park at the end. Paths then lead northwards to the two hides. There is a whole system of paths throughout the park, many of them suitable for the disabled. For those using the main entrance, where there are toilets, a shop and cafe, Far Leys car park is the best base for exploration.

Dosthill Park in the Broomey Croft car park at Kingsbury and walk northwards along the canal towpath. The main pool, which is on the right in about 1 mile (1.6 km), can then be viewed from the public footpaths which cross the river by a temporary bridge and then divert around the water and onto the A51.

Middleton Take the A446 northwards from the M42 junction and in 1 mile (1.6 km) turn right onto the A4091 towards Tamworth. In a little over 2 miles (3.5 km), opposite a turn to Middleton Village, turn right into Middleton Hall. The Hall and the nature trail around the lake are only open to visitors on Sunday afternoons. At other times view from the road. There is also a public footpath from here that leads to Dosthill.

Alvecote Take the A5 westwards from the M42 junction and then turn right at the first roundabout into Pennine Way (B5080). Continue to the next roundabout, turn right again into Glascote Road (B5000) and then take the next turn left towards Alvecote. After about 1 mile (1.6 km) park in the Alvecote Priory picnic area on the right immediately before the

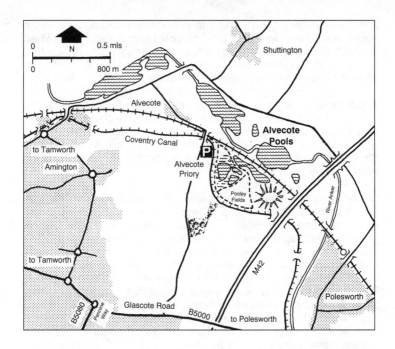

canal bridge. Cross over the canal and follow the waymarked trail to the right to explore the Pooley Field part of the reserve. For the northern area, cross over the railway bridge, pass through Alvecote village and turn either right or left at the end. Good views can then be had from this road, which passes between the larger pools. For access to the reserve itself, contact WWT. A bus service operates from Tamworth to Amington, from where it is a short walk along Shuttington Road to the pools.

Calendar

All Year: Little Grebe, Great Crested Grebe, Great Cormorant, Grey Heron, Mute Swan, Greylag Goose (feral), Canada Goose, Common Shelduck (scarce in autumn), Gadwall, Common Teal (scarce in summer), Mallard, Northern Shoveler, Common Pochard, Tufted Duck, Ruddy Duck, Eurasian Sparrowhawk, Common Kestrel, Red-legged and Grey Partridges, Water Rail, Common Coot, Northern Lapwing, Common Snipe, Black-headed Gull, Little Owl, Tawny Owl, Long-eared Owl (scarce in summer), Common Kingfisher, Meadow Pipit, Grey Wagtail, Tree Sparrow, Common Redpoll, Bullfinch, Yellowhammer, Reed Bunting, Corn Bunting, typical woodland birds and other common passerines.

March–June: Winter visitors depart by April. Garganey (scarce); Oystercatcher, Little and Great Ringed Plovers, Grey Plover, Sanderling, Dunlin, Black-tailed Godwit, Whimbrel, Eurasian Curlew (March roost), Common Redshank, Common Greenshank, Green Sandpiper, Wood Sandpiper, Common Sandpiper, Turnstone and maybe scarcer waders such as Red Knot, Little Stint, Curlew Sandpiper, Ruff, Bar-tailed Godwit and Spotted Redshank; Kittiwake (scarce), Sand Martin, Water Pipit (rare) and Northern Wheatear. From April: Hobby, Little Gull (scarce); Common Tern, Arctic and Black Terns (scarce), Sandwich and Little Terns (rare); Turtle Dove (scarce), Common Cuckoo, Common Swift (after April), hirundines; wagtails including Blue-headed (rare) and White (scarce); Black Redstart (scarce), Whinchat (scarce); warblers including Grasshopper, Sedge and Reed; Spotted Flycatcher and other common passage migrants. Maybe passing raptors. Possible rarity.

July–September: Summer visitors depart. Hobby, Garganey (scarce), Peregrine Falcon (scarce); waders as in spring, but Ruff more likely and Grey Plover, Sanderling, Whimbrel and Wood Sandpiper less so; Little Gull (scarce); Common Tern and perhaps Sandwich, Arctic, Little or Black Tern; and common passage migrants. Maybe passing raptors. Possible rarity.

October–February: Tundra Swan (scarce), Eurasian Wigeon, Northern Pintail (scarce), Greater Scaup (scarce), Common Goldeneye, Smew (scarce), Goosander (scarce), Merlin (scarce), Peregrine Falcon (scarce), European Golden Plover, Woodcock, Jack Snipe (scarce), Eurasian Curlew (October and February roost), Green Sandpiper; gulls including one or two Mediterranean, Yellow-legged, or from December Iceland or Glaucous; Barn Owl (rare), Short-eared Owl (scarce), Rock Pipit (October and November; scarce), Water Pipit (scarce), Common Stonechat (scarce), Fieldfare, Redwing, Siskin and mixed flocks of Tree Sparrows, finches and buntings including Brambling (spring; scarce). Possible diver, rarer grebe, sea-duck or unusual wildfowl. Maybe a passing raptor, late wader or rarity.

14 BENTLEY PARK, MONKS PARK AND HARTSHILL HAYES

OS Landranger Map 140

Habitat

These relics of primary oakwood are reputed to be remnants of the old Forest of Arden. Each has been much altered over the years, but Bentley Park and Monks Park have in part kept their broadleaved character. Here, on a freely draining plateau, acidic soils support oak-birch woodland with an understorey of bracken and bramble. In the wetter areas there are also ash, alder, hazel and elder, while both beech and sycamore are locally dominant.

Much of Hartshill Hayes was clear-felled and replanted with larch, pine and spruce before it became a Warwickshire County Council (WCC) Country Park. Useful pockets of broadleaved timber have survived, however, including several large oak standards that rise above former coppice. Of interest are the limes that used to be coppiced for the hat-makers of nearby Atherstone. Adjoining the Hayes is open, rough grassland and a small, mixed wood of pines and sycamore.

Species

The breeding community includes a good range of woodland birds.

Commoner residents like Wren, Hedge Accentor, Robin, Blackbird, Song Thrush, Blue and Great Tits, and Chaffinch are ubiquitous, but others are scarcer or more restricted in habitat. Eurasian Treecreepers are thinly spread and unobtrusive, though in winter they are more conspicuous as they attach themselves to wandering parties of tits. Marsh Tits often join these parties too. Wood Nuthatches are also thinly spread, mostly amongst the older oaks and beeches. Their ringing calls echo through the woods in spring; a good time also for woodpeckers. The Green Woodpecker's 'yaffle' can be heard at any time, especially in the rough pastures adjoining Hartshill Hayes. Of the other two woodpeckers, Great Spotted is commoner and easier to find with its loud drumming, while Lesser Spotted is the scarcest of the three, with its 'pee, pee, pee' call often the first indication of its presence.

Soon summer migrants add variety. Chiffchaffs come first, closely followed by Willow Warblers. The lofty oaks of Hartshill Hayes seem especially suited to Chiffchaffs, whereas the cheerful song of Willow Warblers can be heard almost everywhere. Blackcaps occur in reasonable numbers, favouring valleys with shrub growth beneath a closed canopy, but Garden Warblers are fewer and generally confined to scrub in open glades and clearings. The more open parts and woodland edges hold a few Common Whitethroats and Spotted Flycatchers. Less fastidious are Eurasian Jays and Turtle Doves, whose respective raucous screams and soft purring might emanate from broadleaved and coniferous woodland alike. The conifer plantations sustain Goldcrests and Coal Tits in plenty, along with a few pairs of Common Redpolls. In winter they are used as a roost by thrushes and finches, while in spring they are sometimes visited by flocks of Siskin or a few Bramblings.

Bentley Park and Monks Park generally have the wider range of migrants. Here a Common Redstart or Wood Warbler might be heard singing, or a Tree Pipit watched in song flight above a suitable clearing. Sometimes a passage Pied Flycatcher stays for a few days.

Overhead, Common Kestrel and Eurasian Sparrowhawk are the usual raptors, though sightings of Common Buzzard are becoming more frequent and Northern Goshawk has been seen. One or two pairs of Woodcock breed, but more are present in winter, while Little and Tawny Owls both nest in the area.

Winter is fairly quiet, but the surrounding fields can hold good flocks of thrushes, Linnets and other finches, or Northern Lapwings and, on occasions, European Golden Plover.

Timing

Early on a bright spring morning, when song is at its height, is the best time. For resident birds try April, before the leaves have opened, but for summer migrants May is best. By high summer most species are difficult to locate. Birds are active throughout the short winter days, frequently roaming together in loose flocks – rewarding when you stumble across one but frustrating otherwise. Hartshill Hayes gets busy in the afternoons, which are best avoided on fine weekends and school holidays.

Access

Bentley Park and Monks Park These are private woodlands, but some of the better areas can be seen from public rights-of-way. Do not trespass

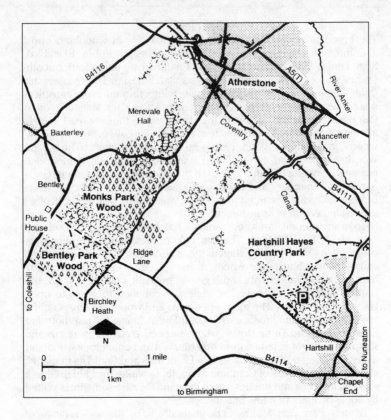

off these paths. Approach along the B4116 Atherstone–Coleshill road to Bentley, park on the verge and take the footpath opposite the public house into the wood. Follow this through to either Ridge Lane or Birchley Heath, using the road between the two to complete a circular walk. A bus service between Nuneaton and Atherstone passes through Ridge Lane village.

Hartshill Hayes Approach along the B4114 Birmingham to Nuneaton road, turning northwards in Hartshill and then left opposite the school playing field. After 0.5 miles (0.8 km) turn right into the Country Park where there is a pay-and-display car park and toilets. Follow the way-marked paths. Several buses run to Hartshill from Nuneaton.

The Centenary Way links Bentley Park and Monks Park with Hartshill Hayes.

Calendar

All Year: Eurasian Sparrowhawk, Common Buzzard (scarce), Common Kestrel, Woodcock, Little Owl, Tawny Owl, all three woodpeckers, Goldcrest, Marsh Tit, Wood Nuthatch, Eurasian Treecreeper, Eurasian Jay, Common Redpoll and other common woodland birds.

April–September: Turtle Dove (scarce), Tree Pipit (scarce), Common Redstart (scarce); scrub and woodland warblers including Wood (scarce); and Spotted Flycatcher. Perhaps a scarce migrant.

126

October–March: Northern Lapwing, European Golden Plover, Fieldfare, Redwing; finches including Brambling (March; scarce) and Siskin (March).

15 SOWE VALLEY, COVENTRY

OS Landranger
Map 140

Habitat
The Sowe Valley is a linear open space along the River Sowe through Coventry. Some 8.5 miles (13.5 km) long, it separates the eastern suburbs from the rest of the city and provides a wildlife corridor from the surrounding countryside into the city. It consists mostly of rough grassland and flood meadows, with overgrown remnants of thorn hedges and patches of scrub woodland. The prime bird areas are the colliery flash pools at Stoke Floods and Wyken Slough, and the alder woodland, scrub and grassland at Stonebridge Meadows. Coventry City Council has designated all three as Local Nature Reserves and manages them in conjunction with Warwickshire Wildlife Trust (WWT).

Wyken Slough covers 80 acres (32 ha) just south of the M6. Its colliery subsidence pool is the largest expanse of open water in Coventry and there is a small marsh with stands of reedmace. Reedmace and willow also grow around the pool, providing cover for waterfowl. The surrounding pastures were mostly severed from their original farms by the M6 and are now used only for grazing ponies. Enclosed by overgrown thorn hedges, some show remnants of ridge-and-furrow with plenty of insects, wildflowers and quaking grass.

The main feature of Stoke Floods is again a subsidence pool, but the marginal vegetation is more extensive and varied with reed-grass, yellow flag and rush in addition to reedmace. All this provides excellent cover for nesting waterfowl, whilst willow and alder scrub and a few mature oaks add to the diversity.

Stonebridge Meadows is a small reserve adjacent to the River Sowe, with acidic grassland that includes harebell, tormentil and field scabious, and wet woodland that includes a stand of mature alder.

Species
Casual visits may be disappointing, but regular watching has produced a good bird list for an urban fringe area, with some unexpected surprises.

The most characteristic birds of Wyken Slough and Stoke Floods are Canada Geese, Mallard, Moorhen and Common Coot. The last three breed in small numbers, along with one or two pairs of Great Crested and Little Grebes, Mute Swans and the occasional Ruddy Duck. Most also occur in winter, but in greater numbers, when they may be joined by Common Pochard and Tufted Duck, with Great Cormorant and Northern Shoveler in autumn. Other wildfowl are sparse, but any of Common Shelduck, Eurasian Wigeon, Common Teal, Gadwall, Common Goldeneye and Goosander might occur. Sometimes scarcer species of suspect origin, such as Ruddy Shelduck or grey geese are seen. Common King-fishers also frequent the valley. At Stoke Floods wildfowl are usually most varied as floodwaters recede.

The pool margins may also hold Water Rail and Common Snipe, while the marsh at Wyken Slough is regularly visited by Jack Snipe and is an important roost for Reed Buntings. Passage Woodcock visit the alder woodland at Stonebridge Meadows. At this time of year, the flocks of Black-headed Gulls usually contain several Common Gulls, with more species and greater numbers passing over at dusk on their way to roost at Draycote Water. Flocks of thrushes and finches, including perhaps Brambling and Siskin, also occur.

Most commoner garden and woodland residents can be found along the valley, including all three woodpeckers. Lesser Spotted Woodpeckers and Willow Tits prefer the damp alder and willow woodland. Summer migrants embrace eight species of warbler, including Reed and Sedge Warblers, Blackcap, Garden Warbler and Common Whitethroat. Most of these breed, as do half-a-dozen pairs of Reed Buntings.

Small numbers of passage migrants move through the valley, too, but few stay long. Most numerous are Common Swifts and hirundines in spring and summer then Sky Larks, pipits and chats in autumn, but records of Yellow and Grey Wagtails, Grasshopper Warbler, Ring Ouzel and Firecrest demonstrate the range that might occur. Waders are scarce, but Common Sandpipers usually appear, while species such as Oyster-catcher and Common Greenshank are occasional visitors. Common Terns are fairly regular, but other terns are only vagrants. In the past, the marsh at Wyken Slough was also used in late summer by roosting Barn Swallows, but this is now rare.

Common Kestrels are regular, Eurasian Sparrowhawk sightings are increasing, Hobbies are seen from time to time and both Common Buzzard and Merlin have occurred in autumn. Among the less expected birds to occur have been Yellow-legged Gull, Rose-ringed Parakeet and Hawfinch.

Timing

All areas are well used by local residents, so early mornings before birds have been disturbed, are invariably best.

Access

Wyken Slough Leave the M6 at Junction 3 and take the B4113 towards Longford, turning right at the next roundabout onto Bedworth Road. After 0.5 miles (0.8 km) turn left into Hurst Road and continue round a sharp left bend, when it becomes Grange Road. Take the second right into Jacker's Road, continue to the end and turn right into Alderman's Green Road. Almost immediately on the left is a small car park and Community Recycling Centre, just before Hawkesbury Field Special School. Follow the footpath from here to the pool and marsh. There are several bus services from Coventry City Centre that pass along Alderman's Green Road.

Stoke Floods Take the A428 Binley Road out of Coventry. At the junction with the A4082 turn left into Hipswell Highway, immediately right at the roundabout into Harold Road and right again into Mayflower Drive. Continue round the left bend into Harry Rose Road, turn right into Barbican Rise and park at the end, taking care not to block the road. Walk down to the pool. There are bus services from Coventry City Centre to Harry Rose Road (Stoke Hill).

Stonebridge Meadows Approach along the eastbound carriageway of the A45 between Finham and Tollbar End and park in the first lay-by after the A46 junction. A gate leads into the reserve just a few yards beyond this lay-by. The nearest bus stops are at Finham and Tollbar End, about 0.75 miles (1.2 km) from the reserve.

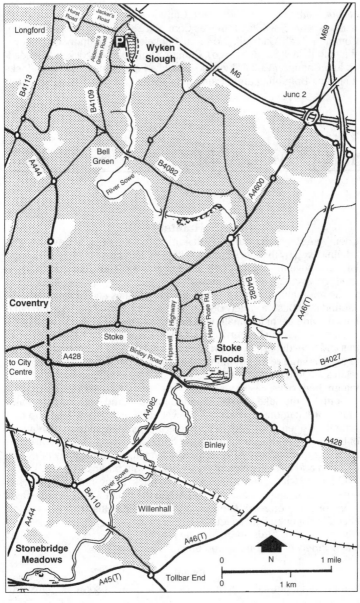

Calendar

All Year: Little and Great Crested Grebes, Mute Swan, Canada Goose, Mallard, Ruddy Duck (scarce), Eurasian Sparrowhawk, Common Kestrel, Moorhen, Common Coot, Common Kingfisher, all three woodpeckers, Willow Tit, Reed Bunting and common passerines.

April–September: Hobby (rare), Common Swift (April–August), hirundines; warblers including Sedge and Reed; and perhaps a wader like Common Sandpiper, tern or scarcer passage migrant.

October–March: Great Cormorant, Common Pochard, Tufted Duck and perhaps scarcer wildfowl such as Common Shelduck, Eurasian Wigeon, Common Teal, Gadwall, Northern Shoveler or Common Goldeneye; Water Rail, Jack Snipe (scarce), Common Snipe, Woodcock, Black-headed and Common Gulls, Sky Lark, Meadow Pipit, thrush and finch flocks including Brambling and Siskin (both scarce). Maybe a passing raptor.

16 COOMBE ABBEY

OS Landranger
Map 140

Habitat

Coombe Abbey is a Country Park 4 miles (6.4 km) east of Coventry and administered by the City Council. Within its 289 acres (117 ha) are a large lake and several smaller pools, extensive woodlands and grasslands, a small grassy heath and formal gardens.

The approach is along a broad avenue of limes and horse chestnuts. Around the house, a variety of evergreens in the formal gardens and parkland provide cover for small birds throughout the year. To the west is the main lake, with the heronry on a small, wooded island. A hide overlooks this and a feeding station, giving excellent views of many birds. Further along is a large reedbed and on the opposite bank the arable farmland retains some of its former parkland appearance, with several scattered mature trees oaks.

North of the lake, mixed deciduous woodland with mature oaks, stands of sycamore, and an area of wet alder and willow leads up to a summit of open grassland. Beyond this are yet more mature plantations of beech, sycamore, larch and Scots and Corsican pines. There are also a few hornbeams, several yews along a stream, an understorey of rhododendron and a small patch of grassy heath, with birch and gorse.

Alder and willow carr surround the old duck decoy, providing soft, rotting timber for nesting and feeding, while the boating lake nearby has a fringe of common reed. The surrounding arable fields are always worth checking for open-field species.

In addition to birds, there are harvest mice in the reeds, grass snakes and a variety of dragonflies and butterflies.

Species

The principal attraction is the heronry which, with some 50 pairs pro-

The heronry at Coombe Abbey is the largest in Warwickshire

ducing up to 100 young, is the largest in Warwickshire. Excellent views of birds at their nests can be had from the hide.

The island trees are also used by roosting Great Cormorants, with as many as 300 present in winter and display noted in spring. Some stay throughout the day, but others move away to Draycote Water to feed, returning again at dusk. Small numbers of the commoner waterfowl breed, with 20 pairs of Canada Geese and Moorhen, a dozen or so pairs of Mallard and Common Coot, 10 pairs of Great Crested Grebes and one or two pairs of Little Grebe, Mute Swan, and Tufted Duck. Northern Shoveler and Common Pochard also breed from time to time. Other riparian species include some 20 pairs of Reed Warbler in the reedbeds, one or two pairs of Sedge Warbler amongst the willow scrub, half-a-dozen pairs of Reed Bunting and a couple of pairs of Common Kingfisher. Northern Lapwings and Yellow Wagtails nest on the farmland south of the lake, where Little Owls inhabit the holes in old pollards.

Water Rails also nest sparingly, though they are more likely to be seen amongst the reeds in winter, along with a couple of dozen Common Snipe and an occasional Jack Snipe. Opposite the hide is a favoured spot for them and for any passage waders. Wildfowl, too, are more numerous and varied in winter, with up to 500 Mallard, 400 Canada Geese, 70 Greylag Geese (often accompanied by a feral Barnacle, Pink-foot or White-front), 40–50 Tufted Duck (usually on the boating lake), Eurasian Wigeon and Common Pochard. A few Common Teal are often present, too, and the pool is especially attractive to Northern Shoveler in autumn, with up to 50 regularly present and sometimes over 100. One or two Gadwall and Common Goldeneye are also likely during the winter and other wildfowl occur from time to time. Flocks of Black-headed Gulls at this time may exceed 1,000.

The woodlands hold an excellent bird community. Most commoner birds are present in good numbers, including ten pairs of Song Thrush and six of Mistle Thrush. The mature trees are especially good for the truly arboreal species, with over 30 pairs of Stock Dove, up to ten pairs of Wood Nuthatch, four pairs of Tawny Owl and three or four of Great Spotted Woodpecker. Eurasian Jays and Bullfinches also breed. Two or three pairs of Lesser Spotted Woodpecker and ten pairs of Eurasian Tree-creeper are also present. The former often nests alongside the path to the hide, drumming from the large poplars, but both species also favour the softer timber of the alder and willow carr around the old duck decoy. This is also a likely area for roding Woodcock. Six species of tit breed, with ten pairs of Marsh Tit and two of Willow Tit noteworthy. Warblers, too, are well represented, with 25 pairs of Chiffchaff, 20 of Blackcap and Willow Warbler, and four or five pairs of Garden Warbler and Common White-throat. A few Lesser Whitethroats sing from hedges on the surrounding farmland, a pair or two of Spotted Flycatchers usually settle in the park-land and the grassland and heath are frequented by Green Woodpeckers.

The surrounding farmland is also good. A few pairs of Tree Sparrows breed on Walsgrave Hill, which also attracts passage Whinchat and Northern Wheatear and can be watched from the Centenary Way (not marked on the Landranger Maps). Parties of Meadow Pipits and Sky Larks pass through in autumn and large flocks of Redwing and Fieldfare, several hundred strong, arrive from October onwards, when they are often attracted to the rich harvest of hedgerow berries. Later in the winter they turn to the fields either side of the main avenue in search of food. The same fields also hold resident Red-legged and Grey Partridges and a large wintering flock of plovers, with 1,000 Northern Lapwings and 500 European Golden Plover. Winter also brings many birds into Coombe to roost, with at times 2,000 Wood Pigeons, 200 Stock Doves, over 300 Rooks and Eurasian Jackdaws, and 200 Chaffinches. The latter settle into the rhododendrons and with them may be a few Bramblings, perhaps as many as 50. Grey Wagtails sometimes visit Smite Brook or the pools and mixed flocks of small birds move restlessly about in search of food, with a few Siskins and Common Redpolls in the birches and alders. Around 100 Blue Tits and half as many Great Tits and Goldcrests have been recorded, the latter often feeding in yews. More interestingly, a Hawfinch was recently seen briefly and a Firecrest frequented the formal gardens.

The regular raptors are Common Kestrel, Eurasian Sparrowhawk and, in summer, Hobby, but Common Buzzard is increasing and a Merlin recently wintered in the area. Waders are scarce visitors, but Common Sandpiper is regular on passage, Eurasian Curlew occur most years and a Green Sandpiper sometimes winters. Among other passage birds to have been recorded are Osprey, Ring Ouzel, Common Redstart, Wood Warbler and Pied Flycatcher. Common Terns are frequently seen in summer.

Timing

On fine summer days the park is very popular, so early morning is recommended. The Grey Herons are most active between March and June, when birdsong is also at its best. For owls and Woodcock, visit at dusk.

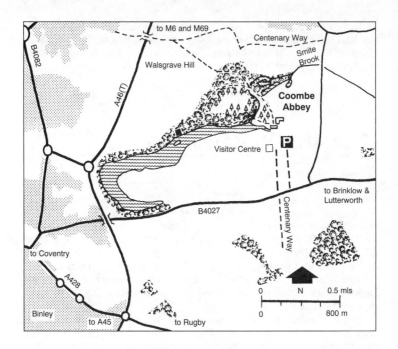

Access

The park is open daily from 7.30 am to dusk. Leave the M6 at Junction 2 (M69) and take the A4600 towards Coventry. Turn left at the third round-about in 1.25 miles (2 km) onto the B4082. Continue for another 1.25 miles (2 km) and then turn left again at the traffic lights, taking the B4027 towards Lutterworth. The entrance to the Country Park is then on the left in 1.5 miles (2.4 km). A charge is made for car parking and there is a visitor centre, toilets, shops and cafe. There are also facilities for the disabled and the hide is accessible by wheelchairs. A bus service between Coventry and Rugby passes the entrance to the park.

Calendar

All Year: Little and Great Crested Grebes, Grey Heron, Great Cormorant (scarce in summer), Mute Swan, Greylag Goose (feral), Canada Goose, Mallard, Northern Shoveler, Tufted Duck, Eurasian Sparrowhawk, Common Kestrel, Red-legged and Grey Partridges, Water Rail, Moorhen, Common Coot, Northern Lapwing, Stock Dove, Little and Tawny Owls, Common Kingfisher, all three woodpeckers, Marsh and Willow Tit, Wood Nuthatch, Eurasian Jay, Eurasian Treecreeper, Tree Sparrow, Bullfinch, Reed Bunting and other common passerines.

April–September: Hobby, Eurasian Curlew (scarce), Common Sandpiper, Common Tern, Common Swift (May–August), hirundines, Yellow Wagtail, Whinchat, Northern Wheatear, warblers including Sedge, Reed and Lesser Whitethroat; and Spotted Flycatcher. Maybe passing raptor or scarce migrant.

October–March: Eurasian Wigeon, Gadwall, Common Teal, Common Pochard, Common Goldeneye, European Golden Plover, Jack Snipe

133

(scarce), Common Snipe, Green Sandpiper (scarce), Black-headed Gull; Sky Lark and Meadow Pipit (October and November); Grey Wagtail, Fieldfare, Redwing, Siskin, Common Redpoll: and roost of pigeons, corvids and finches including Brambling (scarce). Maybe passing raptor or vagrant.

17 BRANDON MARSH

OS Landranger
Map 140

Habitat

Brandon Marsh lies on the south side of Brandon Lane, 3 miles (4.8 km) southeast of Coventry, and is the headquarters of the Warwickshire Wildlife Trust (WWT). It covers 167 acres (68 ha) of old colliery subsidence pools and gravel pits, with habitats including open water, reedbeds, willow carr, rough grassland and two small areas of woodland. Some of these have been very actively and successfully managed by local conservationists for 30 years.

The original colliery flash, known as River Pool, lies in a meander of the River Avon, to which it is connected at its western end. As a result, the water level can fluctuate markedly leaving a dry expanse of mud in summer, but flooding the surrounding marsh in winter. The eastern end has therefore been made into a separate pool, Teal Pool, where water levels can be controlled. The main body of water is Eastern Marsh Pool, which has two substantial islands to provide wildfowl with safe breeding, loafing and roosting sites. Other flooded gravel pits also have several small, well vegetated islands as sanctuaries for wildfowl, while the old silt beds are now colonised by dense growths of sallows and osiers that make ideal roost sites.

Areas of rush, sedge, reed-grass and reedmace, plus a good stand of common reed complete the habitats. Unfortunately pumping stopped with the cessation of gravel extraction and the latter is now drying out and losing its interest. However, a new reedbed is being created nearer the river. On the edge of the reserve are two small woods, which house a few woodland species that add further to the diversity of this interesting site.

Species

Wildfowl, passage waders and warblers are the main attractions.

Among the wildfowl, Common Teal are especially numerous, with around 200 in the autumn, after which there is often a slight decline before numbers approach a peak of 300 in January providing the marsh remains unfrozen. Mallard numbers, by comparison, are small, with a few breeding pairs contributing to a peak of 200 to 300 in late summer, but often only 100 or so through the winter, when a few Eurasian Wigeon can also be expected. Small numbers of Gadwall can generally be seen throughout the year, with an influx to 30–40 in winter, while Northern Shoveler are also resident, with a pair or two breeding, and influxes up to 50 in autumn and perhaps again in late winter. In some years one or two Northern Pintail appear in winter as do Common Shelduck at passage times, though numbers of the latter are poor. Garganey are also seen most years, both in spring and autumn.

Of the diving duck, Tufted Duck is generally the commonest, with numbers steadily increasing through the autumn to a winter peak of just over 100. Pairs breed very occasionally. Small numbers of Common Pochard are always present, except in high summer, but numbers seldom exceed 50 or so. A couple of Common Goldeneye or Goosander might also be expected and Smew has been seen. One or two pairs of Ruddy Duck sometimes breed and up to 50 Common Coot are usually present in autumn.

Two or three pairs of Little and Great Crested Grebes also breed and small numbers of both species are usually present in winter, while a Black-necked Grebe is occasionally seen in spring. Canada Geese are invariably around in good numbers, with some 15 breeding pairs, 300 or so in late summer and 100–200 through the winter. One or two pairs of feral Greylag Geese also breed, sustaining a small resident flock of 25–30. Sometimes other feral geese join them. Mute Swans, though, have variable breeding success and seldom number more than a dozen.

As the winter wildfowl depart, wader passage begins. The first Great Ringed Plovers, Dunlin, Little Ringed Plovers and Common Redshank are often seen in March, with one or two pairs of the latter two species settling in to breed. By April and May a steady stream of waders will be moving through. Numbers are small, but variety can be good with Common Greenshank and Green and Common Sandpipers most likely; and perhaps Ruff, Wood Sandpiper or Spotted Redshank. Less frequently seen are Oystercatcher, Black-tailed Godwit and Whimbrel, while Little and Temminck's Stints are very rare visitors.

Four or five pairs of Northern Lapwing breed and post-breeding flocks begin to form in late June. Up to 1,000 may be present on the marsh in July, when return wader passage starts. Brandon is an excellent site for Green Sandpipers and 20 or so gather by August, with sometimes twice that number. In addition, Common Sandpipers and a few Great Ringed Plovers, Dunlin, Common Greenshanks and Spotted Redshanks are generally recorded, with less often Black-tailed Godwit and Wood Sandpiper. Ruff are very irregular these days, while Oystercatcher and Little Stint are rare.

Autumn usually brings a small influx of Common Snipe, perhaps up to 30, of which some will then remain until the following spring. One or two Jack Snipe usually pass through between October and December, then return again the following March or April. Just occasionally, when the weather is mild, one remains throughout. A few Green Sandpipers often linger well into November and one or two are usually about in winter, as are a couple of Woodcock.

Terns are scarce, but one or two Common or a small party of Black Terns appear sporadically, particularly in late spring. Other terns, Kittiwakes or Little Gulls rarely appear. Of the gulls, Black-headed Gulls number around 500 in winter.

Common Kingfishers are frequent visitors at all seasons and on the East Marsh Common Cuckoos watch patiently for potential hosts. This is an excellent spot for predators too. Apart from the resident Eurasian Sparrowhawks and Common Kestrels, Hobbies are frequently around in summer, a Hen Harrier or Merlin is always a possibility in winter and Red Kite has been recorded. Sometimes a Short-eared Owl quarters the marsh during the short winter days or a roosting Long-eared Owl emerges from the marsh at dusk.

The reedbeds hold up to 30 pairs of Reed Warbler and a few breeding pairs of Water Rail. The latter, though, are much more evident in winter,

Cetti's Warblers have recently bred in the region for the first time at Brandon

especially during hard weather. The elusive Spotted Crake is a very rare visitor, but this appears to be a favoured site with several records over the years. Most occurrences have been between August and November. It is also a favoured haunt of Bearded Tits, whose periodic arrivals coincide with autumnal irruptions from the East Anglian and Continental breeding grounds. With the main reedbed drying out, recent occurrences have been few, but hopefully this will change as the new reedbed becomes established. The sallows are home to several pairs of Sedge Warbler, while at least one pair of Cetti's Warbler is now breeding. The two coverts hold most common woodland birds, including all three woodpeckers and probably one or two Woodcock in winter.

In spring the whole area is alive with birdsong as Blackcaps, Garden Warblers, Common Whitethroats and Lesser Whitethroats return to defend their territories in wood or scrub. From somewhere on the marsh the mechanical reel of a Grasshopper Warbler can usually be heard as well. Goldfinches are especially numerous in autumn, while in winter the marsh becomes a feeding and roosting ground for small flocks of thrushes, finches and buntings. Amongst them a few Common Redpolls and Siskins can usually be found in the alders of the Central Marsh, while any Goldcrest flocks are always worth checking for a rare Firecrest.

Most of the usual migrants such as Northern Wheatear, Whinchat and Yellow Wagtail pass through each spring and autumn and sometimes a scarcer one like Common Redstart or Pied Flycatcher. A big surprise recently was a Bluethroat – the first county record – but summer sightings of Savi's Warbler, Little and Great White Egrets, and an autumn Great Bittern more appropriately exemplify what an excellent marsh this is.

Timing

Timing is not too important from the disturbance point of view. Nevertheless, mornings are still the best time, especially for songsters, but remember the Nature Centre does not open until 10.00 am at weekends. In summer raptors are more active towards midday, but in winter late afternoons can also be good for raptors and owls. The open water freezes solid in hard weather, forcing many birds to forsake the area. Southerly winds in late spring or easterlies in autumn may well bring a rarity.

Access

For non-members of WWT there is an admission charge payable at the Nature Centre, which is open 9.00 am–5.00 pm Monday–Friday and 10.00 am–4.00 pm at weekends. Members can obtain access outside these hours. There are toilets in the Nature Centre. Approach from the A45 Birmingham–Coventry–Northampton road. Entry to Brandon Lane is from the eastbound carriageway only, so if you are coming from the east, go right around the roundabout at the junction with the A46 and retrace your route back towards Northampton. Brandon Lane is almost immediately on your left. The entrance to the Nature Centre is on the right in just over 1 mile (2 km). Follow the right-hand track to the car park. Paths around the reserve are shown on a map in the Nature Centre. There are five hides and a nature trail with disabled access. Buses from Coventry go to the Tollbar End roundabout (A45/A46 junction).

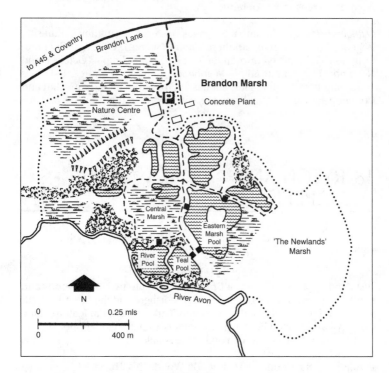

Calendar

All Year: Little and Great Crested Grebes, Mute Swan, Greylag Goose (feral), Canada Goose, Gadwall, Mallard, Northern Shoveler, Tufted

Duck, Ruddy Duck, Eurasian Sparrowhawk, Common Kestrel, Water Rail, Common Coot, Northern Lapwing, all three woodpeckers, Common Kingfisher, Cetti's Warbler, Reed Bunting and other common woodland birds and passerines.

March–June: Winter visitors depart by April. Black-necked Grebe (rare), Common Shelduck, Garganey (scarce), Hobby, Little Ringed Plover, Jack Snipe (March/April; scarce), Common Snipe (March/April), Common Redshank; other common waders such as Great Ringed Plover, Dunlin, Common Greenshank, Green and Common Sandpipers and perhaps scarcer waders such as Oystercatcher, Ruff, Black-tailed Godwit, Whimbrel, Spotted Redshank and Wood Sandpiper. From mid-April: perhaps terns mainly Common or Black, Common Cuckoo, Common Swift (after April); common passage migrants such as Yellow Wagtail, Whinchat or Northern Wheatear; hirundines and warblers including Grasshopper, Sedge, Reed and Lesser Whitethroat. Maybe scarce migrant, passing raptor or rarity.

July–September: Common Shelduck (scarce), Garganey (scarce), Hobby; common waders such as Little and Great Ringed Plovers, Dunlin, Common Redshank, Common Greenshank, Green and Common Sandpipers and perhaps scarcer waders such as Ruff, Black-tailed Godwit and Wood Sandpiper; perhaps terns, mainly Common and Black; returning passage migrants and departing summer visitors as in spring. Maybe scarce migrant, passing raptor or rarity.

October–February: Common Shelduck (scarce in autumn), Eurasian Wigeon, Common Teal, Northern Pintail (scarce), Common Pochard, Common Goldeneye, Goosander (scarce), Jack Snipe (October and November), Common Snipe, Woodcock, Long- and Short-eared Owls (rare) and flocks of thrushes, finches and buntings including Siskin and Common Redpoll. Possible scarce wildfowl or raptor. Maybe a rarity.

18 RYTON AND WAPPENBURY

OS Landranger
Map 140

Habitat

Just 2 miles (3.2 km) south of Brandon Marsh are two large woods and two former gravel pits – one restored as a fishery and the other used for landfill and then reclaimed as a Country Park. The central feature of the Country Park is Ryton Pool, which contains a small island to shelter wild-fowl. There is also a stream linking to the smaller Pagets Pool, grasslands and newly planted trees.

Adjoining the Country Park is Ryton Wood. This 210-acre (85 ha) oak-birch wood is a Warwickshire Wildlife Trust (WWT) reserve. Here, in one of the county's largest ancient woodlands, pedunculate oak predomi-nates above birch, hazel and some old coppiced small-leaved limes.

Further south, the regenerated Wappenbury Wood is another WWT reserve, where oak is again the dominant tree. Some parts have a dry, light, sandy soil with a sparse shrub layer and carpet of bracken. Others have a wet, heavy clay, with a dense, impenetrable understorey of hazel, blackthorn and rose.

A little to the north, behind Ryton-on-Dunsmore village, are two further lakes, known as Jubilee Pools, with some steep, sandy banks interspersed with a gently shelving shoreline. There is a dense growth of willow scrub around the margins and open farmland beyond.

Species

There are few outstanding species, but a good range of woodland birds and a few waterfowl.

At any time of year noisy flocks of Rooks and Eurasian Jackdaws spar with one another over Ryton Wood, or join the Carrion Crows in mobbing the resident Eurasian Sparrowhawks. In both woods, Wrens, Hedge Accentors, Robins, thrushes, tits and finches go about their daily routines. In the more mature woodland, all three woodpeckers, Wood Nuthatch, Eurasian Treecreeper and Marsh Tit can be found.

Spring sees most activity when the residents are joined by a good variety of summer visitors. In the scrub around the edges of the woods, Willow Warblers, Common Whitethroats, Blackcaps and Garden Warblers nest, while here and there Tree Pipits sing. From deep within the thick hedges that line the lanes, Lesser Whitethroats can be heard. Inside the woods Chiffchaffs sing and Eurasian Jays call noisily to one another, while Turtle Doves can still be heard in one or two places. Spotted Flycatchers also breed and any recently felled areas are always worth checking for a Grasshopper Warbler. Try listening at dusk when Woodcock will also be roding.

As well as Eurasian Sparrowhawks, Common Kestrels are regularly present and Hobbies sometimes come in summer to hunt for dragonflies. In summer the woods are quiet, but from autumn onwards nomadic parties of tits roam through sheltered areas. Small finch flocks, including Common Redpolls, can also be seen, while at dusk many more, together with corvids and thrushes, come into the woods to roost. Occasionally in winter a Woodcock is flushed from a bracken ride. Scarce or rare birds are few, but Hawfinch and Arctic Redpoll have been seen.

For their size, Ryton and Jubilee Pools hold a good range of waterfowl, with the latter often picking up birds disturbed from Brandon or Draycote. Canada Geese and a few pairs of Little and Great Crested Grebes, Mute Swan, Mallard, Tufted Duck and Common Coot nest. Numbers and variety increase in winter, with 50 or so Mallard and Tufted Duck, smaller numbers of Gadwall and Common Pochard, and often 100 or so Eurasian Wigeon at Jubilee Pools by the end of the year. A few Common Goldeneye may also be present and other common wildfowl occur irregularly. Rarities have included Black-necked Grebe, Greater Scaup and Long-tailed Duck. Winter also brings small numbers of gulls and those at Ryton Pool can be easily watched from the comfort of your car. Black-headed Gulls predominate, but a few Common Gulls pass through in spring whilst a scarcer species, such as Little or Mediterranean Gull, might be seen in autumn.

One or two of the common waders are usually seen on passage, mainly at Jubilee Pools, and if conditions are right Little Ringed Plover and Common Redshank might nest. Among the scarcer species to have been seen are Temminck's Stint and Grey Phalarope. Passage also brings an occasional tern, a few wagtails and one or two chats.

Timing

Spring is best, especially early mornings in May, but evening visits are always worthwhile for Woodcock and to check for Grasshopper Warblers. The winter bird population is often greatest when a covering of snow on the open fields forces birds into the woods to feed. All pools freeze readily, so little will be seen in icy weather.

Access

Ryton Country Park From the roundabout junction between the A423 and A445 at Ryton-on-Dunsmore follow the latter towards Leamington. The entrance to the Country Park is on the left in about 1 mile (1.6 km). There are three pay-and-display car parks, one overlooking the pool which is ideal for the disabled. Toilets are available.

Wappenbury Wood Continue on the A445, take the next turn left into Pagets Lane, fork left where the road splits and park on the verge. Proceed on foot along this private road (public footpath), past Shrubs Lodge and along the footpath into the wood. WWT has yet to finalise access arrangements with the owners of the shooting rights, but all the typical birds can be seen from this public path.

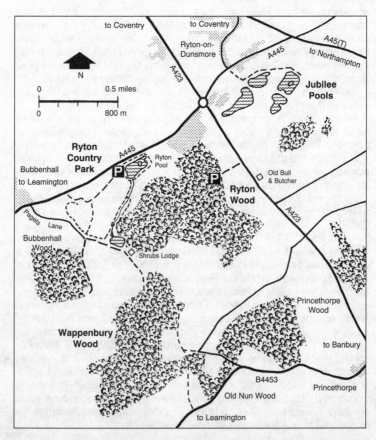

Ryton Wood Take an access track southwestwards off the A423, 0.5 miles (0.8 km) on the Banbury side of the A423/A445 roundabout, just before the Old Bull and Butcher pub. There is a small car park through a locked gate at the end of this track. Access is restricted to WWT members only.

Jubilee Pools The pools are a private fishery, but can be viewed from the east side of the A423 just on the Banbury side of the roundabout and from a public footpath at the rear of houses in Ryton-on-Dunsmore. Access to the latter is from the A445 at the south end of the village, by the last house on the east side.

There are bus services from Coventry along both the A423 and A445 giving access to all sites.

Calendar

All Year: Little and Great Crested Grebes, Mute Swan, Canada Goose, Mallard, Tufted Duck, Eurasian Sparrowhawk, Common Kestrel, Common Coot, Woodcock, all three woodpeckers, Marsh Tit, Wood Nuthatch, Eurasian Treecreeper, corvids and other common woodland birds.

April–September: Hobby (scarce), Turtle Dove (scarce), hirundines, Tree Pipit (scarce), Grasshopper Warbler (rare); scrub and woodland warblers including Lesser Whitethroat; and Spotted Flycatcher. Perhaps a passage wader or tern and commoner migrants.

October–March: Eurasian Wigeon, Gadwall, Common Pochard, Common Goldeneye (scarce); Black-headed Gull, Common Gull (March) or occasionally a rarer gull; tit flocks; Common Redpoll; and thrush, corvid and finch roosts.

19 DRAYCOTE WATER

OS Landranger
Maps 140 & 151

Habitat

Draycote Water is a water-supply reservoir administered by Severn Trent Water (STW) and lying 4 miles (6.4 km) to the southwest of Rugby. Covering 700 acres (280 ha), this is the second largest water in the region. Half of its shoreline comprises earth dams, which are grassed to landward and stone-pitched against the water to prevent erosion. The northern shoreline is most natural. It shelves quite steeply, but two or three bays are shallow and sheltered enough for marginal vegetation to establish. Of these, Toft Bay in the extreme northeastern corner is best for birds.

Recreational activity is intense, with a large sailing club, game fishing from March to October, windsurfing and other activities. Disturbance, and the lack of cover, islands or a designated reserve, severely limit the breeding species, except when the water level is lowered and islands become exposed. In all other respects, though, this is one of the best places in the region for birds.

Draycote is replenished by water pumped during winter from the nearby River Leam. Consequently it is highest in spring, so wader passage is meagre, and lowest in autumn, when most waders appear. However, this cycle produces outstanding concentrations of wildfowl from October to March. The grassy banks are also attractive to feeding wildfowl and passerines, while the latter are increasing as the many trees planted around the reservoir mature. The adjoining small sewage works discharged effluent into a marshy field with a good stand of reedmace.

Like other large waters in the region, Draycote also has a penchant for turning up rarities.

Species

Winter wildfowl are of most interest, with over 2,000 regularly present. Numbers begin to build up from September and are normally good throughout the winter, declining again the following March. Often they reach their maximum in severe weather, when smaller waters are frozen solid.

Draycote is strong in some species, but weak in others. Averaged over the years, dabbling and diving birds have been present in equal numbers. Mallard usually reach 600 in late summer or autumn and over 800 Eurasian Wigeon graze the grassy banks in winter along with 500 Common Coot. Common Teal regularly reach 500 around the turn of the year, good numbers of Gadwall are quite common in late autumn, with 25 a normal count, and up to 40 Northern Shoveler and a dozen Northern Pintail might be seen during the course of the winter. In spring and autumn, small parties of three or four Common Shelduck and one or two Garganey usually pass through.

Mute Swans and Canada Geese were once scarce and irregular, but are now well established, with a herd of 20-30 swans and post-breeding flocks of over 500 geese. Parties of Tundra Swans or a skein of White-fronted Geese are seen most years, usually between November and March. Other geese also occur on occasions, but few give any indication of being wild, though the occasional autumn flocks of Barnacle and Brent Geese may be. From Hensborough Bank, check the river meadows to the south as Eurasian Wigeon, geese and swans sometimes settle there to graze.

In recent years diving waterfowl have been less numerous. Peak counts normally occur in midwinter, when there are approaching 150 Great Crested Grebes, 300 Common Pochard, 500+ Tufted Duck and 100–150 Common Goldeneye. Goosander have increased recently and are now present throughout the winter, with as many as 50 at times. Great Cormorants have recently become established too, with 200 or more regularly to be seen. Draycote has a reputation for seabirds and scarce wildfowl. One or two Shags regularly arrive in autumn and birds have been resident throughout the year. Smew are also very consistent, with two or three usually present between November and March. Most are females or immatures, sometimes accompanied by a snow white drake. Red-breasted Mergansers are occasional visitors. This is one of the best sites in the Midlands for sea-duck. A few Greater Scaup almost invariably occur in winter; Common Scoter are fairly regular on passage; Long-tailed Ducks appear periodically; and both Common Eider and Velvet Scoter have been recorded.

Divers are another of Draycote's regulars. Great Northern Diver, especially, is virtually an annual visitor, with one or two usually arriving in November or December and sometimes staying a few weeks. Recently Red-throated Diver has been almost as consistent, but Black-throated has

Draycote is one of the more consistent haunts of Smew (foreground)
and divers, such as Great Northern

become extremely scarce. The three rarer grebes are erratic, with Red- or Black-necked Grebes being occasional spring or autumn visitors, while a Slavonian Grebe might appear in winter.

The gull roost is huge, with some 40,000 birds comprising 30,000 Black-headed Gulls, 5,000 Common Gulls, 3–4,000 Lesser Black-backs, 2–3,000 Herring and up to 300 Great Black-backed Gulls. Searching for the rarer birds therefore requires infinite patience, but this is rewarded most years by a few Mediterranean and Yellow-legged Gulls plus one or two Iceland and Glaucous Gulls. Real rarities such as Bonaparte's, Ring-billed and Sabine's Gulls have also been seen.

Midwinter sometimes brings an occasional Kittiwake or Little Gull and in recent years there has been a tendency for one or two early waders to show. By March, fishing commences and wildfowl depart. Anglers and high water levels following a winter's pumping normally portend a poor wader passage, though there are notable exceptions. In any case, birds generally pass through very rapidly, mostly in May. Great and Little Ringed Plovers, Dunlin, Common Redshank and Common Sandpiper are the more regular waders, though they only occur in single figures. Even less numerous are species such as Oystercatcher, Grey Plover, Sanderling, Red Knot, Ruff, Whimbrel, Common Greenshank and Turnstone. Others, such as the two godwits, Little Stint, Curlew Sandpiper and Wood Sandpiper are very infrequent visitors. Occasionally there is a real surprise, perhaps an Avocet, Kentish Plover, Temminck's Stint or a splendid Spotted Sandpiper in summer plumage. If the water level is low enough to expose islands, then numbers are higher and Little and Great Ringed Plovers may stay to breed along with two or three pairs of Black-headed Gull and Common Tern.

Less affected by anglers, terns and gulls are often just as interesting as waders in spring. A few Little Gulls and Kittiwakes pass through most years, while late April and early May bring the main passage of terns. Arctic and Common Terns are regular, with exceptionally parties of 50 or more of the former appearing with passing weather fronts. Black Terns also pass through, but in very erratic numbers, while Sandwich and Little Terns are even scarcer and less reliable, though one or two are sometimes seen. Of the migrant passerines, the early Meadow Pipits are followed in

April by a trickle of Northern Wheatears and a few White Wagtails and Whinchats. With luck, something like a Water Pipit, Black Redstart, Common Redstart or Pied Flycatcher might also drop in briefly. Good numbers of Yellow Wagtails also pass through and a pair or two could stay to breed. The grassy banks are good for pipits and wagtails. By May, Common Cuckoos are well established, Sedge Warblers sing from the willow scrub, a pair of Reed Warblers may take up residence, and Blackcaps, Garden Warblers, Common Whitethroats and Lesser Whitethroats can all be heard singing from scrub or thick hedges. Reed Buntings nest and a Grasshopper Warbler might also be heard from within a patch of bramble or tussocky grass.

By high summer the reservoir is deserted, save for a few broods of Mallard and Tufted Duck, and hordes of Common Swifts and hirundines feeding on myriad midges. Soon young Grey Herons begin to arrive from the nearby heronry to fish. Given a low water level, in July and August they will be joined around the shoreline by up to 20 Common Sandpipers, about 10 Little Ringed Plovers, 30 Great Ringed Plovers, 20–50 Dunlin and perhaps a solitary Green Sandpiper. This is also a favourite staging post for Common Greenshank, with two or three usually present during August and September. Other species such as Oystercatcher, Red Knot, Little Stint, Curlew Sandpiper, Ruff, Black-tailed Godwit, Common Redshank or Turnstone appear fairly regularly, with perhaps up to half-a-dozen of each and sometimes a small flock. Sanderling, Whimbrel, Spotted Redshank and Wood Sandpiper are irregular, while site rarities have included a dowitcher, Avocet, American Golden Plover, and Pectoral, Purple and Buff-breasted Sandpipers.

Later, from September to November, a few Grey Plover, or perhaps an Oystercatcher or Red Knot, might pass through, or more Dunlin arrive to stay perhaps through the winter. With them may be an overwintering Green Sandpiper or Ruff.

Autumn is not just a time for waders. Terns pass through once more on their way south. Common Terns, their numbers perhaps boosted by locally-bred birds, may top 50, while Black Terns characteristically can range from a few dozen to a few hundred. Very small numbers of Sandwich and Arctic Terns are noted most years, but Little Terns are scarcer. Three or four Little Gulls often pass through with the terns, followed later in autumn by an occasional Kittiwake. There is always the chance of an Arctic Skua (exceptionally a Long-tailed Skua) moving with the terns or an Osprey pausing to fish around the same time.

Among the migrant passerines, Northern Wheatears, Whinchats and Yellow Wagtails pass steadily through. By October, just as the last Barn Swallows and House Martins are leaving, Meadow Pipit passage is in full swing, a Rock Pipit might feed along the shoreline and the first Redwings and Fieldfares arrive. A few Siskin and Common Redpoll may also settle into the alders along the northern shore. Late autumn or winter usually produces something of interest, be it a Water Rail or Jack Snipe amidst the Common Snipe, a Common Stonechat, or perhaps a couple of Snow Buntings along one of the dams. Each year autumn gales are eagerly awaited as strong westerlies in September or October often bring a Shag, skua or other seabird.

In winter, large flocks of Northern Lapwing and European Golden Plover come from the surrounding fields to feed or roost. Flocks of Common Starlings and finches, predominantly Linnets, also resort to the shoreline or the rough, grassy banks, though numbers recently have been low. Exceptionally they are joined by a few Bramblings or even a Twite or two. A flock of Stock Doves is sometimes present, Green Woodpeckers are commonly seen and a Grey Wagtail occasionally frequents the small stream beneath Draycote dam. Common Kingfishers are scarce, usually appearing only when other waters are frozen over.

With the abundance of prey, raptors and owls are frequently seen. Eurasian Sparrowhawks and Common Kestrels are commonest, both breeding nearby, while Little Owls roost in surrounding trees. Hobbies are frequently seen from spring through to autumn, sometimes torment-ing the large flocks of hirundines. Occasionally a Marsh or Hen Harrier passes through and a Red Kite recently roosted nearby. In autumn or win-ter a Merlin, Peregrine Falcon, Long or Short-eared Owl might stay around for a while to further enliven the birdwatching at this excellent site.

Timing

Public access is restricted to a short length of the southern shore, so the main disturbance comes from sailing, windsurfing and angling. The worst times are between March and October, particularly on weekend after-noons, when sailing and fishing are both taking place. Early morning vis-its are best, but for roosting gulls, many of which come in very late, try the last hour of daylight. Extremely cold winter days often yield the highest wildfowl counts and cold nights bring the most gulls. In spring, many migrants arrive during overcast conditions with light southerly winds, but Arctic Terns and waders are more likely in strong winds and deep depres-sions and Black Terns with light easterly winds. In autumn, try a visit after a spell of easterly winds or a day or two after a vigorous depression has crossed the Atlantic.

Access

The only entrance to Draycote Water is on the right-hand side of the A426 Rugby to Southam road, almost 2 miles (3.2 km) south of Dunchurch. Access is by permit only, available on an annual basis from the fishing lodge, just before the sailing club. The sheer size of the reservoir makes a telescope essential for complete coverage.

For casual access there is a small country park on Hensborough Hill, which overlooks the reservoir from a distance. Access is the same as for the reservoir and there is a pay-and-display car park and toilets. From here a small section of shoreline can be reached on foot. There is also a pub-lic footpath which skirts the northeastern perimeter of the reservoir. However, neither offer adequate views for serious birdwatching, even with a telescope. Bus services from Rugby pass the entrance.

Calendar

All Year: Great Crested Grebe, Great Cormorant (scarce in summer), Grey Heron, Mute Swan, Canada Goose, Mallard, Tufted Duck, Eurasian Spar-rowhawk, Common Kestrel, Common Coot, Northern Lapwing, Black-headed Gull, Stock Dove, Green and Great Spotted Woodpeckers, Pied Wagtail and other common passerines.

March–June: Winter visitors depart by April. Common Shelduck (scarce), Garganey (scarce), Common Scoter (scarce); common waders such as Little and Great Ringed Plovers, Dunlin, Common Redshank, Common Sandpiper and perhaps scarcer waders such as Oystercatcher, Grey Plover, Red Knot, Sanderling, Ruff, Whimbrel, Common Greenshank and

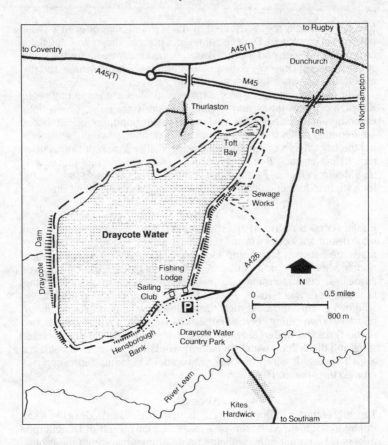

Turnstone; Little Gull (scarce), Kittiwake (scarce) and Meadow Pipit. From April, Hobby; terns including perhaps Sandwich, Little or Black; Common Cuckoo, Common Swift (after April), hirundines; wagtails including White (scarce) and Blue-headed (rare); Whinchat (scarce), Northern Wheatear and warblers including Grasshopper (scarce), Sedge, Reed and Lesser Whitethroat. Possible passing raptor, scarce passage migrant or rarity.

July–September: Common Shelduck (scarce), Common Scoter (scarce), Hobby; common waders such as Little and Great Ringed Plovers, Dunlin, Common Greenshank, Green and Common Sandpipers and perhaps scarcer waders such as Oystercatcher, Red Knot, Little Stint, Curlew Sandpiper, Ruff, Black-tailed Godwits, Common Redshank or Turnstone; Little Gull (scarce), Kittiwake (scarce); terns including perhaps Sandwich, Arctic or Little; Common Swift (July and August), hirundines, Yellow Wagtail, Whinchat (scarce), Northern Wheatear and warblers. Possible vagrant seabird, passing raptor or rarity.

October–February: Tundra Swan (scarce), White-fronted Goose (scarce), Eurasian Wigeon, Gadwall, Common Teal, Northern Pintail (scarce), Northern Shoveler, Common Pochard, Greater Scaup (scarce), Common Scoter (scarce), Common Goldeneye, Smew, Red-breasted Merganser (scarce), Goosander, Water Rail, European Golden Plover, Grey Plover (October and November; scarce), Dunlin, Ruff (scarce), Jack Snipe (scarce), Common Snipe, Green Sandpiper (scarce); gulls including one or two Mediterranean, Yellow-legged, Iceland or Glaucous (latter two from December); Little Gull and Kittiwake (autumn and January; both scarce); Short-eared Owl (scarce), Common Kingfisher (rare), Meadow Pipit (autumn), Rock Pipit (October; scarce), Grey Wagtail, Common Stonechat, Fieldfare, Redwing, Siskin, Common Redpoll and flocks of finches and buntings including Brambling (rare) and Twite (rare). Possible diver, rarer grebe, seabird, sea-duck, passing raptor or rarity.

20 UFTON FIELDS

OS Landranger
Map 151

Habitat

The 77 acres (31 ha) of Ufton Fields are a Warwickshire Wildlife Trust (WWT) reserve. Formerly limestone quarries, the site comprises a series of ridges, between which are several wet areas. There are also six larger pools of varying size and depth, some heavily enclosed by trees and others more open, showing a gradual transition from water, through reed-beds or reedmace to rush and sedge marsh, willow carr and dry scrub.

Plants and insects of limestone grassland are the primary interest, with five species of orchid and several rare or locally scarce butterflies and moths, while the pools are also good for dragonflies. Past planting has turned the centre of the reserve into a woodland of alien pines, poplars and spruce, but elsewhere natural regeneration is mostly of oak, ash, alder, willow and hawthorn.

Species

Although unlikely to produce very many birds or any great rarities, this site is important as good birdwatching habitats are extremely scarce on the heavy Lias clays of southeast Warwickshire.

The shallow, reedy pools harbour a few pairs of Little Grebe, Mallard, Common Coot and perhaps Tufted Duck, their nests and broods well concealed. In autumn they are joined by a few Common Teal and Common Snipe, and all will stay for the winter unless driven out by frost and ice. Both Grey Heron and Common Kingfisher also make sporadic visits, while Common Pochard are infrequent visitors. Water Rails are present throughout the year, being more often heard than seen in summer, but sometimes venturing into the open in winter. Waders are rare, but a Green Sandpiper or other common species might pause briefly in late summer or exceptionally spring. Late summer could also see a Hobby hunting dragonflies or harassing a pre-roost gathering of Barn Swallows and House Martins, while autumn might bring a passing raptor like Peregrine Falcon.

In autumn and winter there is often a small influx of Woodcock and thrushes congregate to roost in the blackthorn, with Blackbirds, Fieldfares and Redwings most numerous. Of the specialised feeders, Bullfinches come to feed on bramble and privet, while the alders along the western side hold mixed flocks of tits, including Long-tailed, and finches such as Goldfinch, Siskin and Common Redpoll. One or two Tree Sparrows might also be seen.

The return of spring may still bring Grasshopper, Sedge and Reed Warblers. In the past all three nested, but now they are very scarce, staying only for a short time. However, scrub and sylvan warblers such as Blackcap, Garden Warbler, Common Whitethroat, Lesser Whitethroat, Chiffchaff and Willow Warbler are well represented. One or two Common Cuckoos are usually present, a few pairs of Reed Buntings nest in the tangled vegetation and scrub and the willow carr may hold a pair of Willow Tits. Elsewhere on the reserve nest boxes are regularly used by Blue and Great Tits.

The conifers are of less value to birds, but Goldcrest, Coal Tit and perhaps Wood Pigeon, Collared Dove and Turtle Dove all nest in them, though the last named has become very scarce. Great Tits also exploit them to some extent. In winter the pines and spruce are used for roosting by finches and buntings. Just occasionally a roosting Long-eared Owl or a party of Common Crossbills might be seen. Anthills are plentiful, particularly on the dry ridges, and these attract Green Woodpeckers. Other hole-nesters breeding in the vicinity are Little and Tawny Owls and Great Spotted Woodpeckers, while Lesser Spotted might be seen outside the breeding season. Birds of prey include Common Kestrel and Eurasian Sparrowhawk. Spring or autumn might bring a passage migrant such as Common Stonechat, Whinchat, Northern Wheatear or even Pied Flycatcher, but their occurrences are very sporadic.

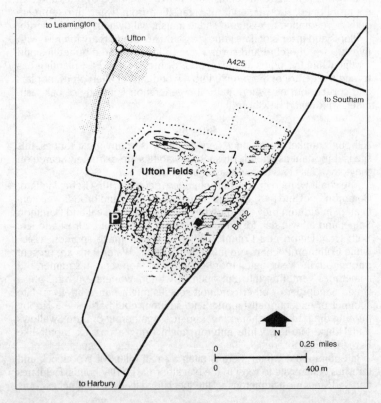

South of the reserve is a rough pasture with rushy, boggy areas that occasionally flood. In winter this sometimes attracts a few Canada Geese, Northern Lapwings, European Golden Plover or Common Snipe. Rarities are not expected, but Great Grey Shrike has occurred several times.

Timing

Early morning or evening in spring and early summer are best, particularly on calm days. High summer is generally poor for birds, but it is the best time for flowers and insects. In autumn and winter, weather is the most important consideration. Avoid wet or windy weather and be prepared for few birds in very frosty or icy conditions.

Access

Approach from the A425 Leamington to Southam (Daventry) road. At the roundabout in Ufton Village turn southwards into a small lane. Follow the lane round a sharp left-hand bend and onto the following right-hand bend, where the reserve is on the left. There is a car park on the left a few yards further on. Access is restricted to WWT members only.

Calendar

All Year: Little Grebe, Grey Heron, Canada Goose, Mallard, Tufted Duck, Eurasian Sparrowhawk (scarce in summer), Common Kestrel, Water Rail, Common Coot, Northern Lapwing, Little and Tawny Owls, Green and Great Spotted Woodpeckers, Long-tailed and Willow Tits, finches including Bullfinch, Reed Bunting and other common passerines.

April–June: Turtle Dove (scarce), Common Cuckoo, and warblers including Grasshopper, Sedge and Reed (all scarce). Perhaps common passage migrant such as Common Stonechat, Whinchat or Northern Wheatear.

July–September: Hobby (scarce), perhaps a passage wader like Green Sandpiper, Common Kingfisher, Lesser Spotted Woodpecker (rare), Barn Swallows and House Martins. Perhaps common passage migrant such as Common Stonechat, Whinchat, Northern Wheatear or Pied Flycatcher.

October–March: Common Teal, Common Pochard (scarce), European Golden Plover (scarce), Common Snipe, Woodcock, Common Kingfisher, Lesser Spotted Woodpecker (rare), thrushes including Fieldfare and Redwing, Tree Sparrow (rare), Siskin and Common Redpoll. Perhaps passing raptor.

21 UPTON WARREN

**OS Landranger
Map 150**

Habitat

Upton Warren, or the Christopher Cadbury Wetland Reserve as it is now known, is a Worcestershire Wildlife Trust (WWT) reserve of some 60 acres (24 ha) midway between Bromsgrove and Droitwich. It consists of two parts, centred respectively on the Moors Pool to the north of the River Salwarpe and the flash pools to the south.

The Moors Pool is the largest and deepest, with a good margin of sedge, rush and reedmace for nesting. Generally this pool holds most of the wildfowl. To the east is Amy's Marsh, a new scrape designed especially for waders, and at the northern end a smaller pool with stands of reedmace. Between this and Moors Pool, the hedge alongside the track is good for migrants. Willows are plentiful and a good stand of mature bankside alders line the River Salwarpe.

South of the river, the County Council uses an old gravel pit for sail training. With steep banks and little marginal vegetation, it attracts mainly Canada Geese and a few gulls and passage terns. Between here and the flash pools is a small stream lined with dense impenetrable scrub, within which a feeding station is maintained. This is particularly good for passerines in winter, while the scrub is always worth checking at migration times. Highlight of the reserve are the three shallow flash pools. These result from subsidence following underground salt extraction and their natural salinity impedes freezing, except in the very coldest weather. It also prevents vegetation growing over a large area, leaving an expanse of mud that is a great attraction to waders.

Species

Wader passage is the main interest, but there is a good variety of breeding and wintering wildfowl as well.

Wader numbers are never spectacular, but variety is good. Spring passage usually begins in March with one or two Oystercatchers, Great Ringed Plovers and Common Redshanks, and an increase in the small winter Eurasian Curlew roost to some 50 birds. Exceptionally they may be joined by an early Whimbrel, although this species is more likely to be seen in April or May. Towards the end of March or early in April the first Little Ringed Plovers arrive and soon around a dozen are running fitfully around the flashes. If conditions are right a few pairs of Northern Lapwing, Little Ringed Plover and Common Redshank attempt to breed, though the latter two often fail.

April and May see the peak passage, with up to a dozen Great Ringed Plovers and Dunlin and nearly as many Common Sandpipers. Green Sandpipers, one or two of which may have overwintered along with a few Dunlin, are also regular in small numbers. Most springs bring Black-tailed Godwits and Common Greenshanks, with less regularly Sanderling and occasionally Grey Plover, Little Stint, Bar-tailed Godwit, Spotted Redshank, Wood Sandpiper or Turnstone. Exceptionally a Temminck's Stint appears in May, this seemingly being a favoured site for this erratic species. A few terns often come with the waders. Most consistent are Common Terns, a pair or two of which attempt to breed on the tern raft provided, but Arctic and Black Terns appear most years in typically variable numbers. Little Terns and Little Gulls, however, are only occasional visitors.

Normally it is July before the first waders begin to move south, but after a poor summer a few may return in June. Black-tailed Godwits and Green and Common Sandpipers are usually first to show. By late July and August anything up to 20 Green Sandpipers may have gathered. Counting can be difficult, as they prefer to feed along the flowing stream where they are hidden from view. Common Sandpipers are less numerous, seldom exceeding a dozen, and similar numbers of Little Ringed Plovers, mostly the resident birds, are around until the beginning of September. Passage

*Upton Warren is excellent for passage waders such as
Green Sandpiper (left) and Common Sandpiper*

also brings a dozen or so Dunlin, Great Ringed Plover and Ruff, with smaller numbers of Whimbrel, Common and Spotted Redshank and Common Greenshank. There is also a chance of Oystercatcher, Little Stint, Curlew Sandpiper, Bar-tailed Godwit, Wood Sandpiper or Turnstone, while Eurasian Curlew return again, with perhaps 100 roosting.

August and September usually bring a few terns or a Little Gull. Passage is generally very weak, but small flocks of Arctic, Common and Black Terns sometimes appear and Sandwich Tern might be seen. Even an Arctic Skua could pass through at this time. About the same time Common Snipe begin to congregate around the muddy, rushy margins. By November, 50 or more may be present, accompanied by four or five Jack Snipe. Provided there is no prolonged frost, several Common Snipe, one or two Jack Snipe, Woodcock or even a Ruff will winter, being joined in March by a few more passage birds. Jack Snipe are very secretive, however, and seldom seen unless forced out into the open by a cold snap. Water Rails are more confiding, with one of several wintering birds quite often coming to the feeding station.

On the fields, flocks of Northern Lapwings often exceed 2,000, with several European Golden Plover amongst them. All the commoner gulls occur, but only in small numbers, which makes it easier to pick out any Mediterranean, Yellow-legged or Iceland Gulls that are occasionally with them. Sometimes a Kittiwake or Little Gull appears in midwinter

Both Water Rails and Common Kingfishers breed, as do several pairs of Great Crested Grebes, Canada Geese, Mallard, Common Coot, and one or two pairs of Little Grebe, Mute Swan and Tufted and Ruddy Ducks. Garganey also appear annually on spring and autumn passage. Post-breeding flocks of wildfowl start to assemble in late summer, when Canada Geese exceed 300 and Mallard often approach the same figure. Other species peak somewhat later, with around 100 Common Teal and Northern Shoveler at some time between September and the new year. A handful of Common Shelduck and Gadwall also occur, mainly in autumn and spring; a few Northern Pintail and Eurasian Wigeon can be expected during the winter, and small numbers of Tundra Swans usually pass through at some time between October and March.

Common Pochard is the most numerous diving duck, with 50 or more often present towards the year end and exceptionally twice that number. By comparison scarcely any Tufted Duck winter, though spring often brings an increase to 20–30. Several Common Coot are also present and Great Cormorants can be seen throughout the year, with up to 20 in autumn. Other diving duck are scarce and irregular, but one or two Common Goldeneye or a Goosander appear most years and Common Scoter make rare appearances in spring and autumn. Autumn and winter sometimes bring one of the rarer grebes or duck, or even a Shag.

Both Little Owl and Green Woodpecker are resident, often frequenting the orchard behind the flash pools, while Eurasian Sparrowhawk and Common Kestrel both breed in the vicinity. Peregrine Falcons are sighted quite regularly and a Barn Owl sometimes occurs outside the breeding season.

Spring migration occurs on a broad front across the valleys of the Severn and Avon and cool, wet weather often produces a 'fall' of Common Swifts, hirundines and Pied and Yellow Wagtails. With the wagtails are always a few White and sometimes a Blue-headed. Small numbers of Water Pipits, Northern Wheatears, Whinchats and Common Redstarts are also regularly noted and there is always a chance of Ring Ouzel or Pied Flycatcher. Spring brings a variety of raptors, with records of Red Kite, Marsh and Montagu's Harriers, and Osprey most notable.

Among the rushy margins, Yellow Wagtails and Grasshopper Warblers nest, though the latter is irregular nowadays. Several pairs of Reed Buntings, Sedge Warblers and Reed Warblers also breed and Cetti's Warbler has been seen on and off for a year or two. Other warblers, woodland and garden birds add their songs too, including Lesser Whitethroats from within tall hedges and dense thickets and Turtle Doves from hawthorn and elder. This is one of the most consistent sites for Hobby, with frequent sightings between April and September, especially in late summer when birds come at dusk to prey on the Barn Swallows and House Martins.

Most of the spring migrants pass through again in autumn, but in addition a Common Stonechat or Rock Pipit might appear, with the former perhaps again in February or March. Less often, a Merlin or Short-eared Owl hunts across the reserve or a Firecrest shelters in a hedge. By October the first flocks of Redwing and Fieldfare appear along the hedgerows and parties of Siskin and Common Redpoll settle into the alders for the winter. Flocks of larks, pipits and finches are joined in their search for weed seeds by a few Yellowhammers. Many are drawn to the feeding station, which is always a good place to study the commoner passerines and look out for something like a Brambling amongst them.

Recent star attractions have included Common Quail, Red-rumped Swallow and Bearded Tit.

Timing

Disturbance is not a problem, but weather is important. Being shallow, the pools will freeze in very cold weather despite their salinity, forcing wildfowl to move elsewhere. Spring migrants are more numerous in cool, wet weather and rarities often occur with southerly or southeasterly winds and overcast skies. Autumn migration is best after prolonged easterly winds or westerly gales. At both seasons early morning is best, especially after overnight rain, as some birds stop very briefly. The flash pools attract waders even after a wet summer. On windy days small birds tend to hide in the thick hedges.

Access

The reserve lies east of the A38 Birmingham to Worcester road, midway between Bromsgrove and Droitwich. It is owned by the WWT and access is restricted to members only. For the Moors Pool turn off the A38 by the AA telephone box onto a track which leads to a small car park on the left-hand side. Park here and follow the paths to the hides. For the flash pools, parking is available at certain times within the sail-training centre (opposite the nursery garden) courtesy of the County Council. From here follow the path between the two buildings and alongside the gravel pit until you see the WWT sign. Then turn right down the bank, cross the stream and continue to the hides. The Birmingham–Worcester bus service passes the site.

Calendar

All Year: Great Crested Grebe, Great Cormorant (scarce in summer), Mute Swan, Canada Goose, Mallard, Tufted Duck, Ruddy Duck, Eurasian Sparrowhawk, Common Kestrel, Water Rail, Common Coot, Northern Lapwing, Little Owl, Common Kingfisher, Green Woodpecker, Cetti's Warbler (rare), Reed Bunting and common passerines.

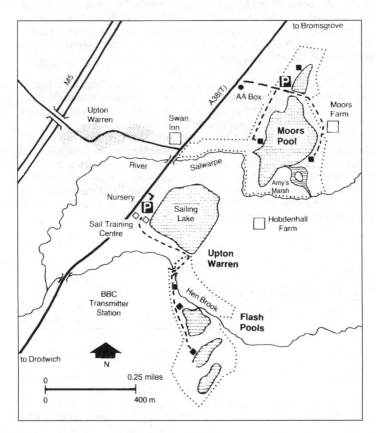

March–June: Winter visitors depart by April. Little Grebe, Common Shelduck, Garganey; common waders such as Oystercatcher, Little and Great Ringed Plovers, Dunlin, Jack and Common Snipe (March/April), Black-tailed Godwit, Whimbrel, Eurasian Curlew, Common Redshank, Common Greenshank, Green and Common Sandpipers and perhaps scarcer waders such as Grey Plover, Sanderling, Little Stint, Bar-tailed Godwit, Spotted Redshank, Wood Sandpiper or Turnstone. From April: Hobby, Little Gull (rare); Common Tern and maybe Arctic and Black Terns (scarce); Turtle Dove (scarce), Common Cuckoo, Common Swift (after April), hirundines, Water Pipit (scarce); wagtails including White (scarce) and possibly Blue-headed (rare); passage migrants such as Common Redstart, Whinchat and Northern Wheatear; and warblers including Grasshopper (scarce), Sedge, Reed and Lesser Whitethroat. Perhaps passing raptor, scarce migrant or rarity.

July–September: Little Grebe, Common Shelduck, Garganey, Hobby, Peregrine Falcon (scarce); common waders such as Little and Great Ringed Plovers, Dunlin, Ruff, Common Snipe (August and September), Black tailed Godwit, Whimbrel, Eurasian Curlew, Spotted and Common Redshanks, Common Greenshank, Green and Common Sandpipers and perhaps scarcer waders such as Oystercatcher, Little Stint, Curlew Sandpiper, Bar-tailed Godwit, Wood Sandpiper and Turnstone; Little Gull (rare), maybe terns including Sandwich (rare); departing summer visitors such as Common Swift (scarce September), hirundines, Yellow Wagtail and warblers; and common passage migrants such as Common Redstart, Whinchat and Northern Wheatear. Perhaps vagrant seabird, passing raptor, scarce migrant or rarity.

October–February: Tundra Swan (scarce), Common Shelduck (early/late), Eurasian Wigeon, Gadwall (scarce; midwinter), Common Teal, Northern Pintail (scarce), Northern Shoveler, Common Pochard, Common Goldeneye (scarce), Goosander (scarce), European Golden Plover, Dunlin (scarce), Jack Snipe, Common Snipe, Woodcock (scarce), Eurasian Curlew; gulls including perhaps Mediterranean, Yellow-legged or Iceland (all scarce); Little Gull and Kittiwake (midwinter; scarce), Barn Owl (rare), Rock Pipit (autumn; scarce), Common Stonechat (early or late), Fieldfare, Redwing, Siskin, Common Redpoll and mixed flocks of finches and buntings including Brambling (scarce) and Yellowhammer. Possible seabird or sea-duck, passing raptor or rarity.

22 PIPERS HILL AND TRENCH WOOD

OS Landranger
Map 150

Habitat

Close to Upton Warren are two woods, Pipers Hill and Trench Wood, which are typical of many to be found in what was once the Forest of

Feckenham. Both are Worcestershire Wildlife Trust (WWT) reserves. Pipers Hill, sometimes known as Dodderhill Common, comprises 40 acres (16 ha) of common land on a plateau which falls away steeply to the west. Within the wood are one or two small pools. The trees are mainly beech, oak and sweet chestnut, many of them very old and therefore attractive to hole-nesting species. Across the plateau the tall beeches shade out all undergrowth save for a patchy cover of bramble, but there is a much better developed shrub layer towards the foot of the west-facing slope.

The 107 acres (43 ha) of Trench Wood are quite different. Although some mature oaks still survive from the traditional coppice-with-standards oakwood, much of the wood was felled by the former owners and replanted with an unusual blend of oak, birch and alder. Some of the rides are floristically rich.

Species

Between them these two woods hold a good range of woodland birds. Pipers Hill is generally the better for arboreal species and Trench Wood for scrub species.

The sparse shrub layer at Pipers Hill restricts the breeding community to birds nesting either in the trees or on the ground. In addition to numerous pairs of Blue and Great Tits, the holes and cavities of the larger, older trees hold Little and Tawny Owls, good numbers of Stock Dove, all three woodpeckers and Wood Nuthatch. Eurasian Treecreepers and Tree Sparrows also breed, although the latter are declining. Of the summer visitors, one or two holes may be occupied by Common Redstarts, while Chiffchaffs, Willow Warblers and perhaps a pair or two of Wood Warblers nest on the ground. Along the western slope, common residents such as Wren, Hedge Accentor, Robin and Blackbird are joined in summer by Garden Warbler, Blackcap and the occasional pair of Turtle Doves. Spotted Flycatchers also occur sparingly, with often a pair or two around one of the pools. Winter birdlife is less varied, but the customary parties of tits and finches wander through the wood in search of food. In particular Great and Marsh Tits, Chaffinches and sometimes Brambling search among the fallen leaves for beechmast.

The commoner woodland birds of Pipers Hill, including Turtle Dove, Willow and Marsh Tits, can also be seen at Trench Wood. This is also a good place for Eurasian Sparrowhawks, while Woodcock can be seen roding in summer and are occasionally flushed in winter. In summer, Garden Warblers and Blackcaps sing from the developing woodland, while a pair or two of Tree Pipits or Grasshopper Warblers might be found around suitable clearings or rough areas. Once this was a stronghold of Rufous Nightingales, but now only one or two birds sing. Winter brings feeding flocks of Goldcrests, Common Redpoll and Siskin, especially to the birches and alders; large numbers of thrushes, including Fieldfare and Redwing, to roost in the dense undergrowth; and sometimes flocks of finches with a few Tree Sparrows and Yellowhammers to the surrounding area.

Neither wood is noted for unusual species, but a Hobby occasionally passes overhead in summer and a Wood Lark was discovered at Trench one autumn.

Timing

Pipers Hill is popular and quite busy at times. Trench Wood is relatively quiet and undisturbed. Both are best in early morning in late April or early

May, but a visit to Trench Wood on a warm, still spring evening is always worthwhile, with the chance of Rufous Nightingale, Grasshopper Warbler and roding Woodcock. As with any woodland, wet and windy weather are best avoided.

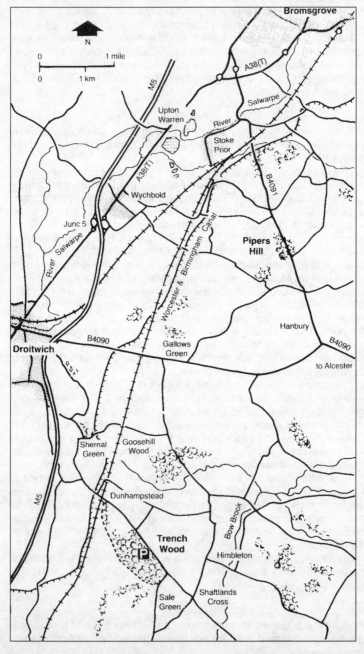

Access

Pipers Hill The common is crossed by the B4091 Bromsgrove to Alcester road some 2 miles (3.2 km) south of Stoke Prior. Park on the edge of the wood and explore on foot. Please do not drive cars too far into the wood.

Trench Wood Approach from the B4090 Droitwich to Alcester road. At Gallows Green, 2 miles (3.2 km) east of Droitwich, turn southwards towards Himbleton. Continue along this twisting lane for 3.5 miles (5.6 km), past the edge of Himbleton, until you come to the crossroads at Shaftlands Cross. Turn right here, continue for about 0.5 miles (0.8 km) and there is a small car park on the left inside the wood. Access to the wood is restricted to WWT members only.

Calendar

All Year: Eurasian Sparrowhawk, Woodcock, Stock Dove, Little Owl, Tawny Owl, all three woodpeckers, Goldcrest, Marsh and Willow Tits, Wood Nuthatch, Eurasian Treecreeper, Tree Sparrow (scarce), Yellow-hammer and other common woodland birds.

April–September: Hobby (scarce), Turtle Dove (scarce), Tree Pipit (scarce), Rufous Nightingale (scarce), Common Redstart (scarce), Grass-hopper Warbler (scarce), most scrub and woodland warblers including Wood (scarce), and Spotted Flycatcher.

October–March: Flocks of thrushes including Fieldfare and Redwing; par-ties of tits and finches including Siskin, Common Redpoll and Brambling (scarce).

23 BREDON HILL AND THE AVON VALLEY

OS Landranger
Map 150

Habitat

Bredon Hill is a limestone outlier of the Cotswolds. Some 3 miles (4.8 km) long and 961 ft (293 m) high, its great dome squats like a recumbent ani-mal, dominating the landscape for miles across the Avon Valley.

Nestling into the foot slopes are picturesque villages of black-and-white cottages in the north and Cotswold stone in the south. The gentler, south-ern slopes are often under arable cultivation or grass leys grazed by sheep. The steeper northern and western slopes are used as rough graz-ing, with the steepest parts clothed in scrub or mixed woodland. Parklands with their specimen ash, chestnuts and oaks, and one or two stone quarries complete a diverse habitat. The best areas for birds are on the summit around the tower, the 'slip' between the tower and Bredon's Norton and the fields west of Great Hill, above Ashton-under-Hill.

North and west of Bredon Hill, the Avon meanders across its wide floodplain. Here the climate is humid, plant growth luxuriant and insects abundant. The river is sluggish, with emergent vegetation including common reed, and the banks are lined with a profusion of nettles, meadowsweet, pollarded willows and remnants of osier beds. It is navigable throughout, with locks by-passing the weirs, creating small, densely vegetated islands. Many riverside meadows were once Lammas lands, or common hay meadows, and waders still breed in a few unimproved ones, except when flash summer floods wash out their nests. Winter flooding, though, provides ideal feeding conditions for large numbers of wildfowl and waders.

At Bredon's Hardwick, gravel extraction has created flooded pits, one of which is now part of a leisure park. These provide a valuable additional habitat for winter wildfowl and passage waders, being ideally located to receive migrants that are funnelled up the Bristol Channel in spring. The southernmost pool, with its two or three islands and regenerating willow, holds most birds.

Six miles (9.6 km) to the north, the lakes, mixed woodland and parkland of Croome Park add yet more diversity. The park, which was 'Capability' Brown's first independent commission, has recently been acquired by the National Trust (NT) and is being restored.

Species

Bredon Hill is not a place for large numbers of birds. Rather it is a peaceful stretch of countryside in which to enjoy many of the commoner species. Nonetheless, it is a good migration watchpoint when conditions are right, with always a chance of something unusual. The Avon Valley is well known for its summer breeding birds and is developing a reputation for its winter and passage wildfowl and waders.

Above the hilltop fields, Northern Lapwings display, Sky Larks and Meadow Pipits sing, Common Pheasants crow and coveys of Red-legged and Grey Partridges scurry between the crops. In the background are noisy Rooks and Eurasian Jackdaws, the latter often nesting in quarries. The larger holes in old parkland trees are used by nesting Little and Tawny Owls, Stock Doves and Eurasian Jackdaws, while tits and Wood Nuthatches occupy the smaller ones made by Green and Great Spotted Woodpeckers. Lesser Spotted Woodpeckers occur sparingly around the foothills.

The hillside scrub and woodlands hold good numbers of breeding warblers, including Chiffchaffs, Willow Warblers, Blackcaps, Garden Warblers, Common Whitethroats and Lesser Whitethroats. Spotted Flycatchers make sorties after insects, as do half-a-dozen pairs of Common Redstarts that nest on the steeper hillsides. Here and there a Grasshopper Warbler might be heard singing, while among the residents are several pairs of Marsh Tits and Yellowhammers. Tree Pipits also breed and Common Buzzards or a Hobby are often seen overhead. The conifer plantations may hold a few Siskin in spring.

In autumn, Bredon Hill is a good place to watch diurnal migration, as small flocks follow the Cotswold Scarp on their journeys south. Passage begins in September, when Sky Larks, Meadow Pipits, Yellow Wagtails, Yellowhammers and finches are on the move. It then reaches its climax in October, when sizeable flocks of Common Starlings, Fieldfares, Redwings, Chaffinches, Greenfinches and Yellowhammers come from the north and east for the winter. Flocks are largest and most frequent during the first two hours of daylight, and are most evident on still, misty mornings. Some drop down to rest and feed, particularly thrushes which are drawn to the abundance of berries. With them could always be something like a Common Stonechat, Black Redstart, Ring Ouzel or perhaps a raptor such as Hen Harrier or Merlin.

Winter flocks of Sky Larks, Chaffinches, Greenfinches and Yellowhammers gather to feed in set-aside or sheltered furrows. During frosty weather they also congregate around sheep feeding stations, where they may fall easy prey to the resident Eurasian Sparrowhawks. In some years they are joined by a few Brambling. Large flocks of Rooks, Eurasian Jackdaws and thrushes are also a familiar part of the winter scene, feeding in the fields by day and roosting in the woods at night.

As the days lengthen, so Sky Larks, Northern Lapwings and Meadow Pipits return to their territories. Spring passage is swifter and less evident than that in autumn. A handful of passage Northern Wheatears usually feed in the summit fields and Whinchat, Ring Ouzel or occasionally Black Redstart might be seen. Raptors pass through too, with recent records of Montagu's and Marsh Harrier, and a 'trip' of Dotterel could rest on the southern slopes.

Down in the Avon Valley, stands of emergent vegetation along the river form breeding sites for many pairs of Moorhen, a few Common Coot and one or two Mute Swans. They also shelter many Mallard ducklings that were hatched in the crowns of pollarded willows. Grey Wagtails frequent the locks and Common Kingfishers are seen throughout the year, although most now prefer to breed along the quieter tributaries than the main river.

The Avon Valley was formerly the stronghold of the rare Marsh Warbler, but numbers have recently collapsed

The luxuriant riverbank vegetation holds many warblers. Sedge Warblers are well distributed in willow and thorn scrub, while a few Reed Warblers nest colonially in patches of common reed. The jewel of the valley though is the Marsh Warbler. With just two or three surviving pairs, you will need to be patient, but in late May and June they should be audible or visible from the footpaths described. Above all do not trespass into sensitive habitats where you can do considerable damage.

Common Snipe, Eurasian Curlew, Common Redshank and Yellow Wagtail all breed sparingly in the damper unimproved meadows, with perhaps an occasional pair of Grasshopper Warblers too. Common Swifts, Barn Swallows and House Martins come regularly to the river to feed throughout the summer, a few Turtle Doves nest, Common Cuckoos are widespread and Hobbies frequently noted.

Passage waders, gulls and terns regularly follow the river, especially in spring when many drop into Bredon's Hardwick if no flood-water remains on the meadows. Wader numbers vary, but most of the commoner species are recorded annually and both Oystercatcher and Little Ringed Plover have attempted to breed. Of the scarcer species, Grey Plover, Sanderling and Whimbrel appear most years and Little Stint, Curlew Sandpiper and both godwits have been seen. Common and Green Sandpipers are usually more numerous in autumn, but otherwise this season generally brings fewer birds and less variety, though Pectoral Sandpiper has occurred several times. One or two Kittiwakes often pass through in March, with perhaps a Mediterranean Gull and then a few Little Gulls in April or May. Terns, too, are more regular in spring, when in addition to the usual Common and Black Terns, a few Sandwich, Arctic or Little Terns might be seen. Even the rare Roseate and Whiskered Terns have been recorded. One or two Garganey are usually seen in spring too.

Winter watching can be equally rewarding as large concentrations of wildfowl and waders gather in the valley when conditions are right. A herd of 20 or more Tundra Swans visits the Bredon's Hardwick area most winters, occasionally being joined by a family of Whooper Swans, while a similar number of Mute Swans frequent the river. Canada Geese breed on the old gravel pits and up to 300 may be present in the winter. More interestingly, a small flock of White-fronted Geese is a regular winter feature, occasionally attracting small gaggles of other apparently wild birds. Bean, Pink-footed, Barnacle and Brent Geese have all been recorded. It is likely the wild swans and geese come from Slimbridge, which is just 22 miles (35 km) away, and they appear to retreat there in the hardest weather, returning again once a thaw sets in.

Flocks of Eurasian Wigeon graze the lush meadows and roost on the pools, with numbers increasing during very cold weather to well over 1,000 in February and March. With them may be a few Gadwall. Up to 70 Mallard, one or two Northern Shoveler and 100 Common Teal are also likely, but receding floodwaters may attract several hundred of the latter along with good numbers of Northern Pintail. Three or four Common Shelduck are also usually present early in the year. One or two Little Grebes can usually be seen on river and some half-a-dozen Great Cormorants regularly fish here or on the pools at Bredon's Hardwick, where they may accompany the resident Great Crested Grebes. Diving duck frequently use the river as well as the pools, especially when still waters are frozen. Up to 100 Common Pochard and Tufted Duck are most probable, but a few Common Goldeneye and Goosander are quite possible and there may even be a Smew. Of the sea-duck, Common Scoter are noted on passage and sometimes one or two Greater Scaup come in winter. A rarer grebe is also possible, with recent records of both Slavonian and Black-necked Grebes.

Large flocks of Northern Lapwings, 2,000–3,000 strong, gather in the fields, often accompanied by 1,000 or more European Golden Plover. As floodwaters subside, the wetter meadows attract plenty of Common Snipe and Dunlin, a few Common Redshank and Ruff, or maybe a Black-

or Bar-tailed Godwit. In very severe weather double these numbers may be present. Large flocks of gulls and thrushes also visit the flooded fields, with up to 2,500 Black-headed Gulls and a few hundred Common and Lesser Black-backed Gulls, especially in spring. A Yellow-legged Gull appears most winters. Spring regularly brings Pied and Yellow Wagtails and sometimes a Common Stonechat. With the former may be a few White Wagtails or a Blue-headed. Such concentrations invariably attract predators. Eurasian Sparrowhawks are seen daily; dashing, twisting Merlins are quite regular in late winter, and sometimes a Peregrine Falcon stoops at breath-taking speed into a flock of roosting birds. In winter a Barn Owl often hunts the meadows, while a Short-eared Owl sometimes appears in early spring.

Almost anything can be expected here, as recent records of Little and Cattle Egrets and Little Auk testify.

Croome Park is best in spring when the resident woodland songbirds are joined by a good range of summer visitors, including Sedge Warbler, Common Whitethroat, Blackcap, Garden Warbler and usually a pair of Rufous Nightingales. Songsters apart, the woods hold Common Buzzard, Common Kestrel and several pairs of Eurasian Jackdaws. Hobbies are also seen in summer, whilst a few of the commoner wildfowl frequent the lake in winter.

Timing

Both Bredon Hill and the Avon Valley are popular, especially at week-ends and summer Bank Holidays, and therefore best visited in the early morning, when they are quietest. Misty autumn mornings immediately after day-break are best for diurnal migration, especially when it is calm or the wind is from the east.

The river is fished and carries a lot of pleasure craft, while in places sailing adds to the disturbance. Winter is quieter and weather then becomes the key factor. Numbers are best in hard weather, but if the ground is frozen solid or covered in snow there may be little to see. Equally birds are scarce in mild weather. Flooding occurs after heavy rain or rapid thaws, with receding floodwaters often most productive.

Access

Bredon Hill The hill lies between the A435/A438 Evesham to Tewkesbury, B4080 Tewkesbury to Pershore and A44 Pershore to Evesham roads. The summit can be reached by a short, sharp climb of nearly 1 mile (1.5 km) from Elmley Castle, a long, steady climb of nearly 2 miles (3.2 km) from Kemerton or a steep and tortuous climb of 2.5 miles (4 km) from Bredon's Norton. The Wychavon Way crosses the eastern end of the hill, between Ashton-under-Hill and Elmley Castle, and there are numerous other public footpaths. Parking is difficult in the narrow village streets, so please take care and avoid blocking access ways.

River Avon The best stretch is the 14 miles (23 km) between Pershore and Tewkesbury. In summer the stretch upstream of Strensham Lock is generally of most interest, whereas in winter the stretch downstream is usually the better. Access points are:

Nafford Leave the A4104 Pershore to Upton-upon-Severn road southwards on the B4080 towards Tewkesbury. Turn left at the first cross roads in Eckington village and continue for 1 mile (1.6 km), where a small car park overlooks the river on the left. Park here, walk a little further along the lane and take the footpath on your left down to the lock. Cross onto the island to view the river, but please do not leave the footpath.

Eckington Proceed as above from the A4104, but immediately after crossing the river bridge park in the small car park on the left-hand side. Cross over the road and take the footpath westwards along the south bank of the river. This can be followed through to Strensham Lock, a distance of 2 miles (3.2 km), or on to Bredon, a distance of 4 miles (6.4 km). There is a bus service from Worcester to Eckington.

Twyning Green At the M50/A38 junction take the lane southwards to Twyning Green. Park at the end and follow the footpath southwards along

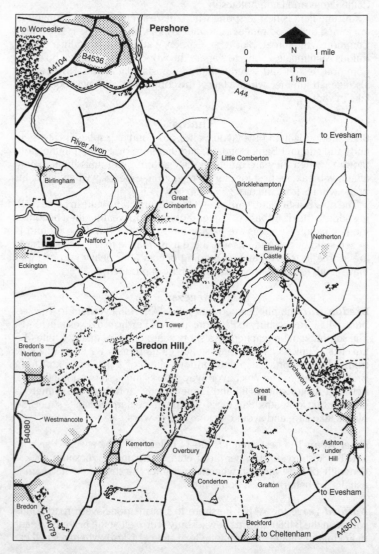

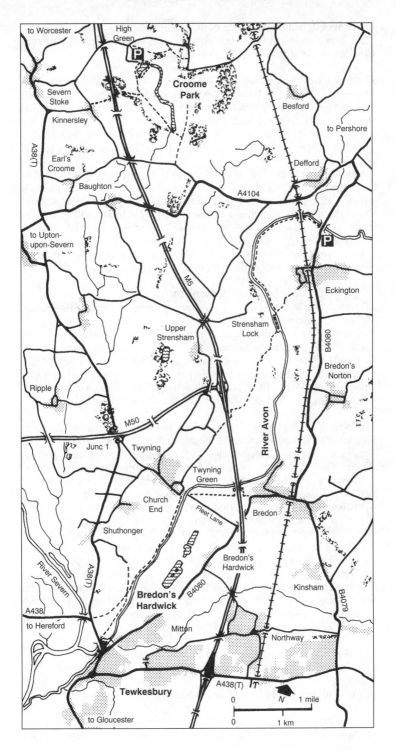

the Gloucestershire bank. This continues for just over 2 miles (3.5 km) until it rejoins the A38 on the edge of Tewkesbury. The Worcester–Gloucester bus service goes into Twyning Green.

Bredon's Hardwick Leave Tewkesbury on the B4080 towards Pershore and after 1·5 miles (2.4 km) park in the lay-by on the right. The pools can then be viewed from the gateways on the opposite side of the road, though the distance is great so a telescope is essential. It is also worth continuing for another mile (1.6 km) through Bredon's Hardwick and then turning left into Fleet Lane and continuing to the end to view the river meadows.

Croome Park Leave the A38 Worcester–Tewkesbury road eastwards at Severn Stoke towards High Green. Cross over the M5, go through High Green and turn immediately right, following the signs to Croome Park. Car parking is on the left-hand side after the next sharp bend. A charge is made for admittance to the Park and the NT should be contacted for opening times. Alternatively, the public footpath heading south-east-wards gives limited access. There are bus services from Worcester to Severn Stoke, from where the park is a 2-mile (3.2 km) walk.

Calendar

All Year: Little Grebe, Great Crested Grebe (scarce in winter), Mute Swan, Mallard, Eurasian Sparrowhawk, Common Buzzard, Common Kestrel, Red-legged and Grey Partridges, Common Pheasant, Moorhen, Common Coot, Northern Lapwing, Common Snipe, Woodcock, Eurasian Curlew (scarce), Common Redshank, Stock Dove, Little Owl, Tawny Owl, Common Kingfisher, all three woodpeckers, Sky Lark, Meadow Pipit, Grey Wagtail, Marsh Tit, Wood Nuthatch, Eurasian Jackdaw, Rook and other common corvids, tits, finches and buntings.

March–June: Winter visitors depart by April. Northern Lapwing, Sky Lark and Meadow Pipit return to Bredon Hill in March. Great Cormorant (March/April), Garganey; common passage waders such as Oystercatcher, Little and Great Ringed Plovers, Dunlin, Common Redshank, Common Sandpiper and scarcer waders such as Grey Plover, Sanderling, Little Stint, Curlew Sandpiper, Black- and Bar-tailed Godwits and Whimbrel; Mediterranean Gull (rare), Kittiwake (March; scarce), Short-eared Owl (March/April; scarce) and Common Stonechat (March/April; scarce) From April: Hobby, Dotterel (May; rare), Little Gull (scarce); maybe Common, Black or perhaps Sandwich, Arctic or Little Terns (last three scarce); Turtle Dove (scarce), Common Cuckoo, Common Swift (after April), hirundines, Tree Pipit; wagtails includ-ing White (scarce) and Blue-headed (rare); Rufous Nightingale (Croome; scarce), Common Redstart, Whinchat (scarce), Northern Wheatear, Ring Ouzel (scarce); warblers including Grasshopper (scarce), Sedge, Marsh (from mid-May; scarce) and Reed; and Spotted Flycatcher. Perhaps a passing raptor, scarce wader or passage migrant, or rarity.

July–September: Hobby; Green Sandpiper and other common waders as in spring, but with less chance of scarcer wader; summer visitors and pas-sage migrants as in spring; larks, pipits, wagtails, finches and buntings move south across Bredon Hill in September.

October–February: Passage of larks, pipits, thrushes, Common starlings, finches and buntings continues in October. Great Cormorant, Tundra

Swan, Whooper Swan (scarce), White-fronted Goose (scarce), Common Shelduck (autumn; scarce), Eurasian Wigeon, Gadwall (scarce), Common Teal, Northern Pintail (scarce), Northern Shoveler (scarce), Common Pochard, Tufted Duck, Common Goldeneye (scarce), Goosander (scarce), Smew (scarce), Merlin (scarce), Peregrine Falcon (scarce), European Golden Plover, Dunlin, Ruff (scarce), Black- or Bar-tailed Godwits (rare); gulls perhaps including Yellow-legged (scarce); Common Stonechat (autumn; scarce), Fieldfare and Redwing. Maybe rarer grebe, unusual wildfowl, sea-duck, passing raptor or rarity.

24 THE MALVERN HILLS   OS map 150

Habitat

The spectacular switchback of the Malverns rises abruptly to a height of 1394 ft (425 m) on Worcestershire Beacon, dominating the skyline for miles in every direction. Eastwards is the broad expanse of the Severn plain and westwards the rolling red fields of Herefordshire. The ridge, 8 miles (13 km) long and comprising some of the oldest rocks in England, is managed by the Malvern Hills Conservators. From its open summits stretches a panorama of wooded slopes, commons, parklands, orchards and rich, fertile farmland studded with tiny villages. Nestling right into the foothills is the elegant spa town of Great Malvern.

The summits have short grass swards with patches of heather and bilberry. These grade quickly into hillsides of bracken and bramble, with the lower slopes invaded by gorse, thorn scrub, rowan and light birch woodland. Lower still, in the more sheltered valleys and foothills, the scrub develops into broadleaved woodlands of oak and ash above birch, hazel and occasionally yew. In autumn, Happy Valley, with its rowans, is one of the best migrant 'traps' in the region. Old orchards with gnarled, lichen-clad trees, the vertical cliffs of old stone quarries, a small reservoir near British Camp and one or two tiny pools complete the mosaic of habitats.

Castlemorton and Old Hills are the best of many commons around the foothills. At Castlemorton, despite sheep grazing, dense clumps of gorse and bramble are invading the rough, low-lying permanent pastures. Traversing the common is a small stream, flanked on either side by marshy areas of sedge and rush. In summer these dry out completely, but in winter they are waterlogged if not flooded. People throng to the hills and commons, especially on sunny summer days, and in places they are causing serious erosion. Yet, despite the ramblers, picnickers, horseriders and hang-gliders, there are still quiet places that hold interesting birds.

The back-bone of the Malverns subsides northwards into a tail of hilly, wooded country dissected by fast-flowing streams. Amidst this delightful, tranquil countryside is the 60-acre (24 ha) Worcestershire Wildlife Trust (WWT) reserve of the Knapp and Papermill. Lying astride a fault which brings Triassic marls and sandstones up against Silurian limestones, it has a particularly rich flora. Through the middle is the narrow, secluded valley of the Leigh Brook with its woodland, old meadows and orchards. The steeper slopes are clothed in ancient broadleaved woodland, their oak standards rising above wild service trees and coppiced hazel and small-leaved lime. On the gentler slopes, the unimproved meadows are full of wild flowers, which in high summer attract countless insects. The brook, which is lined by coppiced alders and pollarded willows, has both fast-flowing shallows and deeper, slower reaches with high banks.

Species

The Malverns are an area for birds of grasslands, commons, woods and streams, with passage migrants especially in autumn.

Sky Larks and Meadow Pipits are the characteristic species of the open summits. In spring and summer the air is full of their songs. In autumn they are joined by passage birds before moving down to the lower pastures and commons for the winter. Much scarcer, but equally at home on the short summit swards, are the two or three pairs of Northern Wheatears which usually nest, often in the vicinity of British Camp. Again many more pass through in spring and autumn. The calls of Common Cuckoos are another familiar sound of spring and Chaffinches, with over 100 pairs, are plentiful wherever there are songposts and cover for nests.

*One or two pairs of Common Stonechat nest on the
Malvern Hills and commons*

Common Stonechats pass through the hills and commons each spring and autumn, with one or two pairs breeding amongst gorse or thorn scrub. Some birds stay well into autumn and may overwinter on the lower ground. The same areas are also the breeding haunt of good numbers of Common Whitethroats, Linnets and the declining Yellow-hammer. Also in decline are Tree Pipits, though several pairs still occur where there are scattered trees or light woodland. Anthills are common amongst the short turf of the hills, so Green Woodpeckers are plentiful. Frequently they choose old orchard trees for their nests – a niche which they share with the scarce Lesser Spotted Woodpecker – while in autumn they may feed on rowan berries.

The woods around Malvern hold a good range of typical species. Warblers, in descending order of abundance, include Willow Warbler, Chiffchaff, Blackcap, Garden Warbler and a few Wood Warblers. The latter are localised, but can usually be heard in beechwoods on Midsummer Hill or in the woods above Wyche Quarry. Other regular summer visitors are Common Redstart (30 pairs), Spotted Flycatcher and, locally in nest boxes, some dozen pairs of Pied Flycatchers. Of the resident species, Eurasian Jays are plentiful and Tawny Owl, Great Spotted Woodpecker, Wood Nuthatch and Eurasian Treecreeper can all be found in small numbers. Eurasian Jackdaws circle high above the quarries, often in flocks of 100 or more in winter, and there is always a chance of Hawfinch at the southern end of the hills around Chase End.

Autumn usually brings a good variety of passage birds to the hills. Once the summer visitors such as hirundines have left, flocks of thrushes and finches, including Fieldfare, Redwing and Mistle Thrush, move westwards through Happy Valley or congregate there to feed on the abundance of rowan berries. With them are normally a few late Ring Ouzels, or perhaps a party of Brambling or Common Crossbill. Autumn also brings small flocks of Siskin and Common Redpoll to birches and alders, while yew and ivy berries may sustain Goldcrests or an overwintering Blackcap. Black Redstarts and even a Yellow-browed Warbler have been seen, while later a Snow Bunting might appear on the summits along with the flocks of larks, pipits and thrushes that are moving south. Occasionally a wintering Short-eared Owl drifts silently across the hills or commons. With the onset of spring comes the promise of a few Ring Ouzels and Whinchats on return passage in April, or perhaps a Black Redstart in March.

Common Kestrels, Eurasian Sparrowhawks and Common Buzzards are frequently seen, the latter especially in the more wooded country to the west and north. All three species breed, as do Common Ravens and at times several birds are airborne together. Hobbies make irregular visits throughout the summer, often in association with movements of Common Swifts and hirundines, and Peregrine Falcon sightings have increased in recent years.

On the commons, passage Whinchats occur sparingly and there is even a chance of hearing a Grasshopper Warbler or Turtle Dove, especially on Castlemorton Common. One or two Rufous Nightingales also linger on the very edge of their range, with Old Hills Common a favoured haunt. Winter brings flocks of Redwing, Fieldfare, finches and buntings which may become the target of a Eurasian Sparrowhawk. Very rarely a Great Grey Shrike makes an appearance. Along the stream on Castlemorton Common, Common Snipe are accompanied by a few Jack Snipe and Woodcock, or an occasional Water Rail.

The woodlands of the Knapp and Papermill reserve hold similar species to those around Malvern, with the exception of Wood Warbler, but the meadows and stream add more diversity. Both Dipper and Common Kingfisher nest along this short stretch of brook, all three wagtails breed in the vicinity and there is a slight chance of Hawfinch. Winter sees flocks of Siskin and Common Redpoll in the alders and thrushes in the meadows and woods, while at dusk a Little Owl, or rarely a Barn Owl, goes hunting.

Timing

At weekends and bank holidays it is best to start early on the hills and commons, before too many people are about. Early mornings from late

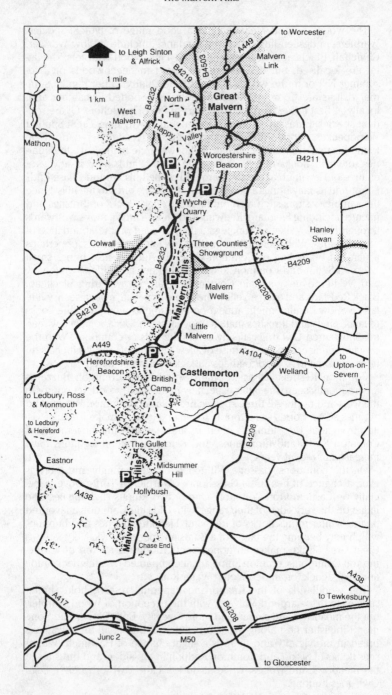

March to early May and more especially from September to November are best for migrants in Happy Valley, particularly with easterly winds. Little will be seen on the hills in very wet or windy weather, but raptors soar on fine, sunny days. Timing matters less at Knapp–Papermill, though song birds are more vocal in the mornings and evenings.

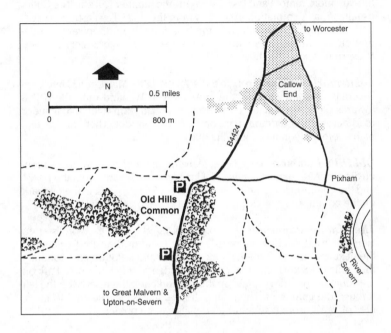

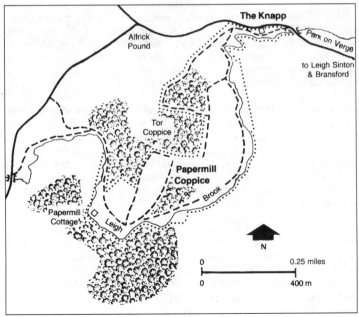

Access

Malvern Hills The northern foothills are encircled by the A449 Worcester to Monmouth and B4232 roads. From these there are innumerable access points onto the hills. Both the A449 and the B4218 cut through the hills *en route* from Great Malvern to Ledbury. South of Little Malvern the hills are more remote and less disturbed. Midsummer Hill and The Gullet usually repay exploration. Access is from the A438 Tewkesbury to Ledbury road at Hollybush, or from the lane running north towards Castlemorton Common. There are bus services from Worcester to Great Malvern that serve the hills.

Castlemorton Common Leave the A4104 Little Malvern to Upton-on-Severn road southwards at the crossroads in Welland onto the B4208 towards Gloucester. In just under 1 mile (1.5 km) turn right onto a minor road across the common, park and explore on foot. There are several paths from the common onto the hills.

Old Hills Common Leave Great Malvern on the B4211 towards Upton-on-Severn. After almost 4 miles (6.4 km) turn northwards onto the B4424 and the common is on the left in 2.75 miles (4.4 km). Park in the car park on the common. There is a bus service from Worcester to Old Hills.

The Knapp–Papermill Approach along the A4103 Worcester to Hereford road, turning westwards by the bend in Bransford village. At the next junction take the left fork towards Alfrick Pound and continue for 3 miles (4.8 km) until you cross the bridge over Leigh Brook. Park on the verge by the bridge, walk up the hill and enter the reserve on the left through the garden of 'The Knapp' house. Access is restricted to members of WWT, from whom further details can be obtained.

Calendar

All Year: Eurasian Sparrowhawk, Common Buzzard, Common Kestrel, Woodcock, Little Owl, Tawny Owl, Common Kingfisher, all three woodpeckers, Sky Lark, Meadow Pipit, Grey Wagtail, Dipper, Common Stonechat (scarce in winter), Mistle Thrush, Wood Nuthatch, Eurasian Treecreeper, corvids including Common Raven, Linnet, Hawfinch (rare), Yellowhammer and other common passerines.

April–September: Hobby (scarce), Peregrine Falcon (April, May and September; scarce), Turtle Dove (scarce), Common Cuckoo, Tree Pipit, Yellow Wagtail, Common Swift (May–August), hirundines, Rufous Nightingale (scarce), Common Redstart, Whinchat (scarce), Northern Wheatear, Ring Ouzel (April; scarce; and September); scrub and woodland warblers including Grasshopper (scarce) and Wood; and Spotted and Pied Flycatchers. Perhaps passing raptors, scarcer passage migrant or rarity, especially in autumn.

October–March: Peregrine Falcon (scarce), Water Rail (scarce), Jack Snipe (scarce), Common Snipe, Barn Owl (rare), Short-eared Owl (scarce), Black Redstart (autumn or March; rare), Ring Ouzel (October), Fieldfare, Redwing, Great Grey Shrike (rare), Brambling (scarce), Siskin, Common Redpoll, Common Crossbill (scarce) and Snow Bunting (November; rare). Perhaps passing raptors, scarcer passage migrant or rarity.

25 KIDDERMINSTER DISTRICT

Habitat

Kidderminster lies near the confluence of the rivers Severn and the Stour and at the heart of some fine birding country, of which five sites are mentioned here.

On the west bank, 3 miles (4.8 km) south of Stourport-on-Severn, is Shrawley Wood – one of England's largest and most important lime-woods. Part has been replanted with conifers, but much of the remainder consists of oak standards above coppiced limes and a rich ground flora with carpets of bluebells; 255 acres (103 ha) are an SSSI. Streams, especially Dick Brook, add further interest.

Further north, at Larford on the edge of Stourport, is a former gravel pit which has now been restored as a fishing lake. This has an island with pollarded willows and some margins of rush and sedge, which provide cover for nesting and roosting birds. Mature trees mark the course of the river and others have been planted as part of the restoration scheme. At the time of writing, there are some 300 acres (120 ha) of set-aside land adjoining to the west which attracts traditional farmland birds. However, it is not known how long this situation will persist.

Between the Severn and Stour, midway between Kidderminster and Bewdley, is 150 acres (61 ha) of the Worcestershire Wildlife Trusts (WWT) Devils' Spittleful and adjacent Rifle Range reserves. Together these form the largest area of heathland in Worcestershire. The Spittleful is dominated by an outcrop of weathered sandstone surmounted by a clump of Scots pines. Beneath is a large tract of heather with scattered birches and a few patches of bracken, gorse and hawthorn scrub. Some developing oak-birch woodland completes the range of habitats.

Along the Stour Valley is another WWT reserve at Wilden. Lying both sides of the river and abutting the Staffordshire and Worcestershire canal, this is a complex area of dry and marshy fields, willow scrub, alder carr, reedbeds and old settling pools used to contain sugar-beet washing from the British Sugar Corporation factory.

To the south of Wilden, the Local Nature Reserve of Hartlebury Common has one of the few inland sand-dune systems in Britain. Again there are extensive banks of heather and bracken and some oak-birch woodland, but here gorse is more abundant, often forming continuous patches. There are also areas of bare sand, an acidic bog and a pool, which provides somewhere for birds to drink and bathe in an otherwise dry habitat.

Species

In combination, these sites provide interesting birdwatching throughout the year.

Winter wildfowl and passage birds are the main attraction at Larford and Wilden. Numbers are small, but regular watching has turned up several quality birds, perhaps reflecting the importance of the River Severn as a migration highway.

Great Crested Grebes, Canada Geese, Gadwall, Mallard, Common Coot and less often Little Grebe, Tufted and Ruddy Ducks nest in small numbers. Most occur at both sites as do small wintering flocks of Great Crested Grebe, Mallard, Canada Geese, Common Pochard, Tufted Duck and Common Coot. A few Mute Swans, Eurasian Wigeon and Gadwall are also likely, the latter more so at Larford. Otherwise Larford is generally better for diving birds, with a few Common Goldeneye and Goosander most winters and several records of divers, rarer grebes or seaduck. Dabbling duck, particularly Common Teal and Northern Shoveler, normally prefer Wilden and Garganey are sometimes seen here in spring and autumn. Great Cormorants, Common Shelduck and Northern Pintail are occasional visitors to both sites. Winter also brings an occasional Kittiwake, Little Gull or wader such as Green Sandpiper or Oystercatcher. The drainage ditches and flooded carr at Wilden are also good for Common Snipe, Jack Snipe, Water Rail and Woodcock, while flocks of Siskin visit the alders.

Spring normally sees Little Ringed Plover, Common Redshank, Dunlin, Common Sandpiper and one or two other waders pass through. Indeed, the first two of these sometimes stay to breed, as have Common Snipe in the past at Wilden. Little Gull and Arctic, Common and Black Terns might also be seen at this time, with easterly winds perhaps bringing a small party of the latter. Sand Martins pass northwards in good numbers and a few Northern Wheatears, Yellow Wagtails and perhaps a White Wagtail are seen most years. Scarcer visitors might include Common Redstart, Whinchat and Rock Pipit, the last two more likely at Wilden. With luck, even an Osprey might pause to fish on its way up the Severn.

At Wilden, one or two Grasshopper and Reed Warblers can usually be heard on the marsh, with Sedge Warblers, Common Whitethroats, Garden Warblers, Reed Buntings and perhaps Turtle Doves amongst the willow scrub. Lesser Spotted Woodpeckers sometimes nest in the alder carr, but are more likely outside the breeding season. Common Kestrels also nest in the area and Hobbies are seen during the summer. Northern Lapwings breed both here and around Larford, while Common Kingfishers are present during the breeding season, Grey Wagtails sometimes nest and Grey Herons are often around.

Autumn passage is generally better at Wilden, with Green and Common Sandpipers likely from July onwards and a chance of other waders such as Oystercatcher, Ruff or Common Greenshank. A few Dunlin occur most years, sometimes staying into November. Terns might also pass through again, but numbers are usually small. Any of the regular migrants such as Yellow Wagtail, Common Stonechat, Whinchat or Northern Wheatear could be seen, with less often a Rock or Water Pipit in late autumn. White-winged Black Tern has been recorded at Wilden.

Good numbers of Grey Partridge and a few Red-legged Partridge frequent the set-aside land around Larford, with perhaps a pair or two of Corn Buntings as well, while Common Quail has been heard calling in summer. The largest coveys of partridges are noted in winter, when large flocks of Sky Larks, Meadow Pipits, Greenfinches and Linnets also gather to feed. Among them are often a few Yellowhammers and Corn Buntings, and maybe one or two Bramblings. The abundance of birds and mammals also attracts predators such as Common Kestrel, Eurasian Sparrowhawk, Common Buzzard, Hobby in summer, and Merlin, Barn Owl and Short-eared Owl in winter.

The woods at Shrawley hold most common woodland birds. The younger coppiced areas are especially good for summer warblers, particularly Garden Warbler and Blackcap, and for scrub species such as Long-tailed Tit and Bullfinch. The older coppices mostly contain resident Robins, Wrens, Blackbirds and Chaffinches. Hole-nesting species like Common Kestrel, Stock Dove, the three woodpeckers, tits, Wood Nuthatch and Eurasian Jackdaw occur where large oaks stand above the coppiced limes. Dippers and Grey Wagtails frequent the streams through the wood.

Among the typical heathland species to occur amongst the gorse at Devils' Spittleful and Hartlebury Common are Linnets, Yellowhammers and, in summer, Common Whitethroats. All breed in fair numbers, as do a few pairs of Meadow Pipits – never a numerous species at low altitude. Green Woodpeckers are also regularly seen searching for ants. Here and there a few pairs of Tree Pipit breed and Garden Warblers nest in the hawthorn thickets. Spring and autumn may bring passage Whinchat or Common Stonechat, both of which formerly bred, or Northern Wheatear. In winter Siskin and Common Redpoll visit the birches along with flocks of tits.

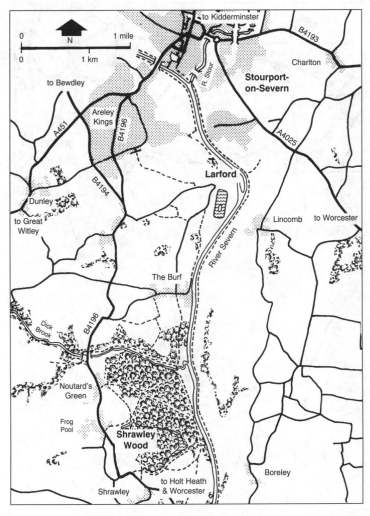

Timing

Early mornings are best at all sites, but especially the heaths where there is disturbance from local people later in the day. High summer may be quiet, as is winter on the heaths, and spring and autumn are generally best. At Larford, viewing from the road is better after midday with the sun behind you. Birds may be frozen out from here and Wilden in severe weather.

Access

Shrawley Wood The wood is at Noutard's Green, 3.5 miles (5.6 km) south of Stourport-on-Severn, on the east side of the B4196 from which several public footpaths lead into the wood. The Kidderminster–Worcester bus service goes along this road.

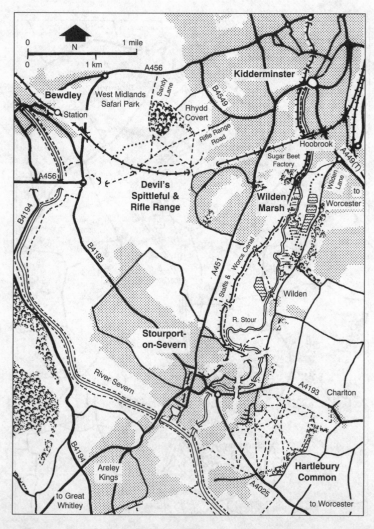

Larford lies just south of Stourport-on-Severn. Leave Stourport south-westwards on the A451 towards Great Witley, then turn left on the B4196 towards Holt Heath. After 1.25 miles (2 km) take the lane to Larford on the left. Continue for another mile (1.6 km) and the pool is on the left immediately after a sharp right-hand bend. Park on the verge. The Kidderminster–Worcester bus service passes the turn to Larford on the B4196.

Devil's Spittleful and Rifle Range The reserves are best reached from the A456 Kidderminster–Bewdley road. Limited parking is available immediately east of the West Midlands Safari Park, in a track known as Sandy Lane. Follow this track (a public footpath) alongside the boundary fence and onto the heath. Kidderminster–Bewdley buses go along the A456.

Wilden Marsh Take the A449 from the Kidderminster ring road, turn right at the first rounadabout (Hoobrook) into Wilden Lane and park along the road in 1.25 miles (2 km) just before Wilden village, taking great care as this is a busy road. Entrance to the reserve is through a gate on the right. Parts of the reserve are dangerous and access is restricted to WWT members only. A permit is required for the northern end of the reserve. The Kidderminster–Wilden–Stourport bus service passes the reserve.

Hartlebury Common The common lies either side of the A4025, 0.75 miles (1.2 km) southeast of Stourport-on-Severn. Park on the verge and explore. The Kidderminster–Wilden–Stourport bus service passes the north end of the common.

Calendar

All Year: Little and Great Crested Grebes, Grey Heron, Mute Swan, Canada Goose, Gadwall, Mallard, Tufted Duck, Ruddy Duck (scarce), Eurasian Sparrowhawk, Common Buzzard (scarce), Common Kestrel, Red-legged and Grey Partridges, Common Coot, Northern Lapwing, Stock Dove, Little Owl, Common Kingfisher (scarce in winter), all three woodpeckers, Sky Lark, Meadow Pipit, Grey Wagtail, Dipper, Wood Nuthatch, Eurasian Treecreeper, Yellowhammer, Reed Bunting, Corn Bunting (scarce) and other common passerines.

April–September: Garganey (scarce), Hobby (scarce), Common Quail (rare); Little Ringed Plover, Dunlin, Common Redshank, Green Sandpiper, Common Sandpiper and maybe a scarcer wader such as Oystercatcher, Ruff or Common Greenshank; Little Gull (scarce); maybe Arctic, Common or Black Tern; Turtle Dove (scarce), hirundines, Tree Pipit (scarce), wagtails including White (spring; scarce), Northern Wheatear; warblers including Grasshopper and Reed; and perhaps scarcer migrant such as Rock Pipit, Common Redstart or Whinchat. Maybe passing raptor.

October–March: Great Cormorant, Common Shelduck (scarce), Eurasian Wigeon, Common Teal, Northern Pintail (scarce), Northern Shoveler, Common Pochard, Common Goldeneye, Goosander, Merlin (rare), Water Rail, Jack Snipe (scarce), Common Snipe, Woodcock, Green Sandpiper or other wader (scarce), Little Gull (scarce), Kittiwake (scarce), Barn and Short-eared Owls (both rare), Rock and Water Pipits (autumn; scarce), Common Stonechat (autumn and March; scarce), Siskin, Common Redpoll and flocks of larks, pipits, finches and buntings, including Brambling (scarce). Perhaps diver, rarer grebe or sea-duck.

26 THE WYRE FOREST

OS Landranger
Map 138

Habitat

The Wyre Forest stands on a plateau immediately west of the River Severn, just upstream of Bewdley. Underlain by sandstones, marls, conglomerates and limestone bands, this remnant of ancient hunting forest contains an outstanding flora and fauna within its 6000 acres (2400 ha). Just over half belongs to Forest Enterprise (FE) and since 1927 this has been progressively converted into conifer plantations. Now that the older ones have matured, clear-felling and replanting has begun. However, the remainder constitutes not only the largest and most diverse woodland in the West Midlands, but one of the best surviving native woodlands in Britain. About a fifth is a National Nature Reserve (NNR) and the Worcestershire Wildlife Trust (WWT) have small reserves too.

The woods of Wyre are a unique blend, with oakwoods recalling the coppices of Wales, mixed broadleaved woods reminiscent of those in East Anglia and diverse valley woods similar to those of the southern Welsh borders. Indeed, several plants and animals here are on the very edge of their range. The glory of the forest is its oakwoods on the acid soils of the plateau. Sessile oak is the commoner species, but pedunculate oak also occurs and many trees show intermediate characteristics. Coppicing has virtually ceased, so the woods are developing the closed canopy of high forest with birch, a field layer of heather, bilberry, bracken and great wood-rush, and here and there a few hollies and yews. The pockets of calcareous clay derived from limestone bands support a very different woodland with ash above an understorey of hazel and dogwood and a field layer of dog's mercury and primrose.

Most diverse are the valley woods, notably along Dowles Brook. Here the stream flows across boulders and between high, overhanging banks above which old orchards and tiny meadows nestle into the narrow valley. Behind them hanging oakwoods rise to merge with those on the plateau. The valley flora is extremely varied, with alder, ash, elm, small-leaved lime and willow as well as oak. Beneath these is a shrub layer rich in autumn berries, with rowan, blackthorn, hawthorn, guelder rose and wild rose. The less acidic areas were cleared for grazing meadows and orchards. Now neglected, the gnarled, twisted trees of apple, damson and plum provide a wealth of nest sites, while the meadows are alive with harebell, yellow rattle, cowslip, green winged orchid, meadow saffron and a host of butterflies.

The Wyre is also renowned for the multitude and variety of its insects. These range from an abundance of wood ants to conspicuous dragonflies and butterflies such as high brown and silver-washed fritillaries. Two moths, Kentish glory and alder kitten, are in fact national rarities. This wealth of insects helps sustain a good population of birds.

Seckley Wood, forming the northeastern extremity of the forest, is a mixed wood with oak and birch on the predominantly light, sandy soils and alder on the wetter clays. There are some fine beeches too, and a few old cherry orchards nearby. The wood ends abruptly in a spectacular sandstone cliff in which pockets of clay cause occasional landslides. From the top the view is superb, with the Severn gliding beneath, while on the far bank steam trains on the Severn Valley Railway puff slowly past the tiny Trimpley Reservoir.

The FE plantations contrast sharply with this idyllic scene. Here the stands of lofty spruce, pine, larch and Douglas fir are dark and lifeless, except where shafts of sunlight along the forest rides admit a limited ground flora. In the New Parks, though, conifers were used only to replace impoverished oakwoods on the higher ground. Lower down, on the more fertile soil, the better oaks were kept and underplanted with beech. Belts of oak were also left alongside roads and tracks. In fact, the FE policy is to maintain hardwoods over a third of its Wyre woodlands, which obviously benefits the birds. As the woodlands have matured, even the plantations have become more attractive and today they hold most birds typical of coniferous woods.

Species

Few forests can boast a better avifauna than the Wyre.

Breeding activity begins quite early, long before the leaf-buds burst, with residents such as Robin, Hedge Accentor, Wren, Blackbird, Song and Mistle Thrushes, and Chaffinch defending their territories. Blue and Great Tits are widespread, but other species can often be found in particular habitats. Eurasian Treecreepers and Willow Tits prefer smaller trees, the latter especially favouring damp areas with rotting timber, while Marsh Tits and Wood Nuthatches tend to keep to the older, broad-leaved trees. The old orchards are good for woodpeckers, with Lesser Spotted much easier to watch in these smaller trees than in the high oaks. Green Woodpeckers also often nest here, or in birches, but Great Spotted is more widely distributed. At Far Forest and Lynall's Coppice, Stock Doves breed in nest boxes.

Once the summer visitors join the resident songsters, the forest reverberates to a symphony of birdsong. First to arrive are Chiffchaffs, whose metronomic notes can be heard as early as mid-March. Most favour the valleys, but a few sing along forest rides. Next to arrive are Willow Warblers, followed soon afterwards by Common Cuckoos. The varied shrub layer along Dowles Brook holds both Blackcap and Garden Warbler, with the former usually under a closed canopy and the latter beneath an open one. Clearings or open glades are also the haunt of Common Whitethroats, while Grasshopper Warblers occasionally nest in rank undergrowth. A few pairs of Tree Pipit also breed, with the abandoned railway line a good place to look. Among the last migrants to arrive, early in May, are Turtle Dove and Spotted Flycatcher, with the latter preferring streams and orchards.

The specialities of the Wyre are that characteristic trio of sessile oakwoods, Wood Warbler, Common Redstart and Pied Flycatcher. All can be seen along the Dowles Brook, where there are about a dozen pairs of each. Wood Warblers prefer the steeper wooded slopes, where there is a good field layer but only a sparse shrub layer, while Common Redstarts and Pied Flycatchers breed in nest boxes or holes in oaks or old orchard trees. Knowles Coppice and Knowles Mill are generally good areas.

The Pied Flycatcher is the most captivating of the Wyre Forest birds

On the deeper, sluggish stretches of the brook, Common Kingfishers nest in the high, sandy banks, while on the faster-flowing reaches two or three pairs of Dippers nest under the overhanging banks and bridges. Sharing their habitat are Grey Wagtails, while Mallard and a pair or two of Mandarin Duck also breed.

The most elusive bird is the Hawfinch. Precisely how many inhabit the Forest is unknown, but small parties are seen from time to time, usually feeding beneath beeches in early spring. Once the leaves open detection is difficult, but if you know their sharp, metallic 'tzik' call you might discover them in midsummer feeding in the canopy on the larvae of the oak tortrix moth. They nest in loose colonies, sometimes in Douglas firs.

The conifer plantations of the Wyre hold much more beside the usual Goldcrests and Coal Tits. Siskin flocks gather in the spruce plantations in March and April, and breeding has been suspected more than once. Common Crossbills too are now regularly present and parties up to 50 are quite common from autumn onwards, with some occasionally breeding. Surprisingly few occur in late summer and early autumn, though, which is the customary time for irruptions. A pair or two of Long-eared Owls also inhabit the plantations, but are hard to find in such a vast area unless you know their calls.

Calm, sunny mornings are best for raptors, when they rise into developing thermals. Eurasian Sparrowhawks, Common Buzzards and Common Kestrels are regularly present, but Northern Goshawks provide only infrequent sightings, often in April. Summer may see a Hobby hunting over the canopy, or a passage Osprey drifting high above the Severn, while Common Ravens are also appearing more frequently. Crepuscular and nocturnal species include Woodcock and both Little and Tawny Owls.

In winter, parties of small birds search sheltered valleys like the Dowles for food. Tits, notably Long-tailed, are most evident, but Willow and Marsh Tits, Goldcrests, Eurasian Treecreepers and even a Lesser Spotted Woodpecker may be loosely associated with their nomadic flocks. Great Tits, Marsh Tits and several hundred Chaffinches come to feast on beechmast, where they are sometimes joined by a few Bramblings, especially in early spring. Flocks of Common Redpoll and Siskin occur from autumn through to spring, with Arctic Redpoll once seen amongst them. To begin with they take birch seeds, but later they move into alders. Fieldfare, Redwing and Blackbird are also numerous, feeding away from the Forest, but coming in to roost at night.

Whilst in the Forest do not forget the Severn and the nearby Trimpley Reservoir. Great Cormorants often move up and down the river outside the breeding season, pausing *en route* to feed on the reservoir. In winter, Common Goldeneye and Goosander do likewise, while spring and autumn might bring Common Shelduck or a party of Red-breasted Mergansers. Even a vagrant diver, Shag or wild swan is a possibility.

Timing

Although a popular spot, few people walk very far from their cars. Spring and summer are the best times, with birds most active early in the morning and late in the day. For resident species, especially Hawfinch, try March or early April, before the trees are in leaf. For summer visitors, May is best. Raptors become more active by late morning as the ground warms up and thermals begin to rise, with March and April again good months. After June most birds are hard to find as they retreat to the canopy with their newly-fledged young. Timing matters less in winter as birds feed throughout the short days, especially during very cold spells.

Access

The Forest is best approached from the A456 Bewdley to Ludlow or B4194 Bewdley to Kinlet roads. There is a bus service between Birmingham, Kidderminster and Bewdley. The best access points are as follows.

Dowles Brook Follow the B4190 Tenbury Wells road up the hill from Bewdley town centre. After 0.75 miles (1.2 km) turn right into the Lakes Road and follow this through the housing estate to Dry Mill Lane. Turn left and follow the lane into the forest, where there is limited parking on the right-hand verge at the bottom of the hill. Continue on foot along the track beside the Brook into the heart of the Forest. After 1 mile (1.6 km) the track passes Knowles Mill, an old stone house on the opposite bank. The footbridge across to the house also leads onto a footpath up through Knowles Coppice (WWT reserve) to an old railway line. A pleasant round walk can be made by taking this path and then returning along the old railway to Dry Mill Lane.

Seckley Wood Leave Bewdley on the B4194 towards Kinlet and after 2 miles (3.2 km) park in the FE picnic site on the right. There are three way-marked forest trails from here. Take the longer (red) trail, but divert from it, past the Seckley Beech and round the forest track that overlooks the River Severn and Trimpley Reservoir. A telescope is needed to view the latter.

New Parks This is the main area of conifer plantations. Leave Bewdley on the A456 towards Ludlow and continue for 2·5 miles (4 km) until you come to the FE Callow Hill car park (pay and display) and Visitor Centre on the right. Park here and follow the red or green trails. The longer (red) route, at 3.5 miles (5.6 km), is usually the best. From this trail footpaths lead down to the Dowles Brook. The Birmingham–Ludlow bus service passes the Visitor Centre.

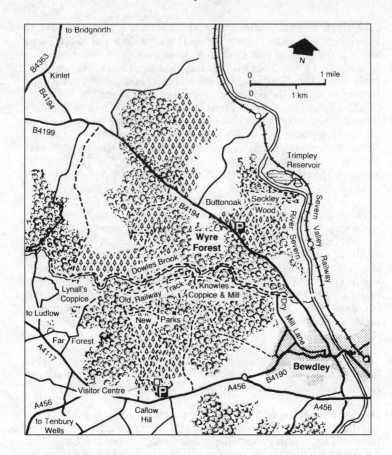

Calendar

All Year: Mandarin Duck (scarce), Mallard, Northern Goshawk (scarce), Eurasian Sparrowhawk, Common Buzzard, Common Kestrel, Woodcock, Stock Dove; Little, Tawny and Long-eared Owls (latter scarce), Common Kingfisher, all three woodpeckers, Grey Wagtail (scarce in winter), Dipper, Goldcrest, Wood Nuthatch, Eurasian Treecreeper, Common Raven (scarce), Siskin (scarce in summer), Common Redpoll, Common Crossbill (scarce in summer; best in irruption years), Hawfinch (elusive) and other common woodland birds.

April–September: Hobby (scarce), Turtle Dove, Common Cuckoo, Tree Pipit, Common Redstart, Grasshopper Warbler (scarce), Common Whitethroat, common woodland warblers including Wood, Spotted Flycatcher and Pied Flycatcher. A few wildfowl along the Severn. Possible passing raptor.

October–March: Roosting thrushes including Fieldfare and Redwing, and flocks of tits and finches including Brambling (scarce). Maybe Great Cormorant, Common Goldeneye, Goosander or other wildfowl along river or at Trimpley Reservoir. Possible passing raptor.

27 DINMORE AREA

This is a beautiful area of wooded hillsides and rich, fertile valleys. At the centre Dinmore Hill rises nearly 400 ft (120 m) above the plain below, forcing the River Lugg into a huge meander round its footslopes. Surmounting the hill is Queenswood Country Park, while in the plain below are two gravel pits, one worked out and the other active. These areas provide the focus of birdwatching interest.

QUEENSWOOD

Habitat

Queenswood Country Park, covering 180 acres (72 ha), was once part of a vast oakwood belonging to the monarchy. Following centuries of coppicing, it was clear-felled during the First World War. Now it is an SSSI and a Local Nature Reserve, managed as a mixture of high forest and coppice.

At the centre is an arboretum, established to commemorate the Queen's coronation, and now regarded as one of the finest collections of young trees in Britain. Surrounding this, notably to north and south, are oakwoods. Where thinning has opened out the canopy, there is a strong secondary growth of hazel whose fruits provide food for dormice. Ash and alder are also locally dominant, while plantations of Scots pine and larch – the latter in the northeast corner – add to the diversity of the habitat. The flora is interesting, too, with carpets of bluebells in spring, herb paris and several orchids. Over 50 nest boxes have been erected to encourage more birds to breed.

Species

Woodland birds in splendid surroundings are the main attraction.

With the onset of spring the resident Robins, Hedge Accentors, thrushes, tits and finches burst into faltering song. Soon the woods are ringing to the calls of Wood Nuthatches and the drumming of woodpeckers. All three species occur, though the Lesser Spotted is elusive. Eurasian Treecreepers, and Goldcrests in the pine and larch plantations, go discreetly about nesting.

Lengthening days bring the first Chiffchaffs and Willow Warblers, followed shortly afterwards by Blackcaps, Garden Warblers and Common Cuckoos. Wood Warblers can also be heard, mostly where the ground cover is sparse, while Pied Flycatchers have increased with the provision of nest boxes. One or two pairs of Tree Pipits also occur, often around recently cleared areas. Aerial skirmishes between Eurasian Sparrowhawks, Common Buzzards and Common Kestrels are frequent. At dusk Tawny Owls begin to call and Woodcock commence their roding flights.

In irruption years Common Crossbills could arrive in the conifer plantations at any time from July onwards. More reliably winter thrushes, especially Redwing and Fieldfare, arrive in October, strip all the berries and then move on, perhaps returning to roost at night. At this time too, a few Siskin and Common Redpoll join the resident tits and finches to roam the woods during winter in search of food. Common Ravens range more widely too, and are regularly seen or heard. Continental birds boost the

Woodcock population in winter, when birds fly down to Bodenham Lake or the Lugg meadows at dusk to feed.

Timing

Early morning in spring, before too many visitors arrive, is best as bird-song is then at its height. For resident birds visit early in the season, before the leaves have opened, as birds are then easier to locate and watch. Visit at dusk for owls and Woodcock. Raptors prefer to soar on calm, sunny days and many other birds are more active then as well.

Access

Queenswood lies to the west of the A49 Leominster–Hereford road at the summit of Dinmore Hill, 5 miles (8 km) south of Leominster. There is a pay-and-display car park, visitor centre, shop and toilets. Of the three trails that lead round the arboretum and the woods, the longer deer trail (2.5 miles or 4 km) is likely to prove most productive. The Hereford–Leominster–Birmingham bus services passes the entrance.

Calendar

All Year: Eurasian Sparrowhawk, Common Buzzard, Common Kestrel, Woodcock, Tawny Owl, all three woodpeckers, Goldcrest, Coal Tit, Wood Nuthatch, Eurasian Treecreeper, Common Raven and other common woodland birds.

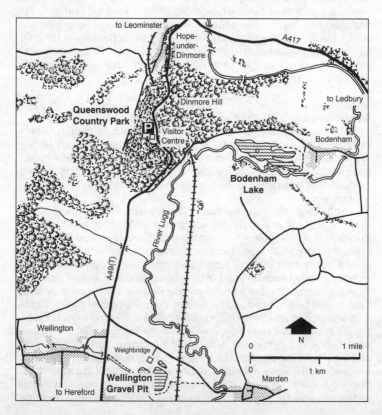

April–September: Common Cuckoo, Tree Pipit (scarce); warblers including Wood; Pied Flycatcher and Common Crossbill (in irruption years).

October-March: Fieldfare, Redwing, Siskin and Common Redpoll.

BODENHAM LAKE AND WELLINGTON GRAVEL PIT

These two sites are dealt with together as similar birds are likely to be encountered at each. Their importance to wildfowl and waders appears to have increased as that of the Wye and Lugg has declined.

Habitat

Bodenham Lake is a former gravel pit which Leominster District Council acquired in December 1994. Set in a narrow part of the Lugg Valley, the lake is around 28 ft (8 metres) deep, with several substantial islands which provide safe nesting and roosting sites. These, and much of the shoreline, are covered by a dense growth of regenerating willow scrub, while the southern shore and the adjacent river are densely lined with alders. The County Youth Service uses the eastern end for sailing and the public have access partway along the northern and southern shores, but the western end is kept as a nature reserve. The District Council hopes to improve the habitat and provide additional facilities, including hides, in the future.

Wellington Gravel Pit is set amidst fertile farmland in an open, expansive plain. There is a large lake with steep banks and smaller settling lagoons in which emergent vegetation and willow scrub are just beginning to develop.

Species

Wildfowl and waders are of most interest.

Little Grebe, Great Crested Grebe, Mute Swan and several pairs of Canada Geese, Mallard, Moorhen and Common Coot breed. Post-breeding flocks then begin to build up, with over 400 Canada Geese and 100 Common Coot at Bodenham and perhaps half these numbers later in the autumn at Wellington GP. A small breeding population of feral Barnacle Geese has also established itself in the area and other geese appear from time to time. Tufted Duck are present throughout the year and probably breed. They peak in autumn, with around 50 at each site, but quickly decline in the new year.

Of the winter visitors, up to 100 Eurasian Wigeon congregate at Bodenham, with much smaller numbers at Wellington; and some 100 or so Common Pochard divide themselves between the two waters, with generally slightly more at Bodenham. Up to half-a-dozen Common Goldeneye regularly visit Bodenham too, but appearances at Wellington are sporadic. Great Cormorants are seen more or less throughout the year, with in excess of 20 often at Bodenham in midwinter, and small numbers of Gadwall and Common Teal occur at both sites. Common Shelduck, Northern Shoveler and Ruddy Duck are occasionally noted too, while Garganey, a diver, rarer grebe or sea-duck is always a possibility.

Little Ringed Plovers breed at Wellington and a couple of hundred Northern Lapwings sometimes come from the surrounding fields to roost. Small parties of Eurasian Curlew also pause briefly to feed in spring and autumn, while a few Common Snipe, or even a Jack Snipe, feed along the muddy edges in winter. Other passage waders are unpredictable, but Oystercatcher, Great Ringed Plover, Dunlin, Black-tailed Godwit, Spotted and Common Redshanks, Common Greenshank and both Green and Common Sandpipers all occurred in a single year. Most were in autumn, with the two sandpipers being the more numerous and regular. Red Knot, Ruff and Whimbrel have also been reported. Passage waders are more likely to be seen at Wellington, where the settling pools ensure suitable feeding areas at all times.

Here, too, gulls often loaf around the pits, with perhaps 200 Lesser Black-backed Gulls present even in midsummer. Black-headed Gulls, though, are much fewer. Terns are scarce, but one or two Common or Black Terns occasionally pass through and Arctic Tern has been seen.

Common Swifts and hirundines congregate over the pits, especially in cold or wet weather, when several hundred may be hawking low-flying insects. Frequently they attract the attention of a Hobby. Among a good variety of passerines, Green Woodpeckers frequent the woods at Bodenham and a few pairs of Sedge Warbler breed in the willow scrub, while a pair or two of Yellow Wagtails nest at Wellington. In a good winter large flocks of Siskin and Common Redpoll visit the alders at Bodenham, while Linnets, Goldfinches and other finches and buntings, including perhaps a Brambling or two, search for seeds amongst the disturbed ground around the pits. Among the unexpected, Red Kite and Osprey have been observed over Bodenham.

Timing

Not particularly critical at either site, though Wellington Gravel Pit is quieter outside operational hours. To avoid looking into the sun, view Bodenham Lake from the road early or late in the day. The depth of the lake inhibits freezing, so visits when other waters are ice-bound might be worthwhile.

Access

Bodenham Lake Leave the A49 eastwards, 0.75 miles (1.2 km) south of Queenswood Country Park – a very sharp turn if approaching from the north. The entrance to the lake is on the right hand side after 1.75 miles (2.8 km). See the notice board for details of access. Continue round the bend in the village, turn right and park opposite the school. Distant views of the western end of the lake can be had from the road *en route*, but a telescope is essential.

Wellington Gravel Pit Continue south on the A49 beyond the Bodenham turn for another 1.25 miles (2 km), turn eastwards at the cross roads and the entrance to the gravel pit is on the right shortly before the level crossing. Redland Aggregates usually allow access during operating hours, so report to the Portakabin by the weighbridge for permission and instructions. At other times continue southwards beyond the cross roads on the A49 for another 0.3 miles (0.6 km), park and follow the footpath eastwards for views across the pits. Again a telescope is useful. Planning permission is being sought for extensions to this quarry which may require further diversions to this path. It is not known how this might affect viewing conditions.

Calendar

All Year: Little Grebe, Great Crested Grebe, Great Cormorant (scarce in summer), Mute Swan, Canada Goose, Barnacle Goose (feral), Mallard,

Tufted Duck, Moorhen, Common Coot, Northern Lapwing, Black-headed Gull (scarce in spring), Lesser Black-backed Gull and Green Woodpecker.

April–June: Little Ringed Plover, Eurasian Curlew, Common Sandpiper and perhaps a scarcer passage wader; possibly Common or Black Tern; Common Swift (after April), hirundines, Yellow Wagtail (scarce) and warblers including Sedge. Maybe a rarity.

July–September: Summer visitors depart. Common passage waders such as Little Ringed Plover, Eurasian Curlew, Green and Common Sandpipers and perhaps a scarcer passage wader; possibly Common or Black Tern. Maybe a rarity.

October–March: Common Shelduck (scarce), Eurasian Wigeon, Gadwall (scarce), Common Teal, Northern Shoveler (scarce), Common Pochard, Common Goldeneye, Ruddy Duck (scarce), Common Snipe, Siskin, Common Redpoll and mixed flocks of finches and buntings including Brambling (rare). Perhaps rarer grebe or vagrant sea-duck.

28 THE WOOLHOPE AREA   OS Landranger
                             Map 149

Habitat

Woolhope is a small village at the heart of beautiful, rolling countryside 7 miles (11 km) east-southeast of Hereford. There are a few special spots for wildlife within the rich, fertile vales and wooded limestone hills, but generally this is an area to be explored from the many roads and footpaths that traverse it.

The largest woodland is the Forest Enterprise's (FE) Haugh Wood, where the plateau and steep hillsides are covered with plantations of pine and larch fringed with beech. Wide sweeps of bracken cover recently felled areas. This is the richest wood in Herefordshire for insects and some rides and paths have recently been opened up to improve the habitat for butterflies and moths. Immediately east of Haugh Wood is Broadmoor Common Local Nature Reserve, a tract of grassy heath with damp hollows, scattered trees, hawthorn thickets, extensive patches of gorse and oak-birch woodland..

Further south, Herefordshire Nature Trust (HNT) owns two small woodland reserves. At Nupend, 12 acres (5 ha) of a steep Silurian limestone ridge are crowned by some magnificent yews, with oak and ash dominant on the slopes. The yews exclude all undergrowth and little but moss grows beneath the oaks on the dry ridge, but on the lower slopes field maple, hazel and wild service trees thrive. The yews are visited by many birds in autumn and the rich flora attracts numerous insects, especially butterflies.

The 22 acres (9 ha) of Lea and Paget's Woods, 1 mile (1.6 km) to the east, also surmount ridges of Silurian limestone that flank a valley cut into the shales lying between them. They are amongst the finest woods in the

Wye Valley Area of Outstanding Natural Beauty. Formerly mixed oak and ash woods, several old oaks still survive in Paget's Wood, but those in Lea Wood have been felled. The latter is now being coppiced, with stools beneath a canopy of spindly ash and birch. Both woods exhibit a diverse understorey with many berry-bearing trees and shrubs. The abundance of wild flowers includes carpets of bluebells and wood anemones, wild daffodils in early spring and several orchids in summer. Along the tiny stream is a belt of mature alders.

Further south still, the oak and ash canopy of Capler Wood drops down to the lush bankside vegetation of the Wye.

Species

Few rare birds can be expected and at times the woods seem almost lifeless. Yet a wide range of woodland birds are here to be enjoyed amidst some superb scenery.

Wrens, Hedge Accentors, Robins, thrushes, tits and finches begin to sing on the first mild days of winter, while Eurasian Sparrowhawks, Common Buzzards and Common Ravens are resolving territorial disputes. By April Chiffchaffs and Willow Warblers are searching the still-bare branches for food, Blackcaps, and more sparingly Garden Warblers, are singing from deep within the shrub layer and Common Cuckoos are calling. Tree Pipits, Common Whitethroats and perhaps a Lesser Whitethroat share the woodland edge with resident Chaffinches and Bullfinches. Open areas such as Broadmoor Common and Common Hill are good for these species, with Common Whitethroats, Linnets and Yellowhammers particularly fond of gorse.

Common Buzzards are a feature of the Woolhope woodlands

Of the scarcer residents, all three woodpeckers are present, though the Lesser Spotted often stays in the canopy, concealed by leaves. Other hole-nesting residents include Little Owl, a few pairs of Willow Tit in damp places, and both Stock Dove and Wood Nuthatch among the more mature, deciduous timber. Notable among the scarcer migrants are a few Common Redstarts, Wood Warblers and Spotted Flycatchers, while sometimes a passage Pied Flycatcher is seen.

Here and there in commons, large clearings or young forestry, the 'reeling' song of a Grasshopper Warbler might be heard, though their appearances are sporadic. Evenings are a good time to listen for them and watch for roding Woodcock or a hunting Barn Owl. Finally, Tawny Owls begin to call, but the flutey notes of a Rufous Nightingale now seem destined to become a mere memory as only one has been heard in recent years, at Fownhope. Coal Tits and Goldcrests are common, even in quite dense stands of conifers, but Turtle Doves are now quite scarce. Common Redpoll have also declined, with dozens rather than hundreds now feeding in the bushy growth around clearings and rides. In irruption years the explosive 'chip' flight calls of Common Crossbills may be heard from July and, with 75 seen in Haugh Wood as late as May, breeding remains a possibility.

Soon winter visitors replace those of summer. October sees migrant Mistle Thrushes, Blackbirds, Fieldfares and Redwings join their resident cousins in plundering yew berries. Finches and sometimes a wintering Blackcap feed with them on yew or honeysuckle. As winter tightens its grip, so tits and finches seek mast beneath the beeches. Great Tits and Chaffinches are commonest, but Marsh Tits or a few Brambling may join them. Small flocks of Common Redpoll and increasing numbers of Siskin feed among birchwoods and streamside alders, sometimes with Goldfinches, Eurasian Treecreepers or a Lesser Spotted Woodpecker. On the hillsides, Woodcock lie camouflaged amongst dead leaves.

By March, Siskin are leaving their winter haunts to form pre-migration gatherings in the conifer plantations. Most then leave during April, but a few remain into May and a pair or two might possibly breed. With luck, a Hawfinch might still be glimpsed in spring as, despite the absence of recent records, it is just possible that this shy species still lingers on.

Although not a prime site for birds, the river at Capler Wood nonetheless increases the range of species that might be seen. Mute Swans are common along the whole river, with a herd of 100 sometimes at Fownhope, and most of the Great Cormorants roost at Carey Islands, just a few miles downstream, so either could pass by. Mallard and Common Kingfishers might be seen as well, while spring and autumn could bring any of the species that typically migrate along the river, most notably Goosander, Common Sandpiper and Sand Martin.

Timing

Early morning in spring is the best time to visit as birds are then most active. For resident species, early spring, before the trees are in leaf, is best, but for migrants a May visit is recommended. Timing matters less in winter as fewer people are about and birds are generally active throughout the short daylight hours. Little is seen in very wet or windy weather.

Access

Haugh Wood Leave Hereford eastwards on Hampton Park Road (B4224), continue for 4 miles (6.4 km) into Mordiford and take the second turning left in the village towards Woolhope. Continue up the hill into Haugh Wood and park in the FE car park and picnic area on the left. From here follow the Butterfly Trail, which has two loops, one on either side of the road.

Broadmoor Common Continue along the same road until reaching the common immediately after leaving Haugh Wood. Take the Woolhope road and park on the left at the far end of the common.

For the two HNT reserves take the lane southwards from Broadmoor Common, continue down the hill and then turn right towards Fownhope.

Lea and Paget's Woods Turn left at the next junction and continue along a narrow lane for about 0.3 miles (0.5 km). As the road begins to descend the hill there is a gate on the left between a derelict stone building and a private drive. This gives access to the reserve, which is restricted to HNT members only. Parking is extremely difficult, so take great care. The Wye Valley Walk also goes through the reserve.

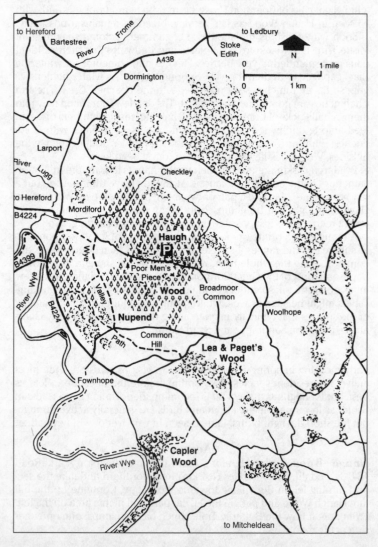

Nupend Wood Carry straight on at the previous junction for a little over 1 mile (2 km) and then, at the foot of the hill where the Wye Valley Path crosses the road, turn into the gateway on the right and park alongside the wood. Again space is limited, so park with care and avoid blocking any gateways. Follow the track up the left side of the wood and access to the reserve, which again is restricted to HNT members only, is up a flight of steps on the right. The Wye Valley Path gives ample opportunity to see the characteristic birds of the area in some magnificent scenery and visitors will do as well walking this as visiting the reserves.

Capler Wood Turn southwards off the B4224 by Fownhope Church and continue for 1 mile (1.6 km). Park in the lay-by on the left, just as the road enters the wood and begins to climb a steep hill. Follow the steep footpath down the edge of the wood to the river, turn south along the riverbank and then return by the track at the landing stage. If desired, use other paths to explore further.

There is a bus service from Hereford to Mordiford and Fownhope, with a limited one onwards from Fownhope to Woolhope.

Calendar

All Year: Eurasian Sparrowhawk, Common Buzzard, Woodcock, Barn Owl (scarce), Little Owl, Tawny Owl, Common Raven, Stock Dove, all three woodpeckers, Goldcrest; Coal, Marsh and Willow Tits; Wood Nuthatch, Eurasian Treecreeper, Common Redpoll (scarce in summer), Linnet, Bullfinch, Yellowhammer and other common woodland birds. River Wye: Great Cormorant (scarce May to July), Mute Swan, Mallard and Common Kingfisher.

April–September: Turtle Dove (scarce), Common Cuckoo, Tree Pipit (scarce), Rufous Nightingale (very rare), Common Redstart; scrub and woodland warblers including Grasshopper (rare), Lesser Whitethroat (scarce) and Wood; Spotted Flycatcher, Pied Flycatcher (scarce), Siskin (mostly April), Common Crossbill (in irruption years; from July to following May) and Hawfinch (very rare). River Wye: Goosander, Common Sandpiper and Sand Martin.

October–March: Thrushes including Fieldfare, Redwing and Mistle Thrush and finches including Brambling (rare), Siskin (increasingly in conifers after February) and Common Crossbill (following irruptions).

29 HEREFORD LUGG AND WYE

OS Landranger
Map 149

Habitat

To the east of Hereford the River Lugg flows through a wide, open floodplain of unimproved pastures, or Lammas lands. Part is an SSSI and some 40 acres (16 ha) have been acquired by the Herefordshire Nature Trust

(HNT), principally for their flora which includes yellow-rattle, pepper-saxifrage, great burnet and fritillary.

South of the city the Wye meanders through its floodplain and the confluence of the two rivers is at Mordiford, some 4 miles (6.4 km) downstream of the city centre. Riverside pastures dominate this open countryside, where hedges are few and trees scarce apart from bankside willows and alders, and the occasional oak. In places the riverbank has been undercut by the current and collapsed, leading to the growth of reed-grass, reedmace and hawthorn scrub. There are also riffles and gravelly islands. Most birds are to be found along the Wye, particularly at Hampton Bishop and Sink Green. During times of flood, however, the Lugg Valley around Tidnor and on the HNT reserve between Lugg and Lugwardine Bridges may hold the best concentrations.

Species

This area is not so rich in birdlife as it once was, but it is still good and certainly repays regular watching. Winter wildfowl and passage waders are the main interest. The former are most numerous following flooding, but in recent years this has been less severe.

Diving birds are few and irregular. The Wye usually holds up to ten Great Cormorants and in late autumn three or four Little Grebes and perhaps a Great Crested Grebe. Goosander are frequently, but not regularly, seen throughout the year, with about a dozen in winter or early spring. By midwinter one or two Common Pochard or Tufted Duck could also have arrived and Common Goldeneye is possible, though not so regular as a decade ago. Exceptionally, Common Scoter have even been noted on the Wye.

Dabbling duck are even more variable. A few dozen Mallard are normally present and one or two pairs breed. Mute Swans and Canada Geese also breed and up to 30 of the former may congregate in autumn or spring. Canada Geese flocks build up in autumn, when over 400 may be present in the Lugg valley, accompanied sometimes by other geese of unknown origin, such as White-fronts. Common Teal, usually less than a dozen, are present during the winter months, when Northern Pintail are almost annual and Eurasian Wigeon, Gadwall and Northern Shoveler occasionally appear. Winter flooding might still bring a small influx of these species and exceptionally one or two Tundra or Whooper Swans. Conditions are best as receding flood-waters leave random pools, with the Tidnor area being especially good. Common Shelduck, too, might pass along the rivers during their spring or autumn migrations.

Waders pass through in spring and autumn and visit the flood meadows in winter. Of the migrants, the first Eurasian Curlew arrive in the Lugg Meadows during March, with a pair or two staying to breed. Many Common Sandpipers also pass up the Wye during April. Movements of Oystercatcher, Dunlin and Common Redshank are erratic and birds rarely stay long. Return passage is more protracted and varied, especially when the rivers are low. Between July and October Green and Common Sandpipers move back downstream, with Green Sandpiper even staying through a mild winter. August and September are best for waders, with very small numbers of Dunlin and Common Redshank, around half-a-dozen Common Sandpipers and one or two Common Greenshank in a good year.

In winter the flood meadows regularly hold 1,000 Northern Lapwings, with twice as many in a good year. With them may be up to 200 European

Golden Plover, though their numbers vary considerably. Common Snipe probe the riverbanks or meadows as flood-waters subside, but numbers rarely reach double figures. Exceptionally one or two Dunlin, or even a Jack Snipe, might be seen. As well as waders, up to 400 Black-headed Gulls, a similar number of Common Gulls, some 200 Lesser Black-backs and a few Herring and Great Black-backed Gulls feed in the riverside meadows each winter. Look closely at gull flocks as Mediterranean, Ring-billed and Yellow-legged Gulls were all recently discovered on the Lugg meadows.

Large flocks of Fieldfare and Redwing are regular in late autumn and winter. Small parties of migrating Sky Larks and Meadow Pipits move westwards in autumn and return again in spring, with some overwintering. Several pairs of Sky Larks breed in the meadows, a few pairs of Sedge Warblers and Reed Buntings nest amongst the bankside willows and scrub and Common Kingfishers and Sand Martins in the riverbanks. Pied Wagtails are most numerous in late autumn, when small numbers of Grey Wagtails also pass through. In spring they are scarcer as they make for their upland breeding streams. Conversely, Yellow Wagtails are more evident in spring. Most common summer migrants occur in small numbers. The flower-rich meadows harbour insects for Barn Swallows and House Martins; Whinchats, Northern Wheatears and Common Redstarts are occasionally seen and a Common Stonechat might visit in late autumn. From late summer onwards, small parties of Linnets and Goldfinches feed on seed heads. In winter, 50 or more Chaffinches, a few Tree Sparrows and Yellowhammers, and less often one or two Bramblings or Reed Buntings add variety. Common Kestrel apart, this is not an outstanding area for predators, though Peregrine Falcons occasionally appear and a Barn Owl might be seen on a misty winter's evening.

A few scrub and woodland birds also occur, with the Lugg Meadows and the alders at Hampton Bishop holding small numbers of Common Redpoll and Siskin in winter. Lesser Spotted Woodpeckers are seen quite often around the village. In summer, passage warblers use the limited cover available, with Lesser Whitethroats regular visitors. Despite its diminished importance, rarities still occur from time to time, the most recent being two Little Egrets on the Wye and a Collared Pratincole along the Lugg.

Timing

Being so close to Hereford, this is a well used area, but weather has a greater influence on birds than disturbance. Spring passage is stronger in poor weather, when birds such as hirundines are forced to follow the river valleys and fly low to feed. Waders need low water levels to expose more mud and shingle spits in the channels.

Several days of heavy winter rainfall or a rapid snow thaw are needed to bring the flooding necessary to attract large numbers of gulls and wildfowl. Receding flood-waters then bring in waders, thrushes and maybe other open ground feeders. Severe frost will quickly force birds to vacate the meadows which become too hard to probe for food.

Access

Main roads across the area provide several access points. The south bank of the Wye can be reached from the B4399 just south of Sink Green, from where a footpath follows the river northwards. Likewise the north bank can be reached from the Wye Valley Path off the B4224 Hereford to Mordiford road. From Hereford, park in the lay-by on the left at the entrance to Hampton Bishop, cross over the road and take the footpath

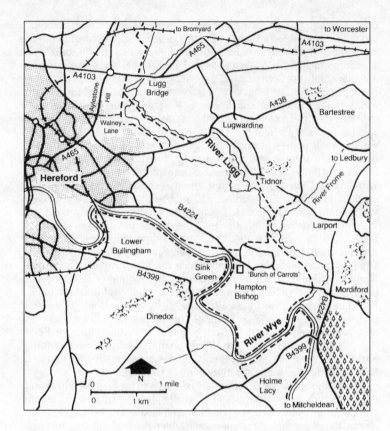

onto the riverbank immediately before the 'Bunch of Carrots' public house. Follow this round to rejoin the B4224 immediately west of Mordiford Bridge.

The Lugg flood meadows are best explored from the A465 Hereford to Bromyard road. Leaving the city, park in the lay-by on the right just as the road begins to descend Aylestone Hill. Walk down Walney Lane and take the footpath at the end onto the meadows. Other footpaths from the A465 near Lugg Bridge, the A438 near Lugwardine Bridge and Hampton Bishop village also give access. During times of flood explore from surrounding roads, especially the narrow lane to the northeast of the river between Lugwardine Bridge, Tidnor, Larport and Mordiford.

There are rail services to Hereford and bus services from there to Hampton Bishop/Mordiford, Lugwardine (Ledbury or Bromyard services), and Aylestone Hill/Lugg Bridge (Worcester or Bromyard services).

Calendar

All Year: Great Cormorant (rare May to July), Mute Swan, Canada Goose, Mallard, Common Kestrel, Common Kingfisher, Lesser Spotted Woodpecker, Sky Lark, Pied Wagtail, Reed Bunting and other common passerines.

March–June: Common Shelduck (scarce), Goosander (March/April), Oystercatcher (scarce), Dunlin (scarce), Eurasian Curlew, Common Redshank (scarce), Sky Lark, Meadow Pipit and Grey Wagtail (scarce).

From April, Common Sandpiper, hirundines, Yellow Wagtail; warblers including Sedge Warbler and Lesser Whitethroat; and passage migrants such as Common Redstart (scarce), Whinchat (scarce) or Northern Wheatear. Perhaps a rarity.

July–September: Summer visitors depart. Common Shelduck (scarce), Goosander (scarce), Northern Lapwing, Dunlin, Eurasian Curlew, Common Redshank, Common Greenshank, Green and Common Sandpipers, hirundines, Yellow Wagtail (scarce), Common Redstart, Whinchat (scarce), Northern Wheatear and flocks of Goldfinch and Linnet in September. Maybe a rarity.

October–February: Little and Great Crested Grebes, Tundra Swan (scarce), Whooper Swan (rare), Common Shelduck (scarce), Eurasian Wigeon (scarce), Gadwall (scarce), Common Teal, Northern Pintail (scarce), Northern Shoveler (scarce), Common Pochard, Tufted Duck, Common Goldeneye (scarce), Goosander, European Golden Plover, Northern Lapwing, Dunlin (rare), Jack Snipe (rare), Common Snipe, Green Sandpiper (scarce), gulls including a possible rare species, Barn Owl (rare), Meadow Pipit (mostly October–November), Grey Wagtail, Common Stonechat (scarce), Fieldfare, Redwing, Siskin, Common Redpoll and flocks of finches and buntings including Tree Sparrow and Brambling (both scarce). Perhaps unusual wildfowl or a rarity.

30 THE WYE GORGE

OS Landranger
Map 162

Habitat

Throughout its entire 156-mile (250 km) course, the Wye must rank as one of Britain's most beautiful rivers. Yet even amidst all its splendour no stretch can compare with the spectacular gorge which can be seen at its best at Symonds Yat. On the Herefordshire side are the Seven Sisters – a series of massive limestone buttresses with a rich and rare flora. Semi natural broadleaved woodland clings precariously to the precipitous slopes. Save for coppicing and the introduction of a few alien species, these woods have been little modified by man and are ecologically among the most important in Britain. They are very varied, with ash, beech, wych elm, small-leaved lime and yew on the more acidic summits; ash, wych elm and hazel on the slopes; alder along the valley; and oak and beech on the Old Red Sandstone. Wild cherry is also widespread and both the shrub and field layers are rich and varied.

West of the gorge, the huge limestone dome of the Great Doward supports an interesting mixture of woodland, scrub and small meadows. The Herefordshire Nature Trust (HNT) has several small reserves here, two of which are interesting for birds. At Woodside, high forest of oak and beech stands above an understorey that contains many berry-bearing species such as blackthorn, hawthorn, holly and yew. Parts are almost pure beechwood, with a typically sparse ground cover, but others have been recently coppiced. In contrast, at Leeping Stocks, which is botanically very rich, a long-neglected tangle of coppiced oak and hazel is now reverting to scrub woodland. Some fine beeches also mark the old field boundaries. Ground cover varies according to the soil and amount of shade cast by the canopy, with acid-loving species such as birch, bracken and common cow-wheat sometimes standing close to calcicoles such as sanicle, marjoram, wood spurge and wood melick.

East of the gorge, within a broad meander of the river, Coppet Hill provides yet more habitat variety. The steep western side is clad with bracken interspersed with patches of gorse and a few scattered trees. Along the footslope is a narrow belt of mature, mixed woodland, beyond which farmland stretches down to the riverbank. This and the meadows on the far bank at Huntsham are also of interest.

Species

The Wye Gorge is best known for its well publicised Peregrine Falcons and is well worth visiting for this alone, although the surrounding woods are also of interest.

The eyrie is on the Gloucestershire side of the river and is best watched from the RSBP's observation post on Yat Rock, where there are telescopes set up and wardens available. Although the adults are resident, observation is easiest during the breeding season, especially from June to August when the young are being fed. Then the birds are very noisy, often announcing their presence with a shrill, repetitive 'kak-kak-kak' long before you catch sight of them. Their behaviour is spectacular, with steep climbs, breathtaking plunges, acrobatic rolls, talon gripping and food passes.

The spectacular display of Peregrine Falcons can be watched above the Wye Gorge

Peregrine Falcons apart, Eurasian Jackdaws nest in crevices amongst the limestone crags and noisy parties are constantly wheeling around the cliffs. Common Buzzard, Eurasian Sparrowhawk, Common Kestrel and Common Raven also breed in the area and are frequently to be seen overhead, with perhaps half-a-dozen Common Buzzards or Common Ravens in the air together. Hobbies, too, appear regularly and sometimes a Barn Owl settles on the cliff face. The woods and scrub along the gorge and on the Doward and Coppet Hill hold Wrens, Hedge Accentors, Robins, thrushes, tits and finches. All three woodpeckers, Wood Nuthatch and Eurasian Treecreeper are resident, but keep mostly to the more mature woodland. In spring the drumming of woodpeckers reverberates around the gorge. Stock Doves and Tawny Owls nest in the older trees and Woodcock amongst the bracken. Summer visitors include Pied and Spotted Flycatchers, a few Common Redstarts and most scrub and sylvan warblers, including one or two pairs of Wood Warbler. Willow Warblers are widespread and, along with Chaffinch, are the commonest birds in the ashwoods. Pied Flycatchers utilise the nest boxes at the HNT reserve at Woodside.

Redwings and Fieldfares arrive in autumn and often join Mistle Thrushes to feed on yew berries. At this time of year, Goldcrests and Long-tailed Tits are much in evidence as well and Yat Rock is a good spot to look for Marsh Tits. Winter is generally quiet as the resident birds move about in search of food, but Common Ravens nest early and a Peregrine Falcon might disturb the tranquillity with an awesome stoop at any time.

For scrub species such as Common Whitethroat, Garden Warbler, Linnet and Yellowhammer try Coppet Hill or Leeping Stocks; and for arboreal ones like woodpeckers, Wood Nuthatch, Blackcap, Chiffchaff, Wood Warbler and Eurasian Jay try Woodside or Coppet Hill. With open views, the latter also lets you keep an eye out for raptors.

The river adds diversity. Great Cormorants and Grey Herons regularly fly past, often at great height, and a dozen or so of the former sometimes roost in riverside trees. Mallard, Moorhen and Little Grebe can all be seen and a passing Common Kingfisher can even be picked out from the top of Yat Rock. Many birds follow the Wye on their migrations and Barn Swallows, Sand Martins and Common Swifts can be seen in good numbers, while House Martins nest beneath Huntsham Bridge. Goosanders, too, are regularly seen, especially in April as they move upstream to their breeding territories. Small numbers of waders also pass along the river and Northern Lapwing, Eurasian Curlew, Common Redshank and Common Sandpiper might be seen along the banks or in the adjoining meadows. The meadows are also visited by Canada Geese and Tundra Swans have been recorded in winter. Recent sightings of Hen Harrier and Red Kite should inspire anyone thinking of exploring this little watched district to do so.

Timing

Symonds Yat, and especially the road up to Yat Rock, get very congested, so avoid fine summer weekends and bank holidays if at all possible. The Peregrine Falcons can be watched at any time, but are most active when feeding young from late May or June to August. For woodland birds, early mornings are the best time of day and May the best month. Raptors soar more on clear, calm days and little will be seen in the wind or rain.

Access

Yat Rock Leave the A40 Ross to Monmouth road 3 miles (4.8 km) beyond the western end of the Ross by-pass by turning southwards and following the signs to Goodrich. Bear right in the village, turn right onto the B4229 and in another 0.75 miles (1.2 km) turn left onto a minor road. Cross over the river at Huntsham Bridge and then in 1 mile (1.6 km) fork left up a narrow steep hill to Yat Rock, where there are pay-and-display car parks, a shop and toilets.

Coppet Hill Take the left fork in Goodrich along the cul-de-sac leading to Welsh Bicknor. Park on the verge in 0.25 miles (0.4 km), follow the track to the right, forking right again down the hill past the restricted road width sign. At the bottom, take the waymarked path to the left of the house and follow this through the wood and down to the river. At the river, turn north and follow the public footpath along the riverbank to Huntsham Bridge. From here, follow the road towards Goodrich and take the public footpath on the right (opposite the turn to Goodrich church) back to your car.

Doward Reserves Continue southwestwards on the A40 to Whitchurch. Leave the main road here and take the old road to Crockers Ash. Then turn southwards into a narrow lane past the Doward Hotel. Continue along this lane, round both right-hand and left-hand hairpin bends. Leeping Stocks is about 160 yds (150 m) along the lane towards the Heritage Centre. Parking is at the top of the track to the Biblins. Access to the reserve is strictly for HNT members only. For Woodside continue on

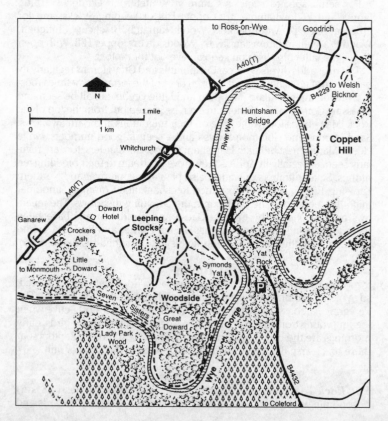

196

the narrow lane for another 200 yds (180 m) beyond the track to Leeping Stocks. Park where the lane turns sharp left and follow the track straight ahead up the hill. At the fork turn right and the reserve is on the right. Again access is strictly for HNT members only.

The Gloucester–Monmouth bus service passes through Goodrich and Whitchurch. It is a 2.5 miles (4 km) walk from Goodrich to Yat Rock with a long, steep ascent. The Doward sites are about a 1.5-mile (2.4 km) walk from Whitchurch.

Calendar

All Year: Eurasian Sparrowhawk, Common Buzzard, Common Kestrel, Peregrine Falcon, Moorhen, Woodcock, Stock Dove, Barn Owl (rare), Tawny Owl, all three woodpeckers, Goldcrest, Long-tailed and Marsh Tits, Wood Nuthatch, Eurasian Treecreeper, Eurasian Jay, Eurasian Jackdaw, Common Raven, Linnet, Yellowhammer, and other common woodland birds. River Wye: Little Grebe, Great Cormorant (scarce in summer), Grey Heron, Canada Goose, Mallard and Common Kingfisher.

April–September: Hobby, Common Swift (May to August), hirundines, Common Redstart; scrub and sylvan warblers including Wood; and Spotted and Pied Flycatchers. River Wye: Goosander and common passage waders. Maybe a rare migrant.

October–March: Thrushes including Fieldfare, Redwing and Mistle Thrush; and flocks of tits and finches. River Wye: Maybe scarce wildfowl.

31 THE BLACK MOUNTAINS OS Landranger Map 161

Habitat

The Black Mountains protrude into west Herefordshire, where, at 2306 ft (703 m), they form the highest part of the region. The county boundary is marked by the Offa's Dyke Path, which wends its way across a high plateau that falls precipitously into valleys on either side. To the west is the Brecon Beacons National Park, to the east the glaciated Olchon Valley. This remote, beautiful valley is penetrated only by a steep and narrow lane which loops back on itself to return on the opposite side of the valley.

The tiny Olchon Brook is flanked by a patchwork of small meadows. These continue up the gentle lower slopes, but as the gradient steepens, gradually give way to banks of bracken above which are scree slopes surmounted by sheer cliffs and crags of exposed sandstone. The summit is a windswept plateau of moorland grass and heather, with crowberry locally abundant.

Woodland is not extensive, but there are some open ashwoods along the higher slopes and tiny sessile oakwoods lower down. Moreover there is a wealth of free-standing and hedgerow timber. Stunted hawthorns are characteristic of the moorland fringe, particularly high in the head of the valley.

Species

The primary interest is upland breeding species.

On the high tops, where winter can be harsh, truly resident birds are few, apart from Red Grouse and corvids. The Black Mountains hold fair stocks of Red Grouse, though the Herefordshire population is small, with just three or four pairs. Common Ravens nest early, so their tumbling display flights begin in winter, while in autumn up to 20 might roost together or flock around a good food source. Common Buzzards also regularly soar above the valley.

*Ring Ouzels breed amongst the high crags and scree slopes
of the Black Mountains*

From mid-March onwards, Eurasian Curlews and Meadow Pipits return to their upland breeding grounds and the latter are soon everywhere across the hills. Close behind them, the first Northern Wheatears and two or three pairs of Ring Ouzels arrive and occupy territories on the high crags and scree slopes. Soon other migrants return to the valley. Willow Warblers are numerous and widespread, Chiffchaffs sing from the tree-tops and Blackcaps from bushy undergrowth. On the valley slopes, Tree Pipits sing from the higher, open woods, Common Whitethroats inhabit patches of scrub, Common Cuckoos call and Whinchats nest here and there. Along the brook, Grey Wagtails and Dippers busily feed young, while in the overhanging branches Common Redstarts and Pied Flycatchers dart after insects. Several pairs of Pied Flycatchers breed in nest boxes at the head of the valley. Most common birds can also be found, including all three woodpeckers. A more unusual migrant might be seen, with recent occurrences of Black Redstart.

After midsummer birds become less obvious, but a family party of warblers, flycatchers or chats, including perhaps Common Stonechats, might stop to feed for a time before moving on again. Mistle Thrushes and Ring Ouzels are often attracted to the rowan berries at this time. As the winds sweep storm clouds across the plateau, so flocks of Redwings and Fieldfares, and occasionally Siskin, shelter in the valley.

As well as Common Buzzard, Eurasian Sparrowhawk and Common Kestrel can always be expected. Less often a Peregrine Falcon soars high above the crags or a Merlin swoops down the valley in pursuit of its prey. The Brecon Beacons were once a Merlin stronghold, but numbers have fallen with the recent national decline. Exceptionally, spring or autumn bring other birds of prey. A Red Kite was recently reported and Short-eared Owl has been seen.

Timing

Weather is the most critical factor. Although the first summer visitors can arrive as early as March, in a cold, late spring they may be delayed until April or even May. Early mornings are the best time of day, before too many people are in the valley or on the hills. If bad weather is forecast it is advisable to think twice about venturing onto the summit, where walking is rough and it is easy to get lost in the mist. Nothing much will be seen in wet, misty weather anyway. On windy days birds tend to seek the shelter of the valley. Calm, clear weather is best for soaring raptors.

Access

The best approach is from the A465 Hereford to Abergavenny road. Turn northwestwards into a narrow lane at Pandy, which is 6 miles (9.6 km) north of Abergavenny. Pass under the railway, over the river and then turn right at the T junction. Continue straight ahead for 3 miles (4.8 km) to Clodock. Turn left in the village, just before the church, and follow the road to Longtown, forking left again in 0.6 miles (1 km). Go through Longtown village and in 0.75 miles (1.2 km) turn left again down a steep hill and across the brook. Follow the lane round to the right and beneath the towering outcrops of the Black and Red Darens. Park at the picnic area on the left and explore. The energetic can make the steep climb up to the top of plateau and follow the Offa's Dyke Path, returning down the head of Olchon Valley and back along the road. For an easier ascent, continue by car past some small woods and at the end turn left to follow the lane into the head of the valley. Park by the bridge, cross the brook and take the footpath on the left up the valley to the plateau top. This walk should produce most of the characteristic birds. On returning to your car, leave the valley by the opposite side and take a track to the left which climbs steeply to another picnic area on the edge of Black Hill. With commanding views, this is a good spot to watch for raptors.

Alternatively, leave Hay-on-Wye on the B4350 towards Brecon and take the first left after the B4348. Continue climbing up a twisty, narrow lane for 2.5 miles (4 km), then take the right fork up a steep hill onto the unfenced moor. In just over 1 mile (2 km) the road crosses Offa's Dyke Path and shortly beyond is a car park on the right beneath Hay Bluff. Park here and take the Offa's Dyke Path southeastwards. This crosses the moor and in just over 2 miles (4 km) another path strikes off left and down into the Olchon Valley.

Calendar

All Year: Eurasian Sparrowhawk, Common Buzzard, Common Kestrel, Red Grouse, all three woodpeckers, Grey Wagtail, Dipper, corvids including Common Raven and other common passerines.

March–September: Eurasian Curlew and Meadow Pipit. From April: Common Cuckoo, Tree Pipit, Common Redstart, Whinchat, Northern Wheatear,

Ring Ouzel, common scrub and woodland warblers, and Pied Flycatcher. Perhaps scarcer migrant such as Common Stonechat or passing raptor.

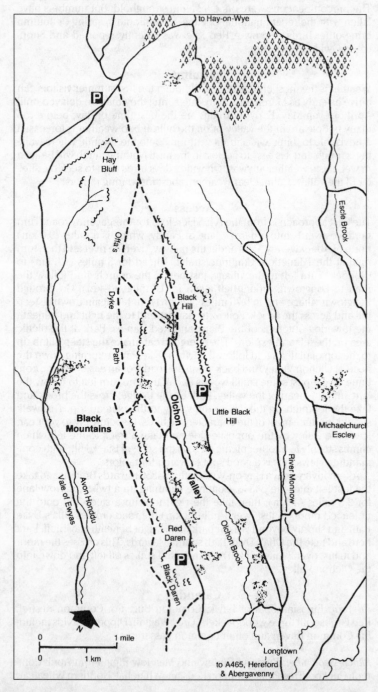

October–February: Thrushes including Fieldfare and Redwing; and Siskin. Perhaps a passing raptor.

32 THE GOLDEN VALLEY

OS Landranger
Maps 148 & 149

The Golden Valley follows the course of the River Dore. This small river rises almost within sight of the Wye, but turns its back on the main river. Instead it flows southeastwards for 12 miles (19 km) through some of Herefordshire's loveliest and most unspoilt countryside to its confluence with the Monnow at Pontrilas.

Habitat

The valley consists of fertile farmland, enclosed by gentle, wooded hillsides. The tiny villages are linked together by narrow lanes winding between high hedge banks.

There are four main sites. At the head of the valley, on the watershed between the Dore and the Wye, is Merbach Hill. The summit is ideal for open-ground species, with a short sward broken up by patches of gorse and several shallow gullies of bare rock. These shelter plants and birds from the wind. From the top, 1045 ft (318 m) above sea level, is a splendid panorama down the Wye. The northern slope is largely wooded, but the others are covered by extensive areas of hawthorn scrub with a few scattered birch trees and a ground flora of bracken and bluebell – a perfect habitat for scrub and woodland fringe birds.

Six miles (9.6 km) southeast is Stockley Hill and Timberline Wood. Stockley Hill is part of a low ridge of hills separating the narrow Golden Valley from the broad plain of the Wye. For much of its length this ridge is clothed in woodland, of which Timberline is a typical example. It is a privately owned oakwood, managed for forestry, and parts have been clear-felled and replanted with a mixture of coniferous and broadleaved species, including pine and beech. There is a dense understorey in which bramble is often dominant.

Some 2.5 miles (4 km) away, on the other side of the valley, the Herefordshire Nature Trust (HNT) has a small reserve of 23 acres (9.2 ha) at Crow Wood and Meadow. Here, within a small area, is a floristically rich meadow dotted with cowslips and common spotted-orchids; wood pasture with some huge, mature oaks; a small area of coppiced woodland dominated by hazel and carpeted with primroses and wood anemones; and three fast-flowing streams.

Lastly, a further 5 miles (8 km) southeast, nearly at the bottom of the valley, is Ewyas Harold Common. This is an extensive area of undulating common land with a range of habitats from open, bracken-clad slopes, through extensive areas of gorse, blackthorn and hawthorn scrub, to small areas of mature woodland.

Species

Birds of woodland and scrub with an upland bias are of most interest. In the valley generally, Common Buzzards and Common Ravens are regularly overhead, Eurasian Curlew may breed in some of the damper pastures, Common Redstarts flit along the roadside hedges and Dippers and Grey Wagtails frequent the streams and rivers. Both Red-legged and Grey Partridge can be found around field margins, while Bullfinches and small flocks of Tree Sparrows and Siskin occur in winter.

The four main sites regularly hold the commoner woodland residents and summer visitors. In addition, the summit of Merbach Hill is typical habitat for Meadow Pipits, either breeding or on passage during early spring and late autumn. Northern Wheatears, too, appear on passage and a pair or two may breed. Lower down the slopes, where scattered trees provide songposts, two or three pairs of Tree Pipits occur. Here the hawthorn scrub holds several Willow Warblers, Blackcaps, Common Whitethroats, Chiffchaffs, Linnets, Yellowhammers and a few Common Redstarts. In autumn the same area provides a well-stocked larder for Redwings and Fieldfares. Common Ravens breed on Merbach Hill and raptors are a feature of the valley. Eurasian Sparrowhawk, Common Kestrel and Common Buzzard are always around and passage can bring other species, with records of Red Kite and a recent spectacle of two Peregrine Falcons being mobbed by five Common Ravens over Merbach Hill.

The woods at Timberline hold a good range of woodland birds, especially the more arboreal species such as woodpeckers, Wood Nuthatch and Eurasian Treecreeper. There are plenty of warblers too, including both Blackcap and Garden Warbler. During the day noisy flocks of Eurasian Jackdaws and Carrion Crows feed on the adjoining fields, coming to roost in the woods at dusk. Many of the former nest in the derelict farm buildings nearby. In addition to most of the above, Crow Wood also holds Tawny Owls, a long established rookery and two upland specialities, namely Common Redstart and Pied Flycatcher. The stream here is equally interesting, with Grey Herons, Common Kingfishers, Dippers and Grey Wagtails to be seen. Lesser Whitethroats may also breed in the area.

Ewyas Harold Common is a good spot to listen for the 'yaffle' call of a Green Woodpecker or the gentle 'purring' of a Turtle Dove. Common Whitethroats and, more sparingly, Common Stonechats nest among the gorse, with the latter more likely after a succession of mild winters. The thorn scrub holds a few pairs of Common Redstarts, and perhaps a pair of Lesser Whitethroats, and Eurasian Curlew sometimes visit the common during spring and autumn. Autumn also brings Redwings and Fieldfares to the hawthorn berries, with one exceptional Redwing count of 1,000. As dusk falls, Little Owls begin to hunt and a Barn Owl might float silently past. Finally, as darkness deepens, the hooting of Tawny Owls carries across the common.

Whilst at Ewyas Harold it is always worth checking the Dulas Brook in the village as this is a favoured haunt of Dipper and Grey Wagtail and a Mandarin Duck was once seen.

Timing

A good range of birds is present at all seasons, but spring and summer are best. For resident species, early spring is best, before the buds break into leaf, as the birds are then easier to see. Raptors will be most active on calm, sunny days. Disturbance is not usually a factor in this quiet area of countryside.

Access

The B4348 and B4347 run the length of the Golden Valley from Dorstone to Pontrilas.

Merbach Hill Leave the A438 Hereford–Brecon road by turning west-wards into Bredwardine at either of the two junctions between Staunton-on-Wye and Letton. Go straight ahead at the cross roads in Bredwardine along a narrow lane up a steep hill and round several bends. In just over 1 mile (1.6 km), where the lane turns sharply left, park on the verge and follow the track ahead on foot, passing through the gate at the end and onto the hill. Take extreme care parking, as space is very limited. The walk to the summit is about 0.75 miles (1.2 km), but is often very wet so suitable footwear is recommended. Public footpaths can be used to make a longer circular walk, taking in part of Westonhill Wood on the northern slope of the hill. There is a limited bus service from Hereford to Bredwardine.

Timberline Wood Leave the B4348 Hay-on-Wye to Hereford road east-wards at the cross roads in Peterchurch. Continue for 1.5 miles (2.4 km) until you reach a track turning off to the right, just beyond the brow of the hill. Park here (space is again restricted, so take care) and follow the way-marked bridleway up the hill alongside a wood, round a sharp left turn and past a derelict farm to Timberline Wood. Continue along the edge of the wood until the bridleway enters it. There are also waymarked public footpaths which can be used to explore the wood further. A limited bus service, operating between Hereford and Brecon, serves Peterchurch.

Crow Wood Leave the B4348 at Vowchurch by turning southwestwards towards Michaelchurch Escley. Continue through the village, over the river and through the village of Turnastone. The reserve is then on the right-hand side by a small bridge about 1.25 miles (2 km) further on. Park here, enter the gate, walk up the field with the hedge on your left until reaching a stile and footbridge on the left which lead into the reserve. Access is strictly for HNT members only. Again a limited bus service, operating between Hereford and Brecon, serves Vowchurch, 1.75 miles (2.8 km) from the reserve.

Ewyas Harold Common Leave the A465 Hereford–Abergavenny road at Pontrilas and take the B4347 northwards. Continue round the sharp bends, across the stream and through Ewyas Harold village. A quarter of a mile (0.4 km) beyond the village turn left into a narrow cul-de-sac. Follow this to the end, park on the common and explore on foot. Alter-natively, continue on the B4347 past Dore Abbey, round the left-hand bend in Abbey Dore and then go straight ahead where the main road turns sharply right. Continue up the hill for 0.5 miles (0.8 km) and turn sharp left onto a narrow track leading onto the common. Park and explore on foot. There is a bus service from Hereford through Ewyas Harold to Abbey Dore.

Calendar

All Year: Grey Heron, Eurasian Sparrowhawk, Common Buzzard, Common Kestrel, Red-legged and Grey Partridges, Little Owl, Tawny Owl, Common Kingfisher, all three woodpeckers, Dipper, Grey Wagtail, Wood Nuthatch, Eurasian Treecreeper, Eurasian Jackdaw, Rook, Carrion Crow, Common Raven and common passerines.

April–September: Eurasian Curlew, Turtle Dove (scarce), Tree Pipit, Meadow Pipit, Common Redstart, Common Stonechat (scarce), Northern Wheatear; common scrub and woodland warblers including Lesser Whitethroat (scarce); Pied Flycatcher, Linnet and Yellowhammer. Possible passing raptor.

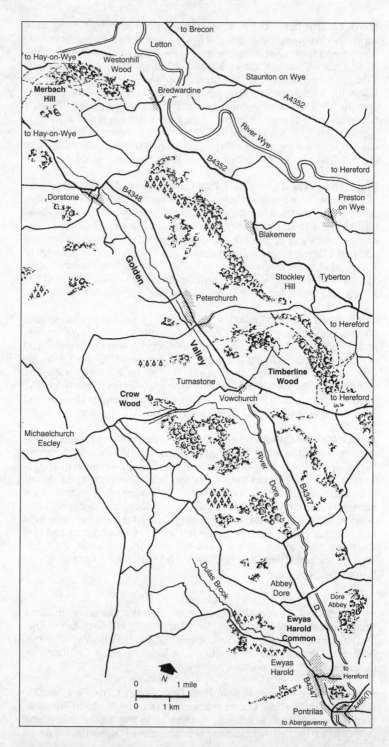

October–March: Barn Owl (scarce), Meadow Pipit (October and March), Fieldfare, Redwing, Tree Sparrow (scarce), Siskin and Bullfinch.

33 THE MIDDLE WYE VALLEY

OS Landranger
Map 148

Habitat

Around Hay-on-Wye, the river leaves Wales and enters Herefordshire. From its narrow valley across mineral-deficient bedrocks upstream, it is abruptly deflected northeastwards by the Black Mountains. For the next 10 miles (16 km) it meanders through a mile-wide floodplain across the nutrient-rich Old Red Sandstone. During this swift transition, life in the river increases sharply, making it much more attractive to birds.

The river is broad, but fairly shallow, with a gravelly bed. At times there are fast currents across shallow runs, at others a sluggish flow through deeper pools. The meanders have deep, undercut sandstone banks on their outsides, and exposed gravelly spits on their insides. Behind these spits are natural levees and flood meadows backed by some beautiful, rolling, wooded countryside. Within the floodplain there are one or two ox-bow lakes and pools and numerous large willows and alders.

Species

Herefordshire has few pools or lakes, so wildfowl and waders make great use of suitable stretches of river such as this. Numbers are seldom large and birds cannot be guaranteed, as much depends on the state of the river and the flood meadows. Nevertheless, regular watching yields an interesting list of species.

Mute Swans are a feature of this stretch of river. Only a pair or two breed, but between late summer and spring small herds of a dozen or so gather, sometimes merging into concentrations of 50 or more. Canada Geese also congregate in late summer, perhaps building to an autumn peak of 400 or more, then dispersing through the winter.

Other wildfowl are sometimes drawn into the valley. Up to ten Whooper Swans come most winters, usually to the stretch from Glasbury (Wales) to Clifford. Further downstream, Tundra Swans favour the reach between Clifford and Winforton. Usually fewer than 20 are present, but herds of more than 50 have been recorded. A party of 12 Barnacle Geese that arrived after a windy December night and a single Brent Goose may have been wild, but otherwise recent years have brought very few wild geese.

Dabbling duck numbers vary with the weather and the degree of flooding. Mallard are most consistent, with several pairs breeding and 100 or more present from September through to February, but Common Teal and Eurasian Wigeon numbers fluctuate. A few Common Teal can often be seen from September onwards, but parties above a dozen are unusual before January or February, when 50–100 may take advantage of

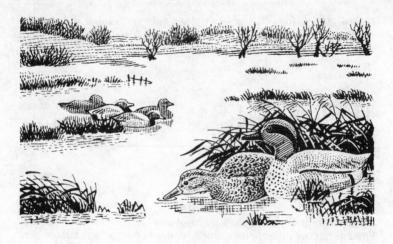

If the Wye meadows flood in winter they attract flocks of dabbling duck such as Eurasian Wigeon (left) and Common Teal

winter flooding. By March most have left again. Eurasian Wigeon seldom appear much before late October, when up to 50 may settle in for the winter. However, flooding or severe cold can bring 100 or more to the meadows between January and March.

Diving birds keep more to the river and pools and depend less on flooding. Up to ten Great Cormorants and about five Little Grebes are regularly present from September through to March. Tufted Duck also occur sparingly, with barely half-a-dozen, while Common Pochard remain scarce and irregular. Great Crested Grebes are uncommon too, though one might appear in spring or autumn. In contrast, Common Goldeneye and Goosander are regular visitors. Typically, one or two Common Goldeneye are around from November to March, with more in severe weather. The Wye is excellent for Goosanders and a few pairs are now breeding. Passage takes place in March and April, when parties up to 20 strong move upriver to their breeding grounds. A small return passage then occurs in late August or September, but it is October or November before the first wintering birds arrive, with some six or so regularly along this stretch of river and on occasions up to 20. As with Common Goldeneye, winter numbers often increase in hard weather. In 1994 the Ministry of Agriculture, Fisheries and Food granted a licence for Goosander and Great Cormorant to be shot.

Grey Herons from the small heronry near Clifford frequently fly along the river or stand around in fields. Common Kingfishers, too, are ever present and might be encountered at any time. Outside the breeding season, small parties of Black-headed Gulls frequent the flood meadows, their numbers highest in winter when they are joined by a few Common and Lesser Black-backed Gulls, and perhaps by one or two Herring or Great Black-backed Gulls.

Northern Lapwings begin to return from their breeding grounds in July and during late summer and early autumn flocks of 600 feed along the valley. Thereafter numbers vary, holding up in some years, but declining in others. Several hundred European Golden Plover used to accompany them, but records are now sparse and numbers barely into double figures. Up to a dozen Common Snipe arrive in August to winter in the valley, their numbers increasing two or threefold when receding floods leave standing water on the meadows. Exceptionally a Jack Snipe or Water Rail is found in early autumn too. A small flock of Eurasian Curlew usually overwinters upstream of Hay, while downstream Woodcock come from the woods to feed at dusk and one or two wintering Green Sandpipers frequent the small pools and ox-bow lakes.

March and April are the main months for passage waders. Parties of six to twelve Common Sandpipers regularly work their way upstream along the river banks in April, while most years bring a solitary Oystercatcher, Great Ringed Plover, Dunlin, Whimbrel or Common Redshank. By late July return passage has begun, but this is seldom as strong or varied as that in spring. First to show are usually a couple of Green Sandpipers and up to half-a-dozen Common Sandpipers, followed in August by the main passage of Common Sandpipers. Once they would have been accompanied by good numbers of Common Greenshanks, but in recent years virtually none has appeared. Other waders appear to have become increasingly irregular too, as do terns, with just one recent record of a solitary Common Tern.

Many migrants follow the valley, especially during a cold spring. Meadow Pipits begin to move through in March and later in the month Sand Martins return to their riverbank nest-holes. The first Northern Wheatears arrive about the same time on their way to the hills. Shortly afterwards a few brilliant Yellow Wagtails, perhaps as many as 20, appear along the riverbanks or in the meadows, Barn Swallows swoop across the river, one or two Common Redstarts establish territories and the occasional pair of Sedge Warblers takes up residence. Late summer and autumn see families of the same species moving back downriver. With them may be Whinchats or Spotted Flycatchers, a wandering Common Whitethroat or Lesser Whitethroat, or a solitary Pied Flycatcher.

With summer visitors gone, resident songbirds such as Linnet and Goldfinch flock together and Fieldfare and Redwing gather in numbers to feed. A small party of the declining Tree Sparrow might also be around. Later, as any winter floods subside, the thrushes transfer to the meadows in search of food. Parties of Siskin and Long-tailed Tits work their way through riverside alders and both Pied and Grey Wagtails feed along the banks. Common Ravens, Stock Doves and all three woodpeckers also frequent the area.

Amongst the birds of prey, Common Kestrel, Eurasian Sparrowhawk and Little Owl are regularly seen, Common Buzzards glide overhead and in the evening twilight a Barn Owl sometimes drifts across the floodplain. Less often a passing Merlin or Peregrine Falcon pauses to harass the wintering wildfowl. Rarities are few, but spring often brings a White or Blue-headed Wagtail, a passing Osprey pauses to fish most years and the biggest surprise of all was the discovery of a Desert Wheatear in 1994.

Timing

Apart from anglers, there is little human disturbance. In winter, flooding is critical. Normally it does not occur until the end of the year, and conditions are usually best sometime between January and March when flood-waters are receding. Hard weather may bring an influx of diving duck from frozen pools and lakes. Spring passage is often best in cool, wet weather, when birds fly low and follow the valley. Periods after gales promise to be interesting, whether in spring or autumn.

Access

The 14 miles (22 km) between Hay-on-Wye and Bredwardine are the most interesting, with the precise whereabouts of birds depending very much on

the time of year and the extent of flooding. North of the valley is the A438 Hereford to Brecon road and south is the B4352 Hereford to Hay road. A few river meadows can be viewed from these roads. The best access points are as follows, but views are distant and a telescope essential.

Hay-on-Wye Leave the B4351 Clyro road immediately north of the river bridge in Hay and take the Offa's Dyke Path to the right, following this along the Welsh shore for 2 miles (3.2 km) through to the A438.

Castleton Take the B4350 (Leominster road) northeastwards out of Hay as far as Clifford. At the far end of the village turn right into a narrow lane and then in 300 yds (0.3 km) turn left. Continue for a little over 1 mile (2 km) until the lane turns sharp right up a hill. Park near this turn (space is restricted) and either follow the Wye Valley Walk eastwards as far as Clock Mills on the B4352, 2 miles (3.2 km) or northwards as far as the toll bridge on the B4350 – just under 1 mile (1.5 km).

Winforton A public footpath leads down to the river from the A438 at the western end of the village.

Bredwardine Turn eastwards at the crossroads in the village, cross over the river bridge and take the left turn towards Letton. Alternatively, turn right just before the river bridge, park by the church and follow the public footpath to the right. This skirts the edge of a wood and eventually rejoins the B4352 in a little over 1 mile (1.8 km), opposite Moccas Deer Park. There is no public access to the Deer Park, but it is always worth checking from the road.

Limited bus services operate from Hereford along the A438 almost as far as Willersley, along the B4352 as far as Bredwardine and along the B4348 to Hay-on-Wye.

Calendar

All Year: Grey Heron, Mute Swan, Canada Goose, Mallard, Eurasian Sparrowhawk, Common Buzzard, Common Kestrel, Stock Dove, Barn Owl, Little Owl, Common Kingfisher, all three woodpeckers, Grey and Pied Wagtails, Long-tailed Tit, Common Raven, and other common passerines.

March–June: Winter visitors leave by April. Great Crested Grebe (passage; scarce), Goosander (March/April) and Meadow Pipit. From April: Common Sandpiper or other common passage wader, Sand Martin, Barn Swallow, Yellow Wagtail, Common Redstart, Northern Wheatear and warblers including Sedge. Perhaps a passing raptor, tern or other rarity.

July–September: Departing summer visitors as in spring, plus Whinchat (scarce), Lesser and Common Whitethroat or Spotted and Pied Fly-catcher. Passage waterfowl and waders including Great Crested Grebe (scarce), Goosander (August/September), Northern Lapwing, and Green and Common Sandpipers. Black-headed Gulls, Goldfinch and Linnet. Perhaps a passing raptor.

October–February: Little Grebe, Great Cormorant, Tundra Swan (scarce), Whooper Swan (scarce), Eurasian Wigeon, Common Teal, Common Pochard (scarce), Tufted Duck (scarce), Common Goldeneye, Goosander, Merlin (scarce), Peregrine Falcon (scarce), Water Rail (rare),

European Golden Plover (sporadic), Northern Lapwing, Jack Snipe (rare), Common Snipe, Woodcock (scarce), Eurasian Curlew, Green Sandpiper (scarce), gulls; thrush flocks including Fieldfare and Redwing; Tree Sparrow (scarce) with finch flocks; Siskin. Maybe wild geese, a passing raptor or rarity.

34 HERGEST RIDGE

OS Landranger
Map 148

Habitat

This large, open hill rises to 1394 feet (426 m). Eastwards and southwards it slopes gently into the valleys of the River Arrow and Gladestry Brook, whereas to the north and west it falls away steeply into a narrow valley. Mixed woodland, with some fine beeches, covers the northern foot-slopes, but otherwise the hillsides are covered with vast sweeps of bracken, relieved only by an area of stunted gorse around the Whet Stone. An unusual and most incongruous feature is the dozen or so stunted monkey puzzle trees in the same area. On the lower slopes bracken gives way to short turf, with a few scattered rowans to the east that attract feeding thrushes in late summer. Some of the perimeter boundaries are defined by overgrown hawthorn hedges.

Species

Open ground species are the main attraction, especially in spring and summer.

At these times the hillsides abound with Sky Larks and Meadow Pipits, with some of the latter fostering the offspring of Common Cuckoos. Several Linnets, Yellowhammers and up to half-a-dozen Common Stonechats usually breed in the areas of gorse. A similar number of Whinchats, several pairs of Northern Wheatear and a few Tree Pipits also breed, the latter often ending their song flights in one of the rowan trees. Other species use the hillsides for feeding, with Common Swifts and Barn Swallows taking insects from above the bracken.

Common Buzzards and Common Raven are regularly overhead, with sometimes a dozen or more of either species in the air at the same time, while Carrion Crows keep a watchful eye on proceedings. The old, over-grown thorn hedges are always worth searching for Common Redstarts, where a pair or two usually nest, while among the typical species in the woods are a few Wood Warblers. Green Woodpeckers and Mistle Thrushes find the blend of scattered trees and open hillsides very much to their liking.

After the breeding season, small flocks of 50 or so Northern Lapwings and a few Eurasian Curlew perhaps visit the hill for a few days. Common Pheasants or a covey of Red-legged Partridge might be found around the farmland fringe on the lower slopes, while in winter the same areas sometimes attract a small flock of Tree Sparrows. Late winter or early spring might bring a small flock of European Golden Plover, or a small passage of Eurasian Curlew.

Timing

Weather is important. There are few landmarks on the hillsides, so it is unwise to venture up in poor visibility. In any case, very little will be seen in wet, windy or misty weather. Raptors are most likely in clear, calm conditions. Severe weather will force most birds to forsake the summit for the lower slopes. Although the Offa's Dyke Path crosses the hill, human disturbance is not usually too great a factor.

Access

Leave the A44 at the western end of Kington by pass, following the signs to Hergest Croft Gardens. Take the first turn right, again following the brown-backed signs to Hergest Croft, continue to the end and park on the verge. The gate straight ahead leads onto the hillside. Follow Offa's Dyke Path to the summit. There is a bus service from Hereford to Kington, from where it is about 1 mile (1.6 km) to the gate leading onto the hill.

Calendar

All Year: Common Buzzard, Red-legged Partridge, Common Pheasant, Green Woodpecker and other common woodland birds, Mistle Thrush, Carrion Crow, Common Raven, Linnet and Yellowhammer.

April–June: Common Cuckoo, Common Swift (after April), Sky Lark, Barn Swallow, Tree Pipit (scarce), Meadow Pipit, Common Redstart, Whinchat, Common Stonechat, Northern Wheatear and woodland warblers including Wood. Perhaps passing raptor.

July–September: Summer visitors depart. Northern Lapwing, Eurasian Curlew (scarce) and thrushes. Perhaps passing raptor.

October–March: European Golden Plover (February/March), Eurasian Curlew (March; scarce) and small flocks of Tree Sparrow.

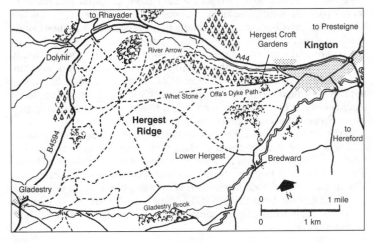

Habitat

Titley Pool, also known as Eywood Pool, is a Herefordshire Nature Trust (HNT) reserve and an SSSI. The reserve extends to 23.5 acres (9.4 ha) and comprises the lake, a herb-rich meadow to the east and Green Wood to the south. The lake, believed to be a glacial kettle-hole, has been enlarged by the construction of a dam at the eastern end. Standing water is scarce in Herefordshire, so this delightfully secluded 15-acre (6 ha) pool, set in private parkland, is of special importance. There is a small island and a narrow belt of perimeter woodland that includes many oaks and alders, together with some ash and birch. Replanted areas also include hornbeam and beech, and the diverse shrub layer attracts many breeding birds, especially warblers. Though modified by man, Green Wood, with its sheets of bluebells, is probably a fragment of ancient woodland which is managed as high forest.

Species

For a small reserve the birdlife is especially rich and, with regular watching, over 100 species have been recorded. Wildfowl are the main interest, although numbers are never high.

A few pairs of Great Crested Grebe, Mute Swan, Canada Goose, Mallard, Tufted Duck and Common Coot regularly breed. By early autumn some 150 Canada Geese and Mallard and up to 20 Tufted Duck may be present, with smaller numbers wintering alongside some 20 Common Pochard and 50 Common Coot. A couple of dozen Common Teal normally arrive around September and remain until the following spring. If the pool freezes over they leave, but some may return again in February or March.

Other species are less regular, but a few Great Cormorants sometimes make winter visits and one or two Northern Shoveler pass through, usually staying just for a day or two in autumn and returning in March. Small numbers of Eurasian Wigeon also occasionally appear in winter, while Garganey, Gadwall and Northern Pintail have all been recorded. In recent years Common Goldeneye appear to have forsaken the pool, but Goosander have become increasingly more regular and numerous. As many as 30 may be present in the autumn, of which 20 might stay through the winter and breeding has occurred. Although not breeding, Ruddy Duck occur in small numbers, particularly in spring and autumn. Wildfowl apart, both Grey Herons and Common Kingfishers often come to seek their next meal. There is little suitable habitat for waders, but a muddy edge in late summer might hold a Green or Common Sandpiper. Water Rail have also been reported in autumn.

In the woods, Little and Tawny Owls, all three woodpeckers, Willow Tit and Wood Nuthatch are resident along with a host of common species, while Common Buzzards frequently circle overhead. Summer visitors include Common Redstart, Sedge Warbler, Garden Warbler, Blackcap, Wood Warbler and Pied Flycatcher. Winter is quieter, but a Woodcock might be flushed from the wood, Fieldfare and Redwing visit in small numbers and parties of Siskin, perhaps with a few Common Redpoll, feed on alder seeds.

Timing
There is little disturbance, but early morning is always the best time to hear and see songbirds in spring and summer. Duck are most numerous in late summer and autumn, but desert the pool altogether when it freezes over. Because it is quiet and secluded, many wildfowl use the pool solely for roosting, so late evening may bring some fresh arrivals from elsewhere.

Access
Titley Pool is owned by the HNT and the surrounding land is all private. The water is small and anyone approaching the shoreline is liable to disturb the birds. Access is therefore strictly limited to HNT members. There is a hide.

Approach from B4355 Kington to Presteigne road, turning westwards between Titley Court and the Stag Inn into the Eywood Park entrance. Drive past the pool on your left, take the first turning left, cross a cattle grid and turn left again after 50 yds (50 m). Go through two field gates and drive on to park in the space provided on the right, just before the

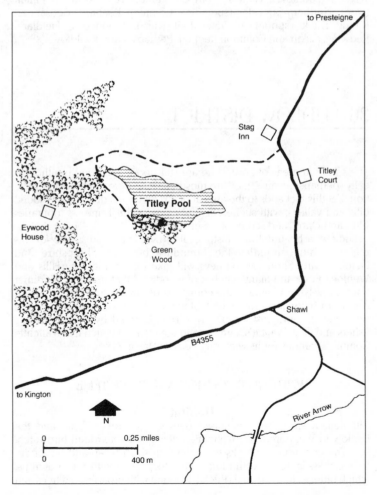

cottage. The hide is on the bank immediately below and HNT members have a right of access on foot around the pool. The nearest public transport is by bus to Kington, which is 3 miles (4.8 km) away.

Calendar

All Year: Great Crested Grebe, Mute Swan, Canada Goose, Mallard, Tufted Duck, Common Buzzard, Common Coot, Little Owl, Tawny Owl, Common Kingfisher; and most common woodland birds including all three woodpeckers, Willow Tit and Wood Nuthatch.

April–June: Garganey (rare), Ruddy Duck (sporadic), Common Redstart; Sedge Warbler, scrub and woodland warblers including Wood; and Pied Flycatcher.

July–August: Grey Heron and Green or Common Sandpiper (both scarce).

September–March: Great Cormorant (sporadic), Grey Heron, Eurasian Wigeon (sporadic), Gadwall (rare), Common Teal, Northern Pintail (rare), Northern Shoveler (sporadic), Common Pochard, Goosander, Ruddy Duck (sporadic), Water Rail (rare), Woodcock, Fieldfare, Redwing, Siskin and Common Redpoll. Perhaps scarcer wildfowl.

36 LUDLOW DISTRICT

The southern areas of Shropshire are still poorly recorded ornithologically, perhaps because they are mostly remote from centres of population. Yet this fact adds to the appeal of this lovely district of low wooded hills and valleys, with such delightful rivers as the Teme, its tributaries Clun and Onny, and scores of lesser streams.

Ludlow, a beautiful and historic old town, is a good centre for this region, which straddles the boundary between Shropshire and Herefordshire. Short car journeys will take one to the Clee Hills and Wenlock Edge, the many patches of woodland that make up Mortimer Forest, low-lying Wigmore, the commons of Bircher and Leinthall, and dozens of other sites worthy of exploration. The town itself is bordered on the south and west by the River Teme, graced by Common Kingfishers and Grey Wagtails, and beyond the water of which lies Whitcliffe Common, famous for its wintering flock of Hawfinches.

WHITCLIFFE COMMON AND RIVER TEME

Habitat

Although a small area, cramped between the River Teme and the Ludlow to Wigmore road, Whitcliffe offers good year-round birdwatching. The common overlooks the town from high level, and the undisturbed grass is dotted with thorns. The steep slope with rock outcrops, which plunges to the river, is thickly wooded with broadleaved trees and a few conifers. A gully, aligned with Dinham Bridge, is generously populated by hornbeams, the seeds of which are avidly sought by Hawfinches and Bullfinches. The river is lined with alders but the water rather tamed by weirs at each end of this stretch.

Species

The river is rarely empty of birds. Grey Wagtails, Pied Wagtails and Dippers feed from the weirs, the first-named sometimes present in numbers at Ludford Bridge. The unmistakable brilliance of a Common Kingfisher will attract attention as a bird arrows low over the water, yet it will be most inconspicuous when perched motionless in the shadow of riverside vegetation. Moorhens leave the water to feed in the small meadows on the town-side bank, and Little Grebes dive in the seclusion of overhanging branches near Dinham Bridge. Small numbers of Mallard are present throughout the year, and the alders are frequented by flocks of Siskins and Common Redpolls in winter.

The open common is not extensive enough to hold many birds. Even so, Wrens, Hedge Accentors, Robins, Blackbirds, Willow Warblers, Chaffinches and Yellowhammers are seen in the bushes, Common Kestrels hunt in quiet periods, whilst Common Swifts and hirundines hawk the area for insect prey. Many species may be seen from here, such as wildfowl including Goosander, following the Teme, and Grey Herons, Common Buzzards and Common Ravens which frequently visit the area.

At Whitcliffe, Hawfinches can be watched against the backcloth of Ludlow Castle

It is the woodland that holds the main attractions. Hawfinches in the hornbeams, Siskins and Common Redpolls in the birches and larches, and even occasional Common Crossbills in the conifers, brighten up winter birdwatching. Commoner finches are present throughout the year, along with resident thrushes, which are joined by Fieldfares and Redwings in autumn and winter. Bramblings arrive in some winters. All three woodpeckers occur, as do Wood Nuthatches and Eurasian Treecreepers, and six species of tits can be found. Of the summer migrants, Common Whitethroats, Garden Warblers, Blackcaps, Chiffchaffs and numerous Willow Warblers breed, along with a few pairs of Wood Warblers. All are well established before Spotted Flycatchers arrive in early May. Wrens and Hedge Accentors skulk in the undergrowth whilst Goldcrests seek food in the tops of conifers, especially at the northern tip of the common. Eurasian Jays, handsome but noisy, are on hand to plunder the nests of some unfortunate victims, and such a proliferation of small birds attracts Eurasian Sparrowhawks into the area on hunting sorties.

Timing

Whitcliffe Common is a great favourite with both locals and visitors, and must be the most popular dog-exercising spot in Shropshire. The river is also a choice spot with anglers. However, the disposition of the woodland, spread along the steep slope between the two, allows all but the very shyest birds to continue their daily routines undisturbed. It is a good area throughout the year, and especially so in spring and early summer with an abundance of breeding species, but also provides good winter birdwatching with flocks of thrushes, tits and finches. Hawfinches, the speciality of Whitcliffe, are present from November until March, peaking in January and February. The flock often topped 40 birds until the early 1980s, but has been much smaller in recent years.

For completely undisturbed birdwatching, very early morning is essential during the months of long daylight hours, and evenings offer a good alternative; in summer, around midday will produce the least bird activity.

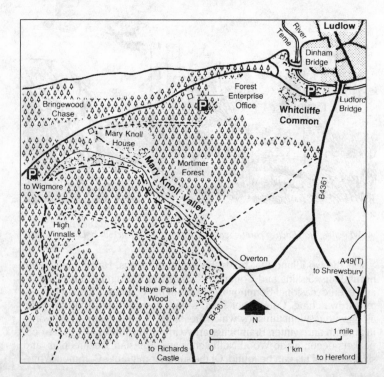

Access

From Ludlow, walk from the castle to cross the Teme at Dinham Bridge. By vehicle, take the unclassified Ludlow to Wigmore road which leaves the B4361 (formerly the A49(T) before the by-pass was constructed) west immediately south of Ludford Bridge. There is a parking area in the woodland on the left and verge parking space on the edge of the common.

The Manchester–Cardiff trains serve Ludlow and there are several bus services to the town. The common and river are only a short walk from the town centre.

Calendar

All year: Mallard, Eurasian Sparrowhawk, Common Kestrel, Moorhen, Common Kingfisher, three woodpeckers, Grey and Pied Wagtails, Dipper, resident woodland songbirds, Goldcrest, six tits, Wood Nuthatch, Eurasian Treecreeper, Eurasian Jay, resident finches, Yellowhammer.

April–June: Resident species breeding, followed by Common Whitethroat, Garden Warbler, Blackcap, Wood Warbler, Willow Warbler. Spotted Flycatcher from May. Feeding Common Swifts and hirundines.

July–September: Mixed flocks of juvenile tits. Finch flocks begin to form.

October–March: Little Grebe. Fieldfare and Redwing from mid-October. Winter finches including Hawfinch, Siskin, Common Redpoll, Brambling and occasional Common Crossbill. Chiffchaff from mid-March.

MARY KNOLL VALLEY AND MORTIMER FOREST
(see map p. 216)

Habitat

Mortimer Forest is made up of many separate woodlands of varying size. One large area commences from the western tip of Whitcliffe Common and runs westward for some 4.75 miles (7.6 km) as Bringewood Chase. At the eastern end the forest swells southwards for 2 miles (3.2 km) to the west of Richards Castle, where it contains the Mary Knoll Valley, Haye Park Wood, and the highest point in the area, High Vinnalls, which reaches 1235 ft (376 m). Practically the whole area is blanketed with conifers, although a few broadleaved sections remain, and the Mary Knoll Valley offers several of these. There is a large area of oak near the entrance to the valley at Overton, and the public footpath descending southeast from Mary Knoll House on the Ludlow to Wigmore road passes through an interesting hillside wood of mixed broadleaves, including oak and birch.

Monoculture on a large scale does not offer exiting birdwatching, but some variety is provided by firebreaks and extraction roads, often lined with weeds which attract tits and finches. Cleared areas, although usually quickly replanted, make good birdwatching sites for a few years. Adders are reputed to bask along the forest tracks and roads, and fallow deer are numerous. The forest contains a unique long-haired variety of the latter.

Species

In the vast coniferous areas Goldcrests and Coal Tits are numerous, and along firebreaks and forest roads are joined by other small passerines, including Chiffchaffs and Willow Warblers in summer. Common Crossbills are often reported but difficult to pin down to a particular site. Look for them in sections bearing a good cone crop. In thinned areas Eurasian Treecreepers feed, Eurasian Jays breed and Eurasian Sparrowhawks dash along the rides with murderous intent. Common Buzzards soar on broad, rounded wings above the woods, and the ominous black shapes of Common Ravens, croaking and tumbling in spring, are often seen.

In recently felled zones Common Kestrels hunt, and where clearance on a large scale has taken place there is always the possibility of Hen Harriers and Short-eared Owls. European Nightjars too should find these areas suit their requirements. Small birds, especially the two common pipits, Hedge Accentors, Wrens, Whinchats, Grasshopper Warblers, Common Whitethroats and Linnets breed here, and Common Cuckoos are attracted by the abundance of host species.

Deciduous areas offer a much greater variety of species. An excellent oak wood stands close to the B4361 Richard's Castle road, and extends along the southwest slopes of Mary Knoll Valley at Overton Common. A small open area still exists between the wood and the beech shaded road which often echos to the drumming of the two pied woodpeckers, the yaffling of the larger Green Woodpecker and where Wood Nuthatches and Eurasian Treecreepers are ever present. Summer visitors include Common Redstarts, Wood Warblers, Chiffchaffs and other woodland songsters. The same species, along with the handsome Pied Flycatchers, are found in the hillside wood at the other end of the valley, where an attractive open area to the north and west falls to the alder-lined stream in the valley bottom and is often favoured by fallow deer. Birches grow alongside the forest road in places and are frequented by Siskins and Common Redpolls in winter. Other birds found in deciduous patches of woodland are Eurasian Sparrowhawks, Tawny Owls, Woodcocks, Common Cuckoos, Eurasian Jays, Spotted Flycatchers, Long-tailed and five other species of tits, all the common woodland songbirds, and finches, including rare appearances by the elusive Hawfinches. Tree Pipits can be seen parachuting in more open areas and along woodland edges.

Timing

Disturbance is mainly from casual visitors who do not normally stray far from their parked cars, and ramblers who stick to paths and forest roads, causing minimal upset. Forestry operations should obviously be avoided.

Spring and early summer give optimum birdwatching conditions, with residents breeding and migrants arriving. Winter can produce large passerine flocks, especially finches, and large raptors may wander into the area, although an appearance by a Snowy Owl in the Mary Knoll Valley in the early 1960s has never been repeated.

In spring and summer, early morning trips are worth the effort, and particularly good for birdsong. Warm days at this time of the year encourage raptors to soar, the midday period being most productive, although this is the least active time for most species. Evenings should not be neglected, with roding Woodcocks, Tawny Owls vociferous, a late hunting sortie from some hungry raptor, and the chance of seeing large mammals in the form of fallow deer, fox and badger. Bats have been encouraged by the provision of bat boxes in some areas.

Access

The minor road which leaves the B4361 (the A49(T) formerly) on the right immediately after crossing Ludford Bridge at the south of Ludlow, bisects this area, with Bringewood Chase to the north and Mary Knoll Valley to the south. There is ample parking space beside the Forest Enterprise (FE) offices 1.5 miles (2.4 km) along the road and this is the best place for starting waymarked walks.

Another large car park is sited a further 1 .75 miles (2.8 km) west along this road and an all-ability trail is provided here. There are many forest roads and paths in this region with Mary Knoll Valley and High Vinnalls easily reached. A more rewarding descent into the valley is by the path leaving the road alongside Mary Knoll House, just over 0.5 miles (0.8 km) east of the car park.

An alternative access point is reached by continuing south along the B4361 for 1 mile (1.6 km), taking the right turn for Richard's Castle to find roadside parking just beyond Overton after a further 1 mile (1.6 km). This gives access to the lower end of Mary Knoll Valley and Haye Park Wood. Consult Ordnance Survey maps to plan circuit walks. The FE also publish maps to supplement the marked trails. (It is worth noting that in long periods of drought the forest may be closed to visitors to prevent risk of fire.)

Bus services from Ludlow pass all the access points mentioned. Additionally the Birmingham–Hereford service passes the lower end of Mary Knoll Valley.

Calendar

All year: Eurasian Sparrowhawk, Common Buzzard, Common Kestrel, Woodcock, Tawny Owl, all three woodpeckers, Wood Nuthatch, Eurasian Treecreeper, Goldcrest, six tits, resident woodland songbirds, Eurasian Jay, Common Raven, resident finches including Common Crossbill.

April–June: Soaring raptors. Residents breeding before being joined by summer migrants including Common Cuckoo, Tree Pipit, Whinchat, scrub and leaf warblers, Pied Flycatchers. Spotted Flycatchers and possibly European Nightjar from early May.

July–September: Soaring family parties of Common Buzzards. Flocks of mixed juvenile tits. Finch flocks forming.

October–March: Chance of wandering large raptors. Finches include Siskin, Common Redpoll and occasional Hawfinch. Common Raven and Common Crossbill breeding from February. Chiffchaff arrives mid-March.

WIGMORE AREA

Habitat

This countryside is an area of contrasts where the flat wet meadows south of the River Teme meet the foothills of the Welsh border. The three principal habitats are the river, the wooded hills of Wigmore Rolls and the flat expanse between the two.

The Teme flows generally southeast from Leintwardine before passing below Criftin Ford Bridge, after which it swings in a huge loop to pass through Burrington Bridge and eventually head northeast through Downton Gorge. The area contains some amazing meanders, especially between the two bridges. Vertical cliffs have formed on the outer bends creating ideal nesting sites for Common Kingfishers and Sand Martins and at low water levels exposed pebble beaches deposited on the inner bends attract waders, wagtails and Dippers. Winter rains bring flooding on either side of Criftin Ford Bridge making the area suitable for wildfowl.

The flat expanse of Wigmore Moor is still labelled Wigmore Lake on some maps, a reminder of the days before the land was reclaimed. The landscape of today is one of fertile fields and hedgerows with an abundance of timber. The land is low-lying, intersected by drainage ditches, and permanently marshy areas have disappeared. Some years ago extensive flooding occurred most winters, bringing in good numbers of wildfowl, and the general wet conditions were suitable for waders at other times of the year, but drain clearing has resulted in considerably less flooding in recent years with a corresponding fall in numbers of wetland species. Now much of the land is given over to agriculture, with many fields producing cereals, especially in the northern parts. Just to the north of Wigmore, however, an area of small fields and dense hedgerows, with willow the dominant tree, still remains.

The extensive woodland to the west of the village of Wigmore is known as Wigmore Rolls and is yet another section of Mortimer Forest. Planted on rolling hill country the forest is a blanket of mostly coniferous trees. Some areas of broadleaved species can be found, especially in Barnett Wood, the woodland to the south of the lane that leaves Wigmore west.

Species

With the Teme at lower levels, Grey and Pied Wagtails feed on pebble beaches, from which occasional Dippers base their underwater explorations, with Common Sandpipers in passage periods and possible Green Sandpipers in autumn and winter. Sand Martins and Yellow Wagtails grace the river in spring and summer, but both species have declined in recent years, whilst the brilliant flash of a Common Kingfisher may be seen negotiating the bends at considerable speed. Grey Herons are regular visitors, and other non-breeding fish-eaters in the area are Great Cormorants and Goosanders. A favourite gathering ground for several species to feed, bathe, preen and rest is the northern tip of the large meander due east of Criftin Ford Bridge, where the river swells into a pool. Little Grebes sometimes feed here, and flocks of Northern Lapwings and Eurasian Curlews use the site, whilst wildfowl include Mallard, small flocks of Common Teal and often large numbers of wintering Eurasian Wigeon. In times of flooding wildfowl numbers increase and less usual species may occur.

Wigmore Moor, where Common Teal have bred in the past, and a flock of seven Black-tailed Godwits was noted in the early 1960s, with a Garganey four years later, is a much quieter area these days. Northern Lapwings and Eurasian Curlews are still present, with a few Common Snipe in the wetter places and ditches. It is the fields and hedgerows now that provide food, shelter and nest sites, with large flocks of Fieldfares and Redwings in autumn and winter, and good numbers of finches, including Common Redpolls, feeding on the seeds of meadowsweet and other weeds growing along the green lanes. Barn Owls, another sadly declining species, may occasionally be seen, emerging on winter afternoons well before dusk to commence hunting. Other predators are Eurasian Sparrowhawks, Common Kestrels and Little Owls, the latter probably nesting in hollow willows. Other species using tree-holes are Stock Doves, Eurasian Jackdaws, Common Starlings, occasional

Common Redstarts and Tree Sparrows, although the last-named are much scarcer now in line with the general decline. Searching the hedgerow timber for insect food are Great Spotted Woodpeckers, Wood Nuthatches and Eurasian Treecreepers. A limited amount of flooding may still occur in some winters, bringing wildfowl and gulls to the area.

The afforested hills to the west of Wigmore hold good numbers of birds, but the conifer domination leads to fewer species. Goldcrests and Coal Tits prefer these areas, but it is Common Crossbills that will probably give birdwatchers more pleasure, and they are regulars in the Rolls. Siskins and Common Redpolls also feed in the conifers, but seek birch seeds too, and commoner finches feed on weed seeds along the edges of forest roads and firebreaks. Great Spotted Woodpeckers and Eurasian Jays find conifers to their liking, and in the more open areas Wood Nuthatches and Eurasian Treecreepers feed on the trunks. There are a few sections of broadleaves, which give a greater variety of species, with thrushes, scrub and leaf warblers, and tits making up much of the breeding population. Eurasian Sparrowhawks hunt the woods, with soaring Common Buzzards and Common Ravens a familiar sight.

Timing

This is an area of little disturbance, and offers good but unspectacular birdwatching throughout the year. Winter has much to offer, with wildfowl attracted by the floods, flocks of thrushes and finches on the moor, and Common Crossbills, Siskins and Common Redpolls in the forest. Low water levels and tall vegetation obscure views of the river in high summer except from the bridges.

The time of day to birdwatch is less critical than some areas, but birds are generally more active in the early morning, and large soaring species are best seen around midday on warm days.

Access

The river can be watched from the lane running at a higher level on the northern side, the best point being the T-junction just to the east of Nacklestone Farm. Approach by car along the Ludlow–Wigmore road, leaving Ludlow west immediately after crossing Ludford Bridge. After 4.5 miles (7.2 km) turn right and continue for a further 2 miles (3.2 km). An alternative approach is from Leintwardine, taking the minor road east from the bridge and following the northern side of the river to reach Nacklestone in 1.75 miles (2.8 km).

Wigmore sits on the A4110 and the moor is to the northeast. A good access point is the lane almost opposite the cemetery, on this road and just outside the village, where there is verge parking space. Along the track take the right-hand fork just beyond the sharp bend. A public footpath continues through the fields to the northeast beyond the end of the lane.

For Wigmore Rolls, take the lane leaving the village west at the southern end. This lane, hilly and narrow, reaches the forest in about 1 mile (1.6 km).

There are bus services from Ludlow to Wigmore and Leintwardine.

Calendar

All year: Grey Heron, Mallard, Eurasian Sparrowhawk, Common Kestrel, Barn and Little Owls, Common Kingfisher, Great Spotted Woodpecker, Grey Wagtail, Goldcrest, Coal Tit, Wood Nuthatch, Eurasian Treecreeper, Common Raven, Tree Sparrow, Common Crossbill.

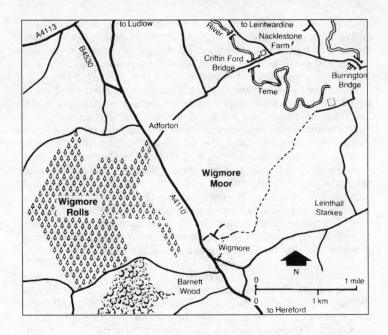

April–June: Soaring raptors. Common Sandpiper passage. Summer migrants from mid-April including Common Cuckoo, Sand Martin, Yellow Wagtail, Common Redstart, scrub and leaf warblers.

July–September: Post breeding flocks of Northern Lapwing and Eurasian Curlew form. Common and Green Sandpiper passage. Tits and finches start flocking.

October–March: Great Cormorant. Winter wildfowl including Eurasian Wigeon, Common Teal, Goosander. Common Snipe, Dipper, Fieldfare, Redwing, Siskin, Common Redpoll.

37 COLSTEY WOOD AND BURY DITCHES

OS Landranger Map 137

Habitat

The southwest corner of Shropshire contains many modern coniferous plantations, which clothe the slopes and even the summits of some of the numerous hills. Most are accessible by track and path, but usually to a very limited extent. One of the better ones to visit is the large area of woodland referred to as Colstey Wood, and containing the ancient hill fort of Bury Ditches, which is situated to the east of the A488 between

Bishop's Castle and Clun. Formerly completely planted with conifers, the site of the fort is now cleared, with the rings of the ramparts clearly defined. In spring it abounds with pipits and is an excellent vantage point from which to see soaring raptors, in addition to providing superb views of the Welsh Marches.

The wood can be explored from several waymarked trails of varying lengths, set out by the Forest Enterprise (FE), so that the birdwatcher has options from a very short walk to a more adventurous ramble of 4 miles (6.4 km) or more. Although at first glance the wood may appear to be almost completely coniferous, there is actually a surprising amount of broadleaved timber, and the walks can be planned to take in a good variety of woodland habitats including a small pool and a woodland stream.

Species

Although the conifers contain a selection of birds including Wood Pigeons, Eurasian Jays and Chaffinches, the specialists here are Goldcrests, Coal Tits, Siskins in winter, and Common Crossbills. The last-named are recorded here more often than at any other site in Shropshire.

In the deciduous and mixed areas of the woods, a greater variety of bird life is seen. Eurasian Sparrowhawks breed, often siting their nest in a larch isolated amongst broadleaved trees, and their prey includes most of the common woodland passerines. All the typical species can be found, such as Wrens, Hedge Accentors, Robins, Common Redstarts, scrub and leaf warblers, including Wood Warbler, Spotted and Pied Flycatchers, six species of tits, Wood Nuthatches, Eurasian Treecreepers, Greenfinches and Bullfinches. All three woodpeckers occur here, along with Turtle Doves, Eurasian Jays, Eurasian Jackdaws and the crepuscular Woodcocks and Tawny Owls.

Eurasian Sparrowhawks can often be seen in the Clun Forest

Along the woodland edges, in clearings, rides and the more open areas, Tree Pipits are numerous in summer, with Siskins and Common Redpolls being attracted by birch seeds during winter months. Where thistles and other desirable weeds grow, dancing flocks of Linnets and charms of brilliant Goldfinches are numerous in late summer and autumn. A Great Grey Shrike spent some weeks here during one recent winter.

Bury Ditches provides a glorious panorama, and is also a commanding observation point from which to see large birds in flight. Soaring Eurasian Sparrowhawks, Common Buzzards, Common Kestrels and Common Ravens are ever present, and other large raptors may be seen including rare non-breeding season visits by Red Kites. Both common pipits breed here, and Common Crossbills regularly overfly the fort when moving between feeding areas. Common Cuckoos are attracted by the pipits, whilst Common Swifts, Barn Swallows and House Martins find a good food supply. Northern Wheatears, upright in stance, and further betrayed by flashing white rumps, occur on passage.

Timing

The area is mainly visited by ramblers and casual walkers, with summer weekends, especially Sundays, bringing greatest numbers. However, this part of the county does not attract the hordes of tourists as do the more publicised areas. The only other likely cause of disturbance is from forestry operations.

Spring and summer are the best times to visit, although there is enough interest at any time of year to warrant a trip.

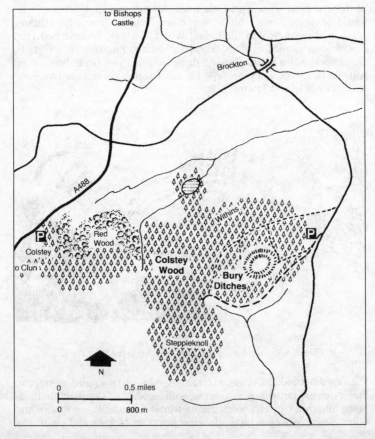

Early morning is the time for maximum bird activity, but raptors are best seen around midday, especially in warm weather, when the formation of strong thermals encourages soaring. Evening trips are also worthwhile, with Woodcocks, Tawny Owls and late hunting raptors the attraction.

Access

The FE has provided a car park, with waymarked trail information, to the east of Bury Ditches hill fort, and 2 miles (3.2 km) north of Clunton, off the unclassified narrow lane which joins the B4385 at Brockton. Motorists using this lane from the north should take the easternmost of the two roads through Brockton, the ford on the other being unsuitable for family cars. There is also limited roadside parking on the A488 Bishop's Castle–Clun road.

A bus service from Ludlow and Craven Arms runs along this road which passes the western end of Colstey Wood.

Calendar

All year: Eurasian Sparrowhawk, Common Buzzard, Common Kestrel, Woodcock, Tawny Owl, three woodpeckers, resident thrushes, Goldcrest, six species of tits, Wood Nuthatch, Eurasian Treecreeper, Eurasian Jay and common crows, Common Raven, resident finches including Common Crossbill, Yellowhammer.

April–June: Soaring raptors. Roding Woodcock. Summer migrants from mid-April including Common Cuckoo, feeding Barn Swallows and House Martins, Tree Pipit, Common Redstart, scrub and leaf warblers including Wood Warbler, Pied Flycatcher. Turtle Dove, Common Swift and Spotted Flycatcher from early May.

July–September: Residents and summer migrants still breeding in July. Family parties of raptors. Flocks of juvenile tits. Finch flocks forming, especially Goldfinch and Linnet.

October–March: Raptors, Siskin, Common Redpoll. Common Raven courtship from January. Resident species such as Meadow Pipit moving back to territories at end of period. Chiffchaff from mid-March.

38 CLEE HILLS AND CATHERTON COMMON

OS Landranger
Map 138

Habitat

The Clee Hills are made up of Brown Clee with its twin summits and Titterstone Clee, the eastern slopes of which merge into the extensive unenclosed Catherton Common. The hills are aligned north to south with the summit of Titterstone Clee less than 6 miles (9.6 km) from the Worcestershire border.

Consisting of old red sandstone, capped by harder dolerite which has protected underlying coal through the ages, the hills have suffered at the hands of man and show the scars.

The northernmost hill is Brown Clee, its major summit of Abdon Burf the highest point in Shropshire at 1772 ft (540 m). Almost 1.5 miles (2.4 km) further south the minor summit of Clee Burf is 100 ft (30 m) lower. Both summits carry masts, the price we pay for modern technology, but at least they make good perches for Common Kestrels. Spoil heaps and derelict buildings near Abdon Burf are gradually weathering into the landscape.

Brown Clee is a huge sprawling hill containing a large variety of habitats. The western flanks are open, covered by acid grassland, some extensive patches of gorse and bracken. The plateau contains heather moorland south of Abdon Burf and wet heath south of Clee Burf. Several pools dot the high ground. The woodlands lie along the eastern slopes, a large proportion consisting of modern coniferous plantations, but with generous areas of oak, birch and hawthorn scrub. There is also some fine open parkland. The nature trail in the northeast is set out in mainly coniferous woods. The streams are rather insignificant, being mainly hidden in woodland; even the one flowing west from the col to Cockshutford is hidden by hedges and trees. Nordybank, a well defined hill fort, sits on the end of a spur of high ground running west from Clee Burf.

Approached from the west, Titterstone Clee is impressive. The northern and western slopes, a mixture of heath-grasses, bracken, some scrub gorse and rushy wet flushes, rise to merge into boulder scree leading to the rocky eminence of the Giant's Chair near the summit of 1749 ft (533 m). Approach from the south is disappointing, the scars, spoil heaps and derelict buildings of former quarrying operations giving an air of desolation, and the science fiction installations of the Civil Aviation Authority radar station, looking like giant tee-ed up golf balls, are very prominent. Do not be put off by this despoilation of the hill, there is much left to admire. Once clear of the eyesore, the eastern slopes swell into a wide flat plateau of wet heath, with a few dragonfly-haunted small pools, patches of soft rush and elevated dry islands of gorse. Finally the hill runs down into Catherton Common. Streams are not a distinctive feature of the landscape, but the one flowing north to pass beneath the road near Cleeton St Mary attracts occasional Grey Wagtails. The working quarry near Clee Hill village is far enough removed from the hill as to cause no disturbance to birdwatching in the more favourable areas.

Managed by the Clee Hill Commoners Association, Catherton Common forms a substantial part of the unenclosed common land to the east of Titterstone Clee. It is 300 acres (120 ha) of heathland, on which heath-grasses, heather and bilbury dominate, with patches of gorse and birch scrub. Water filled depressions, fringed with willow and aquatic vegetation, are the present day evidence of mediaeval coal mining by bell-pits. The wet areas attract dragonflies, insectivorous sundew and butterwort, with a breeding population of Reed Buntings. Adders are recorded on the common, making stout footwear an essential, especially on hot sunny days when they bask in the open. The smallholdings scattered about the common have tall sheltering hedges which add diversity to the habitat as do the coniferous plantations along the southeast boundary.

Species

Common Buzzards and Common Kestrels are found throughout the area, and families of both species may be found hovering in line abreast, using the updraughts of the west-facing slopes in late summer. Other birds found in all areas are Common Snipe in wet heath, Common Cuckoos with their favoured host species, Meadow Pipits, and Tree Pipits along woodland fringes and scrub areas. Large flocks of Common Swifts gather to feed on the summer insect bonanza, with good numbers of Barn Swallows and House Martins, whilst fruit in the form of bilberries attracts Mistle Thrushes. All areas contain some gorse scrub and bracken, suitable for Whinchats, Common Stonechats, Linnets and Yellowhammers. Eurasian Jays, often seen in floppy flight heading for the woods, Magpies and the common black crows are all numerous. Reed Buntings breed in the wet heaths, and many common passerines are found in the fringe areas.

*The Common Raven's croaking call and thrilling flight
are symbolic of wild hills such as Clee*

Common Ravens, the scarce Merlin, and numerous breeding Northern Wheatears are found on the higher ground. Ring Ouzels may occasionally breed, but are more frequently seen in numbers on spring and autumn passage. Eurasian Curlews are surprisingly scarce on the hills, but breed in surrounding fields.

Brown Clee, with a larger variety of habitats, provides the longest species list. Woodcocks and Tawny Owls breed in the broadleaved woods, which are also home to Eurasian Sparrowhawks, the three woodpeckers, and most woodland passerines, including Wood Warblers, Pied Flycatchers, Wood Nuthatches and Eurasian Treecreepers. Birch scrub also holds the woodpeckers, with Common Redstarts, tits, warblers, Siskins and Common Redpolls. Common Crossbills are seen regularly in the coniferous plantations, with other small passerines including numerous Goldcrests and Coal Tits. The exciting Northern Goshawk is occasionally sighted in these conifers. The well wooded parkland shows evidence of extensive Common Pheasant rearing on the estate, and Green Woodpeckers are regulars. Sadly, the Wood Larks once found here have never recolonised after being wiped out by a dreadful winter in the early

1960s. The high altitude pools on Brown Clee are shunned by swamp warblers, but Common Teal, Mallard and Tufted Duck are found on them. Passage Common Redshanks and Green Sandpipers have been known to call at the more open pools near Abdon Burf. Boyne Water, at 1470 ft (448 m), holds the highest nesting Common Coots in Shropshire. A few Red Grouse are found in the heather south of Abdon Burf.

The boulder scree and rocks of Titterstone Clee are visited by Peregrine Falcons, and often used as look-out posts by Common Kestrels and Common Ravens. Snow Buntings have been seen here in late winter, and Dotterels recorded on passage. Pied Wagtails haunt the old quarry buildings, but more exciting are the occasional Black Redstarts that show up in spring.

Catherton Common has been deserted by European Nightjars for many years now, but the habitat is suitable and re-colonisation is a much hoped for possibility. Eurasian Curlews and Sky Larks breed on the heath, with Short-eared Owls hunting over the heather in some winters. Mallard and Reed Buntings nest in damp areas and around the pools, with birch scrub holding Great Spotted Woodpeckers, Willow Warblers, tits, Siskins and Common Redpolls. The woodland on the southeast boundary of the common holds Eurasian Sparrowhawks, Woodcocks and Tawny Owls. Little Owls can be seen in daytime, perched on posts and wires, and the sheltering hedges of the smallholdings provide nest-sites, songposts, food and shelter for the common passerines.

Timing

Although attracting many visitors, the area is not as disturbed by summer hordes as some of the more accessible Shropshire hills. Serious walking is required to get the best from this hill country, and most tourists are content to walk around the nature trail on Brown Clee, or drive to the old quarries to enjoy the view from Titterstone Clee. In conditions of good visibility the Clee Hills offer panoramic views which are unsurpassable, and as the same conditions produce good birdwatching, opportunities to visit at these favourable times should not be missed. Winter weather makes the higher regions inhospitable, although Common Ravens, the hardy crows and occasional raptors will be present. Late spring will give the maximum number of species.

The best time of day depends upon observers' requirements. Early morning will give greatest bird activity, but soaring raptors perform best in thermals around noon. Evenings can also be excellent, with raptors looking for a late kill and crepuscular species beginning to stir. Take the necessary precautions if you expect to be on the hills when darkness falls. Catherton Common can be quite magical at dusk, with roding Woodcock, drumming Common Snipe, crowing Common Pheasants, hooting Tawny Owls, yelping Little Owls, the rush of Mallard wings through the gathering gloom, and anxiety calls of Eurasian Curlews, disturbed perhaps by some prowling fox.

Access

Brown Clee is surrounded by a maze of narrow winding country lanes which form a network between the B4364 Bridgnorth to Ludlow road, and the B4368 Morville to Craven Arms road. The former passes below the eastern slopes of the hill, but the only access point from the road is along the wide track leaving due north 1.25 miles (2 km) south of Burwarton, where there is space to park. To approach from the west, leave the B4364 west for Stoke St Milborough to park at The Yeld, 0.5 miles (0.8 km) south of Clee St Margaret, or continue through the village

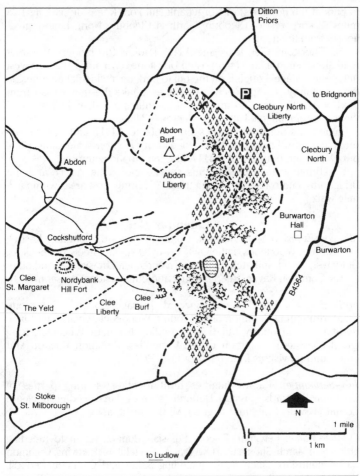

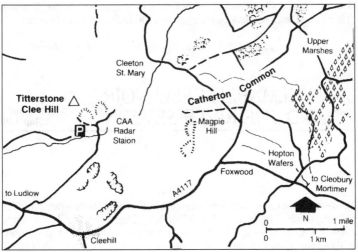

229

to park at the northwest of Nordybank Hill Fort. Roadside parking 1.25 miles (2 km) west of Cleobury North at Cleobury North Liberty gives access from the north.

For Titterstone Clee leave the A4117 Ludlow to Cleobury Mortimer road along a minor lane (signposted Dhustone) 0.75 miles (1.2 km) west of Cleehill village. Fork left on the hill to park on a wide flat area beside the old quarry. To approach from the east, take the minor road from Foxwood, 2.25 miles (3.6 km) east of Cleehill and park at the bottom of the track from Magpie Hill, or at Cleeton St Mary.

Catherton Common also lies north of the A4117 and can be approached from Foxwood. Minor roads from Hopton Wafers and Cleobury Mortimer, both on the A4117, also lead to the common.

The Birmingham–Hereford bus service along the A4117 and the Bridgnorth–Ludlow service along the B4364 bring most areas within a 2-mile walk.

Calendar

All year: Eurasian Sparrowhawk, Common Buzzard, Common Kestrel, Red Grouse, Woodcock, Little Owl, Tawny Owl, the three woodpeckers, Goldcrest, Wood Nuthatch, Eurasian Treecreeper, Eurasian Jay and other crows, Common Raven, Reed Bunting and other resident passerines.

April–June: Soaring Common Buzzard, passage Dotterel (Titterstone Clee), drumming Common Snipe, roding Woodcock, occasional Black Redstart in old quarry buildings, breeding Northern Wheatear, Ring Ouzel (passage), Common Crossbill families. Common Cuckoo and other summer visitors from mid-April.

July–September: Raptor families hunt together, soaring parties of Common Buzzards, passage Dotterel (scarce), large feeding flocks of Common Swifts (until mid-August), Mistle Thrush flocks.

October–March: Peregrine Falcon. Eurasian Curlews return to breeding grounds in March, Short-eared Owl (vagrant), Fieldfare, Redwing. Common Raven courtship. Finch flocks including Siskin and Common Redpoll. Common Crossbills breeding from February, occasional Snow Bunting (Titterstone Clee), resident passerines return to high ground in March.

39 CHELMARSH RESERVOIR AND THE RIVER SEVERN

OS Landranger
Map 138

Habitat

The reservoir at Chelmarsh – constructed in the early 1960s – lies 3.5 miles (5.6 km) south of Bridgnorth. The 0.75-mile (1.2 km) long stretch of water is aligned from northwest to southeast, and at the southernmost, deep end, is about 0.5 miles (0.8 km) wide. The northern end, much narrower and comparatively shallow, is separated by a causeway carrying a public bridleway from a tract of marsh, 250 yds (230 m) long and 100 yds (93 m) wide.

The marsh is bisected along the longest axis by a drainage ditch and conservation work over the past few years has been carried out to improve the habitat. The marsh to the west of the ditch now contains a large shallow scrape with controllable water level and a hide is situated at the southern end. An extensive *Phragmites* bed has been established on the eastern side of the ditch.

The reservoir is surrounded by a variety of habitats. Alders have been planted along much of the shoreline, rough grassland lines the northeast shore, and the opposite flank supports dense willow growth to the south, which gives way to thorn scrub further north. A small hide is situated on the southwest shore, just to the north of the bay. The reservoir is owned by the South Staffordshire Waterworks Company (SSWC). A bird-rich deciduous wood lies outside the SSWC property but adjacent to the boundary fence in the southwest and gives added interest. The dam embankment is grassed but kept short by mowing or occasional grazing and access is strictly forbidden. The area to the southeast of the embankment is a mixture of rough grasses and mixed woodland including some yews which are favourites with roosting Tawny Owls. Many new trees have been planted in recent years and a small outlet stream flows through here from the base of the dam.

There are no feeder streams into the reservoir, the water being pumped from the River Severn which is a mere 0.5 miles (0.8 km) distant. The great advantage of this is to keep at least a section of water unfrozen in severe weather when most other pools in the Midlands are icebound.

The close proximity of the reservoir to the Severn, with the woods and pools of Dudmaston Hall to the east of the river, creates a varied area within which birds can move to suit weather conditions and food supply. In freezing spells waterfowl leave the pools to join the river, but when the latter runs discoloured and bank-full they can reverse the move.

This stretch of river is rather straight, with the water flowing deep and fast on either side of Hampton Loade. There is no spectacular flooding, but in prolonged wet spells some riverside fields become waterlogged and hold shallow pools which attract a few wildfowl, Northern Lapwings and gulls. Pasture and arable fields border the river, but the extensive mixed woodland of Long Covert closes on the east bank and the area is dotted with smaller coverts. The confluence of the Mor Brook with the parent river creates an interesting habitat, the water widening here and showing a few pebbly beaches at low water levels.

Species

From an initial stretch of sterile water lying in a somewhat bare and desolate setting, Chelmarsh Reservoir has built up into a first-class wetland habitat giving exciting birdwatching. It is an excellent winter wildfowl site, with both migrant swans appearing, although scarce, and hundreds of Canada Geese being joined by small numbers of wild Pink-footed and White-fronted Geese, feral Greylag and Barnacle Geese, and Snow Geese escapes. Ducks present in good numbers are the ubiquitous Mallard, Eurasian Wigeon, Common Teal, Northern Shoveler, Common Pochard and Tufted Duck, with smaller numbers of Common Goldeneye, Goosander and Ruddy Duck. There are annual sightings of Common Shelduck, Gadwall, Northern Pintail and Greater Scaup, with Long-tailed Duck and Common Scoter most years, and scarcer ducks on rare occasions.

Winter brings other waterfowl to join the resident but non-breeding Great Crested Grebes, with a few Little Grebes each year and scarce Red-necked, Black-necked and Slavonian Grebes. Great Cormorants in good numbers, and an occasional Shag, share the water with uncommon divers, the Red-throated Diver being the most frequent visitor. Grey Herons fish the reservoir throughout the year, having formerly nested in the adjoining wood, and they still use the old nests to stand on during resting periods. Little Egrets recently paid a first visit to the site.

Being supplied from the river, the water level does not fall during dry spells, hence wader passage has not been a strong feature of the reservoir, due to lack of suitable shoreline. A few species occur annually, feeding along the water's edge on the concrete dam, or staying briefly where minute areas of mud show in one or two places. These include Oyster-catchers, Dunlins, Common Redshanks, Common Greenshanks and Green Sandpipers, with Common Sandpipers numerous in some years. Terns are also regular passage visitors, usually Arctic and Common Terns, but also the delicate Black Tern, with occasional appearances of Sandwich Terns. A rare White-winged Black Tern was recorded in early June 1982.

An exciting passage migrant is the Osprey, which usually appears in the post-breeding period as the birds move leisurely south. Their visits are becoming more frequent and they should be looked for on dead trees in surrounding hedgerows, as they tend to sit immobile for long spells, despite the attention of Magpies and other crows.

The open water of the reservoir is an ideal gull roost, with the most numerous species being Black-headed and Lesser Black-backed Gulls, with combined figures of up to 12,000 in December and January. Herring Gulls reach only a few hundred, with very small numbers of Common and Great Black-backed Gulls. Annual sightings of rarer gulls occur, with first arrivals being Little Gulls in August, followed by Mediterranean Gulls from October. Iceland and Glaucous Gulls usually arrive after the turn of the year, and in recent winters Ring-billed Gulls have been reported in the same period. The graceful, normally pelagic Kittiwake shows up in most winters, sometimes as late as April.

Two very different winter visitors are the Common Kingfisher and Dipper, which leave their more usual river haunts to seek food in the reservoir and outlet stream respectively. The stream also attracts Grey Wagtails.

The marsh holds breeding Grasshopper Warblers and Common White-throats, with populations of Sedge and Reed Warblers, and Reed Buntings, increasing with the spread of the *Phragmites*. A pair of Common Snipe breed regularly, but are mainly wintering birds in good numbers, along with two or three Jack Snipe. Water Rails also occur at this time, often feeding in the drain, and breeding has been recorded. Common Stonechats visit in winter, almost always in pairs. A Cetti's Warbler was recorded in the mid-eighties. The marsh is a regular hunting ground for Common Kestrels, but Barn Owls, formerly familiar visitors, are now scarce. The provision of the scrape has created a favourable habitat for waders and should compensate for lack of suitable shoreline on the reservoir, although results to date have been disappointing.

The woodland adjoining the reservoir holds all the expected birds, including Eurasian Sparrowhawks, Woodcocks, Turtle Doves, Tawny Owls, the three woodpeckers, Wood Nuthatches, Eurasian Treecreepers and a wide selection of woodland songsters. A Firecrest was recorded on one occasion. Many of these birds are also found in the scrub, especially warblers, with Fieldfares and Redwings arriving for the berry harvest in autumn.

Many species are seen generally around the area, or overflying, and these include both partridges, Northern Lapwings and Eurasian Curlews. Little Owls are resident, and Short-eared Owls, which hunt the grassland, are infrequent visitors. Several Common Cuckoos are usually vociferous on arrival, whilst Sand Martins and Barn Swallows make this a first port of call before dispersing to breeding sites.

Many species found on the reservoir also occur on the river. Grey Herons are ever present, as are Common Kingfishers except after harsh winters. Breeding along the river are Mallard, Moorhens, Sand Martins, Sedge Warblers and Reed Buntings, with Yellow Wagtails in the bordering fields.

Little and Great Crested Grebes move to the river after breeding, with Grey Wagtails and Dippers moving down from the tributary streams. Mute Swan families appear at this time and regularly nest on the eyots. Mandarin Duck are frequently seen and breed in the area, perhaps originally escapes from a large bird collection that was formerly housed nearby. Species coming in as winter visitors include Great Cormorants, Common Pochard, Tufted Duck, Common Goldeneye and Goosander.

The Severn also carries passage migrants, including the terns seen at the reservoir, with Dunlins, Common Redshanks, Common Greenshanks, Green and Common Sandpipers the likeliest waders. Common Snipe feed along the river in winter.

If riverside fields are holding flood pools, they attract swans including scarce Tundra and Whooper Swans, and surface-feeding ducks, mainly Eurasian Wigeon, Common Teal and Mallard, but also Northern Pintail and Northern Shoveler. Geese feed on the arable fields between the reservoir and river, the species being as previously listed.

The woods hold good numbers of birds and there is usually some activity to arouse interest, such as the mobbing of a Common Cuckoo or Tawny Owl. Families of Eurasian Jays fly floppily between woods and Eurasian Sparrowhawks may be seen hunting, and soaring Common Buzzards are on the increase. The area is good for wintering flocks of passerines, with tits, Fieldfares, Redwings, Chaffinches, Greenfinches, Goldfinches, Yellowhammers and Reed Buntings often very numerous. Bramblings arrive most winters but the once familiar Tree Sparrows become ever scarcer.

Timing

Winter is the best season at the reservoir, especially from mid-November on. The water tends to be devoid of birdlife in high summer. April to mid-May and August to mid-September should produce passage species.

There is disturbance at the reservoir from sailing and angling, with the latter also a favourite sport on the river. An early morning visit will avoid the sailors but not the anglers. Weekends are the worst times. Visits following strong westerly gales often pay dividends in winter and, contrary to most lakes, the reservoir should be visited during freezing spells.

The position of the sun can adversely affect birdwatching across large sheets of water, and this should be checked on arrival before deciding on a route. Both hides are good for most of the day in this respect.

Access

To reach the area from Bridgnorth, take the unclassified road leaving the B4363 near the sharp bend near the railway station and travel south. After 2.75 miles (4.4 km) roadside parking just before reaching a sharp bend beside a railway bridge will give access to the river along the Mor Brook.

To reach Hampton continue along this road, turning left at Sutton into a no-through-road which leads to the river. The Severn can be walked for miles in either direction from these spots, and the Hampton starting point has the novelty of a foot ferry should one care to walk the opposite bank from Hampton Loade. This point is also easily reached from the A442 Bridgnorth–Kidderminster road.

Access to Chelmarsh Reservoir is restricted to members of the Shropshire Ornithological Society (SOS) and the Shropshire Wildlife Trust (SWT). Access is from Hampton on the no-through-road. Non-members can view the reservoir and marsh from the public bridleway which starts from near Chelmarsh Church, or from various public footpaths to the north, east and south. Birdwatchers who enjoy a good ramble can choose a circuit around the complete area.

Hampton Loade station (Severn Valley Railway) is beside the river and 1 mile (1.6 km) from the reservoir. The Kidderminster–Bridgnorth bus service passes through Chelmarsh village.

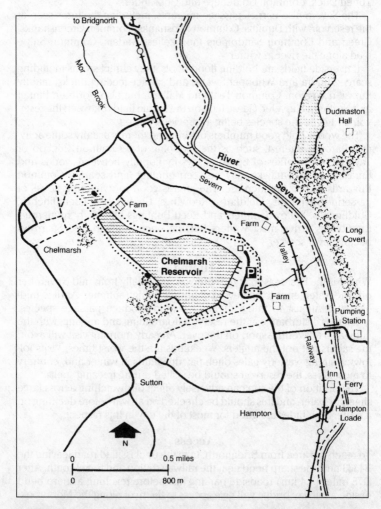

Calendar

All year: Great Crested Grebe, Grey Heron, Mute Swan, Canada Goose, Mallard, Tufted Duck, Eurasian Sparrowhawk, Common Kestrel, Common Snipe, Woodcock, Little Owl, Tawny Owl, Common Kingfisher, three woodpeckers, Grey Wagtail, Dipper, Goldcrest, Wood Nuthatch, Eurasian Treecreeper, Reed Bunting.

April–June: Summer visitors from mid-April including Common Cuckoo, Yellow Wagtail, Grasshopper, Sedge and Reed Warblers, scrub and leaf warblers. Turtle Dove, Common Swift and Spotted Flycatcher from early May. Passage waders including Oystercatcher, Dunlin, and Common Sandpiper. Passage terns, including Black Tern.

July–September: Possible Osprey. Passage waders including Dunlin, Common Redshank, Common Greenshank, Green and Common Sandpiper. Passage terns including Black Tern. Occasional Little Gull.

October–March: Occasional divers, especially Red-throated Diver, grebes including rare Black-necked, Red-necked and Slavonian grebes, Great Cormorant. Small numbers Tundra and Whooper Swans, Pink-footed and White-fronted Geese. Ducks include Eurasian Wigeon, Gadwall, Common Teal, Northern Pintail, Northern Shoveler, Common Pochard, Greater Scaup, Long-tailed Duck, Common Scoter, Common Goldeneye and Goosander. Water Rail, Jack Snipe. Gull roost including scarce gulls. Short-eared Owl, Common Stonechat, winter thrushes, finch flocks including Brambling. Sand Martins arrive from late March.

40 MUCH WENLOCK AND WENLOCK EDGE

OS Landranger
Maps 127 & 138

Habitat

The internationally famous Wenlock Edge, a low, wooded limestone escarpment, runs some 20 miles (32 km) southwest from Ironbridge to Craven Arms. Originally clothed in ash and oak, with a mixture of other trees, it has been converted to conifers in some areas during recent decades. A beneficial development has been the acquisition of substantial areas by the National Trust (NT), with a management plan of reconversion to ash woodland. The woods lie on the steep scarp slope, rarely exceeding 0.25 miles (400 m) in width, and the gentle dip slope is mainly given over to cereal production, with some pasture for sheep and cattle. South of Much Wenlock, as far as Hilltop, the Edge is much scarred by quarrying, but this does create some interesting waste areas. The occasional rock outcrops, usually well hidden by trees, are not extensive enough to attract cliff-nesting birds, although Common Kestrels, Stock Doves and Eurasian Jackdaws do take advantage of disused quarry faces in which to breed. There is little running water, and no standing water apart from the occasional small pond, but one substantial stream, known in different localities as Hughley Brook or Sheinton Brook, flows below the Edge, passing through Harley, the amusingly named Wigwig and Sheinton before joining the Severn. The disused railway track between Much Wenlock and Farley is now an attractive habitat for hedgerow birds, offering both food and shelter to newly arriving migrants in both spring and autumn. Other stretches of this track can be walked in NT-owned areas but much of it has passed into private ownership. The whole area is worth exploring for woodland species, but it is also rich in lime-stone flora and good for butterflies. The early riser may be rewarded by sightings of foxes and fallow deer, whilst the late evening visitor may also see badgers.

Species

The Ordnance Survey map shows an area of woodland bisected by Sheinton Brook lying 2 miles (3.2 km) north of Much Wenlock and labelled The Springs. This is known locally as Bannister's Coppice. It is about 220 acres (90 ha) of deciduous woodland, mainly oak with birch and hazel, and is accessible by public right of way. Eurasian Sparrowhawks and Common Buzzards are regulars here, and there has been one winter sighting of a Red Kite. The woodland provides roding Woodcocks in the breeding season, but they may also be disturbed on winter days if they roost near the paths, and all three woodpeckers, Wood Nuthatches and Eurasian Treecreepers. Many small passerines breed here, and in spring the wood is loud with birdsong; Garden Warblers, Blackcaps, Wood Warblers and Chaffinches are very prominent. Tawny Owls are abundant in the area and the coppice echoes with Common Cuckoo calls in May. Mallard and Dippers breed along the brook and Grey Wagtails can be seen feeding on shallow boulder-strewn stretches and pebbly margins. The presence of fallow deer is betrayed by many slots and it is not unusual to see them.

Woodcock may be disturbed on winter days in the Wenlock woodlands,
but are more likely to be seen roding in the breeding season

The excellent track leading from Much Wenlock to Blakeway Coppice was once the coach road to Shrewsbury. This area is the Wenlock Edge and in spring and summer the track is bordered by wild flowers, butterflies abound, and the hedgerows provide a suitable habitat for Common Whitethroats, Linnets and Yellowhammers. Old quarry workings to the right as one gradually ascends are now clothed in permanent grass and thorn scrub, producing an abundance of berries to the delight of Redwings and Fieldfares, whilst the seeds of ground vegetation attract Greenfinches, Goldfinches and Bullfinches. Turtle Doves, absent in recent years, once crooned here through summer afternoons. Hopefully, they may one day return.

The woodlands on this part of the Edge are owned and managed by the NT who have cleared footpaths, provided marker posts and generally made the area much more accessible. Coniferous sections contain Goldcrests and Coal Tits, with a good mixture of species in the broadleaved woods. Larger birds found here are Common Buzzards, Eurasian Sparrowhawks, Woodcocks, Wood Pigeons, Common Cuckoos, Eurasian Jays and Carrion Crows, whilst Chaffinches and Willow Warblers are the most numerous small passerines in spring and summer, and all the English tit species are present through the autumn and winter, sometimes in large mixed flocks. Great Spotted Woodpeckers are the commonest of their family, drumming noisily in late winter and early spring, and Green Woodpeckers are often seen ground-feeding along the woodland edge. Lesser Spotted Woodpeckers are uncommon, but may be overlooked. Both Wood Nuthatches and Eurasian Treecreepers are to be found here in all months. Tawny Owls are more often heard than seen in the woods and Little Owls call noisily in spring from hedgerow timber. Both are most frequently seen by road users, perched on wayside posts and wires at dusk.

Do not be put off by the extensive quarry workings bordering the upper boundary of the woodlands. Stock Doves breed here, large flocks of Eurasian Jackdaws perform thrilling aerobatics and Common Kestrels can be seen at close quarters as they glide below the observer. Often, during summer evenings, large numbers of Common Swifts, Barn Swallows and House Martins feed above the quarries and become an attraction for the increasing number of Hobbies, which now breed in the area.

Large birds appear to use the Edge as a flight route, perhaps even as a navigational aid. No doubt on some days the updraught from the steep escarpment will provide an economical saving of energy, and all the common raptors, swans, geese, Grey Herons, gulls and Common Ravens have been noted following the line of the Edge.

The southern stretches of the Edge should not be neglected. The woods here are less visited by tourists than those in the north, but adequate rights of way exist to allow full exploration. For a first visit the Edge Wood Nature Trail near Westhope, 11 miles (17 km) southwest of Much Wenlock, cannot be bettered. There is parking space here and a picnic site. Longer walks into Wolverton Wood and Harton Wood can be taken from this same starting point. All the previously mentioned species can be encountered in this area, along with Pied Flycatchers in spring and summer, with large flocks of Common Redpolls in late winter. Good numbers of Wood Warblers usually breed here, especially where oaks dominate.

Timing

For small passerines, especially woodland species, March to May for residents and April to May for summer migrants are the best times of the year, before the trees come into full leaf. Early morning is the best time of the day. The development of tourism in recent years has brought more disturbance to late morning and afternoon birdwatching. For Woodcocks and owls, dusk is the only time to be sure of success. Soaring raptors, especially Common Buzzards, are best looked for around noon on warm days.

Access

To reach Bannister's Coppice, park in Homer, 1.5 miles (2.4 km) by road from Much Wenlock. Take the first turn left after leaving the town north on the B4169. The footpath starts between two bungalows and appears to pass through the garden of one of them, the stile being sited beside the gate of the drive.

Wenlock Edge can be reached from the NT car park at the southwest corner of the town, on the northern side of the B4371 just before leaving the built-up section of the road. Continuing along this road there is a smaller NT car park at Presthope, also on the right just before reaching the junction

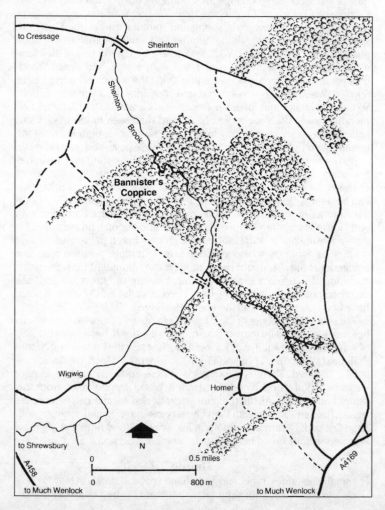

of the minor road to Hughley, and there are several roadside parking spots still further along, between here and the Wenlock Edge Inn at Hilltop.

To reach the southern woods of Wenlock Edge take the B4378 south-west from Much Wenlock, joining the B4368 at Shipton. Continue 0.5 miles (0.8 km) beyond the B4365 turn to Ludlow and take the first road on the

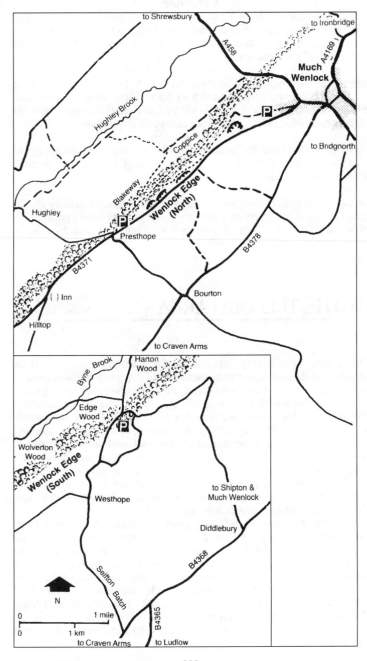

right into Seifton Batch, through Westhope, to the picnic site and Edge Wood Nature Trail, parking on the right just after reaching the woodland.

The Shrewsbury–Bridgnorth bus service passes through Much Wenlock, giving access to the northern sites.

Calendar

All year: Eurasian Sparrowhawk, Common Buzzard, Common Kestrel, Little and Tawny Owls, the three woodpeckers, Grey and Pied Wagtails, Dipper, resident woodland passerines, all common crows, common finches and Yellowhammer.

April–June: Soaring raptors. Roding Woodcock. Summer migrants from mid-April including Common Cuckoo, hirundines, scrub and leaf warblers. Common Swift and Spotted Flycatcher from early May. Common Redstart and Pied Flycatcher mainly passage but both breed.

July–September: Hobbies hawk insects above woodland canopy (from mid-August), mixed flocks of juvenile tits, Eurasian Jays carry acorns, finch flocks reforming.

October–March: Eurasian Curlews return to breeding fields in early March. Large flocks of Fieldfares and Redwings except December and January. Siskin and Common Redpoll from January. Chiffchaff from mid-March.

41 THE TELFORD AREA

OS Landranger
Maps 126 & 127

The underlying rocks in the area occupied by the new town of Telford are mostly middle and upper coal measures of the carboniferous period. Apart from coal, sandstone and limestone are present, outcropping in the south, with various clays such as fireclay. The coming of the Industrial Revolution and with it the practice of intensive mineral extraction, resulted in the creation of many flat-topped mounds, caused by the dumping of waste material; and the mining of open-cast coal and clay, together with balancing reservoirs needed for the canals, left the area dotted with numerous pools. During the century of decay which followed the industrial boom, nature, as always, clothed the eyesores with a great variety of vegetation, which in turn provided ideal conditions for wildlife. It was on this semi-derelict area that Telford was built.

From the start the aim was to preserve a balance between built-up areas and open spaces, retaining some of the habitats for wildlife conservation, and creating others to serve as recreational areas in addition to their wildlife interest. The result is a mosaic of semi-wild habitats, sandwiched between residential and industrial estates, shopping centres, and a network of roads, which contain over 140 bird species, about 80 of which breed, with many species of mammals, invertebrates and flora. There are over 40 spaces with natural history interest, and nearby areas of great ornithological value in The Wrekin, The Ercall, Benthall Edge and the Severn Valley.

TELFORD

Habitat

It would be impractical to describe or map the entire area in detail, and the best plan is to visit the Stirchley Grange Environmental Interpretive Centre (SGEIC) where many leaflets describing all aspects of the new town are available. The Ranger Service is based at the Centre, and there is usually much of interest in the offing, such as guided walks, talks, or visits to places of interest in the area.

Probably by far the most valuable habitat preserved is the ancient woodland and former coppices of the Severn Gorge. Secondary woodland, mainly birch, ash and oak, can be found at Lightmoor, Dawley, Donnington Wood and in the Town Park, these same areas also containing acidic grassland and heath, whilst modern plantations will be found at Jigger's Bank and Nedge Hill. A few unimproved meadows – rarities these days – still exist at Lightmoor and in the Severn Gorge. More than 20 pools are located within the new town boundary, and although some are in built-up areas, others are in semi-wild habitat with a rich variety of wildlife. A few fragments of marshy terrain may still survive at Donnington Wood.

Some sites are extensive and hold a mosaic of habitats, such as Lightmoor with its birch and oak woods, grassy patches, heather and small pools. The Town Park, immediately south of the Town Centre, is 1.75 miles (2.8 km) long and contains no less than nine pools, acres of woodland, and mounds covered with grass and heather.

Species

The woodland holds all the expected species. Eurasian Sparrowhawks are widespread, and there is a year-round abundance of small passerine prey in the form of resident thrushes, tits including Long-tailed Tits, Wrens, Hedge Accentors, Wood Nuthatches and Eurasian Treecreepers. In spring and summer the numbers are augmented by Wood Warblers, Common Whitethroats, Garden Warblers, Blackcaps, Common Redstarts and Pied Flycatchers, with Tree Pipits in fringe areas. Larger birds are Green and Great Spotted Woodpeckers, Eurasian Jays, Stock Doves and Tawny Owls. Coal Tits, Goldcrests and very occasional Common Crossbills are found in the plantations. Birches attract Siskins and Common Redpolls in winter and Linnets and Goldfinches are regulars in scrubby areas such as that bordering the municipal tip near the Jiggers Bank roundabout, where a Red-backed Shrike turned up on passage recently. Rufous Nightingales, formerly heard annually in the Severn Gorge, have been absent in recent summers but still remain a possibility.

Birds of wetland habitats are well represented. Grey Herons, Common Kingfishers, Grey Wagtails and Dippers are all regular on the Severn in the Ironbridge Gorge, with many other species passing along the river on migration. The numerous pools hold good wildfowl numbers in winter, with Priorslee Flash, Priorslee Lake, Holmer Lake and the Town Park pools taking the greatest numbers. Mallard, Tufted Duck and Common Pochard are the commonest species, with Eurasian Wigeon, Common Teal and other ducks in lesser numbers. Occasionally, scarcer species are seen, such as Long-tailed Ducks and Common Scoters. Other waterfowl on the pools are Little and Great Crested Grebes, Mute Swans, Canada Geese, Moorhens and Common Coots, along with fishing experts Grey Herons and Common Kingfishers. A small group of Common Snipe roost regularly each winter on the island in Priorslee Flash. Sedge Warblers and Reed Buntings breed in suitable habitat.

Timing

The woodlands are best visited in spring and early summer, although wintering Siskins and Common Redpolls feed actively in birches and alders, especially after the turn of the year. The pools have good numbers of breeding birds, but really come into their own with the arrival of the northern wildfowl from mid-October.

Angling is permitted on most pools and sailing on Holmer and Priorslee Lakes, with many open spaces used for other recreations. Nedge Hill is a favourite picnic spot being an excellent view point in addition to the woodland making ideal family walking. Most of these activities can be avoided by an early morning birdwatching session, although on most pools many species have become quite tolerant of nearby human presence.

Access

The rapid development of Telford and the continuing construction of new routes within the area, means that available maps rarely show an up-

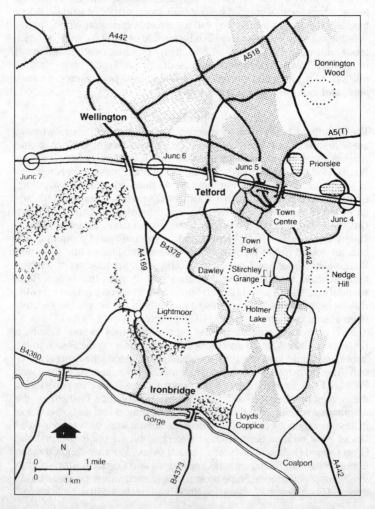

to-date road plan. The large scale street plan produced by Wrekin District Council is indispensible.

SGEIC is to the west of Queensway (A442) from which it can be reached by leaving at the Stirchley Interchange, and proceeding via Stirchley Avenue, Randlay Avenue and Grange Avenue. The Centre is at the eastern end of Grange Pool and has a car park. Queensway (A442) can be found by leaving the M54 at Junction 5 and taking the Rampart Way (A5T) to the Hollinswood Interchange. The Town Park can be entered from SGEIC and also from a car park near the junction of Randlay and Stirchley Avenues 0.5 miles (0.8 km) further north, or from the Town Centre. The Stirchley Interchange is also the point to leave Queensway (A442) for Holmer Lake to the southwest and Nedge Hill to the northeast.

Donnington Wood is in the northeast of Telford and can be reached from the Wombridge Interchange on Queensway via Wrockwardine Wood Way (B4373). The two Priorslee waters lie to the north of the M54 between junctions 4 and 5 and can be reached from either.

The Ironbridge Gorge forms the southern boundary of Telford and there are car parks and picnic sites on the B4373 from Ironbridge and on the unclassified road following the north bank of the river to Coalport. Lightmoor can be explored from roadside parking about 150 yds (140 m) along Lightmoor Road leaving Queensway north 0.5 miles (0.8 km) west of Castlefields Roundabout.

Birmingham–Shrewsbury trains serve Telford and there is a network of local bus services giving access to all sites.

Calendar

All year: Little and Great Crested Grebes, Grey Heron, Mute Swan, Canada Goose, Mallard, Tufted Duck, Eurasian Sparrowhawk, Common Kestrel, both partridges, Woodcock, Little and Tawny Owls, Common Kingfisher, all three woodpeckers, Grey Wagtail, resident thrushes, six tits, Wood Nuthatch, Eurasian Treecreeper, resident finches, Yellowhammer, Reed Bunting.

April–June: Passage waders include Oystercatcher, Little and Great Ringed Plovers, Common Redshank. Passage terns. Summer migrants include Common Cuckoo, hirundines, Tree Pipit, Sedge Warbler, scrub and leaf warblers, with Turtle Dove (scarce), Common Swift and Spotted Flycatcher from early May.

July–September: Residents and summer migrants still breeding. Return passage of waders including Common Greenshank and Green Sandpiper. Passage terns.

October–March: Great Cormorant, Eurasian Wigeon, Common Teal, Northern Shoveler, Common Pochard, Common Goldeneye, occasionally scarcer ducks, Common Snipe, winter thrushes, Siskin, Common Redpoll, Common Crossbill (scarce).

BENTHALL EDGE WOOD

Habitat

This wood is on the southern slopes of the Ironbridge Gorge, and straggles a complicated geological area made up largely of limestones and coal measures. The variety of the underlying rocks leads to a great diversity of plant life, which includes several species of orchids. There are many traces of mineral extraction – here was the cradle of the Industrial Revolution – but most are now clothed in deciduous woodland rich in wildlife. Badger, fox and fallow deer are amongst the mammals that may be encountered here. Ash, beech, birch, wych elm, hazel, holly, oak and the much maligned sycamore all flourish, with at least a dozen other tree species present. Management policy is to remove some sycamore to encourage native trees such as ash and elm.

The wood grows on a very steep slope, and is well served by footpaths. A quite strenuous nature trail of 1.75 miles (2.8 km) has been constructed to show off the more interesting features, but for those requiring a less strenuous walk, the old railway line can be followed until reaching the power station boundary. This track gives views onto the River Severn in places and regularly provides sightings of Mallards, Common Kingfishers and Grey Wagtails.

Species

Observers walking along the old railway track, especially early in the day, may see considerable birdlife on the river from the several viewpoints available. Many species use the Severn as a flight route, and Great Cormorants, Grey Herons, Mute Swans, Mallards, gulls and migrating waders and terns pass through. Low across the water the jerky flight of Common Sandpipers may be seen, the brilliant flash of a Common Kingfisher, or the slender, long-tailed shapes of Grey and Pied Wagtails as they shoot along in characteristic fashion. One unexpected sighting was of an Osprey, fishing the river a little downstream from the Iron Bridge.

The woodland abounds with birds in spring and summer. Tree-holes are plentiful and consequently the species which nest in them are well represented, including Stock Doves, Tawny Owls, Common Redstarts, Wood Nuthatches, Eurasian Jackdaws and Common Starlings. Marsh, Coal, Blue and Great Tits also seek ready made sites, whilst Willow Tits find suitable timber in which to excavate their own holes, as do all three woodpeckers, whilst Eurasian Treecreepers prefer loose bark or crevices to satisfy their requirements. Pied Flycatchers are further encouraged by the provision of nest boxes. Warblers are a strong feature of the wood, advertising their presence by loud song, yet difficult to locate once the trees are in full leaf. Garden Warblers, Blackcaps, Chiffchaffs and Willow Warblers are all numerous, with several pairs of Wood Warblers. Many other common woodland songsters are present, and with so rich a population of small passerines, Common Cuckoos are on hand to practice their parasitic habits, and Eurasian Sparrowhawks find a satisfying supply of food. Nowadays Common Buzzards are seen more frequently above the wood and evening visits during spring should ensure sightings of roding Woodcocks.

The upper boundary of the wood meets agricultural land with small fields and hedgerows. It is worth exploring here to locate species of the woodland edge, where Common Kestrels hunt for small mammals and Eurasian Jays are often seen commuting between fields and wood. Spotted Flycatchers, Long-tailed Tits and Mistle Thrushes breed with Redwings and Fieldfares feeding on the berries in autumn.

Timing

The Ironbridge Gorge has become a 'Mecca' for tourists in recent years, but most of them are absorbed by the attractions of the town, especially by the excellent museums. Away from the peak holiday period and bank holiday weekends, Benthall Edge Wood is surprisingly free of disturbance. April to June is the best time to visit, preferably before the trees are in full leaf.

As usual with woodlands, an early morning visit will bring the greatest reward and as this is not an area noted for soaring raptors the midday period is best avoided. Evenings can also be very enjoyable, with calling Tawny Owls, roding Woodcock and perhaps just the remotest chance of the far-carrying song of a Rufous Nightingale.

Access

Ironbridge sits on the north bank of the Severn, 4.25 miles (6.8 km) south of the M54 and is well signposted, being the tourist centre it is.

There are several large car parks available, but the best one for Benthall Edge Wood is situated at the southern end of the famous Iron Bridge, which now takes pedestrians only. The best starting point is along the old railway track. There is a picnic area here and the beginning of the nature trail. If intending to ascend to the top of the Edge, birdwatchers should wear strong footwear and be prepared for muddy and slippery paths, which may take a considerable time to dry out after heavy rain.

The wood can be approached from the south using the parking area beside Benthall Hall and church, access to which is along a lane on the north of the B4375 Much Wenlock–Brosely road.

There are bus services from Telford to Ironbridge.

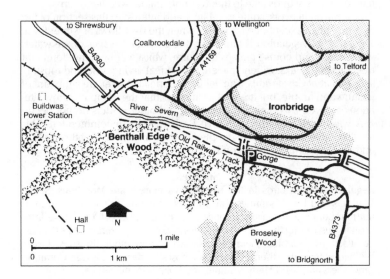

Calendar

All year: Eurasian Sparrowhawk, Woodcock, Stock Dove, Tawny Owl, all three woodpeckers, common woodland songbirds, Long-tailed and five other tits, Wood Nuthatch, Eurasian Treecreeper, Eurasian Jay.

April–June: Woodcock roding. Common Cuckoo and other summer migrants arrive from mid-April, including Common Redstart, Garden Warbler, Blackcap, Wood Warbler, Pied Flycatcher. Spotted Flycatcher from early May.

July–September: Residents and summer migrants still breeding. Mixed flocks of juvenile tits.

October–March: Fieldfare and Redwing along woodland edge. Tawny Owls noisily dispute territories. Resident birds take up territories from late February. Chiffchaff arrives mid-March.

CRESSAGE TO BUILDWAS

Habitat

The Severn Valley is wide and flat in this area, resulting in spectacular meanders and awesome flooding. The outer bends of of these great curves are eroded by the fast-flowing water to form long stretches of vertical cliffs suitable for hole-nesting Common Kingfishers and Sand Martins. The slower current on the inner shore deposits mud, sand and pebbles to create substantial beaches used by many species for resting, bathing, preening, feeding and in some cases breeding. Winter levels submerge these beaches and much of the bankside vegetation. Unseasonal rises in the river level can cause serious damage to riverside breeders, especially grebes (which anchor their nests to trailing willow branches) and Moorhens. Winter flooding converts the valley into a great lake and even after the water has returned between the banks there are flood pools remaining in the fields for several days, or even weeks. In long periods of freezing, with all lakes iced over, many birds take to the river until milder weather returns.

Several small eyots, some vegetated, add interest to this section of the Severn, but all except one disappear when the river flows at winter level. The range of vegetation is limited by the constant ravages of the water, with sedges and course grasses the norm, whilst willow is the dominant tree. Riverside oaks, widely spaced, make ideal drying posts and roosting sites for Great Cormorants. The fields bordering the river are a mixture of pasture and arable, but are well drained so that the damp meadow situations enjoyed by Common Redshanks and other waders do not occur.

A walk upstream from Cressage Bridge is also recommended. This length of river has extensive pebble beaches, a large area of thorn scrub and an interesting hillside wood.

Species

Regular breeding birds in the riverside vegetation are Moorhens, Sedge Warblers and Reed Buntings. The willows attract many species, and from autumn bands of tits, usually Long-tailed, Blue and Great Tits, move from bush to bush along the river. The willows also make good roosting sites, and are used by Magpies, Fieldfares, Redwings and other thrushes. Lesser Whitethroats skulk in them at the end of most summers on passage. Common Kingfishers and Sand Martins tunnel nest holes into the vertical cliffs.

The pebble beaches and eyots exposed at low water periods are favourite haunts of Little Ringed Plovers and Dunlin, particularly on spring passage, although the former breed in small numbers, with elegant Common Greenshanks and Green Sandpipers prominent during the return movement. Common Sandpipers, flicking low above the river surface, appear in numbers at both times. Grey Wagtails and Dippers feed in these areas, although they breed along smaller tributary streams, whilst many species including wildfowl, Northern Lapwing, Eurasian Curlews and gulls gather on them to bathe and preen.

In the fields and hedgerows a wide variety of species can be found, although the once numerous Tree Sparrows, a speciality of the area not too long ago, are now almost a rarity. Stubble, also something of a rarity these days, holds mixed winter flocks of seed-eating species, with Chaffinches, Greenfinches, Goldfinches, Linnets and Yellowhammers present in large numbers. Bramblings and Common Redpolls are likely to appear at the end of winter. Such an abundance of prey, along with voles and field mice, attract predators, and Eurasian Sparrowhawks, Common Kestrels, Little Owls and Tawny Owls are regular here, with occasional Merlins and Peregrine Falcons during the winter months. Sadly, Barn Owls are more conspicuous by their absence now, although irregular sightings still occur, as do those of Short-eared Owls. Sky Larks are residents and both species of partridge breed although in smaller numbers than formerly, and other breeding species are Northern Lapwings, Eurasian Curlews and Yellow Wagtails. The meadows to the east of Leighton Hall are an important wintering ground for wildfowl and up to 1,300 Canada Geese may be counted there in December and January, and a thorough search of the flock may reveal small numbers of Pink-footed, White-fronted and Brent Geese dotted amongst them. A few feral Greylag, Snow and Barnacle Geese add interest and the first named are increasing rapidly in Shropshire. One or two Bar-headed Geese appear most winters, escapes probably from wildfowl collections. Eurasian Wigeon flock here each winter, building up to 400 or so at the turn of the year.

Weather conditions, which dictate the state of the river, bring different species to the area accordingly. Long periods of heavy rain will cause severe flooding, and birds attracted at these times are Tundra Swans, Whooper Swans, Northern Pintail and Northern Shoveler, the last-named remaining on flood pools long after the water has receded within the river banks. Mats of debris, floating on the water surface but trapped between the trunks and branches of willows, obviously provide a useful source of food, as many small birds, including Siskins, feed on them, unlikely though this may seem. Prolonged freezing will increase the numbers of Little and Great Crested Grebes, Common Pochard, Tufted Duck, Common Goldeneye, Goosander and Common Coots. A clear sunny day during a freeze-up, with the river reflecting a blue sky and the smartly pied drakes of Tufted Duck, Common Goldeneye and Goosander diving and resurfacing between ice-floes can be quite magical, especially if there is a carpet of snow to add to the Arctic effect. A falling river level in these conditions will expose a narrow strip of unfrozen banking in a rock-hard countryside, which Common Snipe and Song Thrush are always quick to exploit.

Other species which are commonly seen in the area are Great Cormorants, outside the breeding season – with sometimes up to a score of birds sitting in a riverside oak – Grey Herons, Mute Swans and Mallard. All the commoner gulls are present, especially on flood pools, with Black-headed and Lesser Black-backed Gulls the most numerous, and occasional Kittiwakes pass through in late winter. A very unusual visitor in November 1993 was a drake Common Eider.

Mink are a recent addition to the fauna of the river and reputed to be a threat to native wildlife, especially Moorhens and other riverside nesting birds.

On the upstream side of Cressage Bridge, beneath which Common Kingfishers regularly fly, the pebble beaches are good for the wader species previously mentioned, and Common Redshanks appear each spring. They were regular breeders in a wet meadow near the bridge which has now been improved for cereal production. The thorn scrub provides food, shelter and nest sites for thrushes, warblers, tits, finches and buntings. Newly arrived Redwings and Fieldfares feed here in hundreds each autumn. The hillside wood holds a good selection of birds, including Eurasian Sparrowhawks, all three woodpeckers, Wood Nuthatches and Eurasian Treecreepers.

Timing

There is something of interest throughout the year, with perhaps the leanest spell falling between the departure of summer migrants and the arrival of wintering birds. The winter months produce good birdwatching, especially when pools and lakes in the county are frozen. Visits during periods of flood can be productive, but be prepared for footpaths being inaccessible and footbridges damaged or destroyed. Dry spells are also good, with maximum exposure of beaches and eyots. The worst river condition is when the water runs bank-full but has not yet flooded onto the fields.

There is some disturbance from anglers, although the majority, once settled into position, have little effect on birdwatching. There is also a small amount of shooting in season, but this is insignificant. In summer months canoeing activity may cause temporary disquiet, but parties usually pass quickly through. By far the greatest amount of disturbance on the Shropshire Severn in recent years has been caused by the popular Raft Races. These are noisy social affairs, which raise money for worthy causes, and fortunately only take up one or two Sundays in high summer. The field at Buildwas is sometimes used as a starting point.

Early morning is the best time to visit at any time of the year. Evenings can produce spectacular flights of wildfowl, especially in October when hundreds of Canada Geese fly along the Severn Valley, heading west from the Leighton meadows. From October to March evening flights of Eurasian Wigeon are a delight to see and hear.

Access

There is limited parking space at Cressage Bridge on the spur of the B4380 that runs into the village from the north. Horse-boxes often park here in the morning whilst the occupants are put through their paces on the nearby training circuit. Follow the footpath upstream as far as the second bend for river birds although it is a pleasant and often rewarding walk to continue along the footpath as far as Dryton. It may be necessary to take the route around the outside of the small wood due to severe bank erosion in recent winters, and it is always advisable to go this way when the river is flooded. On the other side of the road a path leaves the field gate and follows the hedgerow towards Leighton, touching the river for a distance from near Eye Farm.

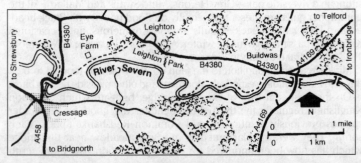

The river is also accessible in the east of the area. Park on the old road near Buildwas Church on the B4380 at the west of the village. The OS map shows a path running through fields, but these are invariably ploughed and the line of the path not maintained. Take the anglers' path alongside the river from the stile 220 yds (200 m) east of the church. The path can be followed for about 1.25 miles (2 km) but footbridges crossing two small streams are often damaged or even swept away after high water levels.

The inaccessible private areas can be viewed from lay-bys overlooking Leighton Park on the B4380, 1 mile (1.6 km) west of Buildwas Church. Grandstand views are obtained from here, but a telescope is essential.

The Shrewsbury–Telford–Birmingham and the Shrewsbury–Bridgnorth bus services serve Buildwas and Cressage respectively.

Calendar

All year: Grey Heron, Mute Swan, Canada Goose, Mallard, Eurasian Sparrowhawk, Common Kestrel, Red-legged and Grey Partridges, Moorhen, Northern Lapwing, Little and Tawny Owls, Common Kingfisher, Sky Lark, common resident thrushes, tits and finches, Tree Sparrow (now scarce), Yellowhammer, Reed Bunting.

April–June: Passage Little Ringed Plover, Dunlin, Redshank, Common Sandpiper. Breeding Eurasian Curlew, Sand Martin, Yellow Wagtail, Sedge Warbler. Resident birds breeding.

July–September: Common Greenshank, Green and Common Sandpipers on passage. Lesser Whitethroat (passage) and juvenile tit flocks in riverside willows. Canada Goose and Northern Lapwing form flocks.

October–March: Little and Great Crested Grebes return to river. Great Cormorants return from coast. Winter wildfowl arrive: Tundra and Whooper Swans (scarce), Pink-footed (scarce), White-fronted and Brent Geese (rare); Greylag, Snow and Barnacle Geese (all feral); Eurasian Wigeon, Northern Pintail, Northern Shoveler, Common Pochard, Tufted Duck, Common Goldeneye, Goosander. Occasional Merlin and Peregrine Falcon. Gulls on floods. Kittiwake (rare) in March. Grey Wagtail and Dipper move down from tributary streams. Fieldfare and Redwing. Large finch flocks include smaller numbers of Brambling, Siskin and Common Redpoll. Sand Martins arrive late March.

THE WREKIN AND THE ERCALL

Habitat

Aligned from northeast to southwest, these hills of ancient volcanic lava lie north of the River Severn. The Wrekin is 2 miles (3.2 km) and The Ercall almost 1 mile (1.6 km) in length. Although not particularly high – the former reaches 1334 ft (407 m) and the latter 871 ft (265 m) – the range is made to look impressive by the flatness of the Shropshire Plain from which it rises. Both hills are thickly wooded, but The Wrekin has some open grassland along the summit ridge and a few outcrops of rock. The prominence of the hill made it a natural choice for the site of an Iron Age fort and later a beacon.

Much of the Wrekin woodland is modern forestry plantations, especially along the southeastern slopes and the southern end, but some areas of broadleaved woods remain, including oak, with an extensive beech wood along the northwest slopes towards the northern end. As with all modern forestry, areas are clear-felled on reaching maturity, to be replanted very quickly. This creates woodland blocks of varying ages and adds to the variety of the habitat.

The Ercall is clothed mainly with broadleaved trees, but is scarred in part by a quarry in the south. It provides pleasant birdwatching, but does not afford the spectacular views for which The Wrekin is renowned, nor is the habitat as varied.

A small pool lies in the angle between two unclassified roads, one of which separates the hills. This is the old Wrekin Reservoir. On the other two sides, undisturbed grass and scrub, together with a bordering stream and a number of mature trees, create a habitat which is often rich in birdlife, although only a limited number of species use the pool.

Species

A quick look at the pool may reveal Little and Great Crested Grebes, with Mallard, Common Pochard and Tufted Duck the likeliest wildfowl. Moorhens and Common Coots both breed. The surrounding vegetation holds scrub-loving species such as warblers in summer, and provides a rich feeding ground for finches in winter, including Siskins and Common Redpolls, but also Greenfinches, Goldfinches and Linnets.

The coniferous plantations of The Wrekin shelter Goldcrests, Coal Tits and occasional Common Crossbills. Newly replanted areas are favoured by Grasshopper Warblers, and where isolated birches have been left unfelled, Tree Pipits breed, followed by Garden Warblers, Blackcaps and Linnets as newly planted trees begin to emerge. Whinchats may also be seen here and in 1983 there was a confirmed breeding report of a European Nightjar (but sadly this was followed by the finding of a dead road victim). Recolonisation is always a possibility as this is a traditional European Nightjar area.

The usual broadleaved woodland species are found on both hills. Common Redstarts, Wood Warblers and Pied Flycatchers all breed. Most common woodland songbirds are present, and spring days resound with the melodies of Wrens, Robins, Blackbirds, Song Thrushes, Garden Warblers and Blackcaps. Declining Turtle Doves may croon and Common Cuckoos become monotonous after the first few exciting calls of the early arrivals. Hole-nesting species include five tits, Wood Nut-hatches, all three woodpeckers, Stock Doves and Eurasian Jackdaws, whilst Eurasian Treecreepers place their nests behind loose bark or in ivy crevices. The main predators are Eurasian Sparrowhawks and Tawny Owls, although Eurasian Jays also pose a threat to eggs and nestlings of many passerines. Spring and summer evenings are enlivened by roding Woodcocks and bats are numerous in clearings and along woodland edges. Siskins and Common Redpolls, seeking birch, spruce and larch seeds, are present during the winter, and Bramblings appear most years, feeding on fallen beech mast with Chaffinches.

Along the open ridge, and around the summit rocks, Common Kestrels hunt and a few Meadow Pipits may be seen. Common Swifts, Barn Swallows and House Martins feed across and above the rock faces on which Carrion Crows love to perch, and about which Eurasian Jackdaws practice their considerable flying skills. Other species enjoying the more open areas and hedgerows of neighbouring fields are Yellowhammers, Mistle Thrushes and the winter visiting Fieldfares and Redwings. Both

Common Buzzards and Common Ravens breed in the area and are frequently seen on The Wrekin.

Timing

The Wrekin is a top tourist attraction for hordes of visitors to Shropshire. Most of these tackle the hill from the road at the northern end, following the well-worn path to the summit. Summer weekends are the worst affected, but fine weather at any time of the year can bring visitors in some numbers. Joggers, orienteers, pony riders and ramblers are all attracted to the area, but most disturbance can be avoided by an early morning visit or by taking some of the less used paths. Forestry operations are another cause of disturbance.

There is a Scout Camp on the southeast side. A thrash around the hill during dusk and darkness seems to be some sort of tradition with this movement, so if the peace and tranquillity of the evening is your preference, with roding Woodcocks, hooting Tawny Owls, bats on the wing and perhaps a prowling fox, you must avoid Fridays and Saturdays.

A small military firing range on the northwest side may cause temporary inconvenience, but this is not a major disturbance to the hills generally and poses no threat to public safety. (Warning flags are flown and sentries posted when the range is in use.)

By comparison The Ercall is reasonably quiet, although it is popular with local people, especially family parties.

Spring and summer are the best times to visit, but there is something of interest at most times of the year. August and September are probably the leanest months.

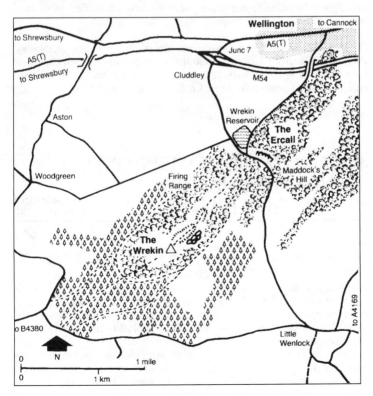

Access

This area is well served by footpaths. The road on the southwest side of the reservoir has a wide verge suitable for parking and can be used for both hills. It is reached by taking the unclassified road south from Junction 7 of the M54, or by meandering through the network of lanes west from the A4169 or north from the B4380. There is limited roadside parking at the southwest end of the Wrekin, but the paths through the plantations from this end are often very muddy in wet periods and footwear should be chosen to suit. With patience and a good navigator the lanes listed above will get you to this spot.

There is a rail service to Wellington Telford West station and buses to Wellington from Shrewsbury and Telford. It is a 2.5-mile (4 km) walk from the station and town centre to the Wrekin.

Calendar

All year: Eurasian Sparrowhawk, Common Kestrel, Woodcock, Tawny Owl, three woodpeckers, resident thrushes, Goldcrest, tits, Wood Nuthatch, Eurasian Treecreeper, Eurasian Jay and other common crows, resident finches.

April–June: Roding Woodcock. Summer visitors from mid-April include Common Cuckoo, Tree Pipit, Common Redstart, scrub and leaf warblers including Wood Warbler, and Pied Flycatcher; but early May for Turtle Dove (scarce), Common Swift and Spotted Flycatcher.

July–September: Residents and summer visitors still breeding. Fledglings on wing. Flocks of mixed juvenile tits.

October–March: Grebes and wildfowl on reservoir (small numbers), Common Buzzard. Fieldfare and Redwing from mid-October, Common Raven. Winter finch flocks include Brambling, Siskin and Common Redpoll. Common Crossbill (scarce). Chiffchaff arrives mid-March.

42 LONG MYND, STIPERSTONES AND THE CHURCH STRETTON HILLS

OS Landranger
Maps 126 & 137

Habitat

This whole area is one of outstanding scenic beauty, and on clear days any high point in the hills offers staggering views in all directions. The three groups are very different in character, from the brooding rocky ridge of the Stiperstones, across the sprawling plateau of the Long Mynd, to the hog-backed Stretton Hills.

The Long Mynd runs north–northeast from Plowden before merging into a patchwork of agricultural land 8 miles (12.8 km) to the north. The greatest width is 4 miles (6.4 km) between Church Stretton and

Ratlinghope. This upland is renowned for its geological interest, the pre-Cambrian rocks forming a plateau rising to an average height of 1500 ft (460 m), with a highest point of 1695 ft (517 m) at Pole Bank. The area is dotted with ancient tumuli and dykes, with Bodbury Ring, an Iron Age hill fort, overlooking the Cardingmill Valley.

The habitat is varied, but dominated by heather moorland, most of which is owned by the National Trust (NT). The heather is managed as a grouse moor, being cut periodically to produce new growth without encouraging the spread of bracken. Bilberries also grow in profusion and attract both humans and wildlife to reap the harvest. Bracken does dominate in some areas, and seems much loved by Whinchats. Gorse flourishes locally, and apart from enlivening the scene with golden-yellow flowers, provides songposts for Yellowhammers and occasional Common Stonechats. Small pools and boggy patches, which hold insectivorous round-leaved sundew and common butterwort, lie hidden between acres of heather. Parts of the Long Mynd have been converted to improved grassland and the whole area is grazed by sheep.

Pure streams flow from springs surrounded by sphagnum moss, to cascade into spectacular valleys cut deeply into the eastern-facing slopes. Known as 'batches', their steep sides are generously dotted with scrub hawthorn and rowan, and small rocky outcrops push through the heather in most valleys. The western-facing slopes are steep, producing updraughts suitable for gliding, hang-gliding and raptors, especially Common Buzzards.

Nestling beneath the slopes of the Long Mynd, on the outskirts of Church Stretton, is Old Rectory Wood. Owned by the Shropshire County Council (SCC), the wood contains a good mixture of trees, mainly hardwoods, including many beech, with oak, chestnut, cherry and Scots pine amongst others. A nature trail has been constructed to cover the most interesting aspects of the wood, and it is an interesting site for all woodland species.

Less attractive, both ornithologically and aesthetically, is the blanket coniferous plantation towards the southern end of the Long Mynd. Even so it is worth a look for Goldcrests and Coal Tits. It also provides nesting sites and shelter for birds feeding on adjacent hillsides, especially Eurasian Jays which commute regularly between wood and valley. Eurasian Sparrowhawks and the occasional rare Northern Goshawk are also encountered here. Recent felling in part of the wood will lead to some variation of habitat which will be of ornithological benefit.

The barren, rocky ridge of the Stiperstones is one of the wildest areas in Shropshire. To walk the hill on one of the not infrequent days of swirling mist can be an unnerving experience. To be caught on the ridge during a summer thunderstorm can be downright frightening, and it is easy to see why the area is steeped in legend. Lying parallel to the Long Mynd, some 4 miles (6.4 km) to the west, it was once a continuous quartzite ridge before excessive frost shatter in the last Ice Age reduced it to the line of jagged tors we see today. The most impressive stretch is the 1.25 miles (2 km) between Cranberry Rock and Scattered Rocks, north of the Bridges to Shelve road. The whole length here is boulder-strewn and strong footwear is recommended. Heather and bilberry make up the dominant vegetation, with some cowberry and the scarce crowberry. Scrub hawthorns and rowans are invading the lower slopes and in the east are joined by conifers straying from the plantation which is now maturing there. This and other extensive plantations further south are comparatively recent developments which brought European Nightjars to the area in the early years, although they now appear to have left. The Stiperstones lacks the streams of the Long Mynd but there are interesting wooded valleys in the northwest at Mytton Dingle and Perkins Beach. The area surrounding the hill is made up of small hill farms and the remains of the former lead mining industry. English Nature (EN) declared a large portion of the Stiperstones to be a National Nature Reserve (NNR) in 1982.

Also parallel to the Long Mynd, and forming the eastern slopes of the Vale of Stretton, the hog-backed Stretton Hills lie in line ahead, aligning on their more northern cousin, The Wrekin. The pre-Cambrian rocks, some of the oldest in Britain, form narrow, steep-sided hills, clothed in acid grasslands, with occasional rocky outcrops making ideal lookout perches for Common Kestrels and Common Ravens. Some patches of oak woodland are to be found, the most extensive being on Helmeth Hill and Ragleth Hill. The former is owned by the Woodland Trust (WT) who have constucted a circuit path within the wood. It is well worth a visit. The dominating hills are Ragleth at 1300 ft (396 m), Caer Caradoc at 1506 ft (459 m) and The Lawley at 1236 ft (377 m), but the outlying hills to the east are worthy of exploration. Wilstone Hill, Middle Hill and Hope Bowdler Hill form a close group, more flat-topped than their neighbours, but rising to similar heights.

Species

These hills are excellent raptor haunts. Hovering Common Kestrels may be seen anywhere, as may soaring Common Buzzards; and Eurasian Sparrowhawks hunt the entire area, even skimming low over the heather of the open moors. All three species breed, and families of Common Kestrels and Common Buzzards are often seen in late summer, lined up with military precision in the updraughts of western-facing slopes. Hen Harriers are passage birds, seen quartering the open moorland of the Long Mynd and the Stiperstones. Seasonal visitors are Hobbies, summer migrants now seen annually in increasing numbers, and scarce Rough-legged Buzzards which appear in some winters. The former may be seen hunting over the Long Mynd, occasionally in pairs, for fox moths and northern eggar moths, whilst the latter are usually seen in the northwest of the Long Mynd and the marginal country between there and the Stiperstones. Peregrine Falcons, great wanderers, may appear anywhere at any time of the year, often as immature birds. In recent years they have become established as regular breeders in Shropshire and are still increasing. Northern Goshawks have also been recorded more frequently over the past decade. The high population of Wood Pigeons should ensure that both species find local food supplies to their liking. The delightful little Merlin is seen hunting the heather moors in most years, when Meadow Pipit numbers are high, and occasional winter birds are seen in bordering lowland pastures. Red Kites also wander into the hills, usually in winter, but more recently in summer too. With the Welsh population increasing significantly, future breeding is a strong possibility.

A number of other species are common throughout the area. Meadow Pipits are very numerous and play host to Common Cuckoos, but Tree Pipits are more local, occurring along woodland edges and on thorn-covered slopes. Up to 500 Common Swifts have been estimated feeding above the Long Mynd, but along with Barn Swallows and House Martins they feed over all the hills, especially when ants are on the wing. Eurasian Curlews breed widely, arriving in early April and small numbers of Common Snipe drum over wet areas in spring and early summer, especially at dusk. The ubiquitous Carrion Crow is rarely out of sight or earshot and large numbers of Rooks and Eurasian Jackdaws feed in the hills. Common Ravens breed here, their croaking calls and thrilling flight being symbolic of wild hill country, and more than compensating for lack of physical beauty. Magpies and Eurasian Jays, handsome but noisy, are commonplace and Red-billed Choughs have appeared on very rare occasions after westerly gales. Mistle Thrushes, lovers of soft fruit, gather in large numbers to feed on bilberies from early summer. Other passerines common to all areas are Northern Wheatears, especially around rocky outcrops with short turf, Linnets and Yellowhammers, the latter two species associating with scrub hawthorn and gorse.

Red Grouse can be seen on the heather moorland of the Long Mynd and Stiperstones

Red Grouse breed on the heather moorland of the Long Mynd and the Stiperstones and Short-eared Owls are vagrants. Common Stonechats, though scarce, breed in both places, but the numerous Whinchats tend to favour the valley slopes and post-breeding families often associate with bracken, perching conspicuously on the taller fronds.

The small pools on the Long Mynd provide breeding sites for Mallard, Common Teal and occasional Moorhens. Green Sandpipers also use them, usually for a very short stay, pausing only to bathe and preen before continuing their journey. Wet areas, habitat of the soft rush, are sought out by breeding Reed Buntings in spring and frequented by solitary Jack Snipe in late winter. Sky Larks feed on the improved pastures, as do Northern Lapwings, and other Long Mynd waders are Golden Plovers, seen on rare occasions in spring and charming trips of Dotterels, seen annually on spring and autumn passage, usually in short vegetation near the Gliding Field.

The Long Mynd valleys are excellent for wildlife when the harshness of winter has passed. Grey and Pied Wagtails along with Dippers breed beside the streams and Grey Herons visit them for small fish. The latter also hunt the moorland pools for frogs. The scrub on the valley slopes is often teeming with small passerines such as Blue and Great Tits,

Chaffinches, Willow Warblers and Robins. Hedge Accentors and Wrens breed almost to the edge of the open moor, and all the major valleys hold Ring Ouzels and Common Redstarts in small numbers. The latter often favour partially dead windblown thorns, lying grounded with bracken growing into the branches. Green Woodpeckers search the slopes for ants and Red-legged Partridges call from rock outcrops, looking far more impressive than their lowland brethren.

Old Rectory Wood and other patches of hardwood found at the foot of most valleys contain Tawny Owls, Great and Lesser Spotted Woodpeckers, Wood Warblers, Wood Nuthatches, Eurasian Treecreepers and many other woodland passerines. The coniferous plantation shelters Goldcrests and tits, with a larger variety of species along the perimeter, including Siskins, which may be found on the lower boundary in Minton Batch.

The Long Mynd is always capable of springing a surprise, and recent years have seen a Great Ringed Plover, Black-tailed Godwits, Wood Sandpiper and Sandwich Terns overflying on passage and a flock of disorientated Canada Geese flying at heather top height through thick fog.

Although less extensive in range and more restricted in habitat than its neighbour, the Stiperstones offers good birdwatching. The abandoned fields and hedgerows surrounding the ruins of former mineworkers' cottages in the north are good for Common Redstarts, Pied Flycatchers, tits and other small passerines. The coniferous plantation north of the Bridges to Shelve road contains large flocks of small birds in autumn, especially Goldcrests and Coal Tits, with birds commuting between here and the oakwood to the east. The northern end of the plantation is more open, containing some mature Scots pine, and the three woodpeckers are found here, with Woodcocks roding on spring evenings. The scrubby hillside between the plantation and the car park is good for pipits, Whinchats, Linnets and Common Redpolls. Ring Ouzels are not recorded on the Stiperstones every year, but have bred in Perkins Beach, an area much frequented by Eurasian Jays.

Birdlife on the tops of the Stretton Hills is rather sparse, but the surrounding low areas can be very good. Common Redstarts in old hedgerow timber with Wood Nuthatches, Eurasian Treecreepers, the three woodpeckers and Tawny Owls in the fragmented woodlands are all typical birds of the area. Winter thrushes join their resident cousins to feed on hawthorn and rowan berries in autumn. The tract of country containing Willstone, Middle and Hope Bowdler Hills is rather neglected by birdwatchers and could hold surprises for the visitor.

Timing

The Shropshire Hills are a tourist area and attract great numbers of visitors from Easter through to September. At first, and towards the end, it is mainly weekends when the crowds arrive, but July and August can be chronic each day. The Long Mynd suffers most, but it is a vast area and many people do not stray far from their vehicles. It is, however, a playground for outdoor activities of all kinds (including birdwatching!) and for educational visits, which may involve more than 100 children spending school hours in one of the valleys. The Cardingmill Valley and Ashes Hollow are usually worst hit. The Stiperstones take fewer visitors, but the area is more compact and cannot absorb large numbers so effectively. Many people come specifically to pick bilberries. Again, July and August are the worst months. On the Stretton Hills ridge walking is a popular pastime, but not particularly disturbing to birdlife.

One sure way to avoid disturbance is to visit early in the day. In spring and early summer the hills are alive with bird movement and song. Return at noon and the difference is unbelievable. Take a word of warning though: temperatures can be below freezing at dawn as late as May, and showers of hail or even a substantial snowfall are not unusual in that month. Rain can be sudden and heavy, even when the lowlands are fine, so be prepared and carry spare clothing if you are walking any distance. Evening visits can be profitable too, and the tranquillity of dusk,

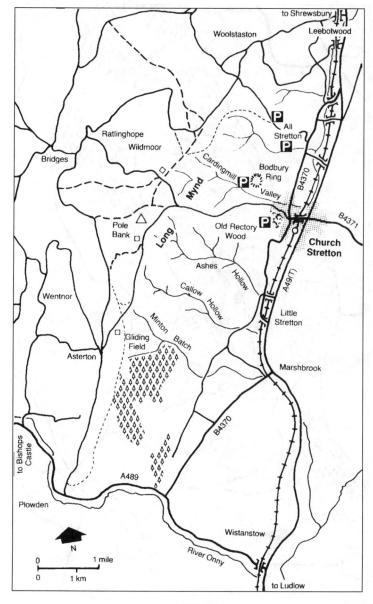

disturbed only by the calls of Red Grouse and Eurasian Curlews, the drumming of Common Snipe and the sudden appearance of a late hunting Hobby, is something very special.

Winter birdwatching is usually very poor, especially at high altitudes, although the occasional raptor may make it worthwhile, and a flock of Common Ravens gathers annually on the Stiperstones. Most birdlife at this time is confined to the lower valleys, woods and marginal land.

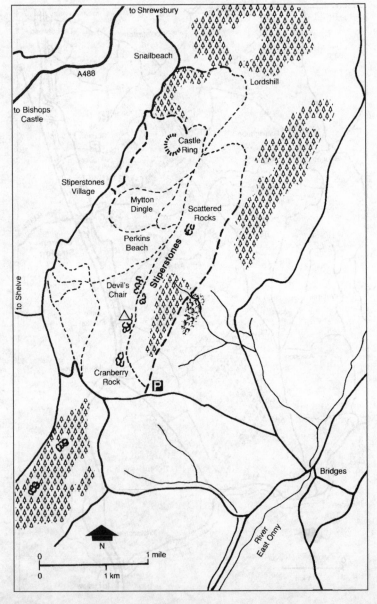

Access

There is open access to those areas of the Long Mynd owned by the NT and the area is well served by roads. The most popular approach is from Church Stretton in the east, but alternative roads may be taken from Bridges in the northwest, or from Plowden via Asterton in the south. The northern end can be reached from Leebotwood on the A49(T). Old Rectory Wood is within easy walking distance of Church Stretton but also has a car park near the Long Mynd Hotel.

The most popular access point for the Stiperstones is the car parking area on the Bridges to Shelve road, below Cranberry Rock. Other good starting points are at Lordshill, near Snailbeach, in the north, and Stiperstones village in the northwest. The area is well served by rights of way and there is open access to the Stiperstones NNR.

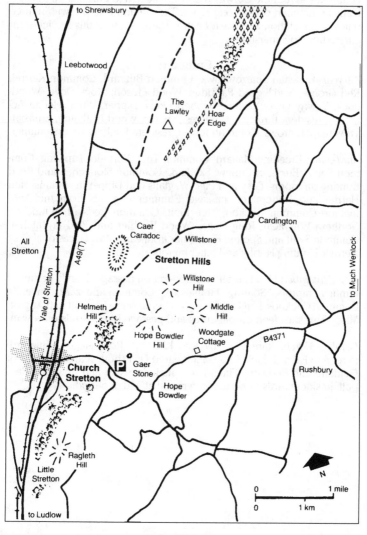

The Stretton Hills are also well served by footpaths. The Lawley is best approached from the minor road passing the northeast end. Hoare Edge, on the opposite side of the valley, can also be gained from this road. Caer Caradoc and Helmeth Hill can be approached from Willstone to the east (the narrow lane from the farms is unsuitable for cars), or from the B4371 beneath the Gaer Stone, 1 mile (1.6 km) east of Church Stretton.

This point also gives access to Willstone, Middle and Hope Bowdler Hills, which can also be walked from paths leaving the same road near Hope Bowdler village or 0.5 miles (0.8 km) further east. Ragleth Hill can be reached via Clive Avenue in Church Stretton through woodland in the northeast, or from the A49(T) at the southwest end.

Church Stretton is served by rail. Also the Ludlow–Shrewsbury bus service passes through the town along the B4370. Several Long Mynd valleys are accessible from this road. Less than 0.5 miles (0.8 km) from the town centre the start of the Burway road (and access to Cardingmill Valley) leads to the heart of the Long Mynd. The Stretton Hills are within three miles of the station and town centre. There is also a bus service from Shrewsbury to Stiperstones.

Calendar

All year: Eurasian Sparrowhawk, Common Buzzard, Common Kestrel, Red Grouse, Red-legged Partridge, Wood Pigeon, Stock Dove, Woodcock, Tawny Owl, the three woodpeckers, Dipper, Wren, Hedge Accentor, resident thrushes, Goldcrest, six tits, Wood Nuthatch, Eurasian Treecreeper, crows, Common Raven, resident finches, Yellowhammer.

April–June: Breeding Mallard, Common Teal, Northern Lapwing, Common Snipe, Eurasian Curlew, Sky Lark, Common Stonechat, and Reed Bunting on moors. Grey and Pied Wagtails and Dipper in streams. Hen Harrier and Dotterel on passage. Summer migrants from mid-April include Common Cuckoo, Tree Pipit, Common Redstart, Whinchat, Northern Wheatear, Ring Ouzel, Wood Warbler and Pied Flycatcher. Common Swift and Spotted Flycatcher from early May. Occasional Grey Herons. Hunting Hobby and other raptors.

July–September: Hen Harrier and Dotterel on passage. Family parties of hunting raptors. Soaring families of Common Buzzard. Juvenile Common Cuckoos. Large gatherings of Common Swifts until mid-August. Mistle Thrushes feed on bilberries and passage Ring Ouzels on rowan.

October–March: Rare visits by Red Kite and Rough-legged Buzzard. Peregrine Falcon. Jack Snipe, Short-eared Owl (both scarce). Flocks of Fieldfare and Redwing. Finch flocks include Siskin and Common Redpoll. Resident birds move to high ground at end of period.

43 VENUS POOL

Habitat

Venus Pool is a small ornithological reserve of some 14.5 acres (6 ha), lying 6 miles (9.6 km) southeast of Shrewsbury in the angle formed by the A458 and the minor road leading south to Pitchford and Acton Burnell. It is owned and managed by the Shropshire Ornithological Society (SOS) and access is restricted to members only. The pool formed in the 1950s due to faulty drainage and quickly acquired a reputation as one of the top sites in the county. Major management in the past decade has resulted in a delightful shallow pool with a deeper channel in front of the large island and several specially constructed smaller islands. The perimeter contains stretches of tall vegetation such as greater reedmace, greater willowherb, rushes and recently introduced *Phragmites* to attract breeding birds, but also areas of open shore to encourage passage waders. Some measure of water-level control provides an additional aid. Areas of pebbles have been laid to provide suitable sites for nesting waders. With some areas of flat, dry and sparser vegetated ground, an area of willow scrub and hardwoods planted around the boundary fence, there is a surprising variety of habitats in a small area. Three hides connected by a well-laid path give excellent viewing over most of the site and a feeding station set out near the North Hide attacts many species including Great Spotted Woodpecker. The reserve is mostly surrounded by pasture and the path running alongside a hedgerow is the sole means of access.

Species

Although supporting good numbers of resident species, it is as a wintering wildfowl and passage wader site that the pool has built a reputation. Little and Great Crested Grebes, Mute Swan, Canada and feral Greylag Geese, Mallard, Tufted Duck, Moorhen and Common Coot are present throughout the year and all breed. Ruddy Duck breed annually but may be absent in winter months. Common Pochard raise one or two broods almost annually, Northern Shoveler breed regularly and Common Teal occasionally, but all three are best known as winter visitors along with Eurasian Wigeon, Northern Pintail in small numbers, Common Goldeneye especially at the end of winter and occasional Goosander. Tundra and Whooper Swans pay brief visits most years, as do occasional Bean, Pink-footed and White-fronted Geese, but with geese species there is always the problem of escapes. There is no doubt that the small number of Barnacle Geese found mingling with the Canada Geese flocks in all seasons are of captive origin. Common Shelduck visit mostly in spring, as do the occasional Garganey, and Gadwall are not unusual but are easy to overlook. Other wildfowl seen irregularly are Red-breasted Merganser, Long-tailed Duck and Common and Velvet Scoter.

Waders now breeding annually are Oystercatchers, Little Ringed Plovers, and Northern Lapwings, but the once annual Common Redshanks are now irregular. Eurasian Curlews nest in the area and use the pool for bathing and preening. Spring passage gets under way in late March with Dunlins, Great Ringed Plovers, Common and Green Sandpipers all regulars, but many other species on a less predictable

Little Ringed Plovers are among the waders that nest annually at Venus Pool

basis. These may include Spotted Redshanks and Ruffs, both in breeding plumage, and the latter have been noted displaying to Common Coots and Mallard in the absence of others of their kind.

All these species return from late July although mid-August to mid-September sees the maximum movement. Little Stints, Black-tailed and Bar-tailed Godwits, Common Greenshanks and Wood Sandpipers are annuals with less regular visits from Red Knots, Sanderlings, Turnstones and recently a Temminck's Stint. Green Sandpipers occasionally over-winter when they share the site with good numbers of Common Snipe and one or two Jack Snipe.

A colony of Black-headed Gulls breed annually and other species visit, including Little and Mediterranean Gulls, but the site is too small to be used as a winter roost. Common, Arctic and Black Terns are regular passage migrants in spring and autumn. Great Cormorants commute regularly between the pool and the nearby River Severn after their post-breeding return in late September and Grey Herons are regular visitors. Two recent vagrants were a Little Egret and Eurasian Spoonbills in two years. Water Rails are seen each winter.

Yellow Wagtails have bred, but are most numerous on passage, whilst many other passerines use the site and breed in the immediate neighbourhood. Sedge and Reed Warblers, along with Reed Buntings, nest in the poolside vegetation. Fieldfares and Redwings abound in the adjacent hedgerows and fields from early October and tits and finches take advantage of the feeding station. Recent provision of nest boxes will encourage more species to breed.

Barn Swallows form pre-migration roosts in some autumns and this attracts Hobbies for a late evening meal. Other predators visiting the site regularly are Eurasian Sparrowhawk, Common Buzzard and Common Kestrel, with increasing Peregrine Falcon sightings and the occasional winter Merlin. Short-eared Owls are winter vagrants but the delightful Barn Owl, not too long ago a regular evening treat, has all but disappeared.

Timing

The main disadvantage of Venus Pool is the lack of land around the reserve to protect it from disturbance. Farming activities in the adjacent fields may cause some inconvenience, but far worse is the shooting that takes place, especially when winter wildfowl are using the site. It is hoped to shortly find a solution to the problem. This apart the time of day to visit is less critical than at a non-reserve site, although early morning visits usually produce better birdwatching.

For wintering wildfowl it is usually early November before birds arrive in numbers. Northbound passage waders visit mostly throughout April and early May with August and early September the best time for returning birds. Evenings in late August produce predatory Eurasian Sparrowhawks and Hobbies when Barn Swallow roosts form.

Access

The entrance to Venus Pool, through a small car park, is 0.5 miles (0.8 km) along a minor road which leaves the A458 south 0.5 miles (0.8 km) southeast of Cross Houses. The pool is omitted from some maps. Entry to the reserve is restricted to members of the SOS. The pool can only be viewed from locked hides, keys to which must be purchased from the Society's treasurer.

The Shrewsbury–Bridgnorth bus service passes through Crosshouses, which is 1 mile (1.6 km) from Venus Pool.

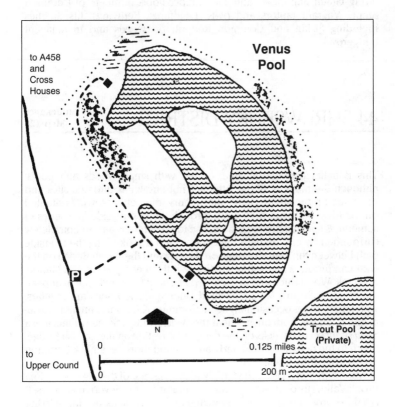

Calendar

All year: Little and Great Crested Grebes, Mute Swan, Greylag (feral) and Canada Geese, Mallard, Tufted Duck, Moorhen, Common Coot, many resident passerines in adjacent fields and hedgerows.

April–June: Common Shelduck. Wader passage includes Great Ringed Plover, Dunlin, Common Redshank, Green and Common Sandpipers. Passage terns including Black Tern. Breeding grebes, Mute Swan, Greylag (feral) and Canada Geese, Mallard, Tufted Duck, Ruddy Duck, Moorhen, Common Coot, Oystercatcher, Little Ringed Plover, Northern Lapwings, Black-headed Gulls, Sedge and Reed Warblers, Reed Bunting.

July–September: Still some late breeding. Juvenile wildfowl, Moorhens, Common Coots, waders and gulls. Return wader passage from late July includes Great Ringed Plover, Little Stint, Dunlin, Ruff, godwits, Spotted and Common Redshank, Common Greenshank, Green, Wood and Common Sandpipers, and possible unusual species. Tern passage including Black Tern. July usually a very quiet month.

October–March: Great Cormorant, Tundra and Whooper Swans (both scarce), geese including occasional White-fronted, perhaps scarce Pink-footed and Bean Geese. Ducks including Eurasian Wigeon, Common Teal, Northern Pintail, Northern Shoveler, Common Pochard, Common Goldeneye and occasional Goosander. Water Rail. Chance of overwintering Green Sandpiper and Jack Snipe, good numbers of Common Snipe. Vagrant raptors and owls. Fieldfares, Redwings, tits, finches including Siskin and Common Redpoll on weeds and in adjacent hedgerows.

44 SHREWSBURY DISTRICT

OS Landranger
Map 126

This is a flat agricultural area, dotted with small woods and pools, although the majority of the latter are not known as bird-rich sites and many are on private property. Shrewsbury, the county town, is situated on the River Severn, which flows through the countryside in a series of sometimes spectacular meanders. The town centre is almost completely surrounded by one of these huge loops, and a walk along the riverside path between the English Bridge on the east and the Welsh Bridge on the west can produce interesting species. Wildfowl escapes such as Mandarin Duck, Wood Duck and Red-crested Pochard frequently put in appearances. Mute Swans, Mallard, Tufted Duck and Moorhens are regulars, with Little Grebes occasionally seen. Common Kingfishers are not unusual and often fish from bushes near the Welsh Bridge. Some winters ago a Shag spent several weeks on the river, often resting on the English Bridge, much to the delight of local birdwatchers and more recently a Common Scoter visited the town.

Also worthy of a visit and within walking distace of the town is the Rea Brook Valley, through which a minor tributary of the Severn meanders. It is a thin corridor of small meadows and hedgerows snaking almost to the town centre which has somehow evaded development. Simply walk into the valley from the large car park opposite the Abbey Church, following the streamside path at the rear of the supermarket.

MONKMOOR

Habitat

In the Monkmoor area the river is at the extreme point of a major mean-der. Within it Shrewsbury Sewage Farm, once the foremost wader site in the county, is situated. There is no public access to the sewage farm, but a nearby pool owned by Severn Trent Water (STW) and known as the Monkmoor Lagoon Nature Reserve, at the end of the road from Monk-moor, often holds a wide range of species. A hide has recently been con-structed at the poolside but access is restricted (see below). The nearby river banks are generally steep, providing suitable nesting cliffs for Common Kingfishers and Sand Martins and the narrow riverside mead-ows on the inside of the bend are left as pasture for grazing cattle. The opposite bank is partially lined with willows and the adjoining fields are arable, with hedgerow removal to the south of Uffington creating what must be one of the largest fields in Shropshire. This reach of the Severn also contains a well vegetated eyot which provides shelter and breeding sites for a number of species, especially Mallard, Sedge Warblers and Reed Buntings. A small tree-lined stream entering the northern side of the river is often a focal point for bird activity in the area.

Species

Little and Great Crested Grebes occur on the pool throughout most of the year and are present on the river in the winter months. Other birds associat-ing with both standing and running water are Mute Swans, Mallard and Moorhens. Common Coots move to the river during spells of prolonged freez-ing. Sedge Warblers and Reed Buntings breed regularly in both habitats.

Birdlife on the river is seasonal. Great Cormorants fish the water outside the breeding season and an occasional immature bird may summer in-land. Grey Herons visit throughout the year, except at times of high water level and Goosanders are encountered in small numbers during the winter months. Passage periods bring sightings of waders and terns. Of the waders, Oystercatchers and Common Sandpipers are seen each spring, with the lat-ter returning early in the autumn, followed by Green Sandpipers, Common Greenshanks and occasional Curlew Sandpipers. Terns are usually Com-mon, Arctic and Black, but Sandwich and Little Terns have been recorded. Common Kingfishers breed but may be scarce following harsh winters. Sand Martins are feeding above the river from the last week in March. Grey Wagtails are regulars, whilst Eurasian Sparrowhawks and Common Kestrels hunt riverside hedgerows and fields.

Tufted Duck are resident on the pool and are joined in winter by Common Teal, Northern Shoveler and Common Pochard. All may be forced to the river in freezing spells. Ruddy Duck visit the pool in spring and autumn. Spring is also the best time to see the delightful Yellow Wagtails, with males resplendent in breeding finery, and a very rare Red-rumped Swallow put in an appearance in 1978. Hobbies, no longer a rar-ity in Shropshire, have been seen here too.

Timing

For passage waders and terns, April, May, August and early September are the best months. Post-breeding Great Cormorants start arriving in September, but it is usually mid-November before winter wildfowl appear in numbers.

The area is popular with anglers and attracts a few local walkers, but dis-turance is rarely great. Early morning is the best time to visit, particularly in spring and summer. For most species low water levels are an advantage, especially waders, Grey Herons and wagtails, and conversely a bank-full river of rushing muddy water will produce very few birds. A visit during or within two or three days of a rainy period will be sure to disappoint.

Access

Drive to the large roundabout beside the police headquarters in Monkmoor (northeast Shrewsbury) and take the road which leads northeast to pass Monkmoor Farm. The road becomes unmetalled and somewhat potholed, but persist to reach a car parking space just short of the river and beside the recently built by-pass. The pool – not shown on maps – is now a nature reserve and enclosed within a security fence. Entry can be gained by collecting a key (returnable cash deposit) from the Shropshire Wildlife Trust (SWT) office in Shrewsbury. Public footpaths run along the riverside in both directions.

There is a local bus service from Shrewsbury to Monkmoor from where the lagoon and river is a short walk.

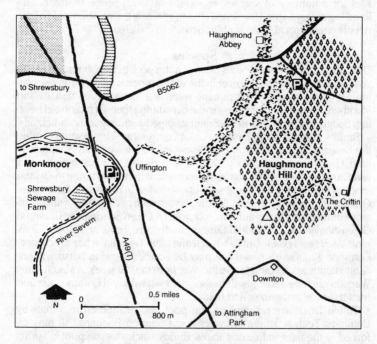

Calendar

All year: Grey Heron, Mute Swan, Canada Goose, Mallard, Tufted Duck, Eurasian Sparrowhawk, Common Kestrel, Moorhen, Common Coot, Common Kingfisher, Green and Great Spotted Woodpeckers, Grey and Pied Wagtails, Reed Bunting.

April–June: Ruddy Duck. Passage waders including Oystercatcher and Common Sandpiper. Passage terns including Black Tern and possible scarce (in Shropshire) Sandwich and Little Terns. Summer migrants from mid-April including Common Cuckoo, Yellow Wagtail, Sedge Warbler. Common Swift from early May.

July–September: Early single Great Cormorants from end of September. Ruddy Duck. Passage waders including Common Greenshank, Green and Common Sandpipers. Passage terns including Black Tern. Finch flocks forming.

October–March: Little and Great Crested Grebes move to river. Main Great Cormorant arrival from end of October. Winter wildfowl including Common Teal, Northern Shoveler, Common Pochard and occasional Goosander move to river in harsh freezing spells. Fieldfare, Redwing, finch flocks including Goldfinch. Sand Martin and Chiffchaff arrive from mid-March.

HAUGHMOND HILL (see map p. 266)

Habitat

Haughmond Hill is a low plateau rising 250 ft (77 m) above the surrounding plain, with rock outcrops and steep wooded slopes on the western and southern-facing boundaries. It lies 3 miles (4.8 km) east of Shrewsbury. Although large sections of the hill have been afforested with regimented conifers, there are enough broadleaved areas remaining to provide a variety of habitats, but there is now much less open country. A forest fire in the late 1970s destroyed many acres of coniferous woodland, creating for a while an ideal habitat for Grasshopper Warblers, Whinchats and Common Stonechats, but it did not, as was hoped, attract European Nightjars back into an area where they were regular breeders not too long ago. Replanting followed quickly and a vagrant Red-footed Falcon was tempted to spend a fortnight hunting the area of infant conifers in 1982. The prolific growth rate of these trees has resulted in a rather dull landscape today.

The most interesting woodlands lie on the western side of the hill, from Haughmond Abbey in the north to Downton in the south, where broadleaved trees still dominate, including many oaks. These occur at low levels and along the slopes. There are areas of birch wood and scrub at high level along this side and a few Scots pines. A quarry in the northwest of the hill has been responsible for the destruction of some habitat but in turn has provided some extensive cliff faces liked by some species. A good area of mature oaks remains to the east of the workings.

Species

A walk through the low-level woods along the western fringe of Haughmond Hill will reveal resident woodland birds at all times of the year and all three woodpeckers may be seen, together with Wood Nuthatches and Eurasian Treecreepers. Long-tailed and other tits form mixed roving bands in autumn and in summer the woods are busy with warblers, especially Blackcaps and Willow Warblers. Turtle Doves croon here and it is one of their few remaining bastions in Shropshire. All the broadleaved areas are good for Eurasian Sparrowhawks, Tawny Owls, Common Redstarts, Pied and Spotted Flycatchers, Eurasian Jays and other common woodland passerines. The old timber provides many sites for hole-nesting species such as Stock Doves, Eurasian Jackdaws, Common Starlings and tits. Common Kestrels are regulars on the hill, hunting the remaining open areas. A few pockets of rough grass can still be found where Grasshopper Warblers are heard and in scrubby growth, or amongst newly planted conifers, Common Whitethroats, Garden Warblers, Whinchats and occasional Common Stonechats are seen. The hill is good generally for small passerines such as Wrens, Hedge

Accentors, Robins, resident thrushes and finches, and Yellowhammers, whilst winter brings Redwings, Fieldfares, Siskins and Common Redpolls. The coniferous plantations contain Goldcrests and Coal Tits. Tree Pipits are present in some numbers, and may play host to Common Cuckoos along with the oft-victimised Hedge Accentors and other small birds. A leading feature of the ornithological year is provided by roding Wood-cocks, which invariably give excellent views in the early dusks of spring and summer. Increasing numbers of Hobbies hunt the hill, especially dur-ing post-breeding dispersal. Common Swifts, sometimes in large num-bers, hunt above the hill in summer months.

Timing

Haughmond Hill is a local beauty spot and well used by walkers. It is not really a tourist attraction, hence disturbance never reaches chronic pro-portions. Summer weekends are the periods of maximum disturbance. There is only a minimum of birdlife in winter, but visits in spring and early summer can be very rewarding, especially after the arrival of most migrants by late April, but before the foliage of high summer makes the viewing of woodland birds difficult. Early morning is the best time of day to visit during this period, although evenings have their own special magic at the approach of dusk, with Woodcocks roding, Tawny Owls hooting, bats on the wing and a good chance of seeing fallow deer.

Access

Haughmond Hill can best be approached from Shrewsbury by taking the B5062 which leaves the A5191 at the Heathgates roundabout 1.25 miles (2 km) north of the town centre to cross the A49(T) – the new by-pass – at another roundabout heading east. To approach from the south take the unclassified road leaving the B4380 (formerly A5(T)) 4 miles (6.4 km) southeast of the town, alongside Attingham Park and proceed via Upton Magna. Limited roadside parking near Haughmond Abbey, on the B5062 north of the hill, enables walkers to explore the western woods at low level before heading for higher ground. For ample parking space turn right into the minor road some 300 yds (277 m) further east to find a pic-nic area, with all-ability trail and information regarding waymarked routes of varying lengths. It is on the right after a very short distance. Roadside parking is also available on the east, just south of The Criftin, where a forest road leads to the coniferous plantations, and on the minor road to the southwest, from which two public rights of way cross fields to reach the hill. An attractive approach is along a strip of woodland from the north of Uffington, but parking may prove a problem.

There is no vehicular access to the hill, nor is there unlimited open access on foot. However, there are good tracks and paths in addition to the waymarked routes.

The Shrewsbury–Newport bus service passes along the B5062 which touches the north of the site.

Calendar

All year: Eurasian Sparrowhawk, Common Kestrel, Woodcock, Tawny Owl, the three woodpeckers, Wood Nuthatch, Eurasian Treecreeper. Resident thrushes, tits, crows, finches.

April–June: Roding Woodcock. Summer migrants from mid-April includ-ing Common Cuckoo, Tree Pipit, Common Redstart, Grasshopper

Warbler, scrub and leaf warblers, Pied Flycatcher. Turtle Dove, Common Swift and Spotted Flycatcher from early May.

July–September: Increasing chance of Hobby. Flocks of mixed juvenile tits. Eurasian Jays carry acorns. Finch flocks form.

October–March: Common Stonechat, Fieldfare, Redwing, finch flocks including Siskin and Common Redpoll.

EARL'S HILL AND PONTESFORD HILL

Habitat

These two hills, almost one feature with separate names rather than two distinct hills, lie south of the A488 7.5 miles (12 km) to the southwest of Shrewsbury. The wild grandeur of Earl's Hill, a pre-Cambrian pile reaching 1040 ft (320 m), forms the southern half of the area, and the heavily afforested Pontesford Hill makes up the remainder. Earl's Hill is a superb spot, with a rich variety of natural features, and is a nature reserve managed by the Shropshire Wildlife Trust (SWT). Views from the summit are magnificent and it is easy to see why Iron Age Man chose the site as a vantage point and to provide protection. Traces of the fort are still clearly discernable today, more than 2,000 years on.

The summit of Earl's Hill is surrounded by open, rough grassland, which also covers the northwest slopes descending to the Craft Valley, there to meet the regimented conifers of Pontesford Hill. The drier grassland on the rockier southern slopes has been invaded by broom and at lower levels by a thicket of scrub and bracken. Mainly ash, elder and hawthorn, with bramble, this is perfect warbler habitat. East of the summit a dramatic rock face towers above scree slopes and a deep wooded valley, through which the Habberley Brook flows, tumbling between boulders and cascading over shelves of bedrock to provide ideal conditions for Dippers and Grey Wagtails. Alders grow along the stream, with the hillside wood containing mainly ash, wych elm and oak. Trees also grow in the gullies which cut into the crags, reaching almost to the summit in places. The scree slopes are enlivened with rock stonecrop and common lizards bask here on sunny days.

The great strength of Earl's Hill as a nature reserve lies in the rich mosaic of habitats crammed into a relatively small area. It is well known for the impressive number of butterfly species to be found there.

Pontesford Hill is much less exciting, due to the blanket of conifers which cover most of the surface. Even so, the woodland edges, a few mixed areas and some small but more open patches at the northern end, provide a good selection of woodland passerines.

The hills are surrounded by agricultural land on three sides, with extensive woodland beyond the Habberley Brook to the east. There is an excellent Visitor Centre in the painstakingly restored barn, sited above the valley and approached by crossing interesting hill meadows to the northeast of the reserve.

Species

Although a visit during any season will be rewarded with some worthwhile sightings, it is in spring and summer, when the woods are vibrant with birdsong, butterflies are on the wing and carpets of flowers and blossoms splash colour across the scene, that the area shows its true splendour.

In the broadleaved woods, Wood Warblers trill, six species of tits perform the hectic chores of their breeding cycle and all three woodpeckers may be heard and seen. Eurasian Treecreepers and Wood Nuthatches, so often overlooked, search the boles for insect food, whilst in more open areas Tree Pipits perform their parachute flights. Sit on a high vantage point and look down onto the woods for a while and the brilliant flash of a Eurasian Jay may be glimpsed momentarily, or the quick dash of a hunting Eurasian Sparrowhawk. The flickering white patches of Pied Flycatchers attract the eye and Common Redstarts are betrayed by their fiery tails, although the white forehead of the cock is always surprisingly conspicuous. Turtle Doves croon, Chiffchaffs sing monotonously from tree-top song posts and Common Cuckoo calls echo across the valley. Common Buzzards soar over these woods and a cacophony of angry alarm cries may betray the presence of a roosting Tawny Owl, discovered perhaps by a Blackbird whose noisy objections lead the chorus of dissent.

The coniferous woods are less productive, but Goldcrests and Coal Tits feed here. The former also breed, but the hole-nesting tits must move out to site their nests. Siskins visit the woods in winter.

In scrubby places, Common Whitethroats, Garden Warblers and Blackcaps are found, together with the ubiquitous Willow Warbler. Linnets and Yellowhammers find this habitat to their liking, whilst in winter Common Redpolls feed in the birches. In rough grassy patches on the edge of scrub towards the southern end of the valley, Grasshopper Warblers are heard though seldom seen, especially at close of day, when Woodcocks are roding overhead.

The stream is closely hemmed in by trees, making it difficult to watch along anything but a short stretch. It is graced by Dippers and Grey Wagtails, with Common Kingfishers seen on rare occasions. Grey Herons may be surprised here occasionally and Mallard, but the flicking white undertail-coverts of Moorhens are usually glimpsed only briefly as the bird swims jerkily for cover, or runs crouching under the stream banking.

Common Kestrels hunt the open hillside grassland and Meadow Pipits occur in some numbers, with a few Sky Larks. In the meadows south of the Visitor Centre, ground-feeding Green Woodpeckers seek their favoured diet of ants and small charms of Goldfinches visit thistles.

Rock-climbers scale the crags during weekends and summer evenings, but are tolerated by noisy Eurasian Jackdaws which nest in the cliff crevices. Common Redstarts also find nest-sites in the tree-clad gullies. In undisturbed periods Common Ravens call from the rocks and Common Swifts scream around the brooding cliff faces in an endless search for insects.

Timing

Spring, with resident breeding birds established on territory, summer migrants newly arrived and broadleaved trees not yet in full foliage, is the best time of the year. Early morning is the best time of the day for maximum bird activity, but evenings can also be good, with reeling Grasshopper Warblers, roding Woodcocks, a late hunting raptor or two and bats on the wing. With care, badgers can be seen and glowworms have been noted in the dusks of summer evenings. For soaring Common Buzzards midday is the best time to visit.

Access

Take the A488 Bishop's Castle road from Shrewsbury and park at the garage beside the junction on the left, 4.5 miles (7.2 km) after crossing the A5(T) and 0.5 miles (0.8 km) before reaching Pontesbury. Visitors are especially asked not to park in the narrow lane at the north of Pontesford Hill, as this could impede the access of emergency vehicles in the event of a fire or a climbing accident.

Follow the lane from the garage (ignoring the turning to the left after 550 yds (500 m)) to reach a wide footpath leaving the road on the left which

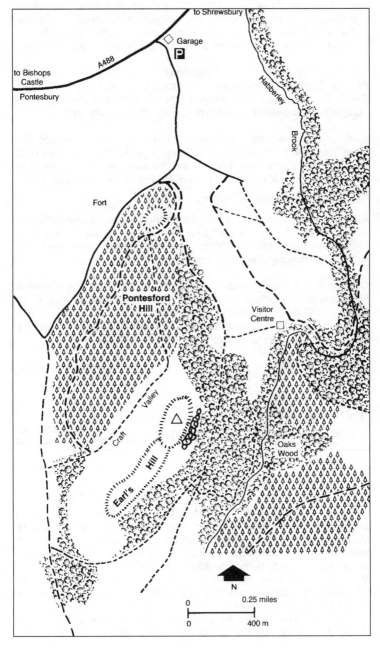

271

is the most direct route to the scree slopes, Habberley Brook and hillside woodland. A short diversion, after passing through a field gate into a meadow, leads to the Visitor Centre (signposted). The Centre has restricted opening hours, but is voluntarily manned during most summer weekends and has a permanent exhibition giving information about the reserve and a nature trail which has been set out to cover the most interesting features of the site. It can be rough walking so take the usual precautions regarding footwear. The area is also well served with public footpaths.

Shrewsbury–Minsterley buses run along the A488. Alight between Pontesford and Pontesbury from where it is a 0.5-mile (0.8 km) walk to the hills.

Calendar

All year: Eurasian Sparrowhawk, Common Buzzard, Common Kestrel, Tawny Owl, all three woodpeckers, Dipper, Goldcrest, six tits, other resident woodland passerines, resident finches, Yellowhammer.

April–June: Summer migrants from mid-April including Common Cuckoo, Tree Pipit, Common Redstart, Grasshopper Warbler, scrub and leaf warblers, Pied Flycatchers. Turtle Dove, Common Swift and Spotted Flycatcher from early May. Soaring raptors. Roding Woodcock. Many breeding species.

July–September: Common Swifts and hirundines feed around crags in large numbers. Large bands of Blue and Great Tits, accompanied by smaller numbers of other tits, Willow Warblers and Goldcrests, feeding in woods. Eurasian Jays carrying acorns. Finch flocks forming.

October–March: Tawny Owls disputing territories at beginning of period. Fieldfares and Redwings from mid-October feeding on berries. Goldcrests and Coal Tits in coniferous woods. Siskins in conifers also join Common Redpolls in birch and alder. Chiffchaffs arrive from late March. Resident species take up breeding territories at end of period.

45 THE NORTH SHROPSHIRE MERES

OS Landranger
Map 126

Habitat

The meres spread southeast from Ellesmere, forming a miniature Lake District in the low-lying North Shropshire countryside. A total of eight meres lie within a compact area of 3 miles (4.8 km) by 2.5 miles (4 km), the more accessible being The Mere, Blake Mere, Cole Mere, Newton Mere and White Mere. Hanmer Mere, 4.5 miles (7.2 km) northeast of Ellesmere, is also well worth visiting although it lies beyond the Shropshire border in Clwyd.

The meres were formed by glaciation. Terminal moraine deposited during the last Ice Age left an uneven surface, hollows in which were water-filled by melting ice. The retreating ice also left behind isolated blocks which melted to form steep sided kettleholes. The result is the delightful, gently undulating, lake-dotted area we see today. Not being fed by rivers or streams, the meres have a water level corresponding with the surrounding water table, resulting in little variation in depth over the year. This makes them particularly good for waterfowl, but less attractive to waders due to the absence of exposed mud which falling water levels would provide. Most of the meres contain good populations of fish, making them ideal for grebes, Great Cormorants, Grey Herons, sawbills and the occasional wintering divers.

Two man-made features add to the ornithological interest of this area. The Shropshire Union Canal runs alongside Blake Mere and Cole Mere, linking the two with a waterway passing through interesting habitats of woodlands, open fields and marshy hollows of rough herbage. At dusk on spring and summer evenings, bats abound, the flittering pipistrelle and Daubenton's bat, skimming rapidly just above the canal surface, being easiest to identify. Wood Lane gravel pit, between White Mere and Cole Mere, provides suitable habitat for nesting Sand Martins and is a good staging post for passage waders.

Between the meres, the land is given over to agriculture, mainly cereals and pasture, but with generous pockets of mixed woodlands, ideal for woodpeckers and small passerines.

Species

Many of the common species are found on most of the meres and it is usually quite easy to locate Little and Great Crested Grebes, Mute Swans, feral Greylag Geese, Canada Geese, Mallard, Tufted Duck, Ruddy Duck, Moorhens, and Common Coots; and in winter Great Cormorants, Eurasian Wigeon, Common Teal, Northern Shoveler, Common Pochard, Common Goldeneye, Goosander and the commoner gulls. Less usual species which occur annually and may appear on any water are Tundra Swan, White-fronted and Barnacle Geese, Common Shelduck, Northern Pintail, and Smew. Common, Arctic and Black Terns are regulars on passage.

Young Great Crested Grebes can be seen on the Shropshire meres in summer

Other birds arrive less frequently, perhaps storm-driven by westerly winds, or as part of a cold weather movement due to harsh conditions further north. These include Red-throated Divers, Black-necked Grebes, Whooper Swans, Bean and Pink-footed Geese, Gadwall, Greater Scaup, Long-tailed Duck, Common Scoter and Red-breasted Merganser. Scarcer still are Black-throated and Great Northern Divers, Red-necked Grebes and Brent Geese. Some wildfowl are difficult to categorise, occurring in Britain as wild birds, but more often met with as escapes, and the meres have hosted Snow Geese, Ruddy Shelduck, Mandarin Duck and Feruginous Duck in recent years. Should you come across such species, better not to worry about their status, simply enjoy them, for they are all handsome birds. Water Rails are heard in winter and several meres have suitable habitat to attract them, but the southern tip of The Mere is as good a place as any to look.

Some species have definite preferences for particular meres. The Mere has a heronry on its island which has grown in recent years, courtesy of a succession of mild winters, to at least 16 nests. This large expanse of water holds a large gull roost, building up from late summer to maximum numbers in midwinter. Black-headed Gulls dominate, sometimes making up three-quarters of the total, which has reached 15,000 birds in some years. Lesser Black-backed, Herring and Common Gulls make up the numbers. Great Black-backed Gulls rarely reach a dozen and Kittiwakes are unusual visitors. Scarcer gulls now recorded annually are Little Gulls arriving in late summer, followed by Mediterranean Gulls from late autumn with Iceland and Glaucous Gulls usually appearing after the turn of the year. The Mere usually takes the very few terns on spring passage, and many of those on the return autumn journey, when the birds are more numerous and longer staying. Common Terns arrive from mid-August followed by Arctic Terns in early September. Black Terns, always the most recorded, have a protracted passage from late August to late October. Single birds are the norm with up to five on occasions. In 1994 a White-winged Black Tern spent a month here until the exceptionally late date of 1 December. The alders on the western corner of The Mere often contain feeding Siskin in winter and the wood on the northwest shore is good for Lesser Spotted Woodpeckers.

Cole Mere also holds a large gull roost which in some years may reach 10,000 in January. It is also an excellent mere for passage terns. This is the best water to see small numbers of White-fronted Geese in winter; and a few Barnacle Geese bored with life in some wildfowl collection have appeared regularly since the early eighties, and of course they also visit other meres. They have bred, but not in sufficient numbers to maintain their population which is now in decline. Irritatingly they hybridise with Canada Geese. The marshy area at the open southeast end of the mere holds good numbers of wintering Common Snipe with one or two Jack Snipe in some years. The same area is graced with Yellow Wagtails in spring and summer.

Blake Mere holds tree-roosting Great Cormorants, and both Newton Mere and White Mere are favoured sites for storm-driven divers. Crose Mere, viewable only from a distance, is a gathering ground for post-breeding Ruddy Duck before they move across to the large West Midland reservoirs for the winter, with numbers topping 100 in some autumns. Clwyd's Hanmer Mere serves a similar purpose for these now well established but controversial stifftails, and often holds up to 60 wintering Goosander.

The Mere, Blake Mere and Cole Mere have mixed woodland adjacent to their shores in which can be found Eurasian Sparrowhawks, Turtle Doves in much reduced numbers, Tawny Owls, the three woodpeckers, Goldcrests, most of the common woodland passerines and Eurasian Jays.

The Wood Lane sand and gravel pit holds a Sand Martin colony, attracts a few wildfowl, including Common Shelduck, and gulls – a Sabine's Gull was recorded here in July 1983 – but is best known for passage waders. Access to the site has recently been improved but conditions may vary and wader sightings have fallen away in recent years. Spring movement is always weaker than the return passage and often limited to a half dozen species. Dunlins, normally the first arrivals, pass through in small groups, but a flock of 45 was counted in April 1985. Oystercatchers, in parties of up to four, are always well represented and pairs have summered in the area. Little and Great Ringed Plovers, together with Common Redshanks and Common Sandpipers usually appear as singles. Much less usual are Whimbrels and Black-tailed Godwits. Eurasian Curlews gather here at the end of spring days to bathe and preen and a post-breeding flock which may top 120 birds winters in the area. The first of the return passage to arrive are Great Ringed Plovers, Dunlins and Common Redshanks, seen from mid-July, and they are joined in early August by Oystercatchers, Ruffs, Common Greenshanks and Common Sandpipers. Green and Wood Sandpipers are also seen annually, with Whimbrels, Red Knots and Little Stints passing through in some years.

The stretch of the Shropshire Union Canal between Blake Mere and Cole Mere can be very rewarding. It gives the best access to Blake Mere, where Little and Great Crested Grebes, Great Cormorants and a few wildfowl regularly occur. To the east of this mere the woodland is waterlogged, containing many old and decaying trees which often play host to Lesser Spotted Woodpeckers and Common Redstarts. Moorhens nest in emergent vegetation alongside the canal towpath and Common Kingfishers are not infrequent. It is a strange sight to see them disappear into, or emerge from, the long tunnel to the west of Blake Mere. Winter thrushes in large numbers feed in the fields and hedgerows to the north of the canal and the woods on the southern bank produce much bird activity. On spring evenings the melancholy hooting of Tawny Owls echoes from the woodland depth, contrasting with the strident calls of Little Owls in the open.

Timing

The meres are very much a tourist area, and birdwatchers may find too many people for their liking during summer weekends and bank holidays. The canal is used by pleasure craft, especially in these periods. However, most visitors stay in the area of The Mere, and there is a beneficial side effect in the way the birds become accustomed to human presence. The Grey Herons continue to nest on the island opposite one of the busiest areas, with Canada Geese, Mallards and Common Coots walking freely among admiring tourists. Even in busy periods an early morning or late evening visit will give quiet conditions. Gull roosts begin to form from mid-afternoon, with the majority of birds arriving before dusk. During the short winter days there is constant bird activity from dawn to dusk and this is the most rewarding time to visit the area. Weather should be taken into account and a visit following westerly gales may be rewarded with a rarity or two. Long periods of freezing weather may leave little or no unfrozen water and wildfowl move out of the area.

Access

There is no access to Crose Mere or the nearby almost infilled Sweat Mere, which lie almost 1.5 miles (2.4 km) to the south of the main group, although the former can be seen from the A528 to the west. However, the mere is fringed by tall trees and viewing from here is unsatisfactory. A public right of way passes between the two meres but gives no access to the shores.

Three other meres can only be viewed from adjacent roads: White Mere lies alongside the A528 with a minor road along the northern shore; Newton Mere can be viewed from the minor road passing the southern tip; and Kettle Mere can be seen from the A495. The former two should not be missed, especially after westerly gales.

Another roadside site is Wood Lane gravel pit which lies south of the minor road from the A528 to Colemere. Permission has recently been

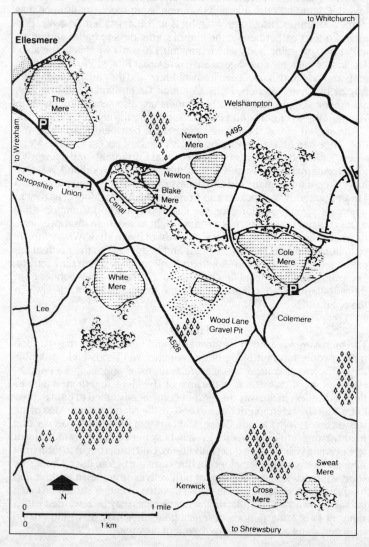

granted by the owners, the Tudor Griffiths Group, for Shropshire Ornithological Society members to enter the site, which is also used by anglers.

The Mere has official car parking on the southwest shore alongside the A528 and limited roadside parking along the minor road to the northwest. There is open access from the southern tip along some three-quarters of the perimeter, until a meadow halfway along the northeast shore is reached, at which point it becomes private property. Parking space has been provided at the junction of the A528 and A495 which gives access to the canal towpath, from which Blake Mere can be seen and from which Cole Mere may be reached by birdwatchers wanting an interesting and picturesque walk. Cole Mere is a Country Park owned by Shropshire County Council (SCC) and a large car park is situated at the southern end of the mere on the Colemere to Lyneal road. SCC have also provided a super footpath which circumnavigates the mere.

Hanmer Mere (not shown on maps) is reached by driving along the A495 Ellesmere to Whitchurch road and taking a minor road northwest after 5 miles (8 km). There is a public right of way along the eastern shore.

The Shrewsbury–Ellesmere bus service runs along the A528 and passes within a mile of most meres.

Calendar

All year: Little and Great Crested Grebes, Mute Swan, Canada Goose, Mallard, Tufted Duck, Eurasian Sparrowhawk, Common Kestrel, Moorhen, Common Coot, Little and Tawny Owls, Common Kingfisher, the three woodpeckers and common resident passerines.

April–June; Young Grey Herons stand on nests from mid-May. Common Shelduck. Passage waders at Wood Lane include Oystercatcher, Dunlin, Little and Great Ringed Plover, Common Redshank and Common Sandpiper. Light passage of Common, Arctic and Black Terns. Most summer migrants from mid-April but Common Swift, Turtle Dove (scarce) and Spotted Flycatcher from early May.

July–September. Passage waders at Wood Lane include Dunlin, Ruff, Common Redshank, Green, Wood and Common Sandpipers and post breeding flock of Eurasian Curlew gathers. Common, Arctic and Black Terns on meres. Possibility of Little Gulls. Passage Yellow Wagtails at Cole Mere.

October–March: Divers (scarce) usually from January after storms. Main Great Cormorant arrival from mid-October. Grey Herons breeding from mid-February. Main arrivals of wintering wildfowl from late October or early November, including Eurasian Wigeon, Common Teal, Mallard, Northern Shoveler, Common Pochard, Tufted Duck, Common Goldeneye, and Goosander (especially Hanmer Mere) in good numbers, but also Tundra Swan, the scarcer Whooper Swan, White-fronted Goose, Northern Pintail and Smew. Ruddy Duck gather on Crose Mere and Hanmer Mere in October. In some years Bean, Pink-footed and Brent Geese, Gadwall, Greater Scaup, Long-tailed Duck, Common Scoter and Red-breasted Merganser. Common Goldeneye gather on The Mere in late March. Water Rail (scarce). Gull roost reaches maximum numbers December–January. Occasional Mediterranean Gull from October. Iceland and Glaucous Gulls. Common Snipe and occasional Jack Snipe, Cole Mere. Winter thrushes and finches include Siskin and Common Redpoll. Chiffchaff and Sand Martin arrive mid-March.

The present day landscape of northern Shropshire bears little resemblance to the countryside of yesteryear, when much of this area would have contained many meres. These filled in naturally over the centuries as successional vegetation encroached and eventually formed mosses of peat. Reclaimation has replaced the area with fertile farmland, but one large area of 3 x 1.5 miles (4.8 x 2.4 km), made up of Fenn's, Whixall and Bettisfield Mosses and the smaller remnant of the 50 acres (20 ha) Wem Moss still remain. The former is now in the safe keeping of English Nature (EN) as a National Nature Reserve (NNR), after a recent successful campaign to prevent further peat extraction and the latter is a Shropshire Wildlife Trust (SWT) reserve. Although the three large mosses are adjoined, the county boundary runs through the area and only Whixall Moss is in Shropshire although the EN nature reserve base at Manor House is within the county – but only just. Bettisfield Moss is now thickly wooded, with no public access and less characteristic of mossland than its neighbours. The density of the woodland is unfavourable for high populations of any species but it does hold the usual arboreal birds including Great Spotted Woodpeckers, Goldcrests and Eurasian Treecreepers.

FENN'S, WHIXALL AND WEM MOSSES

Habitat

The two large mosses, once a superb example of a raised mire, have been much exploited by man. From the 16th century the right to cut peat was granted by the Lord of the Manor, but from early this century new methods of hand cutting with new tools, accompanied by laying down a network of deep drains, speeded up the process. The introduction of machinery in the 1960s increased the assault on the natural landscape until large scale cutting ceased in 1991 when EN acquired the site. A small amount of hand cutting by local peatmen with long established rights still continues. The result of this activity is a much drier habitat which has enabled birch, willow and Scots pine to colonise. The perimeter of the mosses is well wooded with tall trees, which decline into shrubs before the open central areas of heather and cotton-grass are reached. There are many pools, rectangular and steep-sided, the result of abandoned peat cuttings. The whole site is crisscrossed with a network of 3–6 ft (1–2 m) wide, 3 ft (1 m) deep drains, but there is also a deeper main drainage network. Management policy is to dam the drains so as to raise the water table and encourage the growth of sphagnum moss, gradually restoring the mosses to their former condition. A few wet areas have always retained some now rare species of wildlife, especially plants and insects, but the recent change to sympathetic management is already paying dividends as these species begin to spread and the habitat becomes more suitable for wetland birds, particularly wildfowl and waders. The area has a network of firebreaks which are bridged where they cross drains and these serve as footpaths, but they are not rights of way. Entry is strictly by permit (annual) only, but these are readily available from EN.

Wem Moss is also an excellent and important example of a raised mire. It is a small plain of mainly heather, its surface pitted with water-filled depressions, and surrounded by fields and woods. A wet woodland dominated by alder and willow borders the eastern edge and a spur of this extends westwards, bisecting the bog. The reserve, which requires an access permit from SWT, is mostly of botanical and entomological interest, being the home of sundews and other scarce plants, with some interesting butterflies and dragonflies. Ornithologically it is a poorly recorded area, but it does hold breeding Common Snipe, Reed Buntings and Meadow Pipits. Although a small area, the going is rough and requires strong boots or wellingtons, which will also give protection against the numerous adders to be found on the site.

Species

Fenn's and Whixall Mosses have vast potential as ornithological sites, although they were very under-recorded until the recent change in ownership. Wildfowl breeding on the mosses are Canada Geese, Common Teal and Mallard. The increasing feral Greylag Geese will no doubt soon join them, and Common Shelduck are occasionally seen on spring passage. Wader cries and display flights betray the presence of nesting Northern Lapwings and Eurasian Curlews, Little Ringed Plovers have bred and Common Snipe are usually present during the summer. Black-headed Gulls regularly attempt to breed, but are thought to suffer heavily from predation, probably from foxes. With an increase in wetter areas they may be more successful. Such an ideal habitat must host European Nightjars, despite their scarcity, and they are heard churring in some years. They almost certainly breed here. Green Woodpeckers regularly nest, but the expected increase in wetter conditions may force them into the drier and more wooded fringe regions. Small birds raising families in the open areas are Sky Larks, Meadow Pipits, Whinchats, Common Stonechats, Northern Wheatears, Grasshopper Warblers and Reed Buntings. Tree Pipits parachute along the scubby edges and Common Cuckoos are on hand to delegate their parental duties amongst the numerous insect-eating foster-parents available. The area is a haven for dragonflies, moths and butterflies, some of them quite rare, such as the white-faced darter and the large heath.

Hobbies hunt the mosses for large insects and small birds and are thought to have nested in the area for some years.

Other raptors seen regularly are Eurasian Sparrowhawk and Common Kestrel, with increasing sightings of Common Buzzard and Peregrine Falcon. Hen Harriers and Merlins are likely during autumn passage with further visits during the winter months. Short-eared Owls grace the scene with bouyant flight in some winters, when occasional Common Ravens utter their guttural croaks as they range away from their hill-country breeding haunts.

Lesser Black-backed Gulls congregate in late April and May, with over 300 in 1994, but the increasing wader passage is mostly in autumn, with Dunlin, European Golden Plover, Ruff, Spotted Redshank, Common Greenshank and Green Sandpiper seen in recent years. Single Jack Snipe join the growing numbers of Common Snipe that winter on the mosses, with up to 30 present in 1993. The wetter conditions will bring in greater wildfowl numbers, and more species, especially surface-feeding duck, and Eurasian Wigeon, Northern Pintail and Northern Shoveler should join the Mallard and Common Teal which are already regulars.

Common Cuckoos delegate parental duties to Reed Warblers
along the Prees Branch Canal

The woodland and scrub that encircle the mosses hold the usual species, including Great Spotted Woodpeckers, Wood Nuthatches and Eurasian Treecreepers. Woodcocks should find this habitat to their liking, Stock Doves and Wood Pigeons are residents, but Collared Doves concentrate around the dwellings and farms. Passerines are numerous, especially in spring, producing a cacophony of birdsong in which Wrens, Robins, Blackbirds, Song Thrushes, Garden Warblers, Blackcaps, Willow Warblers, Great Tits and Chaffinches are to the fore. The screeching of Eurasian Jays brings a reminder that fine feathers are not always accompanied by a melodious voice.

The peaty, heather-clad Wem Moss hosts a few wetland species in the breeding season, notably Common Snipe and Reed Bunting. Meadow Pipits in the drier areas and Tree Pipits on the woodland fringe are also present. This latter habitat will hold the most species, including common woodland passerines, the pied woodpeckers and possibly a pair of Woodcock. Common Cuckoos linger with intent to seek out prospective foster-parents, Eurasian Sparrowhawks visit to snatch unwary victims, Common Kestrels hover above open ground, whilst small avian and large insectivorous prey attracts occasional hunting Hobbies. The seeds of alder and birch prove irresistible to Goldfinches, Siskins and Common Redpoll at the end of the year.

Timing

Spring and summer are the best times of year to visit at the moment, but the change in management policy will undoubtedly bring in increased numbers of wildfowl in winter and probably encourage passage waders to visit in autumn. Disturbance is not a problem making the time of day less critical than for many sites. Early morning birdwatching always carries an advantage, but spring and summer evening trips may provide churring European Nightjars, the wailing cries of Northern Lapwings, drumming Common Snipe, the bubbling calls of Eurasian Curlews, the echoing calls of Common Cuckoos and reeling Grasshopper Warblers

Access

For Fenn's and Whixall Mosses it is necessary to obtain a permit from EN who will provide with it a detailed map and advice on safety for visitors. The mosses are hazardous terrains and birdwatchers should never stray

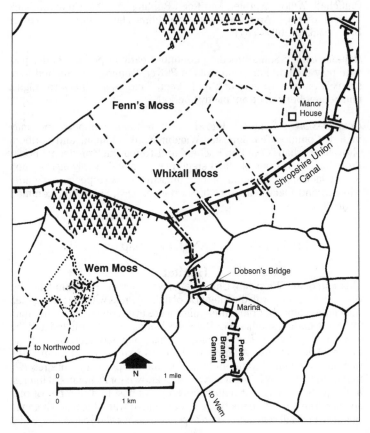

from the adequate tracks, should always wear adder-proof footwear and take particular care in failing light. The southern boundary of this area is formed by the Shropshire Union Canal and there is a right of way along the northern towpath, but this does not give good views of the mossland. There are other rights of way, particularly one running north between woodland and mossland on the eastern side. The area is approached via a network of lanes between the B5476 Wem–Whitchurch road to the east and the B5063 Wem–Welshampton road to the west.

A bus service from Whitchurch runs along the A495 which passes within 0.75 miles (1.2 km) of some northern access points.

Calendar

All year: Mallard, Eurasian Sparrowhawk, Common Kestrel, Stock Dove, Wood Pigeon, Green and Great Spotted Woodpeckers, Wren, Hedge Accentor, Robin, Blackbird, Song Thrush, tits, Eurasian Jay and other common crows, and resident finches.

April–June: Canada Goose, Common Teal, Hobby, Little Ringed Plover, Northern Lapwing, Common Snipe, Eurasian Curlew, Black-headed Gull, probable European Nightjar, Common Cuckoo, Sky Lark, Tree and Meadow Pipits, Whinchat, Common Stonechat, Northern Wheatear, Grasshopper Warbler, Common Whitethroat, Garden Warbler, Blackcap, Chiffchaff, Willow Warbler, and Reed Bunting. Possible Common Shelduck on passage (April–early May). Sometimes large numbers of Lesser Black-backed Gulls (May).

July–September: Some breeding continues early in period. Wader passage may include European Golden Plover, Dunlin, Ruff, Spotted Redshank, Common Greenshank and Green Sandpiper, otherwise August and September can be an inactive period.

October–March: Winter wildfowl swell resident numbers and may include Common Teal, Eurasian Wigeon, Northern Pintail and Northern Shoveler; perhaps Common Pochard and Tufted Duck on deeper pools. Probable Hen Harrier, Merlin, Peregrine Falcon and overflying Common Raven. Jack Snipe, Common Snipe, Eurasian Curlew (especially in milder winters) and Black-headed Gull. Short-eared Owl, Siskin and Common Redpoll.

PREES BRANCH CANAL (see map on p. 281)

Habitat

This spur of the Shropshire Union Canal was constructed around the end of the 18th century with the intention of linking Prees with the main canal, hence the name, but only three miles were ever completed. In the mid-1970s the marina southeast of Dobson's Bridge was constructed and the section of by then overgrown canal to that point had been cleared and brought back into use. A further 0.5 miles (0.8 km) of canal south of the marina still retained water and this became the present nature reserve, managed by the SWT. The reserve is best known for its botanical interest and aquatic insects, but naturally also plays host to a number of bird species. The towpath bank of the canal is lined with alders and a generous growth of tall vegetation such as sedges, rushes and yellow flag, whilst the opposite bank is quite open to the bordering meadows. A mature hawthorn hedge marks the site boundary on the towpath side beyond which are more small grassy meadows, separated by hedgerows containing a substantial amount of oak and ash. The reserve is a long wildlife corridor winding through an undisturbed rural scene that has changed little over the past few decades. If you are in the area do not miss it.

Species

The reserve may be regarded as an elongated pond. Breeding waterbirds are Mute Swan, sometimes two pairs, the ubiquitous Mallard and Moorhens. The tall fringing vegetation on the towpath side is suitable for Sedge and Reed Warblers and Reed Buntings which all probably breed, although this part of the county is poorly reported. The boundary hedgerow is full of spring birdsong, especially Wren, Robin, Blackbird, Chaffinch and other resident passerines, before they are joined by Common Whitethroat, Garden Warbler, Blackcap, Chiffchaff and Willow Warbler. The surrounding hedges and fields, with the numerous mature oaks and ash, provide feeding, roosting, song posts and nesting sites for many species. Northern Lapwings and Eurasian Curlews breed in the area, newly arrived Barn Swallows skim above the meadow grasses from mid-April, and resident passerines such as thrushes, tits, Chaffinches, Greenfinches, Linnets and Yellowhammers inhabit the hedges and trees. A sad bundle of feathers on the towpath indicates the presence of Eurasian Sparrowhawks and Common Kestrels hover as they scan the ground for small mammal prey, more leisurely than their dashing cousins but just as deadly to the victims.

Acrobatic Siskins and Common Redpolls feed in the lining alders in winter and are joined by Goldfinches, especially in milder years.

Timing

April to mid-June is the best time of the year when breeding residents are joined by summer migrants, the flowers are at their best and dragonflies on the wing. From early July the vegetation tends to run riot. The time of day is not so critical in this quiet corner of the county and once clear of the boat enthusiasts the reserve is secluded and seldom disturbed. As always, early mornings hold most bird acivity, but spring and early summer evenings have their special charm.

Access

This area is a maze of minor roads. Head for Dobson's Bridge, midway between the B5063 Wem–Welshampton road on the west and the B5476 Wem–Whitchurch road on the east. The reserve is 0.25 miles (0.4 km) southeast of here. There is limited roadside parking and the reserve is reached by walking along the towpath on the west bank, the only access route. There is usually parking space at the marina, 0.25 miles (0.4 km) eastwards, especially away from the obvious busy spells, but please ask for permission at the shop.

Calendar

All year: Eurasian Sparrowhawk, Moorhen, Wood Pigeon, Wren, Hedge Accentor, Robin, resident thrushes, Long-tailed and other tits, Chaffinch, and Bullfinch. In adjacent fields: Common Kestrel, partridges, Common Pheasant, Stock Dove, Barn (scarce) and Little Owls, Green Woodpecker, Magpie and other common crows.

April–June: Mute Swan and Mallard breeding. Chance of hunting Hobby. Summer migrants include Common Cuckoo, possible Sedge and Reed Warblers, scrub and leaf warblers. Greenfinch, Goldfinch, Linnet, Yellowhammer and Reed Bunting. In adjacent fields: Northern Lapwing, Eurasian Curlew, Common Swifts, Barn Swallows and Yellow Wagtail (scarce).

July–September: Mute Swans with cygnets. Mallard families and groups of drakes in eclipse. Still a few residents and migrants with second or later broods. Flocks of juvenile tits. Mostly a quiet spell.

October–March: Flocks of Redwing and Fieldfare. Goldfinches, Siskins and Common Redpolls feed in alders. In adjacent fields: mixed feeding flocks of sparrows, finches and buntings.

BROWN MOSS

Habitat

Brown Moss lies 1.5 miles (2.4 km) southeast of Whitchurch and is owned and managed as a nature reserve by Shropshire County Council (SCC). Something of a misnomer, Brown Moss is very different from the typical peaty areas at Whixall and Wem. If peat ever existed here it has been long removed, for the ground is now light and dry, consisting mainly of sand and gravel. The 80 acres (33 ha) area is well wooded with birch and oak dominant, but with significant numbers of rowan, holly and Scots pine. A few areas of open heath remain and the site is further enhanced by a ring of shallow pools, the largest of which may be 10 acres (4 ha), although the pools shrink in periods of drought until almost non-existent. A few years ago such a spell completely dried out the large pool. Long rainy periods raise the water level so that some of the pools may join together and footpaths then become waterlogged and impassable. These pools are rich with aquatic plants, being fringed with willows and reedmace, with an abundance of emergent and floating vegetation. For the birdwatcher who appreciates other forms of wildlife, such as dragonflies, this is an enchanting area.

Species

The presence of aquatic species is dependent upon the amount of water held by the pools. In years of high levels breeding species will include Little and Great Crested Grebes, Canada Geese, Mallard, Moorhens and Common Coots. Reed Buntings breed regularly and both Sedge and Reed Warblers have been recorded in some seasons. A few wildfowl visit, particularly during spring passage periods and these include feral Greylag Geese, Common Shelduck, Eurasian Wigeon (scarce), Common Teal, Northern Shoveler, Common Pochard, Tufted Duck, Common Goldeneye (scarce) and Ruddy Duck. Occasional Black Terns call on passage with small numbers of Black-headed and Common Gulls visiting to bathe and preen outside the breeding season. Water Rails skulk in the poolside vegetation in winter but Grey Herons may appear at any time of the year. Common Kingfishers are seen very occasionally.

The pools are not noted for hosting waders due to lack of suitable shorelines, but Common Sandpipers and Common Snipe have been seen in spring passage periods. Northern Lapwings and Eurasian Curlews breed in nearby fields and use the water of the large pool for bathing and preening. Jack Snipe are rare winter visitors, usually towards the end of the period, and it is the woodland haunting Woodcock that spends most time on the reserve, albeit a difficult species to locate except during the roding period.

The woodland, especially in spring and early summer, is usually alive with birds. Resident Wrens, Hedge Accentors, Robins, Blackbirds, Song Thrushes, all the common tits, Wood Nuthatches, Eurasian Treecreepers, and Chaffinches are filling the wood with song and well into their breeding cycles before the summer migrants begin to arrive. These include the early arriving Chiffchaff with its monotonous notes, soon followed by the look-alike Willow Warbler with a delicate cascade of silvery song. Blackcaps, Garden Warblers and Common Whitethroats seek out suitable areas to nest, but Lesser Whitethroats appear merely to call in passage periods as do Common Redstarts. Common Cuckoos take advantage of so many host species, the pied woodpeckers are both found here, and predators are represented by Tawny Owls and Eurasian Sparrowhawks. Noisily screeching Eurasian Jays have recently increased, heard throughout the year but most easily seen as post-breeding family parties or carrying acorns in September. Magpies, Eurasian Jackdaws and Carrion Crows form winter roosts, sometimes in large numbers. In winter the residents are joined by Siskins and Common Redpolls, attracted by the birch. This is the time when Goldcrests feed in small numbers, often joining the tit flocks, and on one occasion a Firecrest was seen.

Species preferring more open areas are Pied, Grey and Yellow (scarce) Wagtails, Meadow Pipits and occasional Northern Wheatears. The first named breed locally but the others are passage visitors. Yellowhammers also breed but usually move away in winter when good numbers of Redwings and Fieldfares feed in the boundary hedgerows, most numerous in November and again in March. Other fringe birds are Common Kestrels and Little Owls.

Timing

Brown Moss is popular with locals, being an ideal area for family outings and dog walking. Anglers formerly visited the large pool in numbers, but it dried up completely for a lengthy spell and appears not to have been restocked. This also affects the fish-eating birds of course. To avoid this disturbance follow the usual rule of early morning visiting, which gives the best birdwatching anyway. Spring and summer evenings are also good.

Mid-March to the end of May is probably the best time to visit, certainly for woodland birds, but there is much of interest for most of the year. Fine winter days can produce a lengthy species list, although the more open shallow pools may quickly freeze in a cold snap. July to September are the least productive months.

Access

The best approach is from the A41(T). The reserve is signposted 0.5 miles (0.8 km) north of Prees Heath roundabout, indicating the minor road easterly towards Ash. Even if travelling from the north it is probably quicker to take the Whitchurch by-pass and use this approach rather than negotiate the lanes from the town via Ash. Ample parking space has been provided.

A bus service runs from Whitchurch to Prees Heath. The reserve is less than 1 mile (1.6 km) walk by quiet roads from the A 41(T), and two shorter public rights of way link it with the same road.

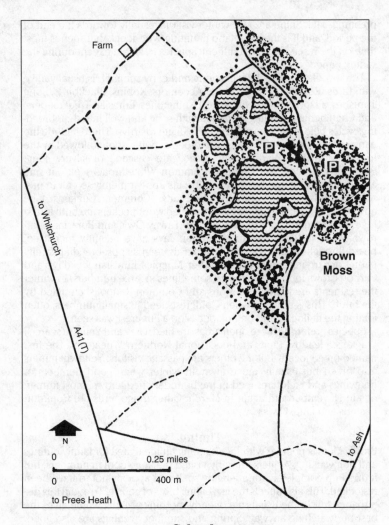

Calendar

All year: Canada Goose, Mallard, Moorhen, and Common Coot all breed and Grey Herons visit regularly (depending on suitable water levels). Eurasian Sparrowhawk, Common Kestrel, Woodcock, Tawny Owl, Great and Lesser Spotted Woodpeckers, Pied Wagtail, Wren, Hedge Accentor, Robin, Blackbird, Song Thrush, six tit species, Wood Nuthatch, Eurasian Treecreeper, Eurasian Jay and other common crows (except Rook), Chaffinch and Reed Bunting.

April–June: Little and Great Crested Grebes breed (if water levels suitable). Common Sandpiper and Common Snipe on passage. Yellowhammers return to breed. Most summer migrants from mid-April including Common Cuckoo, possible Sedge and Reed Warblers, scrub and leaf warblers. Spotted Flycatcher from early May. Passage passerines such as Meadow Pipit, Yellow and Grey Wagtails, Northern Wheatear, Common Redstart and Lesser Whitethroat.

July–September: A few residents and migrants with second or third broods. Return passage of above listed species not so noticeable. Feeding flocks of juvenile tits. Generally a slack period.

October–March: A few Greylag Geese and occasional escapes such as Bar-headed Goose. Common Pochard and Tufted Duck. Other wildfowl mainly March, including Common Shelduck, Eurasian Wigeon, Common Teal, Northern Shoveler, Common Goldeneye and Ruddy Duck. Water Rail and Jack Snipe (both singles). Redwings, Fieldfares, Goldcrests, finch flocks including Siskin and Common Redpoll. Chiffchaff from mid-March.

APPENDIX OF ADDITIONAL SITES

Site Grid Ref	Habitat	Species	Timing	Access
Allscott Sugar Factory SJ 605127	Settling pools, river and marsh	Wildfowl, waders, terns and aquatic passerines	All year, but spring and autumn best	Strictly permit only to SOS members
Berkswell SP 240791	Parkland and lake	Grey Heron, common wildfowl and woodland birds	Spring, summer	Public footpath from Berkswell Church
Bircher Common SO 457665 and Leinthall Common SO 450674	Grass and bracken hillsides, scrub and mixed woodland	Raptors, pipits, common scrub and woodland birds	Spring, summer	Bircher Common NT: open access Leinthall Common public footpaths
Brockhampton Wood SO 690555	Mixed woodland, parkland	Common Buzzard, Pied Flycatcher, common woodland and parkland birds	Spring, summer	NT: general access
Chaddesley Wood SO 914736	Mixed woodland	Common woodland birds	Spring	NNR: follow waymarked paths
Chesterton SP 357582	Pools and farmland	Common wildfowl and passerines	Spring, winter (avoid freezes)	Public footpath from Chesterton Church
Clent Hills SO 940796	Hills with grass, bracken, scrub and mixed woodland	Passerines including Tree Pipit, passage upland birds	Spring, summer, autumn	NT: Several car parks and general access
Copmere SJ 805295	Glacial lake, reedbed, Woodland	Wildfowl (more in winter), waterside birds and common woodland birds	All year	View from adjoining lanes
Crewe Green SJ 330158	Extensive river floods	Wildfowl, including wild swans	Winter	View from road
Croft Castle SO 463655	Parkland and mixed woodland	Raptors, Pied Flycatcher, Common Crossbill (following footpaths irruptions), common woodland birds	Spring, summer	NT: nature walks and
Crinshill including Corbet Wood SJ 519237	Sandstone cliffs, heath and mixed woodland	Eurasian Sparrowhawk, Common Kestrel, Woodcock, common woodland birds	All year	Public footpaths SWT nature trail in Corbet Wood
Downs Banks SJ 902366	Bracken hillsides, deciduous woodland, stream	Common passerines, Grey Wagtail, thrush roost in winter	Spring, winter	NT: general access from adjacent lane

Earlswood Lakes SP 114742 and Clowes Wood: SP 098738	Lakes, deciduous woodland	Common wildfowl (mostly in winter), passage terns, woodland birds	All year	Public footpaths around lakes and through woods. Clowes Wood WWT reserve members only
Edge Hill SP 380480 and Burton Dassett Hills SP 395520	Ironstone hills. Edge Hill: deciduous woodland. Burton Dassett: grass and scrub	Common passerines	Spring	General access from adjacent roads
Enville SO 836865, Sheepwalks SO 813853 and Kinver Edge SO 834830	Heaths and open hillsides. Also coniferous woods at Enville and oak-birch woods at Kinver	Heronry, raptors especially Common Buzzard, Common Raven, Common Crossbill (after irruptions), common heath and woodland birds.	All year	Kinver Edge: general access to NT and Kingsford Country Park. Elsewhere public footpaths
Feckenham Wylde Moor SP 012603	Marsh, pool	Common wildfowl, Common Snipe, Woodcock, common passerines	All year	WWT(2) reserve: members only
Grimley SO 840607 Holt SO 826622	Gravel pits and marsh	Wildfowl (most winter), passage waders, passerines	Spring, autumn, winter (avoid freezes)	View from roads and and public footpaths
Hanchurch Hills SJ 840397	Coniferous woodland	Common woodland birds	Spring	FE: public footpaths
Highgate Common SO 843900	Heath, birch and conifer woodland	Common heath and woodland birds	Spring	Country Park: car parks and general access
Hunthouse Wood SO 705702	Deciduous woodland in steep valley	Common Buzzard, common woodland birds	Spring	WWT(2) reserve: members only
Hurcott Pool SO 851779	Millpool	Common wildfowl, Common Kingfisher	Winter (avoid freezes)	View from adjacent road
Kings Bromley SK 111167	Gravel pit and river	Great Cormorant (roost), wildfowl	Winter (avoid freezes)	View from road
Llanymynech SJ 266218 and Llynclys SJ 273237	Limestone quarry, scrub, heath, grassland and woodland	Raptors (including occasional Peregrine Falcon), Tree Pipit, Common Redstart, Pied Flycatcher, Common Raven, common woodland birds	Spring, summer	SWT reserves: permits not required
Merrington Green SJ 465209	Scrub, woodland, pools and grassland	Eurasian Sparrowhawk, Common Kestrel, common passerines	Spring, summer	SWT: nature trail
Monkwood SO 804607	Mixed deciduous woodland and scrub	Woodcock, common woodland birds	Spring, summer	WWT(2): members only
Nescliffe SJ 386195	Sandstone outcrop, scrub, heath and mixed woodland	Small raptors, passage Northern Wheatear, common scrub and woodland passerines	Spring, summer	Public footpaths

Newbold Comyn SP 335655	Flood meadows, fields and hedges	Common passerines, a few wildfowl when flooded	Spring, winter	Car parks and general access
Ravenshill Wood SO 739539	Mixed woodland	Woodcock, warblers, other common woodland birds	All year	Privately owned reserve: entrance charge (free for WWT(2) members)
Romers Wood SO 602629	Woodland, hillside, stream	Common Redstart, Pied Flycatcher, Common Raven, common woodland birds	Spring, summer	HNT reserve: members only
Seeswood Pool SP 329904	Subsidence pool	Wildfowl, passage waders, gulls and terns	Spring, autumn, winter (avoid freezes)	View from adjacent road
Shobdon SO 402621	Pools, mixed woodland, open farmland	Few wildfowl (most winter), European Golden Plover (winter), Reed Warbler, common woodland birds	All (avoid freezes)	View from roads and public footpaths
Soudley Wood SO 330806	Mixed hillside woodland, conifer plantations	Raptors, Woodcock, Tawny Owl, woodpeckers and many passerines including Common Redstart, Pied Flycatcher and Common Crossbill	Spring, summer	Public footpaths
Valley Park SJ 895004	Grassland, scrub, woodland, canal	Common waterbirds, woodland and farmland passerines	All year	General access
Whichford Wood SP 298341	Mixed woodland	Common woodland birds	Spring	Footpaths from nearest road
Whittington Sewage Farm SO 872839	Sewage works and fields	Common Snipe, Eurasian Curlew, passerines: roost site	Winter	View from road
Wormleighton Reservoir SP449518	Canal-feeder reservoir	A few wildfowl, waders	Autumn, winter	Along towpath

Abbreviations

FE	Forest Enterprise	SOS	Shropshire Ornithological Society
HNT	Herefordshire Nature Trust	SWT	Shropshire Wildlife Trust
LNR	Local Nature Reserve	WWT	Warwickshire Wildlife Trust
NNR	National Nature Reserve	WWT(2)	Worcestershire Wildlife Trust
NT	National Trust		

GLOSSARY OF TERMS

Calcicole A plant more frequently found upon, or confined to, soils containing lime.

Carr Woodland, usually willow or alder, growing in waterlogged ground.

Chat Collective name for Robin, Black Redstart, Common Redstart, Whinchat, Common Stonechat and Northern Wheatear.

'Commic' tern Collective name for Common and Arctic Terns.

Commoner gulls Collective name for Black-headed, Common, Lesser Black-backed, Herring and Great Black-backed Gulls.

Corvid Collective name for the crow family. Includes Eurasian Jay, Magpie, Eurasian Jackdaw, Rook, Carrion Crow and Common Raven.

Dabbling Duck A duck, such as Mallard or Common Teal, which feeds whilst sitting on the water, often by up-ending. Also known as surface-feeding duck.

Diurnal migration Daytime movements of birds migrating overhead, which can be seen mainly in autumn.

Diving Duck A duck, such as Common Pochard or Tufted Duck, which feeds by diving below the surface.

Drumming (1) The sound made by woodpeckers rapidly striking a dead branch. (2) The sound that Common Snipe make with their tail feathers during display flights.

Fall (of migrants) Sudden arrival of migrant birds, usually overnight, that are grounded by adverse weather such as rain or mist.

Feral Birds that have either escaped or been released from captivity and are now living successfully in a wild state.

Flash An area of open water frequently the result of underground mining and sometimes only temporary.

Grey Geese Collective name for Bean, Pink-footed, White-fronted, Lesser White-fronted and Greylag Geese.

Hirundine Collective name for martins and swallows. Applied particularly to Sand Martin, Barn Swallow and House Martin.

Immigrant A bird moving into the area from elsewhere.

Irruption Periodic (every few years) mass arrival of birds from elsewhere, usually because of high populations and/or food shortages in their normal areas. Applied particularly to birds such as Common Crossbill.

Lammas land Common land used for growing hay between Candlemas (2 Feb) and Lammas (1 Aug), before being opened up as commoners' grazing land for the rest of the year.

Larger gulls Collective name for Lesser Black-backed, Herring, Iceland, Glaucous and Great Black-backed Gulls.

Leaf warbler Collective name for Wood Warbler, Chiffchaff and Willow Warbler.

Lek Communal display ground. Applied particularly to Black Grouse.

Loaf/loafing Term applied to gulls and waterfowl resting after bathing or feeding.

Migrant/passage migrant A bird passing through, usually in spring and autumn, *en route* between its breeding and wintering grounds.

Overshooting Term usually applied to spring migrants which are blown further north than their intended destination by strong winds from the southern quarter.

Passage Movement of birds through an area, usually in spring and autumn.

Passerine Collective term for perching birds. Includes larks, swallows and martins, pipits and wagtails, dippers, wrens, accentors, chats, thrushes, warblers, flycatchers, tits, nuthatches, treecreepers, shrikes, crows, starlings, sparrows, finches and buntings.

Pied woodpeckers Collective term for Great and Lesser Spotted Woodpeckers.

Predator Collective name for species which kill and eat live prey, applied usually to raptors and owls.

Raptor Collective term for birds of prey, which includes kites, harriers, hawks, buzzards, osprey and falcons but excludes owls.

Rarer Grebes Collective name for Red-necked, Black-necked and Slavonian Grebes.

Rarer Gulls Collective name for Mediterranean, Yellow-legged, Iceland and Glaucous Gulls.

Rarity Used here to refer to birds which are rare in the West Midlands.

Reel/reeling The rapid, uniform, sustained trill of the Grasshopper Warbler, which is reminiscent of an angler's reel.

Rode/roding The display flight of Woodcock at dusk, during which it flies with a peculiar, deliberate wing action and utters a short grunting note.

Roost/roosting Birds gathering to rest communally at a safe site, usually at night.

Sawbill Collective name for Smew, Red-breasted Merganser and Goosander.

Scrape Shallow, man-made excavation in wet ground to provide habitat for wildfowl and waders.

Scrub warblers A collective term for warblers of scrub habitats, especially Lesser Whitethroat, Common Whitethroat, Garden Warbler and Blackcap.

Sea-duck Duck normally found in coastal waters such as Greater Scaup, Common Eider, Long-tailed Duck, Common and Velvet Scoters, and Red-breasted Merganser.

Set-aside Areas of farmland left fallow under the European Union's Common Agricultural Policy. This provides winter food for birds.

Sink-hole A hole into which streams disappear in limestone districts.

Six species of tits Collective term for Long-tailed, Marsh, Willow, Coal, Blue and Great Tits.

Stifftail Used as an alternative name for Ruddy Duck.

Sylvan/woodland warblers Collective term for warblers that inhabit woodland, especially Garden Warbler, Blackcap, Wood Warbler, Chiffchaff and Willow Warbler.

Tern raft Artificial floating platform designed specifically to encourage Common Terns to nest.

Three woodpeckers Collective term for Green, Great Spotted and Lesser Spotted Woodpeckers.

'Trip' Term for a party of Dotterel.

Vagrant A bird many miles from its normal range, such as seabirds inland.

Wader Collective name for oystercatcher, plovers, sandpipers, snipe, godwits, curlew etc. that generally feed in mud or shallow water. Also known as shorebirds.

Waterfowl Collective name for birds which have evolved to an aquatic lifestyle. Includes divers, grebes, swans, geese, ducks, Moorhen and Common Coot.

Wildfowl Collective name for the Anatidae family *i.e.* swans, geese and ducks.

Wild/winter swans Collective name for Tundra and Whooper Swans as opposed to the introduced Mute Swan. Also referred to as migrant swans.

Winter(ing) thrushes Refers mainly to Fieldfares and Redwings, but also includes Blackbirds and Song Thrushes arriving for the winter.

Wreck Term used to describe seabirds, such as Shag, which are driven inland by gales or storms.

FURTHER READING LIST

Anon (1993) *The 'British Birds' List of English Names of Western Palearctic Birds*, British Birds Ltd., Biggleswade.

Belsey, J.T. *The Birds of Upton Warren*, published annually by J.T. Belsey, 6 Newent Close, Winyates Green, Redditch B98 0QW.

Easterbrook, T.G. (Ed.) (1995) *The New Birds of the Banbury Area 1982–1994*, Banbury Ornithological Society, Banbury.

Green, G.H. and B. Westwood (1991) *The Nature of Worcestershire*, Worcestershire Wildlife Trust and Barracuda Books, Buckingham.

Green, G.H. (1995) *A Year in the Life of Worcestershire's Nature Reserves*, Worcestershire Wildlife Trust, Hindlip.

Harbird, R. (1992) *The Birds of Draycote Water*, Severn Trent Water and West Midland Bird Club, Studley.

Harrison, G.R., A.R. Dean, A.J. Richards and D. Smallshire (1982) *The Birds of the West Midlands*, West Midland Bird Club, Studley.

Harrison, G.R. (1996) *Draycote 25 – A review of wildfowl and waders at Draycote Water*, Severn Trent Water and West Midland Bird Club, Studley.

Herefordshire Nature Trust (1990) *Guide to Nature Reserves*, HNT, Hereford Herefordshire Ornithological Club *Annual Reports*.

Jenkinson A. (1992) *Shropshire's Wild Places*, Shropshire Wildlife Trust, Countryside Commission and Scene Setters, Little Stretton.

Parr, Joyce D. (Ed.) *Birds on the Malvern Hills and Commons* an annual report to the Malvern Hills Conservators.

Rutter, E.M., F.C. Gribble and T.W. Pemberton (1964) *A Handlist of the Birds of Shropshire*, Shropshire Ornithological Society, Shrewsbury.

Shropshire Ornithological Society *Shropshire Bird Reports* published annually.

Smallshire, D (1987) *Belvide Bird Reserve – A Natural History*, West Midland Bird Club, Studley.

Smith, L (Ed.) (1992) *An Atlas of the Breeding Birds of Shropshire*, Shropshire Ornithological Society, Shrewsbury.

Staffordshire Wildlife Trust (1993) *Nature Reserves Handbook*, SWT, Sandon.

Tasker, Dr. A. (Ed.) *(1990) The Nature of Warwickshire*, Warwickshire Nature Conservation Trust and Barracuda Books, Buckingham.

Voous, Dr K.H. (1977) *List of Recent Holarctic Bird Species*, London.

Walker, C.W. and A.J. Smith (1975) *Herefordshire Birds*, Woolhope Naturalists' Field Club, Hereford.

Warwickshire Wildlife Trust (1993) *Nature Reserves Handbook*, WWT, Brandon.

Warwickshire Wildlife Trust, *Brandon Marsh Nature Reserve Annual Reports*.

West Midland Bird Club *West Midland Bird Reports* (cover Warwickshire, Worcestershire, Staffordshire and the former West Midlands County) published annually.

West Midland Bird Club *Belvide Report*, published annually.

West Midland Bird Club *Ladywalk Nature Reserve Annual Reports*.

Worcestershire Wildlife Trust (1987) *Reserves Handbook*, WWT, Hindlip.

There are also leaflets on many of the sites covered by this book, but these are too numerous to list. Contact the relevant authority, trust or owner for further details.

USEFUL ADDRESSES

Statutory Bodies

British Waterways
Regional Office, Peel's Wharf,
Fazeley, Tamworth,
Staffordshire B78 3QZ
Tel: 01827 252000

Countryside Commission
Midlands Region
Cumberland House, Broad Street,
Birmingham B15 1TD
Tel: 0121 632 6503

English Nature
West Midlands Region,
Attingham Park,
Shrewsbury SY4 4TW.
Tel: 01743 709611

Warwickshire Sub-Office,
10–11 Butchers Row,
Banbury, Oxfordshire OX16 8JH.
Tel: 01295 257601

Environment Agency
Regional Office,
Sapphire East,
550 Streetsbrook Road,
Solihull, West Midlands B91 1QT
Tel: 0121 711 2324

Lower Severn Area,
Riversmeet House,
Newtown Industrial Estate,
Northway Lane, Tewkesbury,
Gloucestershire GL20 7JG
Tel: 01684 85091

Upper Severn Area,
Hafren House, Welshpool Road
Shelton, Shrewsbury SY3 8BB
Tel: 01743 272 138

Upper Trent Area
Sentinel House, Wellington Crescent
Fradley Park, Lichfieldl WS13 8RR
Tel: 01543 444141

Forest Enterprise
South and West
Avon Fields House,
Somerdale, Keysham,
Bristol BS18 2BD
Tel: 01272 869481

Severn Trent Water
Head Office,
2297 Coventry Road,
Birmingham B26 3PU
Tel: 0121 722 4000

South Staffordshire Water
Green Lane
Walsall WS2 7PD
Tel: 01922 38282

Organisations

Banbury Ornithological Society
P Douthwaite,
Townsend Farm, Radway,
Warwickshire CV35 0UN
Tel: 0129 587319

Birdline Midlands
(Up-to-the-minute bird information
service)
Tel: 0891 700247
Call in sightings on 01905 754154
(Note: The West Midland Bird Club runs
a separate hotline for its members)

British Birds Rarities Committee
M J Rogers (Honorary Secretary),
2 Churchtown Cottages, Towednack,
Cornwall TR26 3AZ.
Tel: 01736 796223

British Trust for Ornithology
The National Centre for Ornithology,
The Nunnery, Thetford,
Norfolk IP24 2PU.
Tel: 01842 750050

Regional Representatives:
Birmingham and West Midlands
J R Winsper,
32 Links Road, Hollywood,
Birmingham B14 4TP.
Tel: 0121 605 4163

Herefordshire
K A Mason,
The Sett, Common Hill,
Fownhope, Herefordshire HR1 4QA.
Tel: 01432 860546

Rugby
Dr D Porter,
60 Stanley Road, Hillmorton, Rugby,
Warwickshire CV21 3UE.
Tel: 01788 543803

Shropshire
A Dawes,
Rosedale, Chapel Lane,
Trefonen, Oswestry,
Shropshire SY10 9DX.
Tel: 01691 654245

Staffordshire North
A Hancock,
12 Sparch Hollow,
Newcastle-under Lyme,
Staffordshire ST5 9PA.
Tel: 01782 615887

Staffordshire Central
F C Gribble,
22 Rickerscote Avenue,
Stafford ST17 4EZ
Tel: 01785 615887

Staffordshire South
P Dedicoat,
2 The Elms Paddock, Pattingham,
Wolverhampton WV6 7DW
Tel: 01902 700514

Warwickshire
J A Hardman,
Red Hill House, Red Hill, Alcester,
Warwickshire B49 6NQ
Tel: 01789 763159

Worcestershire
H Green,
Windy Ridge, Pershore Road,
Little Comberton, Pershore,
Worcestershire WR10 3EW
Tel: 01386 710377

Herefordshire Ornithologial Club
Secretary,
I B Evans,
12 Brockington Drive, Tupsley,
Hereford HR1 1TA
Tel: 01432 860546

Recorder,
K A Mason,
The Sett, Common Hill,
Fownhope, Herefordshire HR1 4QA
Tel: 01432 860546

Herefordshire Nature Trust
25 Castle Street,
Hereford HR1 2NW
Tel: 01432 356872

National Trust
Severn Region
Mythe End House, Tewkesbury,
Gloucestershire GL20 6EB
Tel: 01684 850051
(covers Hereford, Warwicks, Worcester
and part of West Midlands)

Mercia Region
Attringham Park, Shewsbury,
Shropshire SYA4 4TOP
Tel: 01743 709343
(covers Shropshire, Staffordshire,
and part of West Midlands)

Royal Society for the Protection of Birds
The Lodge,
Sandy,
Bedfordshire SG19 2DL
Tel: 01767 680551

Central England Office
46, The Green, South Bar,
Banbury, Oxfordshire, OX16 9AB,
Tel: 01295 253330

Shropshire Ornithological Society
Treasurer
B Andrews,
Cordage Rope Walk, Friar's Street,
Bridgnorth WV16 4BJ
Tel: 01743 369035

Recorder
G R Smith
Church Cottage, Leetbotwood,
Church Stretton, Shropshire SY6 6NE
Tel: 01694 751479

Shropshire Wildlife Trust
167 Frankwell,
Shrewsbury SY3 8LG,
Tel: 01743 241691

Staffordshire Wildlife Trust
Coutts House
Sanndon
Stafford ST18 0DN
Tel: 01889 508534

Urban Wildlife Trust
Unit 310, Jubilee Trading Centre,
130 Pershore Street,
Birmingham B5 6ND
Tel: 0121 666 7474

Warwickshire Wildlife Trust
Brandon Marsh Nature Centre,
Brandon Lane,
Coventry CV3 3GW
Tel: 01203 302912

West Midland Bird Club
Secretary
H M MacGregor,
74 Ivyfield Road, Erdington,
Birmingham B23 7HH
Tel: 0121 373 5489

Permit Secretary
Miss M Surman,
6 Lloyd Square, 12 Niall Close,
Edgbaston, Birmingham B15 3LX

Recorders
Staffordshire
Mrs G N Jones,
4 The Poplars, Lichfield Road,
Abbots Bromley, Rugeley,
Staffordshire WS15 3AA

Warwickshire
S M Haynes,
4 Spinney Close, Old Arley,,
Coventry CV7 8PD

West Midlands
T C Hextell,
49 Cradley Croft, Handsworth,
Birmingham B21 8HP

Worcestershire
R Harbird,
Flat 4 Buckley Court,
16 Woodfield Road,
Moseley, Birmingham B13 9UJ

Wildfowl and Wetlands Trust
Slimbridge,
Gloucestershire GL2 7BT
Tel: 01453 890333

Worcestershire Wildlife Trust
Lower Smite Farm,
Smite Hill, Hindlip,
Worcestershire WR3 8SZ
Tel: 01905 754919

Public Transpost Information

Herefordshire
Environmental Services
Department,
Hereford and Worcester County
Council,
County Hall, Spetchley Road,
Worcester WR5 2NP
Tel: 0345 125436

Warwickshire
Department of Planning, Transport
and Economic Strategy,
Warwickshire County Council,
PO Box 43, Shire Hall,
Warwick CV34 4SX
Tel: 01926 414140

Shropshire
Public Transport Unit,
Shropshire County Council,
The Shirehall, Abbey Foregate,
Shewsbury, SY2 6ND
Tel: 0345 056785

West Midlands
Centro,
Centro House,
16 Summer Lane,
Birmingham B19 3SD
Tel: 0121 200 2700

Staffordshire
Joint County Transport Unit,
Staffordshire County Council,
Highways House, Riverway,
Stafford ST16 3TJ
Tel: 01782 206608

Worcestershire
See Herefordshire

Reserves and Sites

Brandon Marsh (Tel: 01203 302912)
Branston Water Park (Tel: 01283 508573)
Buckpool and Fens Pool (Tel: 01384 70642)
Cannock Chase Visitor Centre (Tel: 01543 871773)
Clayhanger Common (Tel: 01543 374782)
Consall Visitor Centre (Tel: 01782 550939)
Coombe Abbey (Tel: 01203 453720)
Coombes Valley (Tel: 01538 384017)
Draycote Water (Tel: 01788 811107)
Greenway Bank (Tel: 01782 518200)
Hartshill Hayes (Tel: 01827 872660)
Kingsbury Water Park (Tel: 01827 872660)
The Knapp/Papermill (Tel: 01886 832065)
Long Mynd (Tel: 01694 722631)
Park Hall Country Park (Tel: 01782 326602)
Park Lime Pits (Tel: 01922 722668)
Peak District Ranger Service (Tel: 01629 814321 or 01433 670216 at weekends)
Queenswood Country Park (Tel: 01568 797052)
Saltwells Local Nature Reserve (Tel: 01384 261572)
Sandwell Valley RSPB Reserve (Tel: 0121 358 3013)
Nature Centre (Tel: 0121 553 0220)
Stiperstones (Tel: 01588 660618)
Whixall Moss (Tel: 01948 880362)
Wyre Forest Visitor Centre (Tel: 01299 266302)

CODE OF CONDUCT FOR BIRDWATCHERS

Today's birdwatchers are a powerful force for nature conservation. The number of those of us interested in birds rises continually and it is vital that we take seriously our responsibility to avoid any harm to birds.

We must also present a responsible image to non-birdwatchers who may be affected by our activities and particularly those on whose sympathy and support the future of birds may rest.

There are 10 points to bear in mind:
1. The welfare of birds must come first.
2. Habitat must be protected.
3. Keep disturbance to birds and their habitat to a minimum.
4. When you find a rare bird think carefully about whom you should tell.
5. Do not harass rare migrants.
6. Abide by the bird protection laws at all times.
7. Respect the rights of landowners.
8. Respect the rights of other people in the countryside.
9. Make your records available to the local bird recorder.
10. Behave abroad as you would when birdwatching at home.

Welfare of birds must come first
Whether your particular interest is photography, ringing, sound recording, scientific study or just birdwatching, remember that the welfare of the bird must always come first.

Habitat protection
Its habitat is vital to a bird and therefore we must ensure that our activities do not cause damage.

Keep disturbance to a minimum
Birds' tolerance of disturbance varies between species and seasons. Therefore, it is safer to keep all disturbance to a minimum. No birds should be disturbed from the nest in case opportunities for predators to take eggs or young are increased. In very cold weather disturbance to birds may cause them to use vital energy at a time when food is difficult to find. Wildfowlers already impose bans during cold weather: birdwatchers should exercise similar discretion.

Rare breeding birds
If you discover a rare bird breeding and feel that protection is necessary, inform the appropriate RSPB Regional Office, or the Species Protection Department at the Lodge. Otherwise it is best in almost all circumstances to keep the record strictly secret in order to avoid disturbance by other birdwatchers and attacks by egg-collectors. Never visit known sites of rare breeding birds unless they are adequately protected. Even your presence may give away the site to others and cause so many other visitors that the birds may fail to breed successfully.

Disturbance at or near the nest of species listed on the First Schedule of the Wildlife and Countryside Act 1981 is a criminal offence.

Copies of Wild Birds and the Law are obtainable from the RSPB, The Lodge, Sandy, Beds. SG19 2DL (send two 2nd class stamps).

Rare migrants

Rare migrants or vagrants must not be harassed. If you discover one, consider the circumstances carefully before telling anyone. Will an influx of birdwatchers disturb the bird or others in the area? Will the habitat be damaged? Will problems be caused with the landowner?

The Law

The bird protection laws (now embodied in the Wildlife and Countryside Act 1981) are the result of hard campaigning by previous generations of birdwatchers. As birdwatchers we must abide by them at all times and not allow them to fall into disrepute.

Respect the rights of landowners

The wishes of landowners and occupiers of land must be respected. Do not enter land without permission. Comply with permit schemes. If you are leading a group, do give advance notice of the visit, even if a formal permit scheme is not in operation. Always obey the Country Code.

Respect the rights of other people

Have proper consideration for other birdwatchers. Try not to disrupt their activities or scare the birds they are watching. There are many other people who also use the countryside. Do not interfere with their activities and, if it seems that what they are doing is causing unnecessary disturbance to birds, do try to take a balanced view. Flushing gulls when walking a dog on a beach may do little harm, while the same dog might be a serious disturbance at a tern colony. When pointing this out to a non-birdwatcher be courteous, but firm. The non-birdwatchers' goodwill towards birds must not be destroyed by the attitudes of birdwatchers.

Keeping records

Much of today's knowledge about birds is the result of meticulous record keeping by our predecessors. Make sure you help to add to tomorrow's knowledge by sending records to your county bird recorder.

Birdwatching abroad

Behave abroad as you would at home. This code should be firmly adhered to when abroad (whatever the local laws). Well behaved birdwatchers can be important ambassadors for bird protection.

This code has been drafted after consultation between The British Ornithologists' Union, British Trust for Ornithology, the Royal Society for the Protection of Birds, the Scottish Ornithologists' Club, the Wildfowl Trust and the Editors of *British Birds*.

Further copies may be obtained from The Royal Society for the Protection of Birds, The Lodge, Sandy, Beds. SG19 2DL.

INDEX OF PLACE NAMES
BY SITE NUMBER

INDEX OF SPECIES BY SITE NUMBER

The new English bird names have been used throughout this book. Where different, the old names are shown in brackets in this Index.